New Explor

COMPLETE ANTHOLOGY FOR LEAVING CERTIFICATE
(HIGHER AND ORDINARY LEVELS)
POETRY FOR EXAMINATION IN 2003 AND ONWARDS

EDITED BY

John G. Fahy

CONTRIBUTORS

Carole Scully
John G. Fahy
Bernard Connolly
Martin Wallace
Marie Dunne
Sean Scully
John McCarthy
Ann Hyland
Mary Shine Thompson
David Keogh

GILL & MACMILLAN

Gill & Macmillan Ltd
Hume Avenue
Park West
Dublin 12
with associated companies throughout the world
www.gillmacmillan.ie

© editorial material John G. Fahy, Carole Scully, Bernard Connolly, Martin Wallace,
Marie Dunne, Sean Scully, John McCarthy, Ann Hyland, Mary Shine Thompson,
David Keogh 2001
0 7171 3177 7

Print origination by O'K Graphic Design, Dublin

Colour reproduction by Typeform Repro, Dublin

*The paper used in this book is made from the wood pulp of managed forests. For
every tree felled, at least one tree is planted, thereby renewing natural resources.*

Course Overview

Poets Prescribed for Higher Level

JUNE 2003 EXAMINATION	JUNE 2004 EXAMINATION	JUNE 2005 EXAMINATION	JUNE 2006 EXAMINATION
Donne (pages 1–21)	Wordsworth (pages 22–45)	Wordsworth (pages 22–45)	Donne (pages 1–21)
Hopkins (pages 101–134)	Dickinson (pages 49–72)	Dickinson (pages 49–72)	Hardy (pages 73–100)
Yeats (pages 135–175)	Hopkins (pages 101–134)	Yeats (pages 135–175)	Hopkins (pages 101–134)
Frost (pages 176–201)	Frost (pages 176–201)	Eliot (pages 202–232)	Yeats (pages 135–175)
Bishop (pages 258–287)	Kavanagh (pages 233–257)	Kavanagh (pages 233–257)	Eliot (pages 202–232)
Plath (pages 288–316)	Plath (pages 288–316)	Heaney (pages 317–343)	Bishop (pages 258–287)
Heaney (pages 317–343)	Heaney (pages 317–343)	Longley (pages 344–368)	Plath (pages 288–316)
Mahon (pages 369–397)	Mahon (pages 369–397)	Boland (pages 398–424)	Longley (pages 344–368)

[Ordinary Level: see pages iv–vii]

Poems Prescribed for Ordinary Level
June 2003 Examination

Donne	The Flea (p. 2) Song: Go, and catch a falling star (p. 4)	Herbert	Love (p. 433)
		Blake	A Poison Tree (p. 440)
Hopkins	Spring (p. 111) Inversnaid (p. 124)	Shelley	Ozymandias (p. 448)
		Sassoon	Everyone Sang (p. 457)

Yeats	The Lake Isle of
	    Innisfree (p. 137)
	The Stare's Nest By My
	    Window (p. 160)
	Politics (p. 170)
		St V. Millay	What Lips My Lips Have
			    Kissed (p. 462)

		Graves	Hedges Freaked with Snow (p. 464)
Frost	Mending Wall (p. 182) Out, Out— (p. 190) The Road Not Taken (p.192)	Smith	Deeply Morbid (p. 466)
		Auden	Funeral Blues (p. 470)
Bishop	The Fish (p. 261) Filling Station (p. 282)	Hewitt	The Green Shoot (p. 475)
		Wright	Request to a Year (p. 481)
Plath	The Arrival of the Bee Box (p. 312) Child (p. 315)	Montague	The Cage (p. 498)
		Hughes	Snowdrop (p. 504)
Heaney	A Constable Calls (p. 332) The Skunk (p. 334) Field of Vision (p. 339)	Silkin	Death of a Son (p. 508)
		Adcock	For Heidi with Blue Hair (p. 511)
Mahon	Grandfather (p. 372) After the *Titanic* (p. 377)	Ní Cuilleanáin	Swineherd (p. 523)
		Duffy	Valentine (p. 537)
		Meehan	Would You Jump Into My Grave As Quick? (p. 542)

Note: Ordinary level candidates sitting the exam in June 2003 may chose *either* the poems in the left hand column *or* the poems in the right hand column

Poems Prescribed for Ordinary Level
June 2004 Examination

Wordsworth	She dwelt among the untrodden ways (p. 24) It is a beauteous evening, calm and free (p. 26) Skating (extract from *The Prelude*) (p. 28)	Anon.	Sir Patrick Spens (p. 427)
		Herbert	Love (p. 433)
Dickinson	'Hope' is the thing with feathers (p. 52) A narrow Fellow in the Grass (p. 71)	Williams	The Red Wheelbarrow (p. 452)
		St V. Millay	What Lips My Lips Have Kissed (p. 462)
Hopkins	Spring (p. 111) Inversnaid (p. 124)	MacNeice	Autobiography (p. 473)
		Levertov	What Were They Like? (p. 486)
Frost	Mending Wall (p. 182) Out, Out— (p. 190) The Road Not Taken (p. 192)	Jennings	One Flesh (p. 491)
		Kinsella	Mirror in February (p. 496)
Kavanagh	Shancoduff (p. 238) A Christmas Childhood (p. 245)	Hughes	Snowdrop (p. 504)
		Silkin	Death of a Son (p. 508)
Plath	The Arrival of the Bee Box (p. 312) Child (p. 315)	Kennelly	The Prodigal Son (p. 516)
		McGough	Let Me Die a Young Man's Death (p. 518)
Heaney	A Constable Calls (p. 332) The Skunk (p. 334) Field of Vision (p. 339)	Carson	Soot (p. 530)
		Duffy	Valentine (p. 537)
Mahon	Grandfather (p. 372) After the *Titanic* (p. 377)	Meehan	Would You Jump Into My Grave As Quick? (p. 542)
		Armitage	It Ain't What You Do... (p. 546)

Note: Ordinary level candidates sitting the exam in June 2004 may chose *either* the poems in the left hand column *or* the poems in the right hand column

Poems Prescribed for Ordinary Level
June 2005 Examination

Wordsworth	She dwelt among the untrodden ways (p. 24) It is a beauteous evening, calm and free (p. 26) Skating (extract from *The Prelude*) (p. 28)	Herrick	Whenas in silks my Julia goes (p. 431)
		Milton	When I Consider (p. 436)
Dickinson	'Hope' is the thing with feathers (p. 52) A narrow Fellow in the Grass (p. 71)	Coleridge	The Rime of the Ancient Mariner (p. 443)
		Williams	The Red Wheelbarrow (p. 452)
Yeats	The Lake Isle of Innisfree (p. 137) The Wild Swans at Coole (p. 142) Swift's Epitaph (p. 166)	Lawrence	Piano (p. 455)
		Muir	The Horses (p. 459)
		MacNeice	Autobiography (p. 473)
Eliot	Preludes (p. 212) Rannoch, by Glencoe (extract from *Landscapes IV*) (p. 228)	Thomas	Do Not Go Gentle Into That Good Night (p. 478)
		Levertov	What Were They Like? (p. 486)
Kavanagh	Shancoduff (p. 238) A Christmas Childhood (p. 245)	Jennings	One Flesh (p. 491)
		Kinsella	Mirror in February (p. 496)
		Fanthorpe	Growing Up (p. 501)
Heaney	A Constable Calls (p. 332) The Skunk (p. 334) Field of Vision (p. 339)	Kennelly	Night Drive (p. 514)
		McGough	Let Me Die a Young Man's Death (p. 518)
Longley	Last Requests (p. 360) An Amish Rug (p. 364)	Grennan	Daughter and Dying Fish (p. 520)
Boland	Child of Our Time (p. 406) This Moment (p. 418)	Olds	The Present Moment (p. 524)
		Rumens	Passing a Statue of Our Lady in Derry (p. 527)
		Carson	Soot (p. 530)
		Cannon	Crow's Nest (p. 544)
		Armitage	It Ain't What You Do... (p. 546)

Note: Ordinary level candidates sitting the exam in June 2005 may chose *either* the poems in the left hand column *or* the poems in the right hand column

Poems Prescribed for Ordinary Level
June 2006 Examination

Donne	The Flea (p. 2) Song: Go, and catch a falling star (p. 4)	Herrick	Whenas in silks my Julia goes (p. 431)
		Vaughan	Peace (p. 438)
Hardy	The Darkling Thrush (p. 76) During Wind and Rain (p. 93)	Coleridge	The Rime of the Ancient Mariner (p. 443)
		Thomas	Adlestrop (p. 450)
Hopkins	Spring (p. 111) Inversnaid (p. 124)	Lawrence	Piano (p. 455)
Yeats	The Lake Isle of Innisfree (p. 137) The Wild Swans at Coole (p. 142) Swift's Epitaph (p. 166)	Muir	The Horses (p. 459)
		Thomas	Do Not Go Gentle Into That Good Night (p. 478)
Eliot	Preludes (p. 212) Rannoch, by Glencoe (extract from *Landscapes IV*) (p. 228)	Morgan	Strawberries (p. 483)
		Beer	The Voice (p. 488)
		Murphy	The Reading Lesson (p. 493)
Bishop	The Fish (p. 261) Filling Station (p. 282)	Fanthorpe	Growing Up (p. 501)
Plath	The Arrival of the Bee Box (p. 311) Child (p. 315)	Hughes	There Came a Day (p. 506)
		Grennan	Daughter and Dying Fish (p. 520)
Longley	Last Requests (p. 360) An Amish Rug (p. 364)	Olds	The Present Moment (p. 525)
		Bushe	Jasmine (p. 532)
		Muldoon	Anseo (p. 534)
		Duffy	Warming Her Pearls (p. 540)
		Meehan	Would You Jump Into My Grave As Quick? (p. 542)

Note: Ordinary level candidates sitting the exam in June 2006 may chose *either* the poems in the left hand column *or* the poems in the right hand column

Poems Prescribed for Ordinary Level
June 1966 Examination

CONTENTS

P = poem also prescribed for Ordinary Level

[Notes and explorations: John G. Fahy]

4—Thomas Hardy (1840–1928)   Pages 73–100
(Prescribed for the Higher Level exam in 2006)

[Notes and explorations: Bernard Connolly]

5—Gerard Manley Hopkins (1844–1889)   Pages 101–34
(Prescribed for Higher Level exams in 2003, 2004 and 2006)

[Notes and explorations: Martin Wallace]

6—William Butler Yeats (1865–1939)   Pages 135–75
(Prescribed for Higher Level exams in 2003, 2005 and 2006)

P = poem also prescribed for Ordinary Level

P = poem also prescribed for Ordinary Level

[Notes and explorations: Ann Hyland]

[Notes and explorations: John G. Fahy]

P = poem also prescribed for Ordinary Level

[Notes and explorations: John G. Fahy]

14—Derek Mahon (1941–)   Pages 369–97
(Prescribed for Higher Level exams in 2003 and 2004)

[CD Tracks 23–32]

[Notes and explorations: Mary Shine Thompson]

15—Eavan Boland (1944–)   Pages 398–424
(Prescribed for the Higher Level exam in 2005)

[CD Tracks 33–42]

[Notes and explorations: John G. Fahy]

P = poem also prescribed for Ordinary Level

Ordinary Level

Contributors:

Carole Scully
John G. Fahy
Bernard Connolly
John McCarthy
David Keogh

1 *John* DONNE

prescribed for Higher Level exams in 2003 and 2006

John Donne was born in 1572 in Bread Street, London, into a prosperous Catholic family. However, Catholicism was banned by the Anglican Queen Elizabeth I. Many Catholics, including some of Donne's relatives, were either imprisoned or died for their faith. Up until the age of twelve, Donne was educated at home by Catholic tutors. He then attended the University of Oxford. After university, he went to study law at Lincoln's Inn, London, where he discovered the pleasures of London life.

When he inherited a sum of money from his father he spent some time travelling on the Continent, probably in Spain and France. Subsequently, he joined two expeditions, one to attack the Spanish port of Cadiz and the other to the Azores. On his return to England, he became personal secretary to a powerful courtier, Sir Thomas Egerton. At about this time, Donne decided to change to the Anglican religion. At the age of thirty, he eloped with Ann More, Sir Thomas's seventeen-year-old niece, to the intense annoyance of her family. Donne lost his job and was unable to find another. For a long time, he had great difficulty supporting his ever-growing family. Ann had twelve pregnancies and seven of their children survived.

Donne began to write religious works and the king, James I, was so impressed that he persuaded him to become an Anglican priest. He became famous for his wonderful sermons, some of which are still read today, and was made a royal chaplain to the king. Donne died on 31 March 1631. He was buried in St Paul's Cathedral.

The Flea

this poem is also prescribed for Ordinary Level exams in 2003 and 2006

Mark but this flea, and mark in this,
How little that which thou deny'st me is;
Me it sucked first, and now sucks thee,
And in this flea, our two bloods mingled be;
Confess it, this cannot be said   5
A sin, or shame, or loss of maidenhead,
Yet this enjoys before it woo,
And pampered swells with one blood made of two,
And this, alas, is more than we would do.

Oh stay, three lives in one flea spare,   10
Where we almost, nay more than married are.
This flea is you and I, and this
Our marriage bed, and marriage temple is;
Though parents grudge, and you, we are met,
And cloistered in these living walls of jet.   15
Though use make you apt to kill me,
Let not to this, self-murder added be,
And sacrilege, three sins in killing three.

Cruel and sudden, hast thou since
Purpled thy nail, in blood of innocence?   20
In what could this flea guilty be,
Except in that drop which it sucked from thee?
Yet thou triumph'st, and say'st that thou
Find'st not thyself, nor me the weaker now;
'Tis true, then learn how false, fears be;   25
Just so much honour, when thou yield'st to me,
Will waste, as this flea's death took life from thee.

Notes   [6] **maidenhead:** virginity

[7] **woo:** courts

[11] **nay:** even

[16] **apt:** have a tendency

[17] **self-murder:** suicide

Explorations

First reading

1. Discuss your reaction to a flea appearing in a piece of poetry. Try to explain why you react in the way that you do. Does it have something to do with how you view poetry? Consider what turns a passage of writing into a poem.

2. Describe, in your own words, what happens to the flea in each of the three stanzas. Are you amused or disgusted by these descriptions? Perhaps you have another reaction. How would you react if you saw a real flea?

3. Examine each stanza and discuss the way in which Donne uses the flea's fate to express his feelings. How do you feel about this approach? Does it help you to understand more about Donne, or is it simply confusing?

4. Describe the situation in which Donne finds himself.

Second reading

5. Can you suggest the tone of voice that should be used to read this poem? Which words in the poem indicate this tone to you?

6. Choose two phrases from the poem that you found surprising or interesting and discuss Donne's use of language and imagery. Try to understand why they affected you in the way that they did.

7. Look at Donne's attitude to love in this poem. In particular, consider lines 1–4, lines 12–13 and lines 25–27. What is your reaction to his view?

Third reading

8. Do you think that this poem succeeded in persuading Donne's beloved to his point of view? Do you find it a persuasive piece of writing? Why?

9. During the sixteenth century many bawdy love poems were written about the activities of fleas on the female body. Do you feel that Donne simply repeated this formula, or did he take a more individual approach?

10. One famous critic, Sir Arthur Quiller-Couch, described 'The Flea' as 'about the most merely disgusting in our language'. Would you agree or disagree with this statement. Refer closely to the text of the poem to support your answer.

Song: Go, *and catch a falling star*

this poem is also prescribed for Ordinary Level exams in 2003 and 2006

Go, and catch a falling star,
Get with child a mandrake root,
Tell me, where all past years are,
Or who cleft the Devil's foot,
Teach me to hear mermaids singing,   5
Or to keep off envy's stinging,
And find
What wind
Serves to advance an honest mind.

If thou be'est born to strange sights,   10
Things invisible to see,
Ride ten thousand days and nights,
Till age snow white hairs on thee,
Thou, when thou return'st, wilt tell me
All strange wonders that befell thee,   15
And swear
No where
Lives a woman true, and fair.

If thou find'st one, let me know,
Such a pilgrimage were sweet,   20
Yet do not, I would not go,
Though at next door we might meet,
Though she were true, when you met her,
And last, till you write your letter,
Yet she   25
Will be
False, ere I come, to two, or three.

Notes   [2] **mandrake root:** a poisonous plant believed to have human qualities

[4] **cleft:** split

[15] **befell:** happened to

Explorations

First reading

1. List the tasks Donne describes in the three stanzas. Do they have anything in common? Could you suggest a similar list of present-day tasks?

2. What language does Donne use to give a magical or supernatural feeling to the poem? Why do you think he does this?

3. In each stanza Donne uses two very short lines (lines 7–8, 16–17 and 25–26)—what effect does this have on the rhythm of the poem? You may find it helpful to read the poem aloud. Discuss why Donne chose to use this structure.

4. Each of the three stanzas seems to build up to the final line. Do the three final lines help you to understand the theme of this poem? Can you explain the theme in your own words?

Second reading

5. Examine two images from the poem that you feel are particularly effective. Explain how they achieve their effectiveness.

6. Consider the feelings that Donne reveals in the following lines:
   'And swear
   No where

Lives a woman true, and fair.'
What is your reaction to these lines?

7. How would you describe the tone of this poem? Would you consider it to be the same throughout? Pay particular attention to lines 19–20.

Third reading

8. In some manuscripts this poem appears in a group entitled 'Songs which were made to certain airs that were made before.' Would the effect of this poem be changed if it were sung? Try making up a piece of music for the poem.

9. Examine Donne's attitude to women in this poem and compare it to the one expressed in 'The Flea'— discuss your findings. Based on this, how would you describe Donne as a person? Finally, try reading 'The Sun Rising' where Donne expresses another view about women.

10. In the sixteenth century, listing impossible tasks in a poem was a popular device used for emphasis or hyperbole. Do you feel that this device is used successfully in 'Song: Go, and catch a falling star'? What was Donne trying to emphasise?

The Sun Rising

Busy old fool, unruly sun,
Why dost thou thus,
Through windows, and through curtains call on us?
Must to thy motions lovers' seasons run?
Saucy pedantic wretch, go chide   5
Late schoolboys, and sour prentices,
Go tell court-huntsmen, that the King will ride,
Call country ants to harvest offices;
Love, all alike, no season knows, nor clime,
Nor hours, days, months, which are the rags of time.   10

Thy beams, so reverend, and strong
Why shouldst thou think?
I could eclipse and cloud them with a wink,
But that I would not lose her sight so long:
If her eyes have not blinded thine,   15
Look, and tomorrow late, tell me,
Whether both th'Indias of spice and mine
Be where thou left'st them, or lie here with me.
Ask for those kings whom thou saw'st yesterday,
And thou shalt hear, All here in one bed lay.   20

She is all states, and all princes, I,
Nothing else is.
Princes do but play us; compared to this,
All honour's mimic; all wealth alchemy.
Thou sun art half as happy as we,   25
In that the world's contracted thus;
Thine age asks ease, and since thy duties be
To warm the world, that's done in warming us.
Shine here to us, and thou art everywhere;
This bed thy centre is, these walls, thy sphere.   30

Notes   [5] **pedantic:** one who strictly adheres to formal rules
[8] **offices:** duties
[9] **clime:** climate
[17] **mine:** gold mines
[24] **mimic:** imitation
[24] **alchemy:** the science seeking to turn base metal into gold

Explorations

First reading

1. Consider the various reactions you might feel on being awakened by the sunrise. Are any of these reactions echoed by Donne in the way he addresses the sun in the first 8 lines of the poem?
2. Donne indicates the reason for his outburst in the first and second stanzas. Can you explain what it is? Do you have a certain sympathy for his feelings?
3. In the third stanza Donne compares his situation to that of the sun. Is there a change in the tone he uses? Can you explain why this happens?
4. Discuss two images from the poem that you find particularly effective.

Second reading

5. Consider the various emotions that Donne expresses in the poem. Is there a dominant one?
6. Examine the language and imagery Donne uses to communicate the intensity of the love he feels. Does he persuade you of his sincerity?
7. Contrast the rhythm and sounds of lines 1–4 with those used in lines 27–30. How do they help to convey Donne's emotions?

Third reading

8. Discuss the way in which Donne uses concepts of time and space within the poem. Do you find them confusing or do they help you to understand Donne's mood? Would you agree with him that emotions can transcend the confines of time and space?
9. This poem is centred on the conceit of 'Love' and 'Royalty'. Trace the development of this conceit in the poem. Do you find it a successful connection of ideas, or irritatingly clever?
10. Read 'The Flea' again. Which poem would you consider to be the most realistic and vivid?

The Anniversarie

All kings, and all their favourites,
All glory of honours, beauties, wits,
The sun itself, which makes times, as they pass,
Is elder by a year, now, than it was
When thou and I first one another saw: 5
All other things, to their destruction draw,
Only our love hath no decay;
This, no tomorrow hath, nor yesterday,
Running it never runs from us away,
But truly keeps his first, last, everlasting day.   10

Two graves must hide thine and my corse,
If one might, death were no divorce,
Alas, as well as other princes, we,
(Who prince enough in one another be,)
Must leave at last in death, these eyes, and ears,   15
Oft fed with true oaths, and with sweet salt tears;
But souls where nothing dwells but love
(All other thoughts being inmates) then shall prove
This, or a love increased there above,
When bodies to their graves, souls from their graves remove.   20

And then we shall be thoroughly blessed,
But we no more, than all the rest.
Here upon earth, we are kings, and none but we
Can be such kings, nor of such subjects be;
Who is so safe as we? where none can do   25
Treason to us, except one of us two.
True and false fears let us refrain,
Let us love nobly, and live, and add again
Years and years unto years, till we attain
To write threescore, this is the second of our reign.   30

Notes   [11] **corse:** corpse
               [27] **refrain:** avoid
               [30] **threescore:** sixty

Explorations

First reading

1. Do you find this poem immediately understandable or rather confusing? Did you feel drawn into the poem on the first reading? Is there any aspect of the poem that would encourage you to explore it further?

2. The poem is entitled 'The Anniversarie', can you explain what type of anniversary Donne is writing about?

3. Consider the way in which Donne conveys a sense of time passing in the poem. Do you find the images depressing?

4. How does Donne describe the love he is celebrating in the poem?

5. Can you express the theme of this poem in a few sentences?

Second reading

6. How would you feel if you received this poem as a gift?

7. Examine Donne's use of images connected with the royal court. Do you find them effective in helping you to understand Donne's feelings?

8. Can you describe Donne's mood in the poem? Is it constant, or can you detect changes as the poem progresses?

Third reading

9. 'True and false fears let us refrain,
   Let us love nobly, and live, and add again
   Years and years unto years, till we attain
   To write threescore, this is the second of our reign.'
   Do you find these lines convincing coming as they do at the end of this poem? Does the poem successfully support this ending?

10. Imagine that John Donne has asked you to read this poem and give him some advice on how, if necessary, it could be improved. Outline what you would say to him.

Sweetest love, I do not go

Notes

[8] **feigned:**
pretended, simulated

[33] **divining:** intuitive

Sweetest love, I do not go,
For weariness of thee,
Nor in hope the world can show
A fitter love for me;
But since that I   5
Must die at last, 'tis best,
To use my self in jest
Thus by feigned deaths to die.

Yesternight the sun went hence,
And yet is here today,   10
He hath no desire nor sense,
Nor half so short a way:
Then fear not me,
But believe that I shall make
Speedier journeys, since I take   15
More wings and spurs than he.

O how feeble is man's power,
That if good fortune fall,
Cannot add another hour,
Nor a lost hour recall!   20
But come bad chance,
And we join to it our strength,
And we teach it art and length,
Itself o'er us to advance.

When thou sigh'st, thou sigh'st not wind,   25
But sigh'st my soul away,
When thou weep'st, unkindly kind,
My life's blood doth decay.
It cannot be
That thou lov'st me, as thou say'st,   30
If in thine my life thou waste,
Thou art the best of me.

Let not thy divining heart
Forethink me any ill,

Destiny may take thy part,   35
And may thy fears fulfil;
But think that we
Are but turned aside to sleep;
They who one another keep
Alive, ne'er parted be.   40

 # Explorations

First reading

1. Describe the setting in which Donne places himself. Does the poem make it easy for you to imagine? Discuss the clues that helped you.
2. What tone of voice should be used to speak this poem? Can you choose some words or phrases that you feel indicate this tone?
3. Trace the ways that Donne attempts to reassure his beloved. Would you feel reassured by this poem?
4. What view does Donne convey of death? Why do you think he approaches it in this way?

Second reading

5. Consider the third stanza. Do you find it different in any way to the other stanzas of the poem? Discuss the part that it plays in the overall structure of the poem.
6. What age do you think Donne was when he wrote this? Do you learn anything about his personality? What evidence is there in the poem to support your views?
7. This poem is addressed to Donne's beloved. Do you feel that the emphasis is on Donne's own feelings or on those of his beloved? What does this tell you about their relationship?

Third reading

8. Discuss the rhythm and rhyme used in this poem. Do they add to the overall effect of the piece? Were you aware of them in your reading of this poem?
9. There are some indications that Donne intended this piece to be sung. What aspects of the poem support this. Could you suggest the type of music that might have been used? Would you react differently to the poem if it were a song?
10. Compare Donne's view of death in this poem with the one he communicates in 'The Anniversarie'. Consider the images and language used in each case. Do you think Donne was trying to achieve different effects? If so, why?

A Valediction: Forbidding Mourning

As virtuous men pass mildly away,
And whisper to their souls, to go,
Whilst some of their sad friends do say,
The breath goes now, and some say, no:

So let us melt, and make no noise,   5
No tear-floods, nor sigh-tempests move,
'Twere profanation of our joys
To tell the laity our love.

Moving of th'earth brings harms and fears,
Men reckon what it did and meant,   10
But trepidation of the spheres,
Though greater far, is innocent.

Dull sublunary lovers' love
(Whose soul is sense) cannot admit
Absence, because it doth remove   15
Those things which elemented it.

But we by a love, so much refined,
That our selves know not what it is,
Inter-assured of the mind,
Care less, eyes, lips, and hands to miss.   20

Our two souls therefore, which are one,
Though I must go, endure not yet
A breach, but an expansion,
Like gold to aery thinness beat.

If they be two, they are two so   25
As stiff twin compasses are two,
Thy soul the fixed foot, makes no show
To move, but doth, if th'other do.

And though it in the centre sit,
Yet when the other far doth roam,   30

Notes

Valediction: words used to bid farewell

[7] **profanation:** treat a sacred thing with irreverence

[8] **laity:** lay people

[11] **trepidation:** agitation, anxiety

[13] **sublunary:** earthly

[16] **elemented:** physically contributed to

[19] **Inter-assured:** mutually convinced

[31] **hearkens:** listens, yearns

[34] **obliquely:** slanting

It leans, and hearkens after it,
And grows erect, as that comes home.

Such wilt thou be to me, who must
Like th'other foot, obliquely run;
Thy firmness makes my circle just,   35
And makes me end, where I begun.

 # Explorations

First reading

1. Describe the scene that Donne conveys in the first stanza. Do you find it an effective opening to the poem? What are your expectations of the content of the rest of the poem?

2. How does this opening scene lead into the second stanza? What is the quality in the opening scene that Donne uses to illustrate the type of separation he desires. Do you feel that this connection works?

3. 'No tear-floods, nor sigh-tempests move,'
Consider the connection between this line from the second stanza and the images in the third stanza.

4. There is a similar connection between a line in the third stanza and the content of the fourth stanza, can you explain what it is? Is it now possible to trace Donne's line of thought through the first four stanzas?

Second reading

5. In the fourth to the sixth stanzas, Donne assures his beloved that their love is special. Examine the language and images used to convey this. Do you find them persuasive?

6. Donne compares himself and his beloved to a pair of compasses in the final three stanzas of the poem. Explain in your own words how this conceit works. Consider the effectiveness of Donne's description of the compasses.

Third reading

7. Dr. Johnson was uncertain 'whether absurdity or ingenuity' underlay Donne's conceit of the lovers and the pair of compasses. Discuss which of the two you feel the conceit represents.

8. What is your reaction to this poem? Did you find the line of thought confusing, or did it lead you further into the poem? Were you irritated or fascinated?

9. Do you feel that Donne became so interested in his intellectualizing that he lost track of the emotional content of his poem? On the other hand, does his intellectualizing enable him to communicate a depth of emotion?

10. Compare this poem to 'Sweetest love, I do not go'. If you were Donne's beloved which one would you prefer to receive. Support your decision by close reference to the two poems.

The Dreame

Dear love, for nothing less than thee
Would I have broke this happy dream,
It was a theme
For reason, much too strong for phantasy,
Therefore thou waked'st me wisely; yet   5
My dream thou brok'st not, but continued'st it;
Thou art so true, that thoughts of thee suffice,
To make dreams truths, and fables histories;
Enter these arms, for since thou thought'st it best,
Not to dream all my dream, let's act the rest.   10

As lightning, or a taper's light,
Thine eyes, and not thy noise waked me;
Yet I thought thee
(For thou lov'st truth) an angel, at first sight,
But when I saw thou saw'st my heart,   15
And knew'st my thoughts, beyond an angel's art,
When thou knew'st what I dreamed, when thou knew'st when
Excess of joy would wake me, and cam'st then,
I must confess, it could not choose but be
Profane, to think thee anything but thee.   20

Coming and staying showed thee, thee,
But rising makes me doubt, that now,
Thou art not thou.

That love is weak, where fear's as strong as he;
'Tis not all spirit, pure, and brave,   25
If mixture it of fear, shame, honour, have.
Perchance as torches which must ready be,
Men light and put out, so thou deal'st with me,
Thou cam'st to kindle, goest to come; then I
Will dream that hope again, but else would die.   30

Notes

[4] **reason:** reality
[7] **suffice:** are enough
[11] **taper:** slim candle
[20] **profane:** irreverent

Explorations

First reading

1. How would you describe the tone of this poem? Compare it with 'The Sun Rising' where Donne is also awakened. What factors contribute to the different tone used by Donne in each of the poems?

2. Trace the narrative line of this poem. Do you feel that it is a convincing incident? How does Donne make the situation seem real?

3. Examine the language and images that Donne uses to describe his beloved. What do they convey about the quality of his love?

Second reading

4. Consider the way in which Donne blends the states of waking and sleeping. Do you find it a successful evocation of a half-waking condition?

5. Is this a particularly revealing poem? Consider how the language Donne uses contributes to the sense of sincerity.

Third reading

6. The final four lines of the poem reveal an anxiety that underlies Donne's love poems, a doubt that he is able to attract true love. Would you agree or disagree?

7. Dryden held the view that Donne 'perplexes the minds of the fair sex with nice speculations of philosophy,

when he should engage their hearts'. Discuss this statement with reference to this poem and two of the other love poems in the course.

8. 'Yet I thought thee
(For thou lov'st truth) an
angel, at first sight,'

'This flea is you and I, and this
Our marriage bed, and
marriage temple is;'

'And swear
No where
Lives a woman true, and fair.'

'She is all states, and all princes, I,
Nothing else is.'
Discuss which of these quotations, if any, reveal Donne's true view of love. Which would you like it to be? Why?

Batter my heart

Batter my heart, three-personed God; for, you
As yet but knock, breathe, shine, and seek to mend;
That I may rise, and stand, o'erthrow me, and bend
Your force, to break, blow, burn, and make me new.
I, like an usurped town, to another due,   5
Labour to admit you, but oh, to no end,
Reason your viceroy in me, me should defend,
But is captived, and proves weak or untrue,
Yet dearly I love you, and would be loved fain,
But am betrothed unto your enemy,   10
Divorce me, untie, or break that knot again,
Take me to you, imprison me, for I
Except you enthral me, never shall be free,
Nor ever chaste, except you ravish me.

Notes
[5] **usurped:** wrongfully seized
[7] **viceroy:** a ruler who exercises authority on behalf of a sovereign
[9] **fain:** gladly
[13] **enthral:** captivate, enslave
[14] **ravish:** rape, enrapture

Explorations

First reading

1. Discuss your initial reaction to this poem. Are you surprised, shocked, overwhelmed? Perhaps you have another reaction?

2. Consider the actual appearance of this poem on the page. What are the differences in the visual impact of this poem and that of 'Song: Go, and catch a falling star'. Does the visual structure of the poems imply anything about their content?

3. Examine the language Donne uses to address God. Choose any words from the poem that you find particularly vivid. How does Donne use the actual sounds of the words to emphasise their effect? What tone of voice do they require?

Second reading

4. Trace the series of images that Donne uses to communicate his relationship with God. Are they what you would expect in a religious poem? Do they help you to understand Donne's feelings?

5. How does Donne convey his inability to commit totally to God? What is the attraction that pulls him away from God? Are you made to believe in his indecision?

6. Consider the rhyme scheme in the poem. How does Donne use it to add impact to his writing? Does it dominate or underpin the sense of emotion?

7. Why do you think Donne wrote this poem? What was he trying to do? Do you feel that it would have helped him?

Third reading

8. 'Take me to you, imprison me, for I
   Except you enthral me, never shall be free,
   Nor ever chaste, except you ravish me.'
   Discuss the effect of Donne's use of the paradox in these lines. Do you find this device helps to communicate the intensity of his feelings, or does it simply get in the way?

9. Robert Graves felt that Donne's opening inspirations frequently wear out after two or three lines and that it is only his wit that moves him forward. Does he 'run out of steam' in this poem? Does he move forward?

10. This poem is one of a group entitled *Divine Meditations*: can you find evidence of either the 'Divine' or the 'Meditation' in it?

At the round earth's imagined corners

At the round earth's imagined corners, blow
Your trumpets, angels, and arise, arise
From death, you numberless infinities
Of souls, and to your scattered bodies go,
All whom the flood did, and fire shall o'erthrow,   5
All whom war, dearth, age, agues, tyrannies,
Despair, law, chance, hath slain, and you whose eyes,
Shall behold God, and never taste death's woe.
But let them sleep, Lord, and me mourn a space,
For, if above all these, my sins abound,   10
'Tis late to ask abundance of thy grace,
When we are there; here on this lowly ground,
Teach me how to repent; for that's as good
As if thou hadst sealed my pardon, with thy blood.

Notes   [3] **infinities:** infinite numbers
         [5] **o'erthrow:** overthrow, conquer
         [6] **dearth:** scarcity
         [6] **agues:** fevers

Explorations

First reading

1. Do you feel that Donne wanted to lead you through this poem or sweep you along? Who was in charge, you or Donne? What was your reaction when you had finished reading the poem?

2. Examine the ways in which Donne communicates the drama of the Day of Judgement in the octet (lines 1–8) of this sonnet. Pay particular attention to the senses that he appeals to in his descriptions.

3. What happens to the focus of the poem in the sestet (lines 9–14)? Is the change gradual or sudden? Were you taken by surprise or did you expect it?

Second reading

4. How would you describe Donne's attitude toward the Day of Judgement? Do you feel that this attitude remains constant or alters in the course of the poem? What do you learn about Donne's emotional state from this?

5. Examine the verbs that Donne uses. Do they help to convey the tone of the poem? Are they reminiscent of any of Donne's other poems?

6. What do you learn about Donne's relationship with (i) God, and (ii) his fellow men, from this poem?

Third reading

7. Consider the way in which Donne uses the sounds of words to add depth and pace to his writing. Do you feel that such attention to detail weakens or strengthens the emotional impact of the piece?

8. Are you convinced of Donne's emotional sincerity, or is this simply an intellectual exercise for him? Support your opinion by close reference to the poem.

9. How do you feel about Donne, the man, as he is revealed in this poem? Would you like him as a friend? Did you prefer the man who wrote the love poems? Are they two separate people or aspects of the same man?

10. The critic Mario Praz felt that Donne was more concerned with 'the whole effect' of his writing rather than a search for truth. Choose any three of Donne's poems and discuss this comment.

Thou hast made me

Thou hast made me, and shall thy work decay?
Repair me now, for now mine end doth haste,
I run to death, and death meets me as fast,
And all my pleasures are like yesterday,
I dare not move my dim eyes any way,   5
Despair behind, and death before doth cast
Such terror, and my feeble flesh doth waste
By sin in it, which it towards hell doth weigh;
Only thou art above, and when towards thee
By thy leave I can look, I rise again;   10
But our old subtle foe so tempteth me,
That not one hour I can myself sustain;
Thy Grace may wing me to prevent his art,
And thou like adamant draw mine iron heart.

Note   [14] **adamant:** magnet

Old St Paul's Cathedral, London, where Donne was ordained an Anglican priest in 1615

Explorations

First reading

1. What age do you think Donne was when he wrote this poem? What words convey a sense of his physical condition?

2. Discuss the tone of voice that would be most suitable for this piece. Is there a connection between the sense of Donne's physical state and the tone of the poem?

3. Psychologically, this poem reveals a great deal about the difficulties Donne faced with his religious faith. Can you trace how he communicates the intensity of his mental struggle? Do you feel that this poem enabled him to arrive at a resolution?

Second reading

4. 'And all my pleasures are like yesterday;'
   How do you think the Donne of this poem felt about his earlier love poems?

5. Donne assigns specific roles to God and himself. Can you describe what these are? Compare Donne's approach here with the one he takes in 'Batter my heart'. Is there a poignancy about Donne's role in this poem?

6. The final couplet (rhyming two lines) can be interpreted in different ways. Discuss what these might be and consider which one seems to be most fitting.

Third reading

7. Joan Bennett wrote:
   'Metaphysical poetry is written by men for whom the light of day is God's shadow.' Consider Donne's religious poetry in the context of this statement.

8. Donne never intended his poetry for mass publication and during his life most of his works were circulated around a small circle of friends. Do you think that this gave him greater freedom to express himself or would he have felt more self-conscious. Refer to the poems you have explored.

9. 'Donne is adept at keeping the ball in the air.' (Robert Graves) The wheels take fire from the mere rapidity of their motion.' (Coleridge)
   'The spell holds for the duration of the poem.' (Michael Schmidt)
   Was Donne simply a poetic trickster, or did he truly create magic?

10. 'But when I saw thou saw'st my heart,
    And knew'st my thoughts'
    In the poems that you have explored, did you see Donne's heart and know his thoughts? Did Donne see your heart and know your thoughts?

2 *William* WORDSWORTH

prescribed for Higher Level exams in 2004 and 2005

William Wordsworth was born on 7 April 1770 in Cockermouth, Cumberland. The family was well-to-do and had a good social standing. Dorothy, his sister, was born in December 1771 and the two children developed a close relationship that was to continue into adulthood. Sadly, when he was eight years old his mother died, and five years later his father also died. Wordsworth attended Hawkshead Grammar School and, at the age of 17, entered St John's College, Cambridge.

In 1790, during his summer holidays, he went on a walking tour through France and the Alps. After receiving his BA, Wordsworth returned to France and became interested in the revolutionary movement. He had an affair with Annette Vallon, who bore him a daughter. Under pressure from his friends, who were anxious about the political instability in France, Wordsworth returned to England and published some of his writing. The books received little attention, but they did lead to his friendship with Samuel Taylor Coleridge. Together they worked on a book of poems entitled *The Lyrical Ballads*, generally recognized as marking the beginning of the Romantic Movement in English poetry. For

1770–1850

much of his life Wordsworth lived with Dorothy, his wife Mary, and his children in the beautiful Lake District. However, he enjoyed travelling on the Continent as well as around Britain and Ireland.

Although Wordsworth's work was not generally popular, among the literary set he was recognized as the initiator of a new form of poetic writing. Toward the end of his life he became more generally appreciated. In 1843, he was appointed Poet Laureate and received a state pension. He died, in 1850, at the age of eighty and is buried in Grasmere churchyard.

A contemporary painting of peaks in the French Alps which Wordsworth visited in 1790

She dwelt among the untrodden ways

this poem is also prescribed for Ordinary Level exams in 2004 and 2005

She dwelt among the untrodden ways
Beside the springs of Dove,
A Maid whom there were none to praise
And very few to love:

A violet by a mossy stone   5
Half hidden from the eye!
—Fair as a star, when only one
Is shining in the sky.

She lived unknown, and few could know
When Lucy ceased to be;   10
But she is in her grave, and, oh,
The difference to me!

Notes   [1] **dwelt:** lived
            [1] **untrodden:** not stepped on
            [2] **springs:** a place where water wells up from the earth
            [3] **Maid:** a girl

Explorations

First reading

1. Describe in your own words the type of life that was led by Lucy? What sort of environment did she live in? Do you think that she was happy with her life? Why? Would you be happy to live like this?

2. Wordsworth does not tell us directly what Lucy looked like. In the second stanza he uses two images to suggest some of her qualities. Discuss what you consider these qualities to be. How would you react if someone compared you to a 'violet' or a 'star'?

3. What is Wordsworth's mood in this poem? Choose one phrase from the poem that you feel clearly signals this mood. What tone of voice should be used to read this poem?

Second reading

4. Do you think that the first stanza is an effective way to open a piece of poetry? Why?

5. What do you learn about Wordsworth himself from reading the poem? Can you suggest what sort of relationship he had with Lucy?

6. Examine Wordsworth's use of rhyme? Were you aware of it as you read the poem? How does the rhyme contribute to the overall effect of the piece?

Third reading

7. Wordsworth claims that Lucy's death made a 'difference' to him. Do you feel that the poem communicates death as distressing? Can you think of a reason why he might not be too upset?

8. Do you think that this poem conveys the flesh-and-blood Lucy, or was Wordsworth more interested in describing something else?

9. Wordsworth wanted to write poetry using 'the language really spoken by men'. Does he succeed in doing this here? How did his choice of words effect your reaction to the piece?

10. Is this poem too simple to be really interesting? Does simplicity in writing necessarily mean that it is easy to understand?

It is a beauteous evening, calm and free

this poem is also prescribed for Ordinary Level exams in 2004 and 2005

It is a beauteous evening, calm and free,
The holy time is quiet as a Nun
Breathless with adoration; the broad sun
Is sinking down in its tranquility;
The gentleness of heaven broods o'er the Sea: 5
Listen! the mighty Being is awake,
And doth with his eternal motion make
A sound like thunder—everlastingly.
Dear Child! dear Girl! that walkest with me here,
If thou appear untouched by solemn thought,   10
Thy nature is not therefore less divine:
Thou liest in Abraham's bosom all the year;
And worshipp'st at the Temple's inner shrine,
God being with thee when we know it not.

Notes

[12] **Abraham:** In the Old Testament Abraham was willing to sacrifice his son Isaac on God's orders. He stands for unswerving faith.

[13] **Temple's inner shrine:** The Temple, in the Old Testamant, where God was worshipped was divided into two areas: one part where the congregation gathered and the more sacred inner shrine which could only be entered by the priests.

Grasmere in the Lake District: a nineteenth-century lithograph

Explorations

First reading

1. What time of day does Wordsworth describe in the first 5 lines of the poem? Choose one phrase that you find particularly effective. Have you ever been moved by a scene in nature? Write about your own experience.

2. Discuss who or what 'the mighty Being' is in line 6. You should find lines 7–8 helpful. What do you feel about this description—is it vivid, surprising, confusing, or do you have a different reaction?

3. Does the way in which Wordsworth describes the scene in lines 1–8 tell you anything about what he felt at the time? Suggest two words to summarize his reaction.

4. In lines 9–14 Wordsworth tells us about his companion's reaction. How is it different to his own? Do you think that the fact she is a child affects the way in which she reacts? Does Wordsworth consider one reaction better than the other?

Second reading

5. Wordsworth uses an image of a nun in the opening four lines of the poem. How does he connect it with the sunset? Do you find this a successful connection of ideas? Why?

6. Why do you think Wordsworth referred to the sunset as 'The holy time'? Does the phrase tell you anything about his attitude to nature?

7. What senses does Wordsworth appeal to in this poem? What effect does this have on the overall impact of his description?

Third reading

8. Wordsworth famously wrote that, for him, poetry was stimulated by 'emotions recollected in tranquility'. Consider how the poem shows evidence of this approach.

9. Look again at 'She dwelt among the untrodden ways'. Do you find any similarities in Wordsworth's attitude to nature in the two poems?

10. Find a picture, or paint one yourself, to illustrate this poem.

Skating (extract from The Prelude)

this poem is also prescribed for Ordinary Level exams in 2004 and 2005

And in the frosty season, when the sun
Was set, and visible for many a mile
The cottage windows blazed through twilight gloom,
I heeded not their summons: happy time
It was indeed for all of us—for me   5
It was a time of rapture! Clear and loud
The village clock tolled six,—I wheeled about,
Proud and exulting like an untired horse
That cares not for his home. All shod with steel,
We hissed along the polished ice in games   10
Confederate, imitative of the chase
And woodland pleasures,—the resounding horn,
The pack loud chiming, and the hunted hare.
So through the darkness and the cold we flew,
And not a voice was idle; with the din   15
Smitten, the precipices rang aloud;
The leafless trees and every icy crag
Tinkled like iron; while far distant hills
Into the tumult sent an alien sound
Of melancholy not unnoticed, while the stars   20
Eastward were sparkling clear, and in the west
The orange sky of evening died away.
Not seldom from the uproar I retired
Into a silent bay, or sportively
Glanced sideway, leaving the tumultuous throng,   25
To cut across the reflex of a star
That fled, and, flying still before me, gleamed
Upon the glassy plain; and oftentimes,
When we had given our bodies to the wind,
And all the shadowy banks on either side   30
Came sweeping through the darkness, spinning still
The rapid line of motion, then at once
Have I, reclining back upon my heels,
Stopped short; yet still the solitary cliffs
Wheeled by me—even as if the earth had rolled   35
With visible motion her diurnal round!
Behind me did they stretch in solemn train,
Feebler and feebler, and I stood and watched
Till all was tranquil as a dreamless sleep.

Notes

[4] **heeded not:** paid no attention to

[8] **exulting:** triumphantly joyful

[11] **Confederate:** allied together

[15] **din:** prolonged loud noise

[16] **Smitten:** struck

[16] **precipices:** sheer cliffs

[19] **tumult:** uproar

[19] **alien:** different

[20] **melancholy:** sadness, depression

[25] **throng:** crowd

[26] **reflex:** reflection

[33] **reclining:** bending back

[36] **diurnal:** daily

Explorations

First reading

1. Do you find this piece immediately understandable or rather confusing? Were you carried along by the speed of the language, or did you feel a little overwhelmed? Why do you think Wordsworth chose to write at such a rate?

2. Choose two phrases and two words that you find particularly effective in suggesting a frozen world. Explain why you chose them.

3. Have you ever been skating? Do you feel that Wordsworth successfully conveys a sense of what it is actually like to go skating? Examine the ways he suggests the freedom and speed of movement. Pay particular attention to his choice of words and the actual sounds of the words.

4. Discuss the senses that Wordsworth appeals to in the piece. Consider how they contribute to the vividness of the scene.

Second reading

5. In lines 7–9 Wordsworth compares himself to a horse. Discuss the qualities he is trying to suggest by using this image. Do you think that the linking of these two ideas works? Does he use animal imagery elsewhere in the extract? Is it effective?

6. Sounds play a very important part in this poem. Can you suggest a reason for this? Try to remember being outside when there is snow and ice. Is there a particular sound word in the poem that you find especially effective?

7. Can you describe Wordsworth's mood in the poem? Does it remain the same throughout the piece, or can you detect a change? Discuss why his mood is affected.

Third reading

8. Wordsworth seems to feel that children have an instinctive ability to connect with nature. Examine this view in relation to this extract and one of his other poems that you have read.

9. We often tend to idealise memories of our childhood. Has Wordsworth done that here or is this a realistic portrayal of being a child?

10. Wordsworth wrote 'The end of Poetry is to produce excitement in co-existence with an overbalance of pleasure.' Did you feel excitement and pleasure when you read this extract?

To My Sister

It is the first mild day of March:
Each minute sweeter than before,
The redbreast sings from the tall larch
That stands beside our door.

There is a blessing in the air,   5
Which seems a sense of joy to yield
To the bare trees, and mountains bare,
And grass in the green field.

My sister! ('tis a wish of mine)
Now that our morning meal is done,   10
Make haste, your morning task resign;
Come forth and feel the sun.

Edward will come with you;—and, pray,
Put on with speed your woodland dress;
And bring no book: for this one day   15
We'll give to idleness.

No joyless forms shall regulate
Our living calendar:
We from today, my Friend, will date
The opening of the year.   20

Love, now a universal birth,
From heart to heart is stealing,
From earth to man, from man to earth:
—It is the hour of feeling.

One moment now may give us more   25
Than years of toiling reason:
Our minds shall drink at every pore
The spirit of the season.

Some silent laws our hearts will make,
Which they shall long obey: 30
We for the year to come may take
Our temper from to-day.

And from the blessed power that rolls
About, below, above,
We'll frame the measure of our souls: 35
They shall be tuned to love.

Then come, my Sister! come, I pray,
With speed put on your woodland dress;
And bring no book: for this one day
We'll give to idleness.   40

Notes   [11] **make haste:** hurry
        [11] **task:** piece of work to be done
        [26] **toiling:** hard work
        [32] **temper:** mood or mental attitude

 # Explorations

First reading

1. What do you notice about the way Wordsworth uses language in this poem? Is it what you would expect in a piece of poetic writing? Do you like it or not?

2. Can you work out the time of year and the type of weather that has inspired Wordsworth? Support your view by close reference to the poem. Do you think that he would have been equally inspired had the day been wet and windy? Perhaps he might have written a different type of poem— discuss what it might have been like.

3. Why does Wordsworth want his sister to come outside? If you were Dorothy would this poem persuade you to do as he asked.

4. How, in Wordsworth's view, will a day outside affect the group? Do you agree or disagree with his opinion. Have you ever been positively influenced by a day in the open air?

Second reading

5. Wordsworth asks his sister to put on her 'woodland dress' twice in the poem. Can you suggest why he repeated this request? Do you think that there is more to it then simply asking her to change her clothes?

6. In the sixth stanza

Wordsworth introduces the idea of 'Love'. Discuss how this connects with the time of year described in the poem. Examine in detail what Wordsworth actually means by his use of the word 'Love'. Would you agree with his interpretation of the word? Why?

7. Wordsworth refers to Time throughout this poem. Consider the different aspects of Time that occur. Does he suggest that there is a fundamental difference in the way that they affect Man?

8. We'll give the day to idleness. Did Wordsworth really believe that the day would be spent in 'idleness'?

Third reading

9. Read 'It is a beauteous evening, calm and free' again. Are there any similarities between these two poems? Consider in particular the use of language, the senses and the underlying philosophy.

10. Wordsworth frequently uses exclamation marks in his writing. Why do you think he does this? Did you notice them, or are they not very important to the overall effect of his poetry?

A slumber did my spirit seal

A slumber did my spirit seal;
I had no human fears:
She seemed a thing that could not feel
The touch of earthly years.

No motion has she now, no force;   5
She neither hears nor sees;
Rolled round in earth's diurnal course,
With rocks, and stones, and trees.

Notes   [1] **seal:** close securely, put barriers around
        [7] **diurnal:** daily

Explorations

First reading

1. What mood do you think Wordsworth is trying to create in this poem? Do the actual sounds of the words help to reinforce the effect? Is there any particular phrase that you feel encapsulates this mood?

2. Wordsworth tries to communicate a particular state in lines 3–6. Try to visualize yourself in this state. Write down any words that occur to you as descriptions of what you feel. Discuss your ideas with a view to choosing the five most successful descriptive words suggested.

3. In the final two lines, Wordsworth uses an image that we have previously met in 'Skating (extract from *The Prelude*)'. What is he describing? Do you find it an effective description? How does it relate to the mood of the piece?

Second reading

4. Discuss the language used by Wordsworth in this poem. What are your initial impressions of it? Are you more aware of a degree of ambiguity after a second reading? Can you locate the cause of this ambiguity?

5. Examine the opening line of the poem. Explain how you interpret it. Does the fact that it is written in the past tense influence how it is interpreted?

6. In the second line Wordsworth appears to make a simple statement. Discuss how his use of the past tense could effect the meaning it conveys. Is there a further alteration in the meaning of this line when you join it with lines 3–4?

7. Wordsworth changes to the present tense in the second stanza. Discuss the ways in which this adjustment influences your reaction to his description.

Third reading

8. Consider this poem as a whole interpreting 'she' as referring to 'my spirit'. Can you express, in your own words, what Wordsworth is trying to communicate?

9. Some critics suggest that there are indications that this poem might have been written about Lucy. Re-read 'She dwelt among the untrodden ways'. Does this change your view of the poem?

10. Look at Question 1 again. In the light of your subsequent readings and consideration of the poem, would you alter your answer?

Composed Upon Westminster Bridge

Earth has not anything to show more fair:
Dull would he be of soul who could pass by
A sight so touching in its majesty:
This City now doth, like a garment, wear
The beauty of the morning; silent, bare,　　　　　　5
Ships, towers, domes, theatres, and temples lie
Open unto the fields, and to the sky;
All bright and glittering in the smokeless air.
Never did sun more beautifully steep
In his first splendour, valley, rock, or hill;　　　　　10
Ne'er saw I, never felt, a calm so deep!
The river glideth at his own sweet will:
Dear God! the very houses seem asleep;
And all that mighty heart is lying still!

Notes

[4] **doth:** does
[11] **ne'er:** never

Westminster Bridge, London: a contemporary painting

Explorations

First reading

1. Do you find the subject of this poem a surprising choice for Wordsworth? Why?

2. Consider Wordsworth's description of the City? Does he successfully convey 'its majesty'? Choose two images that you find especially vivid and explain why they appeal to you.

3. What effect does this scene have on Wordsworth? Why do you think he reacted in this way? Would you have felt the same emotions?

Second reading

4. Do you think that Wordsworth was restricted in any way by choosing to write this poem as a fourteen-line sonnet? Was he able to communicate his theme successfully? Would the impact of the piece be increased or reduced had the poem been longer?

5. Do you feel that Wordsworth suggests that there is a spiritual element to the appreciation of beauty? Is this a valid view? Does the spiritual quality come from the one who appreciates or the object that is being appreciated?

6. Why do you think Wordsworth wrote this poem in the present tense? Would the overall impact of the piece be altered were it written in the past? Try changing the tenses.

7. Which of the senses does this poem appeal to? Why do you think Wordsworth chose to write it in this way? Would the effect of the description be altered had sounds been added?

Third reading

8. The Victorian poet Matthew Arnold believed that Wordsworth had a 'healing power'. Can words heal? Do you find any of Wordsworth's poems healing?

The Solitary Reaper

Behold her, single in the field,
Yon solitary Highland Lass!
Reaping and singing by herself;
Stop here, or gently pass!
Alone she cuts and binds the grain,   5
And sings a melancholy strain;
O listen! for the Vale profound
Is overflowing with the sound.

No Nightingale did ever chaunt
More welcome notes to weary bands   10
Of travellers in some shady haunt,
Among Arabian sands:
A voice so thrilling ne'er was heard
In spring-time from the Cuckoo-bird,—
Breaking the silence of the seas   15
Among the farthest Hebrides.

Will no one tell me what she sings?—
Perhaps the plaintive numbers flow
For old, unhappy, far-off things,
And battles long ago: 20
Or is it some more humble lay,
Familiar matter of to-day?—
Some natural sorrow, loss, or pain,
That has been, and may be again?

Whate'er the theme, the Maiden sang   25
As if her song could have no ending;
I saw her singing at her work,
And o'er the sickle bending;—
I listened, motionless and still;
And, as I mounted up the hill,   30
The music in my heart I bore,
Long after it was heard no more.

Notes   [1] **behold:** see, observe   [9] **chaunt:** chant, sing

[2] **yon:** yonder. over there   [18] **plaintive:** mournful

[7] **profound:** deep   [21] **lay:** song

Explorations

First reading

1. Discuss the way in which Wordsworth opens this poem with the first stanza. Does it draw you into the poem by the vividness of the descriptions? Or perhaps you find it overdramatic in its language and use of exclamation marks?

2. In the second stanza, Wordsworth describes the quality of the reaper's singing. Do you feel that he was justified in devoting eight lines to this? Was it simply an opportunity for him to show off his descriptive powers?

3. 'Will no one tell me what she sings?'
   Can you explain why Wordsworth asks this question—does he need to know what the girl was singing about? Would this affect his reaction to the singing? Do you think that it should? Do you need to know what a song is about to enjoy it?

4. In the fourth stanza Wordsworth communicates his reaction to the singing. Do you find it a believable reaction? Have you ever been stopped by a piece of music? Did it stay with you in the way that it did with Wordsworth?

Second reading

5. There is a sense of immediacy about the first two lines of this poem. Can you explain how Wordsworth achieves this effect? Does it continue through the rest of the piece?

6. Both Wordsworth and the reaper are depicted as being on their own in Nature. Does the way in which each is depicted suggest a difference in their attitude to and relationship with nature?

Third reading

7. This poem describes a scene that comes from a world very different to the one we live in. Does this reduce the relevance of the poem? Is there a time limit on artistic creation?

8. Does the title, 'The Solitary Reaper', suggest the central theme of this poem? Could you suggest a more suitable title?

9. Examine the way in which Wordsworth uses imagery from Nature in this poem and two of his other poems. Do you find it a successful technique or simply an overused piece of elaboration?

10. The critic F.R. Leavis commented: 'For Wordsworth solitude is the condition of a contemplative serenity.' Discuss this statement with reference to three of Wordsworth's poems.

The Stolen Boat (extract from The Prelude)

One summer evening (led by her) I found
A little boat tied to a willow tree
Within a rocky cave, its usual home.
Straight I unloosed her chain, and stepping in
Pushed from the shore. It was an act of stealth   5
And troubled pleasure, nor without the voice
Of mountain-echoes did my boat move on;
Leaving behind her still, on either side,
Small circles glittering idly in the moon,
Until they melted all into one track   10
Of sparkling light. But now, like one who rows,
Proud of his skill, to reach a chosen point
With an unswerving line, I fixed my view
Upon the summit of a craggy ridge,
The horizon's utmost boundary; for above   15
Was nothing but the stars and the grey sky.
She was an elfin pinnace; lustily
I dipped my oars into the silent lake,
And, as I rose upon the stroke, my boat
Went heaving through the water like a swan;   20
When, from behind that craggy steep till then
The horizon's bound, a huge peak, black and huge,
As if with voluntary power instinct
Upreared its head. I struck and struck again,
And growing still in stature the grim shape   25
Towered up between me and the stars, and still,
For so it seemed, with purpose of its own
And measured motion like a living thing,
Strode after me. With trembling oars I turned,
And through the silent water stole my way   30
Back to the covert of the willow tree;
There in her mooring-place I left my bark,—
And through the meadows homeward went, in grave
And serious mood; but after I had seen
That spectacle, for many days, my brain   35
Worked with a dim and undetermined sense

Of unknown modes of being; o'er my thoughts
There hung a darkness, call it solitude
Or blank desertion. No familiar shapes
Remained, no pleasant images of trees,   40
Of sea or sky, no colours of green fields;
But huge and mighty forms, that do not live
Like living men, moved slowly through the mind
By day, and were a trouble to my dreams.

Notes

[4]   **Straight:** without delay

[14] **craggy:** rugged

[17] **pinnace:** a ship's small boat

[17] **lustily:** with passionate enjoyment

[22] **bound:** boundary

[31] **covert:** shelter

[37] **modes:** ways

Explorations

First reading

1. What emotions does the young Wordsworth feel as he takes the boat? How does Wordsworth communicate these feelings to you in the first seven lines of the piece?

2. Consider Wordsworth's emotions in lines 11–20. Describe, in your own words, what he feels.

3. How does the appearance of the peak effect Wordsworth's actions? Can you locate the words or phrases that suggest

his emotional alteration?

4. Can you explain how Wordsworth felt in the days after this incident? What particular aspect of this experience provoked these feelings? Do you feel that his reaction is understandable or rather overdramatic?

Second reading

5. Time plays an important part in this piece. Discuss how it is conveyed during and after the incident. Does Wordsworth's

emotional state affect his perception of time. Has this ever happened to you?

6. Discuss how Wordsworth uses the concept of space to suggest his feelings. Can our emotions affect our awareness of space? Can space effect our emotions?

7. What do you think Wordsworth learned as a result of this experience? Have you ever found yourself in a similar situation? Consider whether such learning experiences are exclusive to the young.

Third reading

8. Compare this extract with 'Skating', which also comes from *The Prelude*. Are there any similarities between the two. Are they different in any way? This piece comes before 'Skating' in the full work. Is there any sense of this in the extracts themselves?

9. In many ways the physical activities described in 'The Stolen Boat' and 'Skating' are less important than the emotional movements stimulated by them. Discuss, supporting your view with references from both extracts.

10. Wordsworth described *The Prelude* as 'a poem on my own poetical education.' Consider what lessons he learned, as suggested in 'The Stolen Boat' and 'Skating'. Do you feel that they serve to underpin his later works?

Grasmere by the Rydal Road, painting by Francis Towner (1739–1816)

Rydal Waterfall, a painting by Joseph Wright (1734–1797)

Tintern Abbey

Five years have past; five summers, with the length
Of five long winters! and again I hear
These waters, rolling from their mountain-springs
With a soft inland murmur.—Once again
Do I behold these steep and lofty cliffs,   5
That on a wild secluded scene impress
Thoughts of more deep seclusion; and connect
The landscape with the quiet of the sky.
The day is come when I again repose
Here, under this dark sycamore, and view   10
These plots of cottage-ground, these orchard-tufts,
Which at this season, with their unripe fruits,
Are clad in one green hue, and lose themselves
'Mid groves and copses. Once again I see
These hedge-rows, hardly hedge-rows, little lines   15
Of sportive wood run wild : these pastoral farms,
Green to the very door; and wreaths of smoke
Sent up, in silence, from among the trees!
With some uncertain notice, as might seem
Of vagrant dwellers in the houseless woods,   20
Or of some Hermit's cave, where by his fire
The Hermit sits alone.
These beauteous forms,
Through a long absence, have not been to me
As is a landscape to a blind man's eye: 25
But oft, in lonely rooms, and 'mid the din
Of towns and cities, I have owed to them,
In hours of weariness, sensations sweet,
Felt in the blood, and felt along the heart;
And passing even into my purer mind,   30
With tranquil restoration:—feelings too
Of unremembered pleasure: such, perhaps,

Notes [9] **repose:** rest, lie
[20] **vagrant:** wandering

As have no slight or trivial influence
On that best portion of a good man's life,
His little, nameless, unremembered, acts   35
Of kindness and of love. Nor less, I trust,
To them I may have owed another gift,
Of aspect more sublime; that blessed mood,
In which the burthen of the mystery,
In which the heavy and the weary weight   40
Of all this unintelligible world,
Is lightened:—that serene and blessed mood,
In which the affections gently lead us on,—
Until, the breath of this corporeal frame
And even the motion of our human blood   45
Almost suspended, we are laid asleep
In body, and become a living soul:
While with an eye made quiet by the power
Of harmony, and the deep power of joy,
We see into the life of things.   50
If this
Be but a vain belief, yet oh! how oft—
In darkness and amid the many shapes
Of joyless daylight; when the fretful stir
Unprofitable, and the fever of the world,   55
Have hung upon the beatings of my heart—
How oft, in spirit, have I turned to thee,
O sylvan Wye! thou wanderer thro' the woods,
How often has my spirit turned to thee!

And now, with gleams of half-extinguished thought,   60
With many recognitions dim and faint,
And somewhat of a sad perplexity,
The picture of the mind revives again:
While here I stand, not only with the sense
Of present pleasure, but with pleasing thoughts   65
That in this moment there is life and food

[39] **burthen:** burden
[44] **corporeal:** physical, bodily
[58] **sylvan:** wooded, rural
[62] **perplexity:** puzzlement, confusion

For future years. And so I dare to hope,
Though changed, no doubt, from what I was when first
I came among these hills; when like a roe
I bounded o'er the mountains, by the sides   70
Of the deep rivers, and the lonely streams,
Wherever Nature led: more like a man
Flying from something that he dreads than one
Who sought the thing he loved. For Nature then
(The coarser pleasures of my boyish days,   75
And their glad animal movements all gone by)
To me was all in all—I cannot paint
What then I was. The sounding cataract
Haunted me like a passion: the tall rock,
The mountain, and the deep and gloomy wood,   80
Their colours and their forms, were then to me
An appetite; a feeling and a love,
That had no need of a remoter charm,
By thought supplied, nor any interest
Unborrowed from the eye.—That time is past,   85
And all its aching joys are now no more,
And all its dizzy raptures. Not for this
Faint I, nor mourn nor murmur; other gifts
Have followed; for such loss, I would believe,
Abundant recompense. For I have learned   90
To look on Nature, not as in the hour
Of thoughtless youth; but hearing oftentimes
The still, sad music of humanity,
Nor harsh nor grating, though of ample power
To chasten and subdue. And I have felt   95
A presence that disturbs me with the joy
Of elevated thoughts; a sense sublime
Of something far more deeply interfused
Whose dwelling is the light of setting suns,
And the round ocean and the living air,   100
And the blue sky, and in the mind of man:

[69] **roe:** small deer

[78] **cataract:** large waterfall

[90] **recompense:** amends

[95] **chasten:** restrain

[98] **interfused:** mixed with

A motion and a spirit, that impels
All thinking things, all object of all thought,
And rolls through all things. Therefore am I still
A lover of the meadows and the woods,   105
And mountains; and of all that we behold
From this green earth; of all the mighty world
Of eye, and ear,—both what they half create,
And what perceive; well pleased to recognise
In Nature and the language of the sense   110
The anchor of my purest thoughts, the nurse,
The guide, the guardian of my heart, and soul
Of all my moral being.
               Nor perchance,
If I were not thus taught, should I the more   115
Suffer my genial spirits to decay;
For thou art with me here upon the banks
Of this fair river; thou my dearest Friend,
My dear, dear Friend; and in thy voice I catch
The language of my former heart, and read   120
My former pleasures in the shooting lights
Of thy wild eyes. Oh! yet a little while
May I behold in thee what I was once,
My dear, dear Sister! and this prayer I make,
Knowing that Nature never did betray   125
The heart that loved her; 'tis her privilege,
Through all the years of this our life, to lead
From joy to joy: for she can so inform
The mind that is within us, so impress
With quietness and beauty, and so feed   130
With lofty thoughts, that neither evil tongues,
Rash judgments, nor the sneers of selfish men,
Nor greetings where no kindness is, nor all
The dreary intercourse of daily life,
Shall e'er prevail against us, or disturb   135
Our cheerful faith, that all which we behold

[116]   **genial:** cheerful
[135]   **prevail:** be victorious

Is full of blessings. Therefore let the moon
Shine on thee in thy solitary walk;
And let the misty mountain-winds be free
To blow against thee: and, in after years,   140
When these wild ecstasies shall be matured
Into a sober pleasure; when thy mind
Shall be a mansion for all lovely forms,
Thy memory be as a dwelling-place
For all sweet sounds and harmonies; oh! then,   145
If solitude, or fear, or pain, or grief,
Should be thy portion, with what healing thoughts
Of tender joy wilt thou remember me,
And these my exhortations! Nor, perchance—
If I should be where I no more can hear   150
Thy voice, nor catch from thy wild eyes these gleams
Of past existence—wilt thou then forget
That on the banks of this delightful stream
We stood together; and that I, so long
A worshipper of Nature, hither came   155
Unwearied in that service: rather say
With warmer love—oh! with far deeper zeal
Of holier love. Nor wilt thou then forget
That after many wanderings, many years
Of absence, these steep woods and lofty cliffs,   160
And this green pastoral landscape, were to me
More dear, both for themselves and for thy sake!

[149]   **exhortations:** urgings
[157]   **zeal:** fervour

Explorations

First reading

1. What was your initial reaction when you saw the length of this poem? Did you find the poem difficult to read once you started or did Wordsworth draw you along with his language and images. Was your interest sustained throughout the poem? Should a poem be limited in its length? Why?

2. Examine Wordsworth's description of the sweep of the view that is before him. Do you find it effective? Would you find such a scene appealing?

3. How does the view affect Wordsworth? What does the way in which he uses this scene suggest about Wordsworth's attitude to the different worlds he lives in? Do you think that most people have favourite scenes which they evoke as an escape from situations they find difficult? Do you?

Second reading

4. Discuss the changes that take place in Wordsworth's relationship with Nature as he matures. Do you feel that altered relationships are part of the human maturing process? Why?

5. 'A motion and a spirit, that impels
   All thinking things, all object of all thought,
   And rolls through all things.'
   What do you think Wordsworth is referring to in these lines? Do you think that he is deluding himself into believing that there is a way to understand this 'unintelligible world'?

6. What does Wordsworth's address to his sister, in the final section of the poem suggest about their relationship? Do you find it surprising that he has someone else with him in this poem? Why?

Third reading

7. 'Thy memory be as a dwelling place
   For all sweet sounds and harmonies;'
   What role does memory play in Wordsworth's poetry? Does he use the past to go forward? In what ways?

8. Discuss the way in which Wordsworth, in his poetry, moves out from himself toward a wider perception. Do you feel that he is expressing a process common to all humans? What makes his experience worthy of being studied?

9. With Wordsworth 'an intense intellectual egotism swallows up everything'. (William Hazlitt)
Wordsworth 'continues to bring joy, peace, strength, exaltation'. (A.C. Bradley)
Wordsworth shows 'a capricious predilection for incidents that contrast with the depth and novelty of the truths that they are to exemplify'. (Samuel Taylor Coleridge)
Discuss these opinions on Wordsworth's writing. Do you agree with any of them? Try to summarize your view of Wordsworth into one sentence.

10. Wordsworth commented: 'I have wished to keep the Reader in the company of flesh and blood, persuaded that by so doing I shall interest him.' Did Wordsworth interest you? Why?

3 *Emily* DICKINSON

prescribed for Higher Level exams in 2004 and 2005

Emily Dickinson was born and lived all her life in Amherst, Massachusetts in the US. The family members were prominent members of the community, lawyers and public representatives. Emily's early years seemed ordinary enough: education at Amherst Academy and Mount Holyoke Female Seminary; trips to Boston, Washington and Philadelphia; and running the family household when her mother became seriously ill. But she seems to have suffered some kind of psychological crisis in her early thirties, which resulted in her withdrawal from society.

She became somewhat eccentric, 'the myth' of Amherst, who didn't meet strangers or visitors and who spoke to friends from behind a half-closed door or shrouded in shadow at the head of the stairs. She produced a great number of rather cryptic poems of a most unusual form. When she died she was found to have left almost two thousand poems and fragments, in which she explored a number of themes including love, pain, absence and loss, doubt, despair and mental anguish, and hope. Hardly any were published in her lifetime, and their true worth and originality were not appreciated for many years.

1830–1886

Note on the Poems

In 1955 an authoritative collection of Dickinson's work, *The Poems of Emily Dickinson*, was prepared by Thomas Johnson. The poems are dated, but as Johnson himself admitted, this is the result of educated guesswork. It is very difficult to be definite, since Dickinson never prepared the poems for publication and did not title them. Each poem below is headed with Johnson's number.

214

I taste a liquor never brewed—
From Tankards scooped in Pearl—
Not all the Vats upon the Rhine
Yield such an Alcohol!

Inebriate of Air—am I—   5
And Debauchee of Dew—
Reeling—thro endless summer days—
From inns of Molten Blue—

When 'Landlords' turn the drunken Bee
Out of the Foxglove's door—   10
When Butterflies—renounce their 'drams'—
I shall but drink the more!

Till Seraphs swing their snowy Hats—
And Saints—to windows run—
To see the little Tippler   15
Leaning against the—Sun—

Explorations

First reading

1. If you first approach the poem as a riddle, does this help you to decipher stanzas 1 and 2? For example, can you suggest an answer to any of the following enigmas:
   - How could there be a liquor that wasn't brewed?
   - Tankards or beer mugs the colour of pearl?
   - 'Inebriate of Air', 'Debauchee of Dew'—who or what might she be? Who or what gets drunk on dew?
   - She is seen staggering from 'inns of Molten Blue'—an unusual colour for an inn as we know it. What or where are the inns?

   Is all revealed in the third stanza? Examine the first two lines. Explain your reading of stanzas 1 and 2.

2. Now explain the central metaphor of the poem.

3. Would you agree that the poet's train of thought becomes more whimsical as the poem progresses?

4. What do the first two stanzas suggest about the speaker's attitude to nature?

Second reading

5. What self-image does the poet attempt to project in this poem? Do you think she sees herself as dissolute, rebellious, assertive, or what? Explain, with reference to phrases or images.

6. It is generally agreed that this is a humorous poem. Comment on some of the methods by which the humour is achieved.

7. Do you think there is a substantial theme beneath the whimsical and humorous surface? Make suggestions.

8. How would you describe the tone of the poem? Refer to words and phrases in the text.

Third reading

9. The literary critic David Porter spoke of a 'tone of ecstatic assurance', reflecting the attitude of the speaker as victor over the pains of life. Would you agree with this?

10. What is your own evaluation of this poem?

254

this poem is also prescribed for Ordinary Level exams in 2004 and 2005

'Hope' is the thing with feathers—
That perches in the soul—
And sings the tune without the words—
And never stops—at all—

And sweetest—in the Gale—is heard—   5
And sore must be the storm—
That could abash the little Bird
That kept so many warm—

I've heard it in the chillest land—
And on the strangest Sea—   10
Yet, never, in Extremity,
It asked a crumb—of Me.

Explorations

Before reading

1. Consider briefly what part 'hope' plays in your own day-to-day life.

2. If you had to represent it figuratively in a painting or an image, how would you describe it?

First reading

3. How does the poet visualise hope?

4. Examine the analogy in detail. List the qualities or characteristics of hope suggested by each of the images in the first stanza. Pry beneath the obvious. For example, what does 'sings the tune without the words' suggest? What is the effect of that description of hope as 'the thing' with feathers?

5. What aspects of hope are suggested in the second stanza? What does the sound effect of the word 'abash' contribute to this picture? What is the effect of the adjective 'little'?

6. In the third stanza, which qualities of hope are a repetition of suggestions already encountered, and which are new?

7. How do you interpret the last two lines? Do they indicate the strength or a weakness in the virtue of hope? It depends on whether you read the third line as part of the meaning of the previous two or read it with the last line. Experiment with both readings. Is there some ambiguity, and does this show a weakness in the virtue of hope?

Second reading

8. Do you think the bird analogy is successful? Explain your views. What other metaphors for hope could you advance?

9. What insights into the nature of hope did you get from reading this poem?

10. How would you describe the mood of the poem? Suggest ways in which this is created in the text.

Third reading

11. What do you notice about the technical features of the poem: punctuation, sentences, capital letters, etc.? What is the effect of these?

12. Would you agree that the extraordinary imagery is one of the best features of this poem? Develop your answer with specific references.

13. Do you find this poem hopeful? Explain your views.

258

There's a certain Slant of light,
Winter Afternoons—
That oppresses, like the Heft
Of Cathedral Tunes—

Heavenly Hurt, it gives us—   5
We can find no scar,
But internal difference,
Where the Meanings, are—

None may teach it—Any—
'Tis the Seal Despair—   10
An imperial affliction
Sent us of the Air—

When it comes, the Landscape listens—
Shadows—hold their breath—
When it goes, 'tis like the Distance   15
On the look of Death—

A contemporary painting of a lock on the Erie Canal, completed in 1825, which linked the Great Lakes with the Hudson River in New York State.

Explorations

Before reading

1. Try to recall the image of any wintry sunlit afternoon you have experienced. Describe the quality of the sunlight as best you remember it.

First reading

2. On a first reading, what do you notice about the quality of the sunlight described by the poet?
3. Attempt to describe this light. What can we say about it from the descriptive details in the poem? Is it possible to say very much? Explain.
4. Do you notice how we are made aware of the light? Is it described objectively or filtered through the speaker's feelings? Give an example.

Second reading

5. Explore in detail the speaker's attitude to this light. Pay particular attention to the images for what they reveal of the speaker's view. Examine in particular the connotations of similes and metaphors ('like the Heft of Cathedral Tunes', 'the Seal Despair', 'like the Distance | On the look of Death').
6. What do you think is meant by 'We can find no scar, | But internal difference, | Where the Meanings, are—'?
7. What religious view or philosophy seems to lie behind this poem?
8. How would you describe the tone of the poem? Refer to particular words and phrases. What do you think the sounds of words contribute to the tone? Explain.

Third reading

9. Briefly set down your understanding of the theme of this poem.
10. Outline your general reaction to the poem. What is your evaluation of it as a nature poem?
11. Can you appreciate that the poem might be seen to reflect the poet's deep despair? In your own words, explain the nature of the despair felt by the speaker.
12. Explore the sound effects—echoes, rhymes, alliteration, etc.—used by the poet. Do you think these musical effects might serve to disguise the deep negative feelings in the poem?
13. What questions have you still got about the poem?

280

I felt a Funeral, in my Brain,
And Mourners to and fro
Kept treading—treading—till it seemed
That Sense was breaking through—

And when they all were seated,   5
A Service, like a Drum—
Kept beating—beating—till I thought
My Mind was going numb—

And then I heard them lift a Box
And creak across my Soul   10
With those same Boots of Lead, again,
Then Space—began to toll,

As all the Heavens were a Bell,
And Being, but an Ear,
And I, and Silence, some strange Race   15
Wrecked, solitary, here—

And then a Plank in Reason, broke,
And I dropped down, and down—
And hit a World, at every plunge,
And Finished knowing—then—   20

Explorations

First reading

1. At a first reading, what images in particular hold your attention? What do these images suggest about the subject matter of the poem?
2. List the images suggestive of funerals as they occur throughout the poem. Do these conjure up for you the usual picture of a conventional funeral, or is it somehow different? Comment on any unusual connotations.
3. Where is the speaker in this poem? What suggests this?

Second reading

4. If we read this poem as primarily about the process of dying, what insights about death does it convey?
5. Try a metaphorical reading of the poem. Examine the metaphor in the first line, and then explore the poem as a psychological experience of breakdown. What insights does this reading bring to you?
6. Which view of the poem do you prefer to take? Could we hold both simultaneously?

Third reading

7. Explore the speaker's feelings in the first stanza. What is suggested by the imagery and the repetitions? How do you understand the fourth line?

8. Explore the connotations of the simile 'a Service, like a Drum' in the second stanza. What do the sounds of the words suggest about the speaker's state of mind in this stanza?
9. Explain the speaker's feelings in stanzas 2 and 3.
10. 'As all the Heavens were a Bell,
    And Being, but an Ear,'
    What image does this conjure up for you and what does it suggest about the speaker's perception of her relationship with the heavens?
11. Is the relationship between the speaker and the universe developed further in the following two lines?
    'And I, and Silence, some strange Race
    Wrecked, solitary, here—'
    Explain your understanding of this. How does the speaker feel about her life, her position here? Read the last line aloud. What does the rhythm, or lack of it, convey?
12. Were you surprised by the actions of the last stanza, or was it predictable? Explain. Do you think it is an effective ending?
13. Experiment with different oral readings of the last line. What implications for meaning have the different readings?

Fourth reading

14. List, briefly, the principal themes and issues you found in the poem.
15. Decide on your own interpretation of the poem, grounding your views in the text.
16. Comment on the effectiveness of the imagery used to convey the ideas.
17. How would you describe the tone of this poem: anguished, oppressed, lonely, helpless, coldly factual, or what? What words, phrases or images do you think best indicate the poet's tone of voice?
18. Explore the writing technique, in particular: the repetitions; the sound effect of words; the truncated phrases; the use of single, isolated words; the effect of capitalisation and the punctuation.
    - What is the effect of 'treading—treading', 'beating—beating' and other repetitions?
    - What is the effect of the poet's continuous use of 'and'? Examine its use in the last stanza in particular.
    - What is the effect when the dash is used for punctuation? Examine 'Kept beating—beating— till I thought'. What is the effect of the dash at the end of stanzas 4 and 5 in particular? Look at the poet's use of conventional punctuation: what is the effect in line 16? Read it aloud.
    - List the capitalised words. Do they provide a guide through the poem? Trace it.
    - What is the effect of the repeated sounds of words ('drum', 'numb'; 'Soul', 'toll')? Explore the suggestions of the onomatopoeic 'creak'. What do these effects contribute to the creation of the atmosphere in the poem?
19. 'Dickinson treats the most tormented situations with great calm' (Helen McNeil). Would you agree with this statement on the evidence of this poem?

The Dickinson Homestead, Amherst, Massachusetts, birthplace of Emily Dickinson and her home for over forty years. She wrote virtually all of her known poetry at the Homestead and died there in 1886.

328

A Bird came down the Walk—
He did not know I saw—
He bit an Angleworm in halves
And ate the fellow, raw,

And then he drank a Dew   5
From a convenient Grass—
And then hopped sidewise to the Wall
To let a Beetle pass—

He glanced with rapid eyes
That hurried all around—   10
They looked like frightened Beads, I thought—
He stirred his Velvet Head

Like one in danger, Cautious,
I offered him a Crumb
And he unrolled his feathers   15
And rowed him softer home—

Than Oars divide the Ocean,
Too silver for a seam—
Or Butterflies, off Banks of Noon
Leap, plashless as they swim.   20

Explorations

First reading

1. What do you notice about the nature drama unfolding on the walk?
2. Examine the bird's movements. What do they suggest about the creature?
3. Where is the speaker in this picture? When does she enter 'camera shot'? What does she do, and what is the bird's reaction?

Second reading

4. What does the speaker actually see, and what does she create?
5. Examine how Dickinson creates the sense of the bird's flight in the last five lines of the poem. There is no actual description of the flight: rather she proceeds by way of negative comparisons ('then', 'or'). What sense of the experience does she give us? What qualities of bird flight are evoked in this way?

Refer to words or phrases in the text.

6. Step back or 'zoom out' from this picture and see the poet watching. What do you think is her attitude to this drama? What does she feel about the scene she is viewing? What words or phrases suggest this?

Third reading

7. What particular insights into the natural world does this poem offer you? Explain, with reference to the text.
8. Do you think Dickinson is being serious or humorous, or a combination of both here? Examine the tone of this poem.
9. 'Dickinson wickedly disturbs a clichéd vision of nature through her ornithological caricature' (Juhasz, Miller and Smith). Comment on this view in the light of your own reading of the poem.

341

After great pain, a formal feeling comes—
The Nerves sit ceremonious, like Tombs—
The stiff Heart questions was it He, that bore,
And Yesterday, or Centuries before?

The Feet, mechanical, go round—   5
Of Ground, or Air, or Ought—
A Wooden way
Regardless grown,
A Quartz contentment, like a stone—

This is the Hour of Lead—   10
Remembered, if outlived,
As Freezing persons, recollect the Snow—
First—Chill—then Stupor—then the letting go—

Explorations

Before reading

1. Have you ever experienced severe pain, such as from a broken bone, or appendicitis, or a severe toothache or headache? Try to recollect how you felt as the pain ebbed away and you were free of it for the first moment in a long while. Were you elated or just exhausted, tired, numbed, or what? Recapture how you felt in short phrases or images.

First reading

2. Explore the images in the poem for some indication of the speaker's feeling 'after great pain'.
   - What are the connotations of 'The Nerves sit ceremonious, like Tombs'?
   - What might 'The stiff Heart' indicate?
   - What does the heart's disorientation, in lines 3 and 4, suggest about the strength of the pain?
   - What do the images of the second stanza intimate about the speaker's present mood and condition?
   - What does the image 'Hour of Lead' conjure up for you?
   - Are the references to snow comforting or threatening? Explain.

Second reading

3. Is there a common thread running through any of these images that might give an overview of the speaker's condition? Consider, for instance, 'The Nerves sit ceremonious', 'The stiff Heart', 'The Feet, mechanical'. Taken together, what do these external physical manifestations reveal of the speaker's inner feelings? What do the natural references to wood, quartz and lead suggest about the speaker's condition?

4. Comment on the poet's own description of this condition as 'a formal feeling'. Is this unusual definition supported by any other evidence from the poem? Explain.

5. Can you express the central concern of this poem in one sentence?

6. Do you find the conclusion of this poem in any way hopeful, or just totally bleak? Explain your reading of it.

Third reading

7. Do you think this poem an effective evocation of the particular feeling? Comment.

8. What do you find most unusual or striking about it?

465

I heard a Fly buzz—when I died—
The Stillness in the Room
Was like the Stillness in the Air—
Between the Heaves of Storm—

The Eyes around—had wrung them dry—   5
And Breaths were gathering firm
For that last Onset—when the King
Be witnessed—in the Room—

I willed my Keepsakes—Signed away
What portion of me be   10
Assignable—and then it was
There interposed a Fly—

With Blue—uncertain stumbling Buzz—
Between the light—and me—
And then the Windows failed—and then   15
I could not see to see—

Explorations

Before reading

1. Have you ever been present at a death, or read about a deathbed scene, or visited someone who was seriously ill and not expected to live? What did you notice, and what were your thoughts?

First reading

2. What do you notice about the deathbed scene here? What elements do you think might be ordinary or common to any such scene? What would you consider unusual about the scene?
3. Who is the speaker in the poem?

Second reading

4. Comment on the atmosphere in the room. Would you consider it to be emotional or controlled, expectant, frightened, indifferent, or what? What words and phrases suggest this?
5. What is your impression of the onlookers?
6. How does the poet suggest that this is a dramatic moment?

Third reading

7. How is the prospect of death viewed (a) by the onlookers and (b) by the speaker?
8. 'There interposed a Fly'. What is your reaction to the fly, and what do you think might be its significance in the poem? Refer to words or phrases.
9. In general, what understanding of death is conveyed by this poem? Explore the connotations of phrases such as 'Heaves of Storm', 'that last Onset', 'the King | Be witnessed', 'With Blue— uncertain stumbling Buzz', 'And then the Windows failed'.
10. Do you find the speaking voice effective? Comment on the tone and the style of speech. What part do the phrasing and punctuation play in this?

Fourth reading

11. 'Few poets have dealt with this all-engrossing subject with such intense feeling under such perfect control' (Richard Sewall). Do you find intense feeling and perfect control here?

512

The Soul has Bandaged moments—
When too appalled to stir—
She feels some ghastly Fright come up
And stop to look at her—

Salute her—with long fingers—   5
Caress her freezing hair—
Sip, Goblin, from the very lips
The Lover—hovered—o'er—
Unworthy, that a thought so mean
Accost a Theme—so—fair—   10

The soul has moments of Escape—
When bursting all the doors—
She dances like a Bomb, abroad,
And swings upon the Hours,

As do the Bee—delirious borne—   15
Long Dungeoned from his Rose—
Touch Liberty—then know no more,
But Noon, and Paradise—

The Soul's retaken moments—
When, Felon led along,   20
With shackles on the plumed feet,
And staples, in the Song,

The Horror welcomes her, again,
These, are not brayed of Tongue—

Notes

[1] **Soul:** psyche or spirit

[3] **Fright:** a personification of fear or horror

[7] **Goblin:** a small malevolent spirit

[10] **Accost:** speak to, question

[14] **swings upon the Hours:** an image of childlike play, lasting through all the hours of the day

[16] **his Rose:** the flower with its nectar, source of the bee's energy

[18] **Noon:** the term is used with different connotations in various Dickinson poems; here it probably symbolises the paradise of earthly love. The bee soul escapes from his dungeon, finds fulfilment in the rose, and is transported into an ecstasy of love ('Noon, and Paradise').

[20] **Felon:** a criminal

[21] **the plumed feet:** could suggest freedom of flight, which is in this case curtailed with shackles. In Greek mythology the messenger of the gods, Mercury, had plumed feet. Perhaps 'poetic inspiration' is the theme in question here.

[22] **staples:** metal fastenings, in this case restricting the song

[24] **These:** refers to the soul's 'retaken moments', the capturing horror

 # Explorations

First reading

1. What images, phrases or sounds made most impression on you on a first reading?
2. What is your first impression of the mood or moods of the speaker? What leads you to say this?
3. Is there a narrative line in this poem? Can you trace the sequence of events?

Second reading

4. Explore the following 'thinking points'. Make notes to yourself, to clarify your thinking on them.
   - 'The Soul has Bandaged moments.' How do you visualise this? What does it suggest about the condition of the soul?
   - What does the second line add to our picture of the soul?
   - The soul is named as feminine. How do you perceive the scene in lines 3 and 4?
   - The situation becomes more threatening in lines 5 and 6. Explain the nature of that threat. What is the impact of the adjective 'freezing'?
   - Do you think there is a change of attitude by the speaker in line 7 ('Sip, Goblin')? Explain.
   - 'lips | The Lover— hovered—o'er—'. What does 'hovered' mean? What does it suggest about the lover, and the nature of the relationship? Is the use of the past tense significant?
   - Do you think lines 9 and 10 refer to the thoughts of the lover or the speaker's present feelings? Could they refer to both? What implications has each interpretation?
   - What is suggested about the speaker's state of mind by the first and second stanzas?

- How would you describe the different mood of the third stanza? Do the verbs help create it?
- Is there any suggestion that this mood too is perilous? Explain.
- In the fourth stanza, this new mood is compared to the activities of a bee escaped from captivity. What does this simile convey about the nature of the mood? (Refer to the notes for the significance of 'Noon'.) Explore the effect of the many long vowel sounds in this stanza.
- In the fifth stanza, how does the poet visualise the soul? Do you think this image effective? Explain the mood in this stanza.
- In the fifth stanza, do you think the true horror of captivity is hidden somewhat by the simple repetitive hymn metre and the musical rhyme of lines 2 and 4?
- Is there any community support for the speaker's predicament? What is suggested in the last line about how this mental suffering must be borne? (Note: 'These' refers back to the retaken moments.)

Third reading

5. What are your impressions of the mental state of the speaker? Refer to the text.
6. Explore the appropriateness of the different images and similes Dickinson uses to symbolise the soul.
7. What do you consider to be the main issues and themes explored in this poem? Refer to the text.
8. After some critical thinking, outline a reading you yourself find satisfactory and can substantiate with references to the poem.

Fourth reading

9. What insights into the human condition does this poem offer?
10. 'This poem deals with the intimate aspects of pain and loss.' Comment on the poem in the light of this statement.
11. What part does the music of words—sound effects, metre, rhyme, etc.—play in creating the atmosphere of this poem?

697

I could bring You Jewels—had I a mind to—
But You have enough—of those—
I could bring you Odors from St. Domingo—
Colors—from Vera Cruz—

Berries of the Bahamas—have I—   5
But this little Blaze
Flickering to itself—in the Meadow—
Suits Me—more than those—

Never a Fellow matched this Topaz—
And his Emerald Swing—   10
Dower itself—for Bobadilo—
Better—Could I bring?

Notes

[3] **St. Domingo:** Santo Domingo, capital city of the Dominican Republic, on the Caribbean
island of Hispaniola (so named by Columbus)

[4] **Vera Cruz:** a city and the main seaport of Mexico. The original settlement was founded in
1519 by Cortés and became the main link between the colony of Mexico and Spain.

[5] **the Bahamas:** islands in the West Indies, the first land touched by Columbus, in 1492

[9] **Topaz:** a yellow sapphire (precious stone)

[10] **Emerald:** a precious stone of bright green colour

[11] **Bobadilo:** probably an allusion to Francisco Bobadilla, a tyrannical Spaniard and Columbus's
enemy, who replaced Columbus as governor of the Indies and sent him back to Spain in
chains. He 'seized the admiral's gold, plate, jewels and other valuables, plus an enormous
treasure in gold wrested from the islanders.' So, jewels equal to a dower for Bobadilla would
be priceless. We can assume that Dickinson read Washington Irving's *Life of Columbus*, which
contains the information about Bobadilla.

Background note

Despite her withdrawal from society, Dickinson kept up an active correspondence. Sometimes she sent flowers or gifts with her notes; at other times she sent poems as gifts. She also sent poems as love tokens.

She often used West Indian images as metaphors—for the glories of summer, blooming flowers, poetic success, etc. Rebecca Patterson feels that these images were 'consistently playful rather than intense'.

 # Explorations

First reading

1. In this poem the speaker is presenting a gift. What do you understand about the gift she is describing? Examine lines 6–8 in particular.

2. What do we learn about her attitude to it?

3. Could it be considered a love token? Explain how the poem might be read as a love poem. Do you think this is a credible reading? Explain your own opinion.

Second reading

4. It has been said that Dickinson delighted in making her poems mysterious. For example, she sometimes structured them as riddles. Is there a sense of the mysterious about this poem?

5. What do you think this poem reveals about the writer?

6. Would you consider the tone playful or serious here? Explain your view, with reference to the poem.

986

this poem is also prescribed for Ordinary Level exams in 2004 and 2005

A narrow Fellow in the Grass
Occasionally rides—
You may have met Him—did you not
His notice sudden is—

The Grass divides as with a Comb—   5
A spotted shaft is seen—
And then it closes at your feet
And opens further on—

He likes a Boggy Acre
A Floor too cool for Corn—   10
Yet when a Boy, and Barefoot—
I more than once at Noon
Have passed, I thought, a Whip lash
Unbraiding in the Sun
When stooping to secure it   15
It wrinkled, and was gone—

Several of Nature's People
I know, and they know me—
I feel for them a transport
Of cordiality—   20

But never met this Fellow
Attended, or alone
Without a tighter breathing
And Zero at the Bone—

Background note

On the other side of the street where she lived was the 'Dickinson Meadow', where
Emily might have encountered the 'narrow Fellow' in a 'Boggy Acre'.

Explorations

First reading

You might approach this poem as a sort of literary riddle and explore the clues carried by the connotations and sounds of words and images.

1. Consider the 'narrow Fellow'. What is actually seen of him? Is this enough to identify the creature with any certainty? What does the title lead you to expect?

2. There are incidental indications of his presence. Where are they, and what do they add to our understanding of the 'narrow Fellow'?

3. How do you imagine the speaker? What persona or character does the speaker adopt for this narrative? (See the third stanza.) Do you think this is in any way significant?

Second reading

4. Consider the metaphorical descriptions of the creature. Perhaps the most exciting is 'Whip lash'. What are the connotations of the words? What does the term suggest about the creature? Do these connotations clash with the image of it 'Unbraiding in the Sun'?

5. How did it move when the speaker bent to pick it up?

6. In general, what is your impression of the qualities and nature of this creature?

7. Are there any attempts to make the creature seem less threatening? Refer to the text.

8. What does 'Barefoot' add to the atmosphere of the scene? Who is barefoot? When did this happen?

9. Was the speaker less troubled by this when in her youth? What is the speaker's present or adult reaction to an encounter with the 'narrow Fellow'? Refer to the text. What does 'Zero at the Bone' suggest about her feelings?

Third reading

10. What does the poem convey to us about the writer's attitude or attitudes to nature? Support your ideas with references to the text.

11. Do you think this an effective evocation of a snake? Support your answer with references to the text.

12. Would you agree that there is real fear beneath the apparent casualness of this poem?

Fourth reading

13. 'When she opened her eyes to the real hidden beneath the daily, it was to the peculiarity, awesomeness, and mystery of it' (John Robinson). Would you agree with this interpretation of the poem?

4 *Thomas* HARDY

prescribed for the Higher Level exam in 2006

Thomas Hardy, a major poet and novelist, was born in Dorset on 2 June 1840. A sickly child, he did not attend school until he was eight years old. He made rapid progress and learned Latin, French and German. The Bible was his main focus of attention, he taught in Sunday school and considered taking holy orders. After leaving school he went to work for an ecclesiastical architect in Dorchester in 1859, and three years later he left for London to further his career. He was influenced by Darwin, Mill and Huxley and became an agnostic in contrast with his earlier religious enthusiasm. Hardy pursued his interest in writing as a career and in 1871 published his first novel *Desperate Remedies*. In 1872 *Under the Greenwood Tree* was published, this was followed by *A Pair of Blue Eyes* in 1873. His first major success, *Far From the Madding Crowd*, (1874) allowed him to become a full-time writer and to contemplate marriage.

He met Emma Gifford on a working visit to Cornwall in 1870 and they married four years later. The marriage was initially happy but came under increasing strain. Emma considered Hardy to be her social inferior and resented his literary success. Her conventional attitudes were offended by the

1840–1928

subject matter of *Tess of the D'Urbervilles* (1891), and especially *Jude the Obscure* (1896) which she tried to have suppressed. This final novel received so much adverse critical reaction on moral grounds that Hardy gave up the novel as a form and concentrated on his first love, poetry. Hardy's first volume of poetry, *Wessex Poems*, was published in 1898 when he was 58 years old. He went on to publish over 900 poems. When Emma died in 1912 Hardy was stricken by intense remorse. He was moved to write a remarkable series of love poems based on the early days of their relationship and the places associated with Emma. Nevertheless, he married Florence Dugdale in 1914 with whom he had enjoyed a relationship since 1905. When Thomas Hardy died in 1928 his cremated ashes were buried under a spade full of Dorset earth at Westminster Abbey. His heart was, according to his wishes, buried in Stinford with his first wife Emma. Hardy published eight volumes of poetry and fourteen novels. He is remarkable for the variety of his themes and his range of poetic styles.

Drummer Hodge

I

THEY throw in Drummer Hodge, to rest
Uncoffined—just as found:
His landmark is a kopje-crest
That breaks the veldt around;
And foreign constellations west   5
Each night above his mound.

II

Young Hodge the Drummer never knew—
Fresh from his Wessex home—
The meaning of the broad Karoo,
The Bush, the dusty loam,   10
And why uprose to nightly view
Strange stars amid the gloam.

III

Yet portion of that unknown plain
Will Hodge for ever be;
His homely Northern breast and brain   15
Grow to some Southern tree,
And strange-eyed constellations reign
His stars eternally.

Notes

[3] **kopje:** a small hill on the African veld (veldt)

[4] **veldt:** grassland of South Africa

[9] **Karoo:** dry tableland of southern Africa

[10] **loam:** a soil consisting of a friable mixture of clay, silt and sand

[12] **gloam:** archaic word for twilight

Explorations

First reading

1. 'They throw in Drummer
   Hodge, to rest
   Uncoffined—just as found'

   What is your reaction to the
   burial afforded to Drummer
   Hodge?

2. What do we learn about
   Drummer Hodge in the poem?
   What kind of person do you
   think he was, based on the
   evidence of the text?

3. How does the speaker feel
   about the dead drummer?
   What words or images suggest
   his attitude?

4. Compose a brief diary extract
   about, or a letter to, the young
   soldier suggesting how he feels
   about South Africa.

5. How do you visualize the scene
   in stanza 3? How does the
   poet suggest its foreignness?
   What impression are you left
   with?

Second reading

6. Compose an epitaph for
   Drummer Hodge that is true to
   the poem.

7. Why do you think Hardy uses
   the Afrikaans vocabulary;
   'kopje-crest', 'veldt' and
   'Karoo'? Does it help to
   visualize South Africa's
   landscape and how alien the
   country was for Drummer
   Hodge?

8. What effect is achieved by the
   mention of: 'foreign
   constellations', 'Strange stars'
   and 'strange-eyed
   constellations'?

9. 'His homely Northern breast
   and brain
   Grow to some Southern tree'
   Is there an element of hope or
   consolation in these lines?

10. What is the mood of this
    poem? Look at the
    descriptions, choice of words
    and style of speech.

Third reading

11. Briefly outline the themes of
    this poem as you understand
    them.

12. Comment on the
    appropriateness of the imagery.
    Do you find any images
    particularly effective?

13. Do you find this poem
    moving? Explore your personal
    reaction to the text.

Fourth reading

14. 'Nature and the heavens
    provide the background and
    foreground to the poem; for
    they are permanent, whereas
    man's life is transitory.' Discuss
    the setting of the poem and the
    imagery associated with it.

15. 'Drummer Hodge' has been
    described as 'a kind of poetic
    equivalent of the grave of the

Unknown Warrior', because it shows how quiet lives are disrupted and destroyed by war. Comment on how the poem has universal relevance while at the same time retaining individuality and a particular sense of place.

16. 'Hardy combines simplicity of language and form with strikingly individual vocabulary.' Discuss. Base your answer on a close reading of 'Drummer Hodge'?

The Darkling Thrush

this poem is also prescribed for the Ordinary Level exam in 2006

I LEANT upon a coppice gate
When Frost was spectre-gray,
And Winter's dregs made desolate
The weakening eye of day.
The tangled bine-stems scored the sky   5
Like strings of broken lyres,
And all mankind that haunted nigh
Had sought their household fires.

The land's sharp features seemed to be
The Century's corpse outleant,   10
His crypt the cloudy canopy,
The wind his death-lament.
The ancient pulse of germ and birth
Was shrunken hard and dry,
And every spirit upon earth   15
Seemed fervourless as I.

At once a voice arose among
The bleak twigs overhead
In a full-hearted evensong
Of joy illimited;   20
An aged thrush, frail, gaunt, and small,
In blast-beruffled plume,
Had chosen thus to fling his soul
Upon the growing gloom.
So little cause for carolings   25
Of such ecstatic sound
Was written on terrestrial things

Notes

[1] **coppice:** a thicket; grove or growth of trees

[7] **haunted:** frequented

{7} **nigh:** near or nearby

[10] **outleant:** laid out or outlined

[13] **pulse:** edible seed of leguminous crops such as peas, beans or lentils

[22] **beruffle:** to roughen; trouble or erect in a ruff

Afar or nigh around,
That I could think there trembled through
His happy goodnight air   30
Some blessed Hope, whereof he knew
And I was unaware.

 # Explorations

First reading

1. 'I leant upon a coppice gate'
   What did the poet see in stanza 1?

2. Examine the funeral arrangements for the 'Century' in stanza 2. What represents the laid-out corpse? Other elements in the description represent the tomb and funeral music. Explain.

3. What details do you consider to be significant in the description of the thrush in the third stanza? How do you think the poet feels about the thrush?

4. Why is the poet so surprised by the bird's song in the final stanza?

Second reading

5. What details make the first two stanzas 'desolate'?

6. Is there a contrast between the bird's physical appearance and the 'joy illimited' of its song?

7. 'Some blessed Hope'. Does the poet share this feeling?

Third reading

8. The poem was originally published under the title 'By the Century's Deathbed'. Do you think this title helps you understand the poet's purpose in writing the poem? Explain your answer.

9. 'At once a voice arose among' Comment on Hardy's use of sound as the birdsong is described.

10. Describe the central mood of the poem, how is it created? Is the mood modified at any stage? Comment on the words or images that help to achieve such a change.

11. What images in the poem appeal to you particularly? Explain why you find them effective.

Fourth reading

12. ' 'The Darkling Thrush' is not just a poem about a bird but a profound and wide-ranging meditation on time, history and faith.' Discuss.

13. Philip Larkin wrote 'the dominant emotion in Hardy is sadness'. Based on the evidence of this poem, do you agree?

14. ' 'The Darkling Thrush' is rich in imagery, personification and contrasts.' Discuss.

The Self-Unseeing

HERE is the ancient floor,
Footworn and hollowed and thin,
Here was the former door
Where the dead feet walked in.

She sat here in her chair,   5
Smiling into the fire;
He who played stood there,
Bowing it higher and higher.

Childlike, I danced in a dream;
Blessings emblazoned that day;   10
Everything glowed with a gleam;
Yet we were looking away!

Note

[10] **emblazoned:** strictly speaking it means to 'adorn with
heraldic devices' but more commonly to celebrate or extol

 # Explorations

Before reading

1. What is your favourite piece of
   dance music? How does the
   music make you feel? Make a
   list of words that help describe
   how the music affects you. Do
   you associate the music with a
   particular person, place or
   time?

First reading

2. How do you visualize the
   setting in the first stanza?
   What do you think is left of
   'the ancient floor' and 'the
   former door'?

3. Hardy as a young man played
   the violin at parties and
   dances. Can you imagine the

scene described in the second stanza? What kind of atmosphere was there? Hardy had been known to burst into tears while playing. Do you get any sense of that kind of intensity from the text? A short paragraph will suffice for your answer.

4. How did the speaker feel as the third stanza opens? Did the feeling last? How does she or he feel now?

5. How do you imagine the speaker as a young person? How do you see him/her as the poem was written?

Second reading

6. 'Where the dead feet walked in' Describe your reaction to this line.

7. 'She sat here in her chair Smiling into the fire'

   Visualize the girl, how do you imagine her? Why do you think she is mentioned in a poem that is so economical in its use of detail?

8. 'Blessings emblazoned that day'

   What does Hardy mean by this phrase?

9. 'Yet we were looking away'

   Read stanza 3 aloud. What

tone of voice would you use for this line?

Third reading

10. State briefly the theme of this poem as you understand it.

11. What is the mood of this poem? How is the mood created? What details contribute to the poem's atmosphere?

12. Comment on Hardy's use of alliteration in the poem. What effects does he achieve?

13. Write a diary entry for any of the characters mentioned in the poem. Imagine their feelings and impressions.

Fourth reading

14. 'Hardy has succeeded in conveying both the musical delight of the past and the evanescent (transient) quality of that past, though perhaps with the compensation that it can be recalled.' Discuss with reference to the text.

15. 'A craftsman with words'. Evaluate Hardy's use of language in 'The Self-Unseeing'. Does the ballad format suit the subject matter? Comment on the verbal music.

Channel Firing

THAT night your great guns, unawares,
Shook all our coffins as we lay,
And broke the chancel window-squares,
We though it was the Judgment-day

And sat upright. While drearisome   5
Arose the howl of wakened hounds:
The mouse let fall the altar-crumb,
The worms drew back into the mounds,

The glebe cow drooled. Till God called, 'No;
It's gunnery practice out at sea   10
Just as before you went below;
The world is as it used to be:

'All nations striving strong to make
Red war yet redder. Mad as hatters
They do no more for Christés sake   15
Than you who are helpless in such matters.

'That this is not the judgement-hour
For some of them's a blessed thing,
For if it were they'd have to scour
Hell's floor for so much threatening...   20

'Ha, ha. It will be warmer when
I blow the trumpet (if indeed
I ever do; for you are men,
And rest eternal sorely need).'

So down we lay again. 'I wonder,   25
Will the world ever saner be,'
Said one, 'than when He sent us under
In our indifferent century!'

And many a skeleton shook his head.
'Instead of preaching forty year,'   30
My neighbour Parson Thirdly said,

Notes

[3] **chancel:** part of the church containing altar and seats for the clergy or choir

[7] **altar-crumb:** referring to the mouse stealing pieces of the consecrated bread

[9] **glebe:** a plot of land belonging or yielding profit to a parish church

'I wish I had stuck to pipes and beer.'
Again the guns disturbed the hour,
Roaring their readiness to avenge,
As far inland as Stourton Tower,   35
And Camelot, and starlit Stonehenge.

 # Explorations

Before reading

1. What do you associate with
   the dates '1914' or '1939'?
   Describe the thoughts, feelings
   and pictures that come to your
   attention. What enduring
   impression are you left with?

First reading

2. How do you imagine the scene
   described in the first two
   stanzas? What details strike
   you on first reading?
3. Who is speaking in the opening
   stanza? What kind of character
   is she or he? How do you see
   the person?
4. What does God have to say?
   What is his attitude to events
   in the world? How do you
   react to his sense of humour
   'Ha, ha'?
5. Why did 'many a skeleton
   shake his head'? What is meant
   by this gesture?

6. What point do you think the
   parson is making 'I wish I had
   stuck to pipes and beer'? Does
   he think his life was spent
   productively?

Second reading

7. What details dramatise the
   effects of the guns being fired?
   Look at the various reactions
   and the words and images
   used.
8. 'The world is as it used to be'
   What do you understand by
   this line? What view of the
   world is apparent in this
   poem?
9. Read the poem aloud. What
   tone(s) of voice would you
   use? How should the poem
   sound? Do you notice anything
   on reading the poem aloud
   that you might have missed in
   a silent reading?

10. What is Hardy suggesting by his references to 'Camelot, and starlit Stonehenge' in the final stanza?

Third reading

11. Outline the main themes of this poem as you understand them.
12. What is the effect of Hardy's use of direct speech? Examine the poem's language.
13. 'I wonder,
    Will the world ever saner be,'
    How do you think Hardy would have answered this question?
14. Comment on the imagery used in the poem. Do you find it effective?

Fourth reading

15. This poem is dated April 1914, it does however have a timeless relevance. Do you agree? What view of the world and humanity is presented in the text?

Thomas Hardy

The Convergence of the Twain

(Lines on the loss of the *Titanic*)

I

IN a solitude of the sea
Deep from human vanity,
And the Pride of Life that planned her, stilly couches she.

II

Steel chambers, late the pyres
Of her salamandrine fires,   5
Cold currents thrid, and turn to rhythmic tidal lyres.

III

Over the mirrors meant
To glass the opulent
The sea-worm crawls—grotesque, slimed, dumb, indifferent.

IV

Jewels in joy designed   10
To ravish the sensuous mind
Lie lightless, all their sparkles bleared and black and blind.

V

Dim moon-eyed fishes near
Gaze at the gilded gear
And query: 'What does this vaingloriousness down here?'...15

VI

Well: while was fashioning
This creature of cleaving wing,
The Immanent Will that stirs and urges everything

VII

Prepared a sinister mate
For her—so gaily great—   20
A Shape of Ice, for the time far and dissociate.

VIII

And as the smart ship grew
In stature, grace, and hue,
In shadowy silent distance grew the Iceberg too.

IX

Alien they seemed to be: 25
No mortal eye could see
The intimate welding of their later history,

X

Or sign that they were bent
By paths coincident
On being anon twin halves of one august event,   30

XI

Till the Spinner of the Years
Said 'Now!' And each one hears,
And consummation comes, and jars two hemispheres.

Notes

Twain: archaic word for two

[5] **salamandrine:** refers to a mythical creature who lived in fire; and a mass of
solidified material, largely metallic, left in a blast furnace hearth

[6] **thrid:** a vibrating noise produced by engines

[6] **lyre:** an ancient stringed musical instrument

[12] **bleared:** blurred

Explorations

Before reading

1. Brainstorm what the *Titanic* suggests to you. Jot down the words and phrases that come to mind. Visualize the ship; how do you see it? Do any details stand out?

First reading

2. 'Deep from human vanity' What aspect of human vanity is referred to in the opening stanza?
3. What point is made about the liner's opulent decoration in stanzas III to V?
4. 'The Immanent Will that stirs and urges everything' What role is played in stanzas VI to VIII by the 'Immanent Will' described above?
5. How is a sense of drama built up in the final three stanzas?
6. How do you visualize 'the Spinner of the Years'? Does this 'Spinner' care about people or the consequences of actions? Is this a conventional Christian picture of God?

Second reading

7. Read the poem aloud. What do you notice about the sounds and rhythms? Do some phrases strike you as particularly effective? Does the sound echo the sense anywhere? Make a brief note of your observations.
8. What is the poet's attitude to the ship? Does he admire it or is he critical of some aspects of its construction?
9. How does Hardy suggest the iceberg's sinister potential? What words and images are employed?

Third reading

10. Analyse how contrast is employed to dramatic effect in this poem. Choose one example to comment on in detail.
11. What is the mood of the poem? Describe how Hardy's choice of words and images establish the atmosphere.
12. 'This is a more public poem in terms of content and style than the others by Hardy on your course.' Discuss.
13. Do you think the stanza form is effective in this poem? What effects does Hardy achieve with the long third lines? Do you find the rhyme scheme off-putting or does it work well for you?

Fourth reading

14. What do you think of the absence of people in the poem? Does the operation of fate and

the depiction of 'human vanity' overshadow the human tragedy of lives lost and separation?

15. Does Hardy display a pessimistic vision of life in 'Convergence of the Twain'? Comment.

The *Titanic* sinking, April 1912: watercolour by C.J. Ashford

Under the Waterfall

'WHENEVER I plunge my arm, like this,
In a basin of water, I never miss
The sweet sharp sense of a fugitive day
Fetched back from its thickening shroud of gray.
Hence the only prime   5
And real love-rhyme
That I know by heart,
And that leaves no smart,
Is the purl of a little valley fall
About three spans wide and two spans tall   10
Over a table of solid rock,
And into a scoop of the self-same block;
The purl of a runlet that never ceases
In stir of kingdoms, in wars, in peaces;
With a hollow boiling voice it speaks   15
And has spoken since hills were turfless peaks.'

'And why gives this the only prime
Idea to you of a real love-rhyme?
And why does plunging your arm in a bowl
Full of spring water, bring throbs to your soul?'   20

'Well, under the fall, in a crease of the stone,
Though where precisely none ever has known,
Jammed darkly, nothing to show how prized,
And by now with its smoothness opalized,
Is a drinking-glass: 25
For, down that pass
My lover and I
Walked under a sky
Of blue with a leaf-wove awning of green,
In the burn of August, to paint the scene,   30
And we placed our basket of fruit and wine
By the runlet's rim, where we sat to dine;
And when we had drunk from the glass together,
Arched by the oak-copse from the weather,
I held the vessel to rinse in the fall,   35
Where it slipped, and sank, and was past recall,

Though we stooped and plumbed the little abyss
With long bared arms. There the glass still is.
And, as said, if I thrust my arm below
Cold water in basin or bowl, a throe   40
From the past awakens a sense of that time,
And the glass we used, and the cascade's rhyme.
The basin seems the pool, and its edge
The hard smooth face of the brook-side ledge,
And the leafy pattern of china-ware   45
The hanging plants that were bathing there.

'By night, by day, when it shines or lours,
There lies intact that chalice of ours,
And its presence adds to the rhyme of love
Persistently sung by the fall above.   50
No lip has touched it since his and mine
In turns therefrom sipped lovers' wine.'

Notes

[9] **purl:** a swirling stream or rill; a gentle murmur of water

[40] **throe:** a pang or spasm

[47] **lours:** darken or threaten

Skelwith Force, Westmoreland: pencil and watercolour by Robert Hills (1769–1844)

Explorations

Before reading

1. Imagine your favourite place. Briefly describe the colours, sounds, sights and smells that come to mind. Do you associate the place with any special memory or person? How do you feel when you think of this place?

First reading

2. 'Hardy could always tell a good story'. What story is told in this poem?
3. What impression do you have of the narrator in this poem?
4. Describe the setting of the waterfall as you visualize it. What details strike you? Is it a romantic location?
5. The narrator speaks of the only love-rhyme 'that leaves no smart'. What do you understand this to mean?
6. What is it about the waterfall that most impresses the narrator? Is it something other than its physical beauty?

Second reading

7. How would you describe the mood of the poem? Select words and images that convey the mood.
8. 'And why does plunging your arm in a bowl
Full of spring water, bring throbs to your soul?'

What gives this incident such significance for the narrator?
9. Imagine the scene as the lovers are about to start their picnic 'In the burn of August'. What details stand out?
10. Write a diary entry that one of the lovers would have written on returning from the picnic. Explore thoughts and feelings.

Third reading

11. Read the poem aloud and explore its rhythms, cadences and musical sound effects.
12. 'From the past awakens a sense of that time,'
What role does nostalgia play in this poem?
13. Explore Hardy's descriptions of nature, which do you consider to be most memorable? Does nature reflect the lovers' feelings?
14. 'There lies intact that chalice of ours,'
Comment on how symbolism is used in the poem.

Fourth reading

15. Based on the evidence of this poem, what is your assessment of Thomas Hardy as a love poet?
16. 'Hardy has the ability to make poetry from slight incidents'. Discuss this statement taking 'Under the Waterfall' as the basis for your answer.

The Oxen

CHRISTMAS EVE, and twelve of the clock.
'Now they are all on their knees,'
An elder said as we sat in a flock
By the embers in hearthside ease.

We pictured the meek mild creatures where   5
They dwelt in their strawy pen,
Nor did it occur to one of us there
To doubt they were kneeling then.

So fair a fancy few would weave
In these years! Yet, I feel,   10
If someone said on Christmas Eve,
'Come; see the oxen kneel

'In the lonely barton by yonder coomb
Our childhood used to know,'
I should go with him in the gloom,   15
Hoping it might be so.

Notes

[13] **barton:** the domain land of a manse (country estate) or a
farmyard

[13] **coomb:** a hollow in a hillside; a shelter

Explorations

Before reading

1. Think back to what Christmas meant to you as a child. Contrast that attitude with what Christmas means as a young adult. Do you have any sense of regret or nostalgia for the childhood experience?

First reading

2. How do you visualize the scene described in the first stanza? Who is present? Where is the scene located? When is it set?

3. 'We pictured the meek mild creatures'
Comment on how the animals are presented. What is the significance of them 'kneeling'?

4. What do you think the poet means by 'so fair a fancy'? Does he suggest that attitudes have changed 'In these years'?

5. How does the speaker feel in the final stanza?

Second reading

6. Describe how you imagine the speaker to be. Is it an old or a young person? Does the speaker feel that the world is a good and happy place?

7. 'Nor did it occur to one of us there
To doubt they were kneeling then.'
What do you think Hardy means by this?

8. How does the poet feel about 'So fair a fancy'? Are his feelings a little mixed?

9. Use headings, or a flow chart or spider diagram to trace the development of thought in the poem.

10. How would you describe the tone in this poem? Which words and images contribute to the tone?

11. What do you notice about the style of language used in the poem? Why is direct speech used?

Third reading

12. Would you agree that the poem displays a sense of nostalgia?

13. Comment on 'as we sat in a flock'. What does the image suggest to you? Did you find the imagery used in the poem effective?

14. What effect did reading this poem have on you? Could you identify with the poet's feelings?

15. 'In Hardy there is a tension between the man who loved the simple things in life and the intellectual sceptic who thought there was no benevolent God guiding the universe.' Discuss this statement and its relevance to 'The Oxen'.

During Wind and Rain

this poem is also prescribed for the Ordinary Level exam in 2006

THEY sing their dearest songs—
He, she, all of them—yea,
Treble and tenor and bass,
And one to play;
With the candles mooning each face....   5
Ah, no; the years O!
How the sick leaves reel down in throngs!

They clear the creeping moss—
Elders and juniors—aye,
Making the pathways neat   10
And the garden gay;
And they build a shady seat....
Ah, no; the years, the years;
See, the white storm-birds wing across!

They are blithely breakfasting all—   15
Men and maidens—yea,
Under the summer tree,
With a glimpse of the bay,
While pet fowl come to the knee....
Ah, no; the years O!   20
And the rotten rose is ript from the wall.

They change to a high new house,
He, she, all of them—aye,
Clocks and carpets and chairs
On the lawn all day,   25
And brightest things that are theirs....
Ah, no; the years, the years;
Down their carved names the rain-drop ploughs.

Note

[15] **blithely:** in a joyous manner

Explorations

First reading

1. Describe what is happening in the first stanza. Who do you think the people are?

2. What does the image of 'sick leaves' suggest to you? How significant is Hardy's choice of the word 'sick'?

3. Explain how you view the people in stanza 3. Is their life comfortable? Is their home important to them?

4. 'Blithely breakfasting all'. What makes the breakfast scene so pleasant? Examine the scene in detail.

5. Is stanza 4 a good description of the organised chaos involved in moving house? Is this family moving up in the world? What is the poet saying about the 'brightest things that are theirs'? Does the inclusion of the clock subtly suggest something?

Second reading

6. What do the images of 'storm birds' and 'rotten roses' mean to you? What are they saying about human happiness?

7. 'Down their carved names the rain-drop ploughs.'
How do you feel about the ending? Do you think the final line is prepared for earlier in the poem?

8. Who do you think the speaker in the poem is? What connection does she or he have with the people? How does she or he feel about them? Are the events described in the poem recent or are they set long in the past? Refer to the text in your answer.

9. Is the title 'During Wind and Rain' appropriate? What do you think Hardy is drawing attention to?

Third reading

10. Briefly describe the four scenes of family life sketched by Hardy? What do the scenes have in common?

11. What does the reader learn about the people? Are the characters individuals or are they meant to represent humanity in general?

12. Contrast is used effectively in this poem; examine the images that occur in the final lines of the four stanzas and explain what you understand by each of them. Do the images increase in power?

13. Music played an important role in Hardy's life: comment on the verbal music. What techniques does the poet use to achieve musical effects in language?

14. In what ways can the poem be considered dramatic? Bear in mind Hardy's use of language and imagery.

Fourth reading

15. Does this poem display Hardy's gifts as a novelist? Pay particular attention to his narrative abilities and his powers of observation and description.

16. Hardy has been accused of being overly pessimistic in his view of life. On the evidence of this poem, what do you think?

17. Compare and contrast Hardy's treatment of death in this poem with 'Afterwards'.

18. Hardy wrote, 'The business of the poet,...is to show the sorriness (sic) underlying the grandest things and the grandeur underlying the sorriest of things.' Is this statement applicable to 'During Wind and Rain'? Explain your answer.

Afterwards

When the Present has latched its postern behind my tremulous stay,
And the May month flaps its glad green leaves like wings,
Delicate-filmed as new-spun silk, will the neighbours say,
'He was a man who used to notice such things'?

If it be in the dusk when, like an eyelid's soundless blink,   5
The dewfall-hawk comes crossing the shades to alight
Upon the wind-warped upland thorn, a gazer may think,
'To him this must have been a familiar sight.'

If I pass during some nocturnal blackness, mothy and warm,
When the hedgehog travels furtively over the lawn,   10
One may say, 'He strove that such innocent creatures should come no harm,
But he could do little for them; and now he is gone.'

If, when hearing that I have been stilled at last, they stand at the door,
Watching the full-starred heavens that winter sees,
Will this thought rise on those who will meet my face no more,   15
'He was one who had an eye for such mysteries'?

And will any say when my bell of quittance is heard in the gloom,
And a crossing breeze cuts a pause in its outrollings,
Till they rise again, as they were a new bell's boom,
'He hears it not now, but used to notice such things'?   20

Notes

[1] **postern:** a back door or gate; also a private entrance

[1] **tremulous:** characterised by trembling; exceedingly sensitive

[10] **furtively:** done by stealth

Explorations

Before reading

1. What does the title suggest to you? Jot down the ideas that come to mind. Share them with your classmates.

2. Imagine you had to deliver a funeral eulogy for someone you admired. What would you have to say about how the person would be remembered? What memories of the person would you refer to? Write the speaking notes you would use.

First reading

3. ' 'He was a man who used to notice such things'?'
   What does the poet notice in the first stanza? How do you visualize the scene?

4. What impression do you get of the hawk in stanza 2? Do you detect a sense of menace?

5. On the evidence of the third stanza what is the poet's attitude to 'such innocent creatures'? What does it tell us about him?

6. What 'mysteries' are present in the sky? Do you think Hardy is referring to his passion for astronomy, or his lifelong interest in philosophy, or both?

7. How do you think the poet feels about his death in the final stanza? Does he believe in any sort of afterlife?

Second reading

8. On the evidence of the poem what kind of a man was Thomas Hardy? Describe how you see him and the things he cared about. Was he a self-important person?

9. List the five expressions (euphemisms: a mild word or phrase instead of a frank one) for death in each of the five stanzas. Are these images intimidating? How would you describe them?

10. This poem deals with death but it is not at all bleak. Would you agree? How would you describe the tone of the poem? Comment on the choice of words and images that convey the tone.

11. Read the poem aloud. What do you notice about the sounds and movement of the poem? Does the use of language reflect the mood and the sense?

Third reading

12. Notice how Hardy appeals to the different senses in the poem. Find examples that you feel are particularly effective. Comment for instance, on his choice of 'mothy' in stanza 3.

13. Hardy was an accomplished musician, examine how he uses verbal music in the poem. It

might be useful to bear in mind the following technical terms: sibilants ('s' sounds); assonance; alliteration; rhyme.
14. What does the imagery contribute to the effectiveness of the poem? Refer to specific examples.
15. Briefly express the theme.

Fourth reading

16. Is Hardy's attitude to death different in this poem from that displayed in the other poems on your course? Sum up your conclusions on Hardy's treatment of death.
17. Do you like this poem? Explain your reaction.

When I set out for Lyonnesse

WHEN I set out for Lyonnesse,
A hundred miles away,
The rime was on the spray,
And starlight lit my lonesomeness
When I set out for Lyonnesse   5
A hundred miles away.

What would bechance at Lyonnesse
While I should sojourn there
No prophet durst declare,
Nor did the wisest wizard guess   10
What would bechance at Lyonnesse
While I should sojourn there.

When I came back from Lyonnesse
With magic in my eyes,
All marked with mute surmise   15
My radiance rare and fathomless,
When I came back from Lyonnesse
With magic in my eyes!

Notes

Lyonnesse: This was the name of his first wife Emma Gifford's house. In legend it is the home of King Arthur and Merlin the magician.

[3] **rime:** frost; an accumulation of ice

[7] **bechance:** happen

[8] **sojourn:** stay for a time

[9] **durst:** dared

Explorations

First reading

1. Briefly tell the story in the poem.
2. 'With magic in my eyes,' How is the sense of magic built up in the poem?
3. What do we know about the speaker? How do you visualize him? Is information deliberately kept from the reader to enhance the sense of mystery?
4. In medieval romance poems the hero is frequently on a quest where he must overcome hardship. What is the hero of this poem on a quest for? Explain your answer.

Second reading

5. What details help to convey the poet's 'lonesomeness' in stanza 1?
6. What is the effect of the archaic language such as 'bechance' and 'durst' in stanza 2? What does such diction contribute to the poem?
7. How do you think the final stanza relates to the rest of the poem? Has it been prepared for in the earlier stanzas?
8. How does the speaker's state of mind alter as he travels? Refer to the text in your answer.

Third reading

9. Does the knowledge that this poem was written against the background of a marriage that later failed affect how you view the poem?
10. Hardy wrote of Cornwall 'The place is pre-eminently the region of dream and mystery'. What does 'Lyonnesse' suggest to you? Do you think of it as a place or state of mind?
11. The poem has many features of the traditional ballad, comment on the subject matter and Hardy's use of simple diction, archaic words, repetition, rhyme and musical sound effects.

Fourth reading

12. Does this poem fit in with the view of Thomas Hardy's work you have gained from reading the other poems on your course? Explain your answer.
13. What does this poem say to you about love? How would you rate 'When I set out for Lyonnesse' as a love poem?
14. 'When I set out for Lyonnesse' is remarkable for the way in which the poet has been able to transmute autobiographical details into that of a medieval romance. Discuss.

Hardy's drawing of the pews at St Juliet's Church, Cornwall. He met his first wife, Emma Gifford, working there—an event commemorated in 'When I set out for Lyonnesse'.

5   *Gerard Manley* HOPKINS

prescribed for Higher Level exams in 2003, 2004 and 2006

On Saturday, 8 June 1889, in 85 St Stephen's Green, Dublin, a Jesuit priest died of typhoid. None of the other priests who shared the rat-infested building with the odd little man from England could have guessed that he would be commemorated a hundred years later as one of the most important poets in the English language.

Gerard Manley Hopkins was born into a prosperous Anglican family on 28 July 1844 at Stratford in Essex. He was the eldest of nine children. The Hopkins household had a great interest in poetry, drawing, music and architecture. In 1854, Gerard was sent to Highgate as a boarder. One of his teachers described him as 'a pale young boy, very light and active, with a very meditative and intellectual face'. He was fiercely independent and an outstanding student, winning prizes for poetry and a scholarship to study Classics at Balliol College, Oxford. At Oxford, Hopkins converted to Catholicism and in 1868 he joined the Jesuit Order. He decided to destroy the poems that he had written because he wished to devote his life totally to the service of God, (an act which he described as 'the slaughter of the innocents').

1844–1889

'In my salad days, in my Welsh days' (St Beuno's College, North Wales 1874–77)

Hopkins was sent to St Beuno's College in North Wales to study theology. In 1875, he was encouraged by one of his superiors to write a poem to commemorate the death of five German nuns in a shipwreck. The result was 'The Wreck of the Deutschland', a poem of extraordinary brilliance and originality; in fact, it was so innovative in its use of language and rhythm that no editor would publish it. Undeterred by the unfavourable reaction, Hopkins continued to write poetry. He corresponded regularly with a friend from his days at Oxford, Robert Bridges. Despite Bridges's dislike for his technical experimentation, Hopkins sensed the importance of his own work. It was Bridges who first published Hopkins's work in 1918, almost thirty years after the poet's death.

The first five poems by Hopkins in this anthology were written in St Beuno's in 1877, between the months of March and August. This was one of the happiest times in the poet's adult life—he called them 'my salad days'. These poems are often referred to as the 'bright sonnets' because of the poet's optimistic mood and obvious delight in the beautiful Clwyd Valley and distant Snowdonia. They contrast starkly with the 'terrible sonnets' which he wrote later.

'the encircling gloom'
(Liverpool and Glasgow 1878–81)

After his ordination, Hopkins spent time teaching classics and doing some parish work. Toward the end of 1879, he was sent to work in a parish in Bedford Leigh, near Manchester and then to St Francis Xavier's in the heart of industrial Liverpool. The poet who had such a love of nature was shocked to see the full impact of England's Industrial Revolution. The population of the city had increased dramatically as a result of immigration from famine-stricken Ireland; and pollution from the factories was unregulated. He found some comfort in the warmth of the local people who made him feel welcome.

One of these local people, a thirty-one-year-old farrier, died from consumption on 21 April 1880. His name was Felix Spencer. A week later, Hopkins wrote the poem 'Felix Randal', which is included in this anthology.

In 1881, Hopkins spent a few months working in St Joseph's Parish in Glasgow. Before he left Scotland, he paid a visit to Inversnaid, on the eastern shore of Loch Lomond (28 September). William Wordsworth's poem 'To a Highland Girl, | (At Inversnayde, upon Loch Lomond)' may well have prompted this visit. He wasn't very happy with the poem that he composed, 'Inversnaid'. It remained unseen until after his death.

'To seem the stranger lies my lot, my life'
(Dublin 1884–89)

His appointment as Fellow of the Royal University of Ireland and Professor of Greek and Latin Literature at the Catholic University of Ireland was not the accolade one might think. The English Provincial of the Jesuits did not know where to employ the eccentric priest and the President of the University wanted a fellow-Jesuit so that he could spend the salary of £400 p.a. on the upkeep of the College. Thus began the most miserable period in the poet's short life.

'Gerald Hopkins was at an opposite pole to everything around him: literary, political, social etc. (a thorough John Bull incapable of understanding Rebel Ireland). No one took him seriously.'
(Fr Joe Darlington, a colleague of Hopkins in the University).

To make matters worse, the poet's primary responsibility for the five years he lived in Dublin was the correction of examinations. Alienation and physical exhaustion took its toll on his spiritual wellbeing. He began to suffer from deep depression. The so-called 'terrible sonnets', 'No worst, there is none' and 'I wake and feel the fell of dark', were written in 1885 and mark the nadir of his life.
Even though there is evidence of a spiritual recovery, his physical deterioration was hastened by the unsanitary conditions in which he lived. One of his last poems, 'Thou art indeed just, Lord' was written on St Patrick's Day 1889, a few months before he died at the relatively young age of forty-four. His final words were, 'I am so happy, I am so happy.' He is buried in Glasnevin Cemetery in Dublin.

St Beuno's College in Wales, where Hopkins wrote the first five poems in this chapter

God's Grandeur

The World is charged with the grandeur of God.
It will flame out, like shining from shook foil;
It gathers to a greatness, like the ooze of oil
Crushed. Why do men then now not reck his rod?
Generations have trod, have trod, have trod;   5
And all is seared with trade; bleared, smeared with toil;
And wears man's smudge and shares man's smell: the soil
Is bare now, nor can foot feel, being shod.

And, for all this, nature is never spent;
There lives the dearest freshness deep down things;   10
And though the last lights off the black West went
Oh, morning, at the brown brink eastward, springs—
Because the Holy Ghost over the bent
World broods with warm breast and with ah! bright wings.

Notes

This poem was written while Hopkins was studying in St Beuno's (pronounced 'Bíno') College in North Wales. The poet sent it as a birthday present to his mother on 3 March 1877.

[1] **charged:** as in electrically charged, suggesting a force rather than a substance
'All things therefore are charged with love, are charged with God, and if we know how to touch them, give off sparks and take fire, yield drops and flow, ring and tell of him'

(Hopkins)

[2] **foil:** as in tin foil, a leaf of metal often used to set something off by contrast
'Shaken gold foil gives off broad glares like sheet lightning and also, and this is true of nothing else, owing to its zigzag dents and creasings and network of small many-cornered facets, a sort of fork lightning too'

(Hopkins)

[3] **ooze of oil:** a reference to the harvesting of fruit, compared with:
'Or by a cider-press, with patient look,
Thou watchest the last oozings hours by hours.'

('Ode to Autumn', Keats)

[4] **reck:** heed
[4] **rod:** authority
[6] **seared:** withered, scorched
[9] **spent:** used up, exhausted
[12] **brink:** brink of daylight

Explorations

Before reading

1. Have you ever been startled by the beauty of a natural scene? Do you ever feel that development, 'progress', the work of mankind, is destroying the beauty of the natural world? Discuss these ideas before reading the poem.

First reading

2. All poetry should be experienced 'through the ears' at first. This is especially true of Hopkins's poetry. Read the poem aloud several times. Experiment with the placing of stresses until you find a version that is satisfactory.

3. Pick out a phrase, image or even a word that appeals to you and say why you chose it. (Imagine that you are thinking up a name for a band, e.g. Crushed!)

4. This is the first of Hopkins's so-called 'bright sonnets'. Can you suggest a reason why the poem is considered 'bright'?

Second reading

5. What qualities of the natural world does the poet admire?

6. How does the poet contrast the different manifestations of God's grandeur?

7. At what point does the poet move from admiration to reflection?

8. What, according to the poet, has been the impact of mankind on the natural world?

9. Identify the ways in which mankind is perceived to have affected the physical world.

10. What is the effect of the last word of the image in line 8, 'nor can foot feel, being shod'? What does it suggest about the poet's attitude to human development?

11. How does the mood of the poem change in the sestet?

12. Consider the possible meanings of the line,
'There lives the dearest freshness deep down things'
What word is missing from this statement? The omission of a word from a line is a stylistic device called 'ellipsis'. Hopkins used it frequently. When you have encountered more examples of it, consider its effect.

13. Lines 11 and 12 state in an unusual way that the sun sets and rises again. How does the poet's manner of expressing this idea add greater significance to this mundane event? Does this image have any religious resonance?

14. What is the effect of the 'ah!' in the final line?

Third reading

15. Identify the changes of tone in the poem? Which one is predominant?
16. There is a great sense of energy in the first quatrain. How does the poet generate this energy? Pay close attention to rhythm and sound.
17. How does the second quatrain differ from the first in terms of sound and rhythm?
18. Consider carefully the implications of the final image of the poem. How is the Holy Ghost represented?

Fourth reading

19. How does the poet perceive the relationship between man, God and the natural world?
20. What words or phrases appeal to your senses?
21. How does this poem vary from the standard Petrarchan sonnet?
22. Consider carefully the meaning, the sound and the position of the word 'Crushed'. Would you agree that the poet draws attention to the word? Watch out for other words in later poems that are highlighted by their position in a similar way.
23. What peculiarities of style can you identify in this poem? Pay particular attention to the sound effects.
24. Is there a tension in the poem between the poet who loves beauty and the priest who feels a duty to moralise? Consider the manner in which the poet moves from joy in the contemplation of the natural world to dismay at the way mankind has abused the world, and finally to the assertion that the Holy Ghost will continue to nurture the world. Do you find this movement satisfying?
25. In what way are the poet's concerns relevant to today's world?
26. If you had to recommend this poem to a friend, what aspect or aspects of the poem would you choose to highlight?

Sunset, St Beuno's
'The World is charged with the grandeur of God.
It will flame out, like, shining from shook foil;'

As kingfishers catch fire, dragonflies draw flame

As kingfishers catch fire, dragonflies draw flame;
As tumbled over rim in roundy wells
Stones ring; like each tucked string tells, each hung bell's
Bow swung finds tongue to fling out broad its name;
Each mortal thing does one thing and the same: 5
Deals out that being indoors each one dwells;
Selves—goes itself; myself it speaks and spells,
Crying *What I do is me: for that I came.*

Í say more: the just man justices;
Keeps gráce: that keeps all his goings graces;   10
Acts in God's eye what in God's eye he is—
Christ. For Christ plays in ten thousand places,
Lovely in limbs, and lovely in eyes not his
To the Father through the features of men's faces.

Notes

'All things therefore are charged with love, are charged with God, and if we know how to touch them give off sparks and take fire, yield drops and flow, ring and tell of him'.
(Notebooks and Papers of G.M.H.)

[1] **kingfisher:** a bird with a brilliant plumage

[1] **dragonfly:** an insect

[3] **tucked:** plucked

[6] **indoors:** within

[7] **Selves:** (verb) asserts its own nature, individuality

[9] **justices:** (verb) acts in a way that promotes justice
'acts in a godly manner, lives fully energized by grace, justness, sanctity'

(R.V. Schoder SJ)

Explorations

Before reading

1. 'I am what I am.' a politician once said in self-defence. What do you think he meant? Was it a declaration of apology or defiance? How many of us have the courage to be what we are? Do we express our individuality or hide it behind a veneer of conformity? Is there any other creature or object in existence that possesses such individuality as we do?

First reading

2. Read the poem aloud several times. What sounds dominate?
3. Pick out a phrase or image that you find appealing, intriguing or strange. Explain your choice.

Second reading

4. This poem can be quite difficult to grasp on a first reading. The language itself is not difficult; however, the poet has concentrated his meaning through the use of ellipsis and unusual syntax. It becomes easier to understand when one realises that the same idea is expressed in different ways throughout the octet. Consider the statement 'What I do is me: for that I came.' It asserts not only the individuality of all

things, but also the notion that everything and everyone has its role in God's creation. With this in mind, attempt an explanation for the first line.
5. Identify the images in the next three lines. What have they in common?
6. What are all these creatures and things doing?
7. The poet seems to give a sense of destiny or purpose to animate and inanimate objects alike. Identify examples of each. Consider the significance of this idea.
8. Do you agree that there is an extraordinary intensity and sense of conviction to the octet? How is this intensity conveyed?
9. How does the sestet develop the thought in the octet? Would you agree that there is a change of emphasis from the philosophical to the religious?
10. What is your reaction to a statement such as 'the just man justices'? Does it read well? Is it poetic? Can you think of a reason why the poet should express himself in such a way? Are there any other expressions in the poem which strike you as odd or unusual?
11. In the last three lines, the poet suggests that the 'imprint' of Christ's love is evident in all

aspects of God's creation. Everything in existence is unique and has its own essence; but each individual person and thing shares in God's design. The poet sees Christ in 'ten thousand places' and in 'men's faces'. This is the unifying and moral principle that governs the universe. This is how Hopkins sees the Incarnation of Christ. Find out what you can about the word 'incarnation'. It is a very important word if you want to understand the way Hopkins relates to the world.

Third reading

12. How does this poem differ from the previous poem? Would you agree that the nature imagery is employed in a different way in this poem?
13. This poem is believed to have been written as a defence of Scotism against Thomism. The teachings of Duns Scotus advocated the uniqueness of all things and the ability of the senses to perceive what is good and beautiful. In this philosophy there is a moral value to what is beautiful. This point of view has great significance for a priest who was made to doubt the value of poetry by his superiors. Thomas Aquinas, on the other hand, was suspicious of the senses and stressed the importance of reason. Try to relate these ideas to the poem! What is your own view on this debate, which is sometimes characterised as a debate between the emotions and reason, the romance and the pragmatism, the heart and the head?

Spring

this poem is also prescribed for Ordinary Level exams in 2003, 2004 and 2006

NOTHING is so beautiful as Spring—
When weeds, in wheels, shoot long and lovely and lush;
Thrush's eggs look little low heavens, and thrush
Through the echoing timber does so rinse and wring
The ear, it strikes like lightnings to hear him sing;   5
The glassy peartree leaves and blooms, they brush
The descending blue; that blue is all in a rush
With richness; the racing lambs too have fair their fling.

What is all this juice and all this joy?
A strain of the earth's sweet being in the beginning   10
In Eden garden.—Have, get, before it cloy,

Before it cloud, Christ, lord, and sour with sinning,
Innocent mind and Mayday in girl and boy,
Most, O maid's child, thy choice and worthy the winning.

Notes

[2] **wheels:** an architectural term that describes a design similar to the wheel of a bicycle with spokes radiating from the centre

[3] **low heavens:** the eggs mirror the pattern of the clouds against the sky (a dappled effect)

[4] **timber:** tree or wood

[4] **rinse and wring:** the effect of the bird's song on the ear

[6] **leaves and blooms:** these nouns are used as verbs here

[8] **fair:** abundant

[9] **juice:** possibly meaning the essence or spirit of a thing

[10] **strain:** a musical term meaning a remembered melody and/or an inherited quality

[11] **cloy:** satiate, fill to the limit, lose its appeal (verb having 'innocent mind' and 'Mayday' as object)

[12] **cloud:** verb having 'innocent mind' and 'Mayday' as object

[12] **sour:** verb having 'innocent mind' and 'Mayday' as object

[13] **Mayday:** Hopkins associates May with the purity of Mary, the Blessed Virgin and Mother

[14] **maid's child:** Jesus

Explorations

Before reading

1. How do you know when Spring has arrived? What aspects of the season appeal to you most?

First reading

2. Read the poem aloud several times. Listen carefully to the rhythm or movement of the lines in order to pick up the mood of the poem. Is this a happy or sad poem? Pick out phrases or images that capture the mood of the first verse.

3. Does this poem remind you of 'God's Grandeur' in any way? Discuss the similarities briefly.

Second reading

4. The opening line of the poem is very simple. What is the effect of such a simple beginning? Does it draw you into the poem?

5. Does it surprise you that the poet enthuses about weeds in the second line? What qualities do weeds have that might appeal to the poet? Does his admiration for weeds tell us anything about his personality? How has your attitude to weeds been developed?

6. What does the poet mean by the phrase 'rinse and wring the ear'? Consider carefully the meanings and associations attached to these two words. Do you think they are unusual words to describe the effect of the bird's song? Suggest a reason for the poet's choice of image.

7. In the previous poem, the poet described how God's grandeur 'will flame out'. Here, he describes the song of the bird striking him 'like lightning'. What effect is the poet creating with these images?

8. Would you agree that there is a great sense of startled delight in the octet? How does the poet achieve this?

9. In the octet, the poet provides us with a rich array of movement, sounds, shapes, textures and colours. Identify each one of them. How does the poet move from weeds to thrush's eggs, to the glassy pear tree and finally to the descending blue? Would you agree that the movement follows the eye naturally? How does the poet return from the sky to the lambs?

10. What is the tone of the sestet? How does it differ from the octet? Consider the effect of the question in line 9.

11. The poet seems to associate Springtime with Paradise. But it is only a strain that will soon disappear. Does the poet

suggest any reason for this?

12. Do you find the reflection in the sestet satisfying or an intrusion on the wonderful description of Spring? Does the complicated syntax (sentence structure) jar the ear after the vibrant octet?

Third reading

13. Look for examples of the following features: alliteration, assonance, rhyme, ellipsis. Explain how they contribute to the poem.

Fourth reading

14. Do you consider this an optimistic or pessimistic poem? Give reasons for your answer.

15. What is the theme of this poem?

16. Do you note any variations in the use of the Petrarchan sonnet?

17. What similarities have you discovered between this poem and 'God's Grandeur' in terms of theme and poetic technique?

18. Which poem do you prefer and why? Do you prefer the poet's descriptions of nature or his meditations on its significance? Or do you find the combination of description and reflection most satisfying?

The Windhover:

To Christ our Lord

I CAUGHT this morning morning's minion, king-
  dom of daylight's dauphin, dapple-dawn-drawn Falcon, in
  his riding
  Of the rolling level underneath him steady air, and striding
High there, how he rung upon the rein of a wimpling wing
In his ecstasy! then off, off forth on swing,   5
  As a skate's heel sweeps smooth on a bow-bend: the hurl and
  gliding
  Rebuffed the big wind. My heart in hiding
Stirred for a bird,—the achieve of, the mastery of the thing!
Brute beauty and valour and act, oh, air, pride, plume, here
  Buckle! AND the fire that breaks from thee then, a billion   10
Times told lovelier, more dangerous, O my chevalier!
  No wonder of it: shéer plód makes plough down sillion
Shine, and blue-bleak embers, ah my dear,
  Fall, gall themselves, and gash gold-vermilion.

Notes

Hopkins described this poem as 'the best thing I ever wrote'.

Windhover: A kestrel, common in the Clwyd area of Wales. At St Beuno's College there was a glass case of stuffed birds on which the following inscription was written: 'The Kestrel or Windhover: The commonest and most conspicuous of British falcons remarkable for its habit of remaining suspended in the air without changing position while it scans the ground for its prey.'

[1] **caught:** caught sight of (an example of ellipsis)

[1] **minion:** favourite

[2] **dauphin:** prince, heir apparent to the French throne (to the kingdom of daylight)

[2] **dapple-dawn-drawn:** a coined adjective meaning 'dappled and drawn out in front of the dawn' or 'dappled and attracted by the dawn'

[5] **rung upon the rein:** (a) a technical term of the riding school, 'to ring on the rein'—said of a horse that circles at the end of a long rein held by its trainer; (b) 'to ring' in falconry means to rise in spirals.

[5] **wimpling:** pleated

[7] **bow-bend:** as the skater forms the figure 8

[7] **hurl:** normally a verb, here it is a noun meaning the vigorous forward motion

[10] **achieve:** verb used as noun meaning 'achievement'

[12] **Buckle:** This complex word is crucial to the meaning of the poem. There are several possible interpretations: (a) prepare for action, come to grips, engage the enemy; (b) clasp, enclose, bring together as one; (c) give way, bend, collapse under stress or pressure. Interpretations (a) and (b) can be combined in the image of the chivalric knight putting on his armour in order to do battle. Perhaps the poet is pleading for the qualities mentioned to be united 'here' in his heart.

[12] **fire:** characteristic energy

[13] **chevalier:** a knight (French), a reference to the Christ

[14] **shéer plód:** sheer hard work

[14] **sillion:** a strip of arable land

[16] **gall:** hurt

[16] **gold-vermilion:** a mixture of gold and red colour

 # Explorations

Before reading

1. Some people erroneously regard poetry as a kind of cryptic puzzle to be solved, a sort of verbal Rubik's Cube. If the primary purpose in reading a poem is to 'find the meaning', then surely the poet would have been better employed writing his or her ideas in understandable prose. Clearly, there is more to a poem than 'meaning'. The way in which the 'meaning' is expressed provides the 'beauty' or aesthetic value of a poem. It is possible to enjoy the beauty of a poem without understanding the meaning. Discuss your attitude to poetry in general and how your view of it has been formed.

First reading

2. In a letter to Robert Bridges about this poem, Hopkins invited him to 'Take breath and read it with the ears, as I always wish to be read, and my verse becomes all right.' Read the first eight lines several times and try to get a sense of the rhythm. Pay particular attention to the changes of pace. Do you agree that the rhythm seems to capture the flight of the bird and that there is a sense of awe and breathlessness as one reaches the end of the octet? How is this achieved?

3. The poet gives a procession of titles to the kestrel 'as in some royal proclamation of medieval pageantry'(Peter Milward SJ). What is the effect of this? How does it lead into the imagery of horse-riding?

4. How does the poet convey the sense that the bird is in complete control of its environment?

5. The poet uses imagery from the world of horse-riding and skating to describe the movement of the bird. Look closely at these images and describe the movements of the bird in your own words. Do you think that the poet's use of imagery is effective in communicating the grace, elegance and energy of the bird?

6. Is there a paradox in the combination of 'hurl' and 'gliding'? Explain.

7. Why is the poet's heart 'in hiding'? Is he afraid, ashamed, humbled, envious? Why might a student priest feel envious of this magnificent bird in flight? Why does he write 'for a bird' rather than 'for the bird'?

8. The first tercet begins with a list of qualities which the bird embodies. Describe these qualities in your own words.

9. Look at the possible meanings of 'Buckle' and arrive at your own conclusions on its meaning. Does the capitalisation of the word 'and' imply a consequence of 'Buckle'? To what does 'thee' refer? His heart? The bird? Christ? Consider the possibilities.

10. The second part of the tercet is addressed to 'my chevalier'. What connection does the poet see between the windhover and Christ our Lord? Is there a physical similarity between the bird with its outstretched wings and Christ on the Cross? Does the poet see the bird battling against the wind as a symbol of Christ battling against evil? Consider these possibilities.

Second reading

11. The poet uses quite a varied diction in this poem. At the start, the language is regal—'minion', 'kingdom', 'dauphin'. What other categories of words are used in the poem? Note the contrast between words like 'Buckle', 'plód' and 'minion', 'sillion', 'billion', 'vermillion'. Describe the texture of these words.

12. The second tercet presents the reader with two images of beauty evolving out of what appears to be unpleasant. The drudgery of ploughing the land brings forth a radiant surface. The embers of a dying fire fall from the grate, break open to reveal the glowing interior.

What resonances do these images create in the context of the whole poem? Do they connect with the image of Christ on the Cross in any way?

13. Would you agree that there is a passionate intensity to this poem? How is this effect created? Is there a mystical quality to this poem. Discuss your understanding of mysticism.

Third reading

14. Compare this poem with the previous three poems under the following headings: theme, mood, development of thought, style and use of the sonnet form. Would you agree that it is quite different in terms of development of thought and use of the sonnet form?

15. Find out what you can about the Spiritual Exercises of St Ignatius Loyola, in particular his 'Meditation on the Kingdom'.

16. Find out what you can about Sprung Rhythm, Inscape and Instress.

17. This poem is written in a remarkably original style. Consider the elements of that style, such as the use of alliteration, assonance, exclamation, ellipsis, inversion, compound adjectives, use of verbs as nouns, sprung rhythm, and rhyme. What is the primary purpose of all these poetic devices? It might be useful to consider their effect.

18. Do the difficulties of interpretation make 'The Windhover' a richer or more frustrating poem? Is it possible to enjoy the parts of the poem without a clear understanding of the whole? Consider this question in relation to poetry in general.

Pied Beauty

GLORY be to God for dappled things—
For skies of couple-colour as a brinded cow;
For rose-moles all in stipple upon trout that swim;
Fresh-firecoal chestnut-falls; finches' wings;
Landscape plotted and pieced—fold, fallow, and plough   5
And áll trádes, their gear and tackle and trim.

All things counter, original, spare, strange;
Whatever is fickle, freckled (who knows how?)
With swift, slow; sweet, sour; adazzle, dim;
He fathers-forth whose beauty is past change: 10
Praise him.

Notes

Pied: of different colours

[1] **dappled:** Irregular patches of different colours, Hopkins was particularly fond of 'dappled' things. It is a word that he used frequently in his writings.

[2] **brinded:** brindled, brownish with streaks of another colour

[3] **rose-mole:** rose-like spots

[3] **stipple:** dotted

[4] **Fresh-firecoal:** In his Journal (17 September 1868), Hopkins refers to 'Chestnuts as bright as coals or spots of vermilion.' (Vermilion is a brilliant red pigment.)

[4] **chestnut-falls:** see 'Fresh-firecoal' above

[5] **fold:** pasture for sheep to graze

[5] **fallow:** unused

[5] **and plough:** planted with crops

[6] **áll trádes...tackle:** the variety of trades with their different implements

[7] **counter:** all things that stand in contrast with other things

[7] **spare:** rare

Explorations

Before reading

1. Make a class list of 'beautiful things' to see if there is any consensus on what constitutes beauty. Consider the view that 'beauty is in the eye of the beholder'. Is there a social pressure to conform to or agree on a single type of physical beauty? If so, from where does this pressure come? Have you ever considered as beautiful someone/something whom/that no one else admires?

First reading

2. This poem seems to be very simple in its message. It is a celebration of 'pied beauty' or the beauty that comes from variety of colour and/or contrast. List all the examples of such beauty to be found in the poem.

3. Are all the poet's illustrations of beauty taken from the natural world? What does the poet mean in line 6 by 'áll trádes, their gear and tackle and trim.'

4. Does his appreciation of variety and contrast extend beyond the mere physical in the last four lines? Do you find it unusual that a priest in the nineteenth century should celebrate 'All things counter, original, spare, strange'? Have you noticed any other aspects of Hopkins's poetry that suggest his unconventionality? Take another look at the descriptive adjectives used in lines 7 and 8.

Second reading

5. How would you describe the tone of this poem?

6. Do you notice a difference between this poem and 'As kingfishers' on the one hand, then 'God's Grandeur' and 'Spring' on the other?

7. Consider the significance of line 10. Who is 'He'? How is his beauty 'past change'?

8. What is the effect of the brief last line?

Third reading

9. The poem supports the views of the painter, John Ruskin for whom Hopkins had great admiration. Find out what you can about his aesthetic theory.

10. The simple opening and conclusion echo the Ignatian mottoes Ad Maiorem Dei Gloriam (AMDG) and Laus Deo Semper (LDS). The poem thus becomes a kind of prayer of praise and a meditation on the glory of God. Consider the efficacy of the poem as a prayer.

Felix Randal

FELIX RANDAL the farrier, O he is dead then? My duty all
ended,
Who have watched his mould of man, big-boned and hardy-
handsome
Pining, pining, till time when reason rambled in it and some
Fatal four disorders, fleshed there, all contended?

Sickness broke him. Impatient, he cursed at first, but mended   5
Being anointed and all; though a heavenlier heart began some
Months earlier, since I had our sweet reprieve and ransom
Tendered to him. Ah well, God rest him all road ever he
offended!

This seeing the sick endears them to us, us too it endears.
My tongue had taught thee comfort, touch had quenched thy
tears,   10
Thy tears that touched my heart, child, Felix, poor Felix
Randal;

How far from then forethought of, all thy more boisterous
years,
When thou at the random grim forge, powerful amidst peers,
Didst fettle for the great grey drayhorse his bright and battering
sandal!

Notes

[1] **farrier:** a blacksmith or horse doctor

[6] **fleshed:** took hold of the flesh

[6] **contended:** competed

[8] **heavenlier:** more focused on the next world

[9] **sweet reprieve and ransom:** Holy Communion

[10] **all road:** in any way (colloquial Lancashire phrase)

[17] **How far from then forethought of:** how far away were the thoughts of death when you were in your prime

[19] **random:** architectural term meaning built with rough irregular stones or it could refer to the untidiness of the forge

[20] **drayhorse:** a horse suitable for pulling heavy loads or dray carts

Explorations

Before reading

1. One of the most challenging roles for a priest is to provide comfort to the sick and the dying. He must reconcile the existence of suffering with faith in a loving God. What must it be like to minister to the terminally ill? Does one become indifferent? Does it become a job? How important is faith in the afterlife? Imagine for a moment how you would cope in that role.

First reading

2. Read the poem through several times. Would you agree that the meaning of the poem is relatively easy to grasp? Write a summary of the thoughts in the poem.

3. The poet provides the reader with a vivid picture of the farrier? What do we learn about his physical appearance and the changes that took place as a result of illness? What do we learn about his personality? Does it undergo any change?

4. How would you describe the relationship between the poet/priest and the farrier? Look at the opening statement and lines 9–11 in particular. Do you see any change or development in the poet's attitude to the farrier?

5. What is the effect of the questions in the first quatrain?

6. The first eight lines of the poem are primarily descriptive. How do the next six lines differ in mood?

7. In the first tercet (lines 9–11) how does the poet convey the idea that his relationship with the farrier was mutually rewarding?

8. In 'The Windhover', the student priest seemed to envy the bird's ability to 'achieve' something. Is there any hint in this poem to suggest that the poet finds satisfaction in his parish work?

9. The second tercet reflects another change of mood. The poet seems to be looking back to a time when the blacksmith was at his physical peak. What is the poet trying to achieve in these lines? How does the ending affect the overall mood of the poem?

10. Suggest reasons why the sandal is described as 'bright and battering'.

Second reading

11. The image of Holy Communion in line 7 ('our sweet reprieve and ransom') is a very rich one. Explore its connotations.

12. What is the effect created by the use of ellipsis (omission of words in phrases such as 'my duty (is) all ended')?
13. Hopkins tended to use complex syntax in his poetry. The final sentence is a good example. What is the effect of such an unusual arrangement of words? Can you suggest a reason for this arrangement? Try arranging the sentence in a more normal manner and consider the merits of each.
14. Show how rhythm and imagery combine to create a powerful and triumphant conclusion to the poem.
15. Are there dramatic elements in this poem? Identify them.

Third reading

16. What elements of the sonnet form are recognisable in this poem? How does it differ from a conventional sonnet? How do the innovations contribute to the impact of the poem?
17. Is this a poem about death or a poem about religious faith? Explain your answer.
18. What significance is there in the phrase 'child, Felix, poor Felix Randal'? Does this phrase have a Biblical resonance?
19. Return to your original summary. Would you agree that there is much more to this poem than you thought at first? Elaborate.
20. There is no record of a man named Felix Randal dying in Liverpool around this time. There is a record for a man called Felix Spencer, who was a farrier. Look up the words 'felix' and 'rand' in the dictionary. Can you suggest a reason why the poet would have changed the man's name in this way?
21. Hopkins writes poetry that appeals to the senses. Discuss.

Inversnaid

this poem is also prescribed for Ordinary Level exams in 2003, 2004 and 2006

THIS darksome burn, horseback brown,
His rollrock highroad roaring down,
In coop and in comb the fleece of his foam
Flutes and low to the lake falls home.

A windpuff-bonnet of fáwn-fróth   5
Turns and twindles over the broth
Of a pool so pitchblack, féll-frówning,
It rounds and rounds Despair to drowning.

Degged with dew, dappled with dew
Are the groins of the braes that the brook treads through,   10
Wiry heathpacks, flitches of fern,
And the beadbonny ash that sits over the burn.

What would the world be, once bereft
Of wet and wildness? Let them be left,
O let them be left, wildness and wet;   15
Long live the weeds and the wilderness yet.

Notes

[1] **burn:** A term frequently used by Scottish poets for a small stream. Arklet Water flows from Loch Arklet among the Trossachs and enters Loch Lomond near Inversnaid.

[3] **coop:** an enclosed space suggesting the idea of water trapped in pockets

[3] **comb:** the water combs over the rocks in contrast to 'coop'

[4] **flutes:** could describe the flute-like shape (an architectural term) of the water falling and/or the sound made by the waterfall

[5] **fáwn-fróth:** the froth is a fawn colour

[6] **twindles:** A verb coined from an obscure noun, 'twindle' meaning 'twin'. It is a combination of 'dwindle' and 'twitch' describing the movement of the water.

[6] **broth:** one of the poet's favourite words to describe the seething water, suggestive of a witch's brew

[7] **féll-frówning:** 'Frowning' suggests the gloomy appearance of the scene. 'Fell' can

mean a mountain, an animal's hide or it can mean 'ruthless'. It could also come from the verb 'to fall' (with theological implications).

[9] **degged:** sprinkled (Lancashire dialect)

[9] **dappled:** one of the poet's favourite words to describe patches of different (contrasting) colours

[10] **groins:** folds, another architectural term to describe the joints of vaulting in an arched roof or possibly a bodily metaphor

[10] **braes:** steep banks (Scottish term)

[11] **heathpacks:** patches of densely-packed heather

[11] **flitches:** strips cut from a tree i.e. ragged tufts

[12] **beadbonny ash:** refers to the beautiful (bonny) orange/red berries of the rowan tree or mountain ash

'THIS darksome burn, horseback brown,'

'His rollrock highroad roaring down,
In coop and in comb the fleece of his foam'

The Falls of Inversnaid

'...the groins of the braes that the brook treads through'

'Wiry heathpacks, flitches of fern,'

Explorations

Before reading

1. Look carefully at the pictures of Inversnaid. Does the place appeal to you? Give reasons for your answer.

2. 'Long live the weeds and the wilderness yet.'
   Do you know any place that remains untouched by human development? Write a brief description of it.

First reading

3. Read the poem aloud several times in the classroom. What sounds are dominant?

4. Choose an image or phrase that appeals because of its sound or association. Explain your choice.

5. In general terms, what sort of scene is evoked by the words in the poem?

Second reading

6. With the aid of the glossary and in your own words, describe the actions and appearance of the water in the first two verses. Does the poet make it easy for you to visualize the scene? How does he do it? Comment on the effect of words such as 'horseback', 'rollrock', 'pitchblack' and 'féll-frówning'.

7. Would you agree that there is a great sense of energy in the first verse? How does the poet achieve this effect? Is the downward movement of the water echoed in the rhythm of the lines?

8. Is there a darkening of mood in the second verse? What words convey the change?

9. In the third verse, the poet describes the terrain through which the stream runs. Describe the scene in your own words. How do the poet's words ('degged', 'groins', 'braes', 'beadbonny') flavour the description?

10. How is the fourth verse different from the previous three? In your own words explain what aspect of Inversnaid appeals most to Hopkins.

Third reading

11. Now that your understanding of the poem is deepened, read it aloud again. Would you agree that this is a very simple poem once the difficulties of language are overcome?

12. Would it surprise you to learn that Hopkins once thought of being a landscape painter? Pick out examples of his attention to detail. Use the accompanying photographs to get a sense of the accuracy of his descriptions.

No worst, there is none

No worst, there is none. Pitched past pitch of grief,
More pangs will, schooled at forepangs, wilder wring.
Comforter, where, where is your comforting?
Mary, mother of us, where is your relief?
My cries heave, herds-long; huddle in a main, a chief-   5
woe, world-sorrow; on an age-old anvil wince and sing—
Then lull, then leave off. Fury had shrieked 'No ling-
ering! Let me be fell: force I must be brief'.

O the mind, mind has mountains; cliffs of fall
Frightful, sheer, no-man-fathomed. Hold them cheap   10
May who ne'er hung there. Nor does long our small
Durance deal with that steep or deep. Here! creep,
Wretch, under a comfort serves in a whirlwind: all
Life death does end and each day dies with sleep.

Notes

[1] **Pitched past pitch:** To pitch (verb) could mean 'to throw' and 'pitch' (noun) could mean either pitch-black, as in tar, or it could be used in a musical sense. There are other possible combinations of meaning. The sense of the line seems to be that the poet has been cast beyond what are considered to be the normal limits of human suffering.

[2] **forepangs:** previously experienced agonies

[3] **Comforter:** the Holy Spirit

[5] **herds-long:** a long line of cries, like a herd of cattle, huddled together

[6] **wince and sing:** words chosen as much for their sound as their meaning; they suggest the beating of a hammer against an anvil

[7] **Fury:** an avenging spirit sent to punish crime, or possibly the personification of a guilty conscience

[8] **fell:** cruel

[8] **force:** perforce, of necessity

[10] **no-man-fathomed:** (coinage) no man has fathomed, or explored the depths of this mental abyss

[10,11] **Hold them cheap ... hung there:** those who ... anguish it causes

[12] **Durance:** endurance

Explorations

Before reading

1. This is a poem about mental suffering and a struggle with despair. If you have ever experienced such feelings, try to describe them.

First reading

2. When you have read the poem several times, pick out the images or impressions that are most vivid. Discuss these with the rest of the class.

3. Does this poem come as something of a shock after the previous poems? Explain your answer.

Second reading

4. The opening sentence is short and dramatic. Note carefully that the poet uses the superlative 'worst', not the comparative 'worse'. How does this change the meaning?

5. The second sentence seems to suggest that the agonies that are about to torment him have been 'schooled' by previous agonies and will, therefore, be even more skilled at inflicting pain. How does the poet's expression of this idea surpass this paraphrase? Would you agree that there is an extraordinary intensity in the line?

6. In his address to the Holy Ghost, Hopkins repeats the word 'where'. What is the effect of this repetition? Are there any other examples of this in the poem? What is the cumulative effect of this technique?

7. How does the second quatrain differ from the first? Is it easier or more difficult to comprehend? Give reasons for your answer. Despite the obscurity of the lines, certain impressions are communicated. What are they?

8. How does the poet engage our senses in the octet?

9. In the sestet, the poet suggests that mental torment can feel like hanging on to the edge of a cliff. Is it a good image? Give reasons for your answer.

10. At the end of the poem, Hopkins seems to find some scrap of comfort in the idea that sleep brings the day to a close just as death brings life to a close. What does this 'comfort' say about his state of mind?

Third reading

11. Are we told at any stage in the poem what it is that is causing such anguish? Is the poet more concerned with the experience of suffering rather than the cause?

12. Do you ever get the feeling that the poet is just feeling sorry for himself? Or is his documentation of suffering a testament to his courage?
13. What variations in the use of the sonnet form are evident in this poem?
14. Consider the overall impact of such poetic devices as alliteration, assonance, ellipsis, repetition, compound words and onomatopoeia.

I wake and feel the fell of dark

I WAKE and feel the fell of dark, not day.
What hours, O what black hoùrs we have spent
This night! what sights you, heart, saw; ways you went!
And more must, in yet longer light's delay.
    With witness I speak this. But where I say   5
Hours I mean years, mean life. And my lament
Is cries countless, cries like dead letters sent
To dearest him that lives alas! away.

I am gall, I am heartburn. God's most deep decree
Bitter would have me taste: my taste was me;   10
Bones built in me, flesh filled, blood brimmed the curse.
    Selfyeast of spirit a dull dough sours. I see
The lost are like this, and their scourge to be
As I am mine, their sweating selves; but worse.

Notes

[1] **fell:** An adjective meaning 'cruel' or a noun meaning 'a stretch of moorland' or 'the skin of an animal'; or a verb meaning 'to strike down'; it could also be a play on the word 'fall'. Here, the word is used as a noun.

[9] **gall:** a bitter substance secreted in the liver

[9] **heartburn:** burning sensation in the lower part of chest

[9] **decree:** judgement

[12] **selfyeast:** Yeast is a fungous substance used in baking bread ; thus, it 'sours' a 'dull dough'. Originally, Hopkins used the phrase 'my selfstuff', i.e. the very stuff of my being or self.

[13] **The lost:** those in Hell

Explorations

Before reading

1. Darkness, nightmares and terror, a sense of abandonment, self-disgust— these are the powerful forces at work in this poem. Which of these images do you find most terrifying? Give reasons for your answer.

First reading

2. To what extent is this poem a sequel or continuation to 'No worst, there is none'?

3. How is the sense of darkness emphasised in the first quatrain?

4. What effect is created by the poet's address to his 'heart'?

5. Does Hopkins use any of the poetic devices found in the previous sonnet?

6. How does the poet create a sense of spiritual desolation? Is it described in abstract terms or does he create a sense in which it is physical as well as spiritual?

7. To whom are his 'dead letters' sent? Why does he describe them as 'dead'?

8. In the sestet, there is a powerful impression of self-disgust. Identify the images used by the poet to create this effect.

9. Hopkins changed the phrase 'God's most deep decree' to 'God's most just decree' and then changed it back to the original. How do the two phrases differ? What do we learn about the poet's state of mind from this information?

10. Lines 11 and 12 are a kind of definition of self. His physical body is described in gruesome terms; his spirit, instead of lifting the dough, sours it and makes it worse. What is your reaction to this self-definition? Does it inspire shock or pity?

11. Does the poem end with despair or consolation? Who is 'worse'?

Second reading

12. Are we told why the poet feels such desolation? Does it matter?

13. Pick out examples of the poet's use of inversion (of normal word order). How does this device contribute to the sense of anguish in the poem?

14. Compare this poem with the previous one. (They are usually referred to as 'the terrible sonnets'.) Which of the two is more effective in communicating the poet's suffering? Give reasons for your answer.

THOU *art indeed just, Lord*

Justus quidem tu es, Domine, si disputem tecum; verumtamen
justa loquar ad te: Quare via impiorum prosperatur? etc.

THOU art indeed just, Lord, if I contend
With thee; but, sir, so what I plead is just.
Why do sinners' ways prosper? and why must
Disappointment all I endeavour end?

Wert thou my enemy, O thou my friend,   5
How wouldst thou worse, I wonder, than thou dost
Defeat, thwart me? Oh, the sots and thralls of lust
Do in spare hours more thrive than I that spend,

Sir, life upon thy cause. See, banks and brakes
Now, leavèd how thick! lacèd they are again   10
With fretty chervil, look, and fresh wind shakes

Them; birds build—but not I build; no, but strain,
Time's eunuch, and not breed one work that wakes.
Mine, O thou lord of life, send my roots rain.

Background note

The Latin quotation is taken from Jeremiah 12: 1. The full text is: 'Thou indeed, O Lord, art just, if I plead with thee, but yet I will speak what is just to thee: why doth the way of the wicked prosper: why is it well with all of them that transgress and do wickedly? Thou hast planted them, and they have taken root: they prosper and bring forth fruit. Thou art near in their mouth and far from their reins. And thou, O Lord, hast known me, thou hast seen me, and proved my heart with thee.'

It was customary for a Jesuit priest to repeat the phrase, 'Justus es, Domine, et rectum iudicium tuum' (You are just, O Lord, and your judgement is right.), like a mantra. It signifies an acceptance of God's will, however unpalatable it may seem.

Notes

[7] **sots:** drunkards

[7] **thralls:** slaves

[9] **brakes:** thickets

[11] **fretty:** fretted or interlaced

[11] **chervil:** cow parsley

[13] **eunuch:** castrated male employed in a harem

[13] **wakes:** comes to life

 # Explorations

Before reading

1. Have you ever felt that life is unfair and that there seems to be no connection between effort and reward? Describe the circumstances and feeling.

First reading

2. Read the poem aloud. Can you hear the sense of hurt, anger and frustration? Identify where you think the feelings are at their most intense.

Second reading

3. The first quatrain takes the words from Jeremiah and arranges them to suit the constraints of the sonnet form. Is there any tension in these lines or is the poet simply repeating the formula from the Bible?

4. Is there a tone of humility or anger in the first quatrain?

5. Is there any evidence in the second quatrain to suggest that the poet's feelings are becoming unmanageable? Look carefully at the metre and syntax.

6. What is the effect of the apostrophes, 'Lord', 'sir', 'O thou my friend', 'O thou lord of life'?

7. It is difficult to separate the third quatrain from the second. Is this deliberate? What does the poet intend to convey by this arrangement?

Third reading

8. What is the poet's complaint?
9. Is there a sense of growing anger as the poem progresses? Does it continue to build until the end of the poem?
10. To what extent does the syntax contribute to the expression of tortured innocence?
11. How does the imagery change in the sestet?
12. What sort of relationship exists between the poet and God?
13. What kind of 'work' does the poet want? Does he write as a poet or as a priest? Or both?
14. Hopkins included this poem in a letter to Robert Bridges. He suggested that it be read 'adagio molto', a musical term meaning very slowly, 'and with great stress'. How would such a reading enhance the impact of the poem?

6 W.B. YEATS

prescribed for Higher Level exams in 2003, 2005 and 2006

In 1865 William Butler Yeats was born in Dublin to a Co. Sligo family. His grandfather had been rector of the Church of Ireland at Drumcliff. His father, the portrait-painter John Butler Yeats, had married Susan Pollexfen, who belonged to a family of substantial traders and ship-owners from Co. Sligo. His brother, Jack B. Yeats, was to become one of Ireland's best-known painters. William Yeats was educated intermittently at the Godolphin School in London, the High School in Dublin and the Dublin Metropolitan School of Art.

He was interested in mysticism and the supernatural and developed a great curiosity for Irish mythology, history and folklore. It became one of his life's great passions to develop a distinctive, distinguished Irish literature in English. His first long poem, 'The Wanderings of Oisin' (1889), established the tone of what became known as the 'Celtic Twilight'. His early volumes of poetry reflect his interest in mysticism, theosophy and mythology but also deal with his hopeless love affairs, most notably that with Maude Gonne. In 1889 he had met and fallen in love with her; and though she would not marry him, he remained obsessed with her for most of his life. With Lady Gregory of Coole Park, Gort, Co.

1865–1939

Galway and John Millington Synge he founded the Irish Literary Theatre Society in 1899 and later the Abbey Theatre in 1904.

By the end of the century Yeats had changed his decorative, symbolist style of poetry and began to write in a more direct style. From *The Green Helmet* (1910) onwards he shows a more realistic attitude to love and also begins to write about everyday cultural and political affairs. *Responsibilities* (1914) contains satires on the materialism of Dublin's middle class. Among the major themes of his mature years are the need for harmony in life, the search for perfection in life and art, and the mysteries of time and eternity. These are to be found particularly in the poems of the later volumes, *The Tower* (1928), *The Winding Stair* (1933), and *Last Poems* (1936–39).

Yeats was made a senator in 1922 and was very active in public life; he supervised the design of the new coinage in 1926. He was awarded the Nobel Prize for Literature in 1923. He died in Rome in 1939, but his body was not brought back to Ireland until after the war, when it was buried in Drumcliff.

William Butler Yeats as a young man, painted by his father John Butler Yeats (1839–1922)

The Lake Isle of Innisfree

this poem is also prescribed for Ordinary Level exams in 2003, 2005 and 2006

I will arise and go now, and go to Innisfree,
And a small cabin build there, of clay and wattles made:
Nine bean-rows will I have there, a hive for the honey-bee,
And live alone in the bee-loud glade.

And I shall have some peace there, for peace comes dropping slow,   5
Dropping from the veils of the morning to where the cricket sings;
There midnight's all a glimmer, and noon a purple glow,
And evening full of the linnet's wings.

I will arise and go now, for always night and day
I hear lake water lapping with low sounds by the shore;   10
While I stand on the roadway, or on the pavements grey,
I hear it in the deep heart's core.

Notes

[1] **I will arise...:** This has echoes of the return of the Prodigal Son in Luke 15: 18—'I will arise and go to my father.' So they were the words of another returning emigrant.

[1] **Innisfree:** (in Irish 'Inisfraoich': Heather Island)—a rocky island on Lough Gill, Co. Sligo

[2] **wattles:** rods interlaced with twigs or branches to make a fence

Explorations

Before reading

1. Read only the title. What comes into your mind when you read the title?

First reading

2. What do you notice about Yeats's island?
3. What sights and sounds will the poet see and hear? List them.
4. Contrast this island with his present surroundings.

Second reading

5. Do you think that the features of the island mentioned by the poet are the usual sights and sounds of everyday life in the country or will this place be special? Explain your thinking on this.
6. What kind of space or place is the poet attempting to create? What does that indicate about his needs and philosophy of life or values? Refer to the poem to support your theories.
7. What is the poet's attitude to nature as suggested in the poem? Refer to specific lines and phrases.

Third reading

8. The poet seems almost impelled or driven to go and create this ideal place. Where is the sense of compulsion in the poem and how is it created? Explore the style of language he uses, the syntax, the rhythms of his speech and the repeated phrases in order to help you with this.
9. What do you think is the meaning and significance of the last line?

Fourth reading

10. State succinctly what you think the poem is about?
11. What mood do you think the poet creates here and how do the images and the sounds of words contribute to this?
12. Does anything about the poet's vision here appeal to you? Discuss this.

September 1913

What need you, being come to sense,
But fumble in a greasy till
And add the halfpence to the pence
And prayer to shivering prayer, until
You have dried the marrow from the bone?   5
For men were born to pray and save:
Romantic Ireland's dead and gone,
It's with O'Leary in the grave.

Yet they were of a different kind,
The names that stilled your childish play,   10
They have gone about the world like wind,
But little time had they to pray
For whom the hangman's rope was spun,
And what, God help us, could they save?
Romantic Ireland's dead and gone,   15
It's with O'Leary in the grave.

Was it for this the wild geese spread
The grey wing upon every tide;
For this that all that blood was shed,
For this Edward Fitzgerald died,   20
And Robert Emmet and Wolfe Tone,
All that delirium of the brave?
Romantic Ireland's dead and gone,
It's with O'Leary in the grave.

Yet could we turn the years again,   25
And call those exiles as they were
In all their loneliness and pain,
You'd cry, 'Some woman's yellow hair
Has maddened every mother's son':
They weighed so lightly what they gave   30
But let them be, they're dead and gone,
They're with O'Leary in the grave.

Background note

During 1913 Yeats had spent a great deal of energy in support of Lady Gregory's nephew, Sir Hugh Lane. A wealthy art collector, who made a gift to the city of Dublin of an extraordinary collection of modern painting provided the city build a suitable gallery. There was a great deal of dispute about the structure, the location and the cost. Yeats was furious at what seemed a mean spirited, penny-pinching, anti-cultural response to the project.

Notes

[8] **O'Leary:** John O'Leary (1830–1907) A fenian who was arrested in 1865 and sentenced to twenty years imprisonment. After a number of years he was released on condition of exile. Returning to Dublin in 1885 he was greatly influential in Yeats's developing views on Irish nationalism.

[17] **the wild geese:** Irish soldiers who were forced into exile after the Williamite victory of the 1690s. They served in the armies of France, Spain and Austria.

[20] **Edward Fitzgerald:** Lord Edward Fitzgerald (1763–98), one of the leaders of the United Irishmen who dies of wounds received while being arrested.

[21] **Robert Emmet:** leader of the rebellion of 1803

[21] **Wolfe Tone:** Theobald Wolfe Tone (1763–98) was leader of the United Irishmen. Captured and sentenced to death, he committed suicide in prison.

 # Explorations

First reading
Stanza 1

1. 'What need you...'. The 'you' here refers to the new Irish relatively prosperous and Catholic middle classes, whom Yeats is addressing. What does he suggest are their main concerns or needs in life?

2. Explore the connotations of the images used in the first five lines, i.e. what is suggested by each of the pictures. List all the suggestions carried by each of the following and discuss them in groups: 'fumble'; 'greasy till'; 'add the halfpence to the pence'; 'add...prayer to shivering prayer'; 'dried the marrow from the bone'.

3. As a consequence of your explorations, what do you think is Yeats's attitude to these people? What words do you think best convey the tone?

4. 'For men were born to pray and save'

Does the poet really mean this? If not, what? How should it be read? Try reading it aloud.

5. (a) Read aloud the last two lines of the stanza as you think the poet would wish it. (b) How is this refrain different from the earlier lines of the stanza? (c) What do you understand by 'Romantic Ireland' and how does Yeats feel about it?

6. Now read the entire stanza aloud, differentiating between the sections that are sarcastic, bitter, or condemnatory and the lines that are wistful, nostalgic, or plaintive.

Second reading

Stanza 2

7. 'They'—the romantic generations of heroes had great power and influence in society. How is this suggested? Explore all the possible suggestions carried by lines 10 and 11.

8. How were they different from the present generation?

9. Is there a suggestion that they were fated to act as they did? Examine line 13.

10. In groups discuss the best possible way of reading this stanza aloud. Then do it.

Third reading

Stanza 3

11. 'for this ... For this ... For this'. Through this repetition Yeats punches out the contrast between past and present. His attitude to the present generation is quite clear by now. But what does this stanza say about his attitude to the heroes of Ireland's past? Explore in detail the suggestions carried by the images.

12. 'All that delirium of the brave'. Discuss what this implies about heroism.

Stanza 4

13. 'All Yeats's sympathy and admiration is with the past generations of heroes'. Discuss this and refer to the text in support of your ideas.

14. 'You'd cry, 'Some woman's yellow hair has maddened every mother's son'.'
What do you think they mean by this?

Fourth reading

15. 'In this poem we find a quite grotesque portrayal of the middle classes in contrast to an unreal and highly romanticised portrayal of past patriots!' Discuss this as an interpretation of the poem.

16. What do you think is the effect of the refrain?

17. Do you think this was a politically risky, even dangerous, poem to publish? Explain.

18. Are you surprised by the passion and strength of feeling here? Outline your reactions.

The Wild Swans at Coole

this poem is also prescribed for Ordinary Level exams in 2005 and 2006

The trees are in their autumn beauty,
The woodland paths are dry,
Under the October twilight the water
Mirrors a still sky;
Upon the brimming water among the stones   5
Are nine-and-fifty swans.

The nineteenth autumn has come upon me
Since I first made my count;
I saw, before I had well finished,
All suddenly mount   10
And scatter wheeling in great broken rings
Upon their clamorous wings.

I have looked upon those brilliant creatures,
And now my heart is sore.
All's changed since I, hearing at twilight,   15
The first time on this shore,
The bell-beat of their wings above my head,
Trod with a lighter tread.

Unwearied still, lover by lover,
They paddle in the cold   20
Companionable streams or climb the air;
Their hearts have not grown old;
Passion or conquest, wander where they will,
Attend upon them still.

But now they drift on the still water,   25
Mysterious, beautiful;
Among what rushes will they build,
By what lake's edge or pool
Delight men's eyes when I awake some day
To find they have flown away?   30

Notes

Coole: Coole Park, outside Gort, Co. Galway and home of Lady Augusta Gregory. She was a friend and benefactor to the poet and collaborated on many of his projects. Yeats regarded Coole Park as a second home and a welcoming refuge and retreat.

[6] **nine-and-fifty swans:** there actually were fifty-nine swans on the lake at Coole Park

[7] **the nineteenth autumn:** Yeats is referring to the summer and autumn of 1897 which was the first time he stayed for a lengthy period at Coole. At that time he was passionately involved with Maude Gonne and in a state of acute nervous exhaustion.

[18 **Trod with a lighter tread:** It is interesting that the poet chooses to recast 1897 as a hopeful and even carefree period, when this was not the case!

Explorations

First reading

Stanza 1

1. Notice all the details that draw Yeats's eyes and ears to the scene. Visualize them intently, with eyes closed, if you can. If you came upon this scene what would your thoughts be?

2. How would you describe the atmosphere of this scene? What particular images or sounds contribute to this atmosphere? Explain.

Stanza 2

3. Read the second stanza with energy, aloud if possible, and see if you can make the swans come alive.

4. Examine the description of the swans here. (*a*) What attributes or qualities of these creatures does the poet wish to convey? (*b*) How are these qualities carried by the language? Look at images, verbs, adverbs, the sounds of words and the structure of the long single sentence.

Second reading

5. In the third stanza the poet introduces a personal note. What does he reveal about himself?

6. In stanzas 3 and 4 he explores the contrasts between the life and condition of the swans and his own life and condition. In your own words explain the detail of these contrasts.

7. Do you think the poet envies the swans? If so, what exactly does he envy? Refer to phrases and lines to support your thinking.

8. Is this a logical or a poetic argument? Explain.

Third reading

9. If we read the first four stanzas as lamenting the loss of youth, passion and love, what particular loss frightens him in the final stanza? Explain.

10. What general issues or themes does Yeats deal with in this poem?

11. Do you think there is any sense of resolution of the personal issues raised by Yeats in this poem? Does he come to any definite conclusion? Explain your thinking.

12. Examine how the poem is structured stanza by stanza, moving from that very particular local opening to the general speculation about love in stanza 4, and then opening up into that rather mysterious ending that seeks to look into the future. What is the effect of this?

13. The poem is built upon a series of antitheses: the swans and

the poet; the poet then and the poet now; contrasting moods. Show how these are developed.

14. What do you think the symbolism adds to the poem? Explore the elements of sky and water; trees and paths; great broken rings; and of course the swans themselves.

Fourth reading

15. Would you agree that the poem creates a 'hauntingly evocative description of the swans'? Discuss or write about this.

16. 'Ageing and the diminution of visionary power are bitterly regretted' (Terence Brown). Discuss this view of the poem, referring in detail to the text to substantiate your argument.

Coole Park: the home of Lady Gregory, now demolished

An Irish Airman Foresees his Death

I know that I shall meet my fate
Somewhere among the clouds above;
Those that I fight I do not hate,
Those that I guard I do not love;
My country is Kiltartan Cross,   5
My countrymen Kiltartan's poor,
No likely end could bring them loss
Or leave them happier than before.
Nor law, nor duty bade me fight,
Nor public men, nor cheering crowds,   10
A lonely impulse of delight
Drove to this tumult in the clouds;
I balanced all, brought all to mind,
The years to come seemed waste of breath,
A waste of breath the years behind   15
In balance with this life, this death.

Notes

[3] **Those that I fight:** the Germans

[4] **Those that I guard:** the English or possibly the Italians

[5] **Kiltartan Cross:** a crossroads near Robert Gregory's home at Coole Park, Gort, Co. Galway

An Irish Airman: The speaker in the poem is Major Robert Gregory, the only son of Yeats's friend and mentor Lady Augusta Gregory of Coole Park, near Gort, Co. Galway. He was a pilot in the Royal Flying Corps in the First World War and at the time of his death, on 23 January 1918, was on service in Italy. It emerged later that he had been accidentally shot down by the Italian allies.

The entrance to Coole Park today

Explorations

Before reading

1. Read only the title. What do you expect to find in this poem? Imagine what this man's thoughts might be. How might he visualize his death? How might he feel about it? Jot down briefly the thoughts, pictures and feelings you imagine might go through his mind.

First reading

2. Who is the speaker in this poem? If in doubt, consult the note (An Irish Airman) at the end of the poem.

3. Focus on lines 1 and 2. Are you surprised by how definite he is? Can you suggest any reasons why he might be so definite about his coming death? How would you describe his mood?

4. How do you think the speaker would say these first two lines? Experiment with various readings aloud.

5. Taking the first four lines as a unit, are you surprised that they are spoken by a military man, a pilot? In your own words, describe how he views his situation.

Second reading

6. In lines 5–8 the speaker talks about the people of his home area. How does he feel about them? Does he identify with them in any way? Have the people and the speaker anything in common? How does he think his death will affect their lives? Does he feel they will miss him? Do you think his attitude to them is uncaring, or that he feels unable to affect their lives in any way? Discuss these questions and write down the conclusions you come to, together with the evidence from the text.

7. What do you think is the purpose of his mentioning his Kiltartan countrymen in the context of his explanation? How does it fit in with his reasoning?

8. Lines 9 and 10. In your own words, explain these further reasons, which the speaker discounts as having any influence on his decision to volunteer.

9. What is revealed about the character of the speaker in the lines you have explored so far?

Third reading

10. Lines 11 and 12. Here we get to the kernel of his motivation. Examine the language very carefully. 'A lonely impulse of delight': can you understand

why he might feel this sense of delight? Explain how you see it. 'Impulse': what does this tell us about the decision? 'A lonely impulse': what does this suggest about the decision and the man? 'Drove': what does this add to our understanding of how he felt and of his decision? 'Tumult in the clouds': in what other context might the words 'tumult' or 'tumultuous' be used? Suggest a few. What does the sound of the word suggest? What does it suggest about the speaker's view of flying?

11. In the light of what you have discovered so far, and in the voice of the speaker, write a letter home, explaining your decision to volunteer as a pilot. Try to remain true to the speaker's feelings as outlined in the poem.

12. Lines 13–16. 'In spite of his hint of excitement earlier, the speaker did not make a rash and emotional decision.' On the evidence of these lines, would you agree with that statement? Write a paragraph.

13. 'The years to come seemed waste of breath …
   In balance with this life, this death.'
   Yet the speaker seemed to want this kind of life very much. Explore how the use of 'breath' and 'death' as rhyming words help to emphasise this.

Fourth reading

14. Having read this poem, what do find most interesting about the speaker?

15. What appeals to you about the poem? Do you find anything disturbing about it?

16. Thousands of Irishmen fought and died in the British army during the First World War; others could not bring themselves to join that army while Ireland was governed by England. How does the speaker deal with this issue? Is the title significant?

17. As well as being a rhetorical device, the repetition of words and phrases emphasises certain ideas and issues. List the main ideas thus emphasised.

18. What are the principal themes or issues the poem deals with? Write a number of short paragraphs on this.

19. 'The pictures and images are sparsely used but very effective.' Comment on any two images.

20. To whom is this being spoken? Read it aloud. Is the tone more appropriate to a letter or to a public statement or speech? Explain your view with reference to phrases or lines in the text.

Easter 1916

I have met them at close of day
Coming with vivid faces
From counter or desk among grey
Eighteenth-century houses.
I have passed with a nod of the head   5
Or polite meaningless words,
Or have lingered awhile and said
Polite meaningless words,
And thought before I had done
Of a mocking tale or a gibe   10
To please a companion
Around the fire at the club,
Being certain they and I
But lived where motley is worn:
All changed, changed utterly: 15
A terrible beauty is born.

That woman's days were spent
In ignorant good-will,
Her nights in argument
Until her voice grew shrill.   20
What voice more sweet than hers
When, young and beautiful,
She rode to harriers?

Notes

Easter 1916: On Monday 24 April 1916 a force of about 700 republicans, who were members of the Irish Volunteers and the Irish Citizen Army, took over the centre of Dublin in a military revolution and held out for six days against the British army. This was known as the Easter Rising.

[1] **them:** those republicans, in the pre-1916 days

[3] **grey:** built of granite or limestone

[12] **the club:** probably the Arts Club where Yeats was a founder member in 1907

[17] **That woman:** Constance Gore-Booth (1868–1927) of Lissadell, Co. Sligo, who married the Polish Count Markiewicz. She became a fervent Irish Nationalist and was actively involved in the Fianna and the Citizen Army. She was sentenced to death for her part in the rising but the sentence was later commuted to penal servitude for life—she was released in 1917 under the general amnesty.

This man had kept a school
And rode our wingèd horse;   25
This other his helper and friend
Was coming into his force;
He might have won fame in the end,
So sensitive his nature seemed,
So daring and sweet his thought.   30
This other man I had dreamed
A drunken, vainglorious lout.
He had done most bitter wrong
To some who are near my heart,
Yet I number him in the song;   35
He, too, has resigned his part
In the casual comedy;
He, too, has been changed in his turn,
Transformed utterly:
A terrible beauty is born.   40

Hearts with one purpose alone
Through summer and winter seem
Enchanted to a stone
To trouble the living stream.
The horse that comes from the road,   45
The rider, the birds that range
From cloud to tumbling cloud,
Minute by minute they change;
A shadow of cloud on the stream

[24] **This man:** Padraig Pearse (1879–1916). Barrister, teacher and poet he was the founder of
    St Enda's school and editor of *An Claidheamh Soluis*. He believed that a blood sacrifice was
    necessary to revolutionise Ireland. A member of the revolutionary IRB and the Irish Volunteers he
    was the Commandant General and President of the Provisional Government during Easter week.
[25] **wingèd horse:** Pegasus, the winged horse, was a symbol of poetic vision
[26] **This other:** Thomas MacDonagh (1878–1916), poet and academic who taught at University
    College Dublin
[31] **This other man:** Major John MacBride who had fought with the Boers against the British in
    South Africa and in 1903 married Maude Gonne, the woman Yeats loved. He too was
    executed for his part in the Rising.
[33] **He had done most bitter wrong:** a reference to rumours of family violence and
    debauchery
[34] **To some who are near my heart:** Maude Gonne and her daughter
[41–43] **Hearts ... stone:** 'Stone' at its simplest is usually taken to be a symbol for the fanatical
    heart—i.e. those who devote themselves fanatically to a cause, become hardened and lose
    their humanness as a result.

Changes minute by minute;   50
A horse-hoof slides on the brim,
And a horse plashes within it;
The long-legged moor-hens dive,
And hens to moor-cocks call;
Minute by minute they live: 55
The stone's in the midst of all.

Too long a sacrifice
Can make a stone of the heart.
O when may it suffice?
That is Heaven's part, our part   60
To murmur name upon name,
As a mother names her child
When sleep at last has come
On limbs that had run wild.
What is it but nightfall?   65
No, no, not night but death;
Was it needless death after all?
For England may keep faith
For all that is done and said.
We know their dream; enough   70
To know they dreamed and are dead;
And what if excess of love
Bewildered them till they died?
I write it out in a verse—
MacDonagh and MacBride   75
And Connolly and Pearse
Now and in time to be,
Wherever green is worn,
Are changed, changed utterly:
A terrible beauty is born.   80

[67–68] **needless death ... England may keep faith:** The Bill for Irish Home Rule had
   been passed in the Westminster Parliament. In 1914, however, it was suspended on the
   outbreak of World War I, but with the promise that it would be put into effect after the war.

[76] **Connolly:** James Connolly (1870–1916). Trade Union organiser and founder of the Citizen
   Army he was military commander of the insurgents in Dublin, Easter 1916.

Explorations

Before reading

1. First re-read 'September 1913' and remind yourself how Yeats felt about the Irish middle class of his time.

First reading

Section One

2. Concentrate on the first fourteen lines. These are the same people who feature in 'September 1913'. Yeats is no longer savagely angry but he certainly has no respect for them. Visualize the encounter he describes—time of day; atmosphere; what the poet does; what he says; how he behaves. Share these ideas.

3. (a) What 'polite meaningless words' might he have said? Invent some dialogue for him. (b) As he speaks these 'polite meaningless words' what is he actually thinking? Script his 'thoughts—inside—the head' and the tale or gibe he might tell later.

4. 'Where motley is worn': what does this tell us about how Yeats regarded Ireland at this time.

5. How would you describe the poet's feelings and mood in this first section?

6. The first fourteen lines are transformed by lines 15 and 16 and given a new context. Framed by use of the perfect tense 'I have met them. I have passed.' The impression is given that that was then, this is now. (a) Re-read the first section, from this perspective. (b) Do you think Yeats is ashamed of his earlier treatment of these people? Discuss this with reference to lines or phrases in the poem.

7. 'A terrible beauty is born'. Explore all the suggestions of this phrase.

Second reading

Section Two

8. According to the poet what are the effects on Constance Markiewicz of fanatical dedication to a political cause.

9. 'This other his helper...'. In contrast to the portrait of Constance Markiewicz which is somewhat masculine, this portrait of Thomas MacDonagh is quite feminised. Would you agree? Explain your thinking with reference to words and phrases in the poem.

10. There is great emphasis on change in this section. List all the instances and comment on them.

11. There is a sense that this

change or transformation was not something actually effected by these people but rather something that happened to them.

'He, too, has been changed in his turn,
Transformed utterly:'

They were changed by death and by executions. Do you think that Yeats is exploring how ordinary people are changed into heroes and what is he suggesting? Discuss this.

Third reading

Section Three

12. Here Yeats is fascinated by flux and the process of change. (*a*) List all the examples he uses. (*b*) Comment on the atmosphere created here. Is it an appealing picture?

13. In this section he is exploring the paradox that only a stone (the fanatical heart) can alter the flow of a stream, i.e. the course of life. But it can only do this at the expense of losing humanness. What does this indicate about Yeats's thinking on revolutionary politics?

Fourth reading

Section Four

14. What is your initial impression of the tone of this section? Is the poet weary, worried, confused; giving up or what? Refer in detail to the text.

15. '...our part

To murmur name upon name'
How does he see the poet's role here?

16. 'sleep ... not night but death ... needless death ... excess of love | Bewildered them...'. The poet is attempting to think through his confusions and uncertainties here. Trace his thoughts in your own words.

17. Finally, at the end of the poem, Yeats lists out the dead, almost as a sacred act. What is the effect of this for the poet, the reader and those who died?

Fifth reading

18. Yeats had been severely disillusioned by the new Irish Catholic middle class but he had to rethink this view after 1916. Explain the process of his rethinking as it happens in the poem.

19. 'Despite his sense of awe and admiration for the change brought about, this poem does not represent a totally unqualified approval of revolutionary politics.' Discuss this view of the poem, support your answer with references to the text.

20. Though written in 1916, Yeats did not have this poem published until October 1920. Speculate on his possible reasons. Do you think they were justified?

Maude Gonne: painting by Sarah Purser

The Second Coming

Turning and turning in the widening gyre
The falcon cannot hear the falconer;
Things fall apart; the centre cannot hold;
Mere anarchy is loosed upon the world,
The blood-dimmed tide is loosed, and everywhere   5
The ceremony of innocence is drowned;
The best lack all conviction, while the worst
Are full of passionate intensity.

Surely some revelation is at hand;
Surely the Second Coming is at hand.   10
The Second Coming! Hardly are those words out
When a vast image out of *Spiritus Mundi*
Troubles my sight: somewhere in sands of the desert
A shape with lion body and the head of a man,
A gaze blank and pitiless as the sun,   15
Is moving its slow thighs, while all about it
Reel shadows of the indignant desert birds.
The darkness drops again; but now I know
That twenty centuries of stony sleep
Were vexed to nightmare by a rocking cradle,   20
And what rough beast, its hour come round at last,
Slouches towards Bethlehem to be born?

Notes

The Second Coming: In its Christian interpretation this refers to the prediction of the second coming of Christ, see Matthew 24. In Yeats's occult and magical philosophy it might also refer to the second birth of the Avatar or great antithetical spirit which Yeats and his wife felt certain would be reincarnated as their baby son whose birth was imminent. In fact the child turned out to be a girl, dashing that theory.

[1–2] **Turning ... falconer:** The bird is rising in ever widening circles and so making the pattern of an inverted cone or gyre. These lines could be read as the trained bird of prey reverting to its wild state or, in a more religious sense, taken to represent Christian civilization growing further away from Christ (the falconer).

[12] **Spiritus Mundi:** 'The spirit of the world', which Yeats describes as 'a general storehouse of images which have ceased to be a property of any personality or spirit'.

[14] **A shape with lion body and the head of a man:** instead of the second coming of Christ, Yeats imagines this horrific creature, a sort of Antichrist

[20] **rocking cradle:** the birth of Christ in Bethlehem began the then two-thousand-year period of Christian history

Explorations

Before reading

1. Read Matthew 24: 1–31 and some of the Book of Revelations, particularly chapters 12, 13, 20 and 21. Discuss these.

First reading

Stanza 1—Focusing on the Images

2. The trained falcon is released and it circles looking for prey. What do you think might happen if the falcon cannot hear the falconer?

3. What do you see and imagine when you read (a) line 3 and (b) line 4?

4. 'The blood-dimmed tide is loosed'
   What does this picture conjure up for you? Do you find it sinister, frightening, or what?

5. Lines 7 and 8 focus on people. What types of people do you think the poet has in mind? Discuss this.

Second reading

6. Taking the first stanza as a whole what does it communicate about Yeats's view of civilisation as he saw it at that time?

7. 'The first stanza or section is full of the tension of opposites.' Discuss or write about this.

8. In the second section of the poem Yeats is looking for some sufficiently weighty reason which would explain this collapse of civilisation. What occurs to him first?

9. His first short-lived thought is replaced by this 'vast image' that 'troubles' his sight. Read Yeats's description carefully and (a) Describe what you imagine (b) What particular qualities are exhibited by this 'rough beast'? (c) What particular images or phrases help create the sense of revulsion?

10. Are you shocked by the association with Bethlehem? What is suggested here? Discuss this.

Third reading

11. Yeats is talking about the end of the Christian era, the end of innocence. This is encapsulated particularly in the horrific image of one of the holiest places in Christianity, Bethlehem, being defiled by this beast. What typically nightmarish elements do you notice in the second section of the poem?

12. In your own words, set out briefly what you think the poem is about.

13. Comment on the power of the imagery.

14. Though this was written primarily as a reaction to

events in Europe, can you
understand how it might be
read as a commentary on the
Irish situation of that time?
Explain your views.

15. Could the poem be seen as
    prophetic in any way?
16. What did this poem make you
    think about? Describe the
    effect it had on you.

Sailing to Byzantium

I

That is no country for old men. The young
In one another's arms, birds in the trees
—Those dying generations—at their song,
The salmon-falls, the mackerel-crowded seas,
Fish, flesh, or fowl, commend all summer long   5
Whatever is begotten, born, and dies.
Caught in that sensual music all neglect
Monuments of unageing intellect.

II

An aged man is but a paltry thing,
A tattered coat upon a stick, unless   10
Soul clap its hands and sing, and louder sing
For every tatter in its mortal dress,
Nor is there singing school but studying
Monuments of its own magnificence;
And therefore I have sailed the seas and come   15
To the holy city of Byzantium.

III

O sages standing in God's holy fire
As in the gold mosaic of a wall,
Come from the holy fire, perne in a gyre,
And be the singing-masters of my soul.   20
Consume my heart away; sick with desire
And fastened to a dying animal
It knows not what it is; and gather me
Into the artifice of eternity.

IV

Once out of nature I shall never take	25
My bodily form from any natural thing,	
But such a form as Grecian goldsmiths make	
Of hammered gold and gold enamelling	
To keep a drowsy Emperor awake;	
Or set upon a golden bough to sing	30
To lords and ladies of Byzantium	
Of what is past, or passing, or to come.	

Notes

Byzantium: The Roman emperor Constantine, who became a Christian in A.D. 312, chose Byzantium as his capital city, renaming it Constantinople in 330. Yeats idealized Byzantium, in particular at the end of the fifth century, as the centre of European civilisation—a place where all life was in harmony.

[1] **That:** Ireland

[4] **The salmon-falls, the mackerel-crowded seas:** all images of regeneration, new life, energy and plenty

[5] **commend:** praise, celebrate

[17] **O sages:** probably refers to the depiction of the martyrs being burned in a fire in a mosaic at the church of San Apollinare Nuovo in Ravenna, which Yeats saw in 1907

[19] **perne in a gyre:** When Yeats was a child in Sligo he was told that 'pern' was another name for spool or bobbin on which the thread was wound. So the idea of circular movement is carried in the word 'perne' which Yeats constructs here as a verb. A 'gyre' is a revolving cone of time, in Yeats's cosmology. Here, Yeats is asking the sages to journey through the cone of time, to come to him and teach him perfection, teach his soul to sing.

[24] **artifice of eternity:** Artifice is something constructed, created—here a work of art. The word can also have connotations of trickery or slight of hand. In a certain sense art is outside time and has a sort of eternal quality about it. Yeats asks the sages to gather him into the eternity of art.

[27] **such a form:** Yeats wrote that he had read somewhere that there existed in the Emperors' Palace in Byzantium 'a tree made of gold and silver, and artificial birds that sang'. Here the golden bird is used as a metaphor for art which is beautiful, perfect and unchanging.

[32] **Of what is past, or passing, or to come:** Though Yeats wished to escape out of the stream of time into the eternity of art, ironically, the golden bird's song is about time.

Explorations

First reading
Stanza 1

1. Read the first stanza carefully for yourself, as many times as you feel necessary. In groups, try out different ways of reading aloud the first sentence. Why do you think it should be read in that way?

2. Notice the perspective. The poet has already left Ireland, either in reality or imagination, and is looking back. (*a*) What does he remember about the country? (*b*) Why is it 'no country' for old men?

3. The first stanza portrays the sensuality of life very vividly. Explore how the poet does this. Consider the imagery; the sounds of words; repeated letters, the crowded syntax; the repetitions and rhythms of the sentence etc.

4. How do you think the poet feels about this teeming fertility? Ostensibly he is renouncing the world of the senses but do you think he dwells on these scenes a little too much if he dislikes or hates them? Consider phrases such as 'The young | In one another's arms, birds in the trees'; 'commend all summer long'; 'Caught in that sensual music'. Do you think there might be a hint of nostalgia and a sense of loss here? Discuss the tone of the stanza.

5. Yet in the midst of all this energy and life there are the seeds of death. Explain the paradox and word punning in 'dying generations'. Where else, in the first stanza, is there an awareness of time?

6. What does the poet value that he feels is neglected in Ireland?

7. Re-read the stanza and list all the reasons you can find for Yeats's departure or withdrawal.

8. Now read aloud the first sentence as you think the poet intended it.

Second reading
Stanza 2

9. In this stanza Yeats asserts that only the soul gives meaning to the human being. (*a*) Explore the contrast between body and soul here. (*b*) Do you think that the imagery used is effective? Explain?

10. 'Nor is there ... own magnificence': (*a*) Tease out the possible meanings of these two lines. Explore the following reading: the only way the spirit learns to sing (achieves perfection) is by studying monuments created by and for

itself, i.e. works of art. In other words, art enriches the soul? (*b*) Explain why the poet has come to Byzantium.

Third reading

Stanza 3

11. In the third stanza Yeats entreats the sages of the timeless city to teach his soul to sing, i.e. perfect his spirit. But perfection cannot be achieved without pain and sacrifice. Where in the stanza is this notion dealt with?

12. What is the poet's ultimate goal as expressed in the stanza?

13. Byzantium was renowned as the city of religion, philosophy and a highly formalised art. Where are these elements reflected in the second and third stanzas?

Fourth reading

14. In the fourth stanza he wishes that his spirit be transformed into the perfect work of art and so live on, ageless and incorruptible. What do you notice about this piece of art?

15. Do you think Yeats achieves the yearned for escape from the flux of time into the 'immortality' of art? Consider carefully the irony of the final line.

16. Essentially, what is Yeats writing about in this poem?

17. 'This poem is built around essential contrasts and polarities.' Discuss this with reference to relevant phrases and lines.

18. Can you appreciate Yeats's dilemma as experienced here as well as his deep yearning?

Mosaic from the church of San Apollinare Nuovo in Ravenna showing a procession of saints carrying crowns, symbols of martyrs. (See the note referring to line 17 in the poem 'Sailing to Byzantium'.)

The Stare's Nest By My Window

this poem is also prescribed for the Ordinary Level exam in 2003

Section VI
From 'Meditations in Time of Civil War'

The bees build in the crevices
Of loosening masonry, and there
The mother birds bring grubs and flies.
My wall is loosening; honey-bees,
Come build in the empty house of the stare.   5

We are closed in, and the key is turned
On our uncertainty; somewhere
A man is killed, or a house burned,
Yet no clear fact to be discerned:
Come build in the empty house of the stare.   10

A barricade of stone or of wood;
Some fourteen days of civil war;
Last night they trundled down the road
That dead young soldier in his blood:
Come build in the empty house of the stare.   15

We had fed the heart on fantasies,
The heart's grown brutal from the fare;
More substance in our enmities
Than in our love; O honey-bees,
Come build in the empty house of the stare.   20

Notes

Stare's Nest: 'Stare' is the term sometimes used in the West of Ireland for a starling.

Meditations in Time of Civil War: This is quite a lengthy poem structured in seven sections. Apart from the first, composed in England in 1921, the other sections were written in Ireland during the Civil War of 1922–23.

[1] **The bees:** There is a possible echo of the bees who were sent by the gods to perform certain tasks in Porphyry's mystical writing. At any rate they may symbolise patient creative endeavour as distinct from the destructive forces all around.

[14] **That dead young soldier:** This is based on an occurrence that reputedly took place beside Yeats's Galway house, Thoor Ballylee, in which a young soldier was dragged down a road, his body so badly battered and mutilated that his mother could only recover his head.

Explorations

Before reading

1. Read only the title. What might you expect to find in this poem?

First reading

Stanzas 1–3

2. Examine the detail of the first three lines of stanza 1. Write about what you see: the details, the sounds, the atmosphere.

3. In the actual historical context many big houses of the establishment class were abandoned or evacuated for fear of reprisals. What do you imagine might have been the poet's thoughts when he first came upon this scene by the window?

4. There are two references to 'loosening' masonry or walls in the first stanza. Do you think these might be significant? Explain.

5. Read the second stanza carefully. What is the atmosphere in the house and what details contribute to this?

6. What single word do you find most powerful in the third stanza? Write about it.

Second reading

7. Tease out the meaning of the fourth stanza, in your own words.

8. Comment on the tones you find in the final stanza and suggest how these are created.

9. How do you think the repeated refrain should be read? Try it.

Third reading

10. Would you agree that Yeats is torn between a bitter disappointment and a desperate hope here? Discuss this.

11. 'The poem captures the atmosphere of war with vivid realism.' Discuss this statement with reference to the text.

12. Explore the music of this piece: the onomatopoeia of words; the effect of the rhyming; the haunting refrain etc.

13. 'This poem is really a prayer.' Discuss.

Fourth reading

14. 'This poem could be read as a metaphor for the situation of the poet's traditional class, the Anglo-Irish ascendancy.' Discuss this.

15. How did this poem affect you. Write about it.

In Memory of Eva Gore-Booth and Con Markiewicz

The light of evening, Lissadell,
Great windows open to the south,
Two girls in silk kimonos, both
Beautiful, one a gazelle.
But a raving autumn shears   5
Blossom from the summer's wreath;
The older is condemned to death,
Pardoned, drags out lonely years
Conspiring among the ignorant.
I know not what the younger dreams—   10
Some vague Utopia—and she seems,
When withered old and skeleton-gaunt,
An image of such politics.
Many a time I think to seek
One or the other out and speak   15
Of that old Georgian mansion, mix
Pictures of the mind, recall
That table and the talk of youth,
Two girls in silk kimonos, both
Beautiful, one a gazelle.   20

Dear shadows, now you know it all,
All the folly of a fight
With a common wrong or right.
The innocent and the beautiful
Have no enemy but time;   25
Arise and bid me strike a match
And strike another till time catch;
Should the conflagration climb,
Run till all the sages know.
We the great gazebo built,   30
They convicted us of guilt;
Bid me strike a match and blow.

Background note

Eva Gore-Booth (1870–1926) was a poet and a reader of Eastern Philosophy. She became involved in social work for the poor and was a member of the women's suffrage movement.

Constance Gore-Booth (1868–1927) married a Polish poet and landowner Count Casimir Markiewicz. A committed socialist republican, she became involved in Irish revolutionary movements and joined the Citizen Army. For her part in the Easter Rising she was sentenced to death, but the sentence was commuted to life imprisonment and she was released in the general amnesty of 1917. She was appointed Minister for Labour in the first Dail Eireann of 1919, the first Irish woman government minister. She took the anti-treaty side in the Civil War.

Notes

[1] **Lissadell:** The Co. Sligo Georgian mansion referred to below, built in the early part of the nineteenth century and home of the Gore-Booth family. Yeats visited in 1894–95.

[3] **kimonos:** traditional Japanese long robes

[4] **gazelle:** A small delicately-formed antelope. The reference is to Eva Gore-Booth.

[7] **The older:** Constance

[8] **lonely years:** her husband returned to his lands in the Ukraine and she was separated from her children

[16] **old Georgian mansion:** Lissadell, an image of aristocratic elegance and good taste for Yeats

[21] **Dear shadows:** both women were dead at the time of writing

[30] **gazebo:** The scholar A.N. Jeffares give three possible meanings: (a) a summer house (b) a vantage point and (c) to make a fool of oneself or be conspicuous (in Hibernian English).

 # Explorations

First reading
Lines 1–4
1. Picture the scene in the first four lines—notice all the details. What do you learn about the lifestyle?
2. What questions are you prompted to ask by these lines? Formulate at least three.

Share your questions.
3. (a) Do you think Yeats treasured this memory? (b) What do the lines reveal about what Yeats valued or considered important in life?

Lines 5–6
4. Do you think these lines are an

---

effective metaphor for the passage of time or a rather tired one? Discuss this.

Lines 7–13

5. Read these lines, consult the notes and then state briefly, in your own words, how the life paths or careers of these two women have developed.

6. Do you think that Yeats approved of their careers? Explain your view with reference to words and phrases in the text.

Second reading

7. 'Two girls in silk kimonos, both Beautiful, one a gazelle'
These lines are repeated at the end of the first section. Do you think the refrain here should be spoken in the same tone as lines 3 and 4, or have intervening lines coloured the poet's feeling? Explain your opinion on this. Read aloud the first section as you think Yeats would want it read.

8. Lines 20–25 carry the kernel of the poet's insight, which he feels certain the spirits ('Dear shadows') of the two sisters will understand. (a) What is this wisdom or insight? (b) Is there a certain weariness of tone here? Explain.

9. What do you understand by Yeats's animated wish to light a bonfire at the end of the poem?

Third reading

10. What are the main issues or themes that Yeats deals with in this poem? Support your view with detailed reference.

11. What could one discern about the poet's philosophy of life from a reading of this poem? Again refer to the detail of the text.

12. Yeats felt that the Anglo-Irish ascendancy class with their great houses and wealth had a duty to set an example of graciousness and cultured living. (a) Do you think he felt that Eva and Con had let the side down? Where and how might this be suggested? (b) Do you think he may have considered their activities un-feminine?

13. 'The off-rhymes that Yeats employs from time to time gives the poem a conversational naturalism and reinforce the theme of imperfection.' Discuss this with reference to the details of the poem.

14. Many of Yeats's poems are about time structured on quite violent contrasts. Do you think this an effective device here? Comment.

15. Think or talk about your personal reactions to this poem. What did it make you think about? What insights did it give you?

Eva Gore-Booth (left) and her sister Constance (Con Markiewicz)

Swift's Epitaph

this poem is also prescribed for Ordinary Level exams in 2005 and 2006

Swift has sailed into his rest;
Savage indignation there
Cannot lacerate his breast.
Imitate him if you dare,
World-besotted traveller; he
Served human liberty.

Background note

Jonathan Swift (1667–1745) was the most famous Dean of St Patrick's Cathedral, Dublin. Poet, political pamphleteer and satirist, he was the author of such well-known works as: The Drapier Letters; A Modest Proposal; A Tale of a Tub and Gulliver's Travels. Politically conservative, Swift voiced the concerns and values of protestant Ireland with an independence of mind and a courage that Yeats admired.

This poem is a translation, with some alterations, of the Latin epitaph on Swift's burial stone in St Patrick's, Cathedral, Dublin. Yeats changed the first line and added the adjective 'World-besotted' in the penultimate line.

The original epitaph, which is in Latin, runs as follows:

> Here is laid the Body of
> JONATHAN SWIFT
> Doctor of Divinity,
> Dean of this Cathedral Church,
> Where savage indignation
> can no longer
> Rend his heart,
> Go traveller, and imitate,
> if you can,
> This earnest and dedicated
> Champion of Liberty.
> He died on the 19th day of Oct.,
> 1745 A.D. aged 78 years.

Explorations

First reading

1. What does the first line suggest about Swift's death?
2. What can we learn about Swift's life from this epitaph?
3. What qualities of Swift's do you think Yeats admired?
4. Comment on the tone of the epitaph. Do you think it is unusual? Refer in detail to words and phrases.

Second reading

5. How do Yeats's alterations in lines 1 and 5 (see question 2) change the epitaph?
6. Contrast Swift's original epitaph with Yeats's own epitaph. (p. 168)

W.B. Yeats in his later years

An Acre of Grass

Picture and book remain,
An acre of green grass
For air and exercise,
Now strength of body goes;
Midnight, an old house   5
Where nothing stirs but a mouse.

My temptation is quiet.
Here at life's end
Neither loose imagination,
Nor the mill of the mind   10
Consuming its rag and bone,
Can make the truth known.

Grant me an old man's frenzy,
Myself must I remake
Till I am Timon and Lear   15
Or that William Blake
Who beat upon the wall
Till Truth obeyed his call;

A mind Michael Angelo knew
That can pierce the clouds,   20
Or inspired by frenzy
Shake the dead in their shrouds;
Forgotten else by mankind,
An old man's eagle mind.

Notes

[2–5] **An acre of green grass ... an old house:** The reference is to Riversdale, a farmhouse with orchards and fruit gardens at the foot of the Dublin mountains in Rathfarnham which Yeats leased in 1932 for thirteen years.

[9] **loose imagination:** unstructured imagination

[11] **rag and bone:** The left-over, discarded bric-à-brac of life. Lines 10–11 might refer to the imagination's everyday, casual focus on the bric-à-brac of life.

[15] **Timon:** An Athenian, died in 399 B.C. who was satirised by the comic writers of his time for his marked misanthropy or strong dislike of humanity. Shakespeare dramatised the story in Timon of Athens.

[15] **Lear:** Shakespeare's King Lear who couldn't accept old age gracefully, lost his reason and lived wild on the heath.

[16] **William Blake:** (1757–1827) By profession an engraver, Blake is best known for his more accessible poems 'Songs of Innocence' and 'Songs of Experience'. Lesser known is a great body and range of work which shows him as mystic, apocalyptic visionary, writer of rude verses and an

independent thinker who challenged the accepted philosophies and values of his age. He was considered mad by his contemporaries. Yeats admired him greatly and co-edited his *Prophetic Books* in 1893. He also wrote an interpretation of Blake's mythology.

[19] **Michael Angelo:** Michelangelo Buonarroti (1475–1564) was one of the premier figures of the Italian Renaissance—sculptor, architect, painter and poet. Among his most famous creations are the statue of David and the ceiling of the Sistine Chapel in Rome.

 # Explorations

First reading

1. Explore the images and sounds of the first stanza. (*a*) What do we learn about the condition of the poet? (*b*) How would you describe the atmosphere created in this stanza? What words and sound contribute most to that?

2. In the second stanza, despite his age the poet is still thinking of poetry. In your own words, describe his dilemma.

3. Examine the metaphor for the mind used in lines 10 and 11. What do you think of it?

4. Comment on the tones found in stanzas 1 and 2. Do you think there is a sense of emptiness at the end of the second stanza? Explore how the sounds of the words contribute to this.

Second reading

5. 'Grant me an old man's frenzy' This is a very unusual prayer. Does the remainder of stanza 3 help to explain this intercession? Consult the textual notes and try to outline in your own words what Yeats is actually praying for.

6. What is the connection that Yeats is making between poetry, madness and truth?

7. There is evidence of a new energy in both language and imagery in stanzas 3 and 4. Comment in detail on this.

8. This extraordinary change or metamorphosis culminates in the final image of 'An old man's eagle mind.' Trace how this conceit (or startling comparison) has been prepared for earlier in the fourth stanza.

Third reading

9. Would you agree that this poem is a most unusual response to the theme of old age?

10. Yeats's theories of creativity (partly inspired by the works of the German philosopher Nietzsche) included the need for continual transformation of the self. Trace the transformation that occurs here.

Politics

this poem is also prescribed for the Ordinary Level exam in 2003

'In our time the destiny of man presents its
meanings in political terms'
(Thomas Mann)

How can I, that girl standing there,
My attention fix
On Roman or on Russian
Or on Spanish politics?
Yet here's a travelled man that knows   5
What he talks about,
And there's a politician
That has read and thought,
And maybe what they say is true
Of war and war's alarms,   10
But O that I were young again
And held her in my arms.

Note

Thomas Mann:
(1875–1955) a German
novelist

Background note

Written in May 1938 the poem was composed as an answer to an article
about Yeats, which has praised his public language but suggested that he
should use it on political subjects.

Explorations

First reading

1. In your own words state the dilemma or conflict that Yeats is experiencing here?

2. 'And maybe what they say is true | Of war'
   From the context of the poem what do you suppose they say? Examine Thomas Mann's epigraph for suggestions.

3. 'That girl standing there'
   To whom or to what do you think he might be referring?

Second reading

4. Write about the essential conflicts that are set up here: politics versus love; public life versus private; public devotion versus private satisfaction etc.

5. 'For all its simplicity of language. This is a very well crafted poem.' Discuss this statement with reference to the text.

6. State what you think this poem is about.

7. 'The vision in this poem is that of an old man.' Argue about this.

From 'Under Ben Bulben'

V

Irish poets, learn your trade,
Sing whatever is well made,
Scorn the sort now growing up
All out of shape from toe to top,
Their unremembering hearts and heads   5
Base-born products of base beds.
Sing the peasantry, and then
Hard-riding country gentlemen,
The holiness of monks, and after
Porter-drinkers' randy laughter;   10
Sing the lords and ladies gay
That were beaten into the clay
Through seven heroic centuries;
Cast your mind on other days
That we in coming days may be   15
Still the indomitable Irishry.

VI

Under bare Ben Bulben's head
In Drumcliff churchyard Yeats is laid.
An ancestor was rector there
Long years ago, a church stands near,   20
By the road an ancient cross.
No marble, no conventional phrase;
On limestone quarried near the spot
By his command these words are cut:
Cast a cold eye   25
On life, on death.
Horseman, pass by!

September 4, 1938

Background note

The final draft of this poem is dated 4 September 1938, about five months before the poet's death. Parts of it were published in 1939. 'Under Ben Bulben' as a whole can be seen as Yeats's poetic testimony, an elegy for himself, defining his convictions and the poetic and social philosophies that motivated his life's work.

Section V: Yeats urges all artists, poets, painters, sculptors to promote the necessary heroic images that nourish civilization.

Section VI: rounds his life to its close and moves from the mythologies associated with the top of Ben Bulben to the real earth at its foot, in Drumcliff churchyard.

Notes

Section V

[2] **whatever is well made:** note [14] comments on the great tradition of art and letters

[3–6] **Scorn the sort ... products of base beds:** Yeats had joined the Eugenics Society in London in 1936 and became very interested in its literature and in research on intelligence testing. ('Eugenics' is the science of improving the human race through selective breeding.)

[11–12] **Sing the lords ... beaten into the clay:** refers to the Cromwellian settlement of 1652 which evicted the majority of Irish landowners to Clare and Connaught to make room for new English settlers

[13] **centuries:** the centuries since the Norman Invasions

[14] **other days:** A reference to the great tradition in European art and letters valued by Yeats. But it could also be a reference to Ireland's literary tradition, particularly of the eighteenth century.

Section VI

[17] **Ben Bulben:** a mountain north of Sligo connected with Irish mythology

[18] **Drumcliff:** at the foot of Ben Bulben, it was the site of a sixth century monastery founded by St Colmcille

[19] **ancestor was rector there:** the Revd John Yeats (1774–1846), Yeats's grandfather, was rector there and is buried in the graveyard

[20–21] **a church stands near ... ancient cross:** as well as the remains of a round tower, there is a high cross and part of an older cross in the churchyard

[27] **horseman:** has echoes of the fairy horseman of folk belief but might also have associations with the Irish Ascendancy class

Explorations

Section V

First reading

1. Yeats's advice to Irish poets to write about the aesthetically pleasing ('whatever is well made') is quite understandable but what do you think of his advice on what they should scorn? Consult the textual notes. (*a*) What exactly is he saying? (*b*) What is your reaction to this rant?

2. In your own words, what does Yeats consider to be the proper subjects for poetry?

3. What image of 'Irishry' does Yeats wish to celebrate? Do you think he is being elitist and superior?

Second reading

4. Would you agree that this section exhibits an abhorrence for the present at the expense of a romanticised past? Explain your opinion with reference to the details of the verse.

5. This reads like an incantation. What features of poetic technique do you think contribute to this? Consider: the metre; the rhyming scheme; choice of diction etc.

6. Write about the poet's attitude of mind as you detect it from these lines.

7. Professor Terence Brown has written of 'Under Ben Bulben':

'Skill (i.e. poetic) here is complicit with a repulsive politics and a deficient ethical sense.' On the evidence of the extract, would you agree with this?

Section VI

First reading

1. Yeats visualized the details of his last resting place very carefully. Without checking back, what details of the churchyard can you remember?

2. How would you describe the atmosphere of the churchyard? What details in the verse contribute particularly to this?

Second reading

3. What do these lines reveal about the poet, how he sees himself and wishes to be remembered?

4. Discuss the epitaph in the last three lines. How does it differ from most epitaphs you have read?

5. The scholar A.N. Jeffares felt that the epitaph embodied Yeats's essential attitude to life and death 'which he thought must be faced with bravery, with heroic indifference and with the aristocratic disdain of the horseman'. Consider this as a possible reading of the lines and write a response to it.

Ben Bulben

Cast a cold Eye
On Life, on Death.
Horseman, pass by!

W. B. YEATS

June   13th   1865
January 28th   1939

Yeats's grave in Drumcliff churchyard

7 Robert FROST

prescribed for Higher Level exams in 2003 and 2004

Robert Lee Frost was born in San Francisco on 26 March 1874. Following his father's death in 1885, he moved with his younger sister Jeanie and his mother to Lawrence, Massachusetts, where his grandparents lived. Robert entered Lawrence High School in 1888. There he studied Latin, Greek, ancient and European history and mathematics. From high school he went to Dartmouth College and Harvard but left the two colleges without graduating. On 19 December 1895 he married Elinor White, a former classmate. For health reasons he took up farming. In later years he recalled that his favourite activities were 'mowing with a scythe, chopping with an axe and writing with a pen'. He supplemented his income by teaching and lecturing. Frost devoted his free time to reading the major poets in order to perfect his own writing. Shakespeare, the English Romantics (Wordsworth, Keats and Shelley) and the Victorian poets (Hardy, Kipling and Browning) all influenced his work. The many biblical references in his poems reflect his scripture studies while his classical education enabled him to write with confidence in traditional forms. He followed the

1874–1963

principles laid down in Wordsworth's 'Preface to the Lyrical Ballads' basing his poetry on incidents from common life described in 'language really used by men'.

Frost and his family emigrated to England in 1912. There he published two collections *A Boy's Will* (1913) and *North of Boston* (1914). The books were well received and he was introduced into the literary circles in London, where he met W.B. Yeats. After the outbreak of World War I Frost returned to America and wrote his next collection *Mountain Interval*. This book contains some of his best known poems including 'Birches', 'Out, Out—' and 'The Road Not Taken' with their characteristic themes of isolation, fear, violence and death. Frost bought another farm in Franconia, New Hampshire and supported his family by college teaching, readings, lectures, book royalties and reprint fees. In January 1917 he became Professor of English at Amherst, Massachusetts. By 1920 he could afford to move to Vermont and devote himself to apple-farming and writing poetry. In recognition of his work he won the Pulitzer Prize four times, in 1924, 1931, 1937 and 1943.

Unlike his public life, Frost's personal life was dogged by tragedy. His sister Jeanie was committed to a mental asylum. His daughter Lesley had an emotionally disturbed life and blamed her father for her problems. His favourite child, Majorie, had a nervous breakdown, developed tuberculosis and died in 1934 aged twenty-nine. Irma, his third daughter, suffered from mental illness throughout her adult life. Elinor, his wife, died of a heart attack on 20 March 1938 and his only son Carol committed suicide in 1940. Frost survived the turbulence of these years with the support of his friend, secretary and manager, Kay Morrison. In his final years, Frost enjoyed public acclaim. He recited 'The Gift Outright' at John F. Kennedy's inauguration, watched on television by over sixty million Americans. He travelled as a celebrated visitor from Brazil to Ireland and Russia. On his eighty-eighth birthday he received the Congressional Gold Medal from President Kennedy and in the same year, 1962, published his final volume *In The Clearing*. On 29 January 1963, two months before his eighty-ninth birthday, Robert Frost died peacefully in a Boston hospital.

Robert Frost

The Tuft of Flowers

I went to turn the grass once after one
Who mowed it in the dew before the sun.

The dew was gone that made his blade so keen
Before I came to view the levelled scene.
I looked for him behind an isle of trees;   5
I listened for his whetstone on the breeze.

But he had gone his way, the grass all mown,
And I must be, as he had been,—alone,

'As all must be,' I said within my heart,
'Whether they work together or apart.'   10

But as I said it, swift there passed me by
On noiseless wing a bewildered butterfly,

Seeking with memories grown dim o'er night
Some resting flower of yesterday's delight.

And once I marked his flight go round and round,   15
As where some flower lay withering on the ground.

And then he flew as far as eye could see,
And then on tremulous wing came back to me.

I thought of questions that have no reply,
And would have turned to toss the grass to dry;   20

But he turned first, and led my eye to look
At a tall tuft of flowers beside a brook,

A leaping tongue of bloom the scythe had spared
Beside a reedy brook the scythe had bared.

I left my place to know them by their name,   25
Finding them butterfly weed when I came.

Notes

[1] **to turn the grass:** to toss the grass so that it will dry

[3] **keen:** sharp-edged, eager

[6] **whetstone:** a stone used for sharpening edged tools by friction

23] **scythe:** a long, curving, sharp-edged blade for mowing grass

The mower in the dew had loved them thus,
By leaving them to flourish, not for us,

Nor yet to draw one thought of ours to him,
But from sheer morning gladness at the brim.   30

The butterfly and I had lit upon,
Nevertheless, a message from the dawn,
That made me hear the wakening birds around,
And hear his long scythe whispering to the ground,

And feel a spirit kindred to my own;   35
So that henceforth I worked no more alone;

But glad with him, I worked as with his aid,
And weary, sought at noon with him the shade;

And dreaming, as it were, held brotherly speech
With one whose thought I had not hoped to reach. 40

'Men work together,' I told him from the heart,
'Whether they work together or apart.'

Explorations

First reading

1. Describe the scene in the first five couplets. What do you see? Who is present? What is he doing?
2. Explore the mood in these opening lines. How does the speaker feel? Do you think you would feel the same way?
3. How does the speaker feel after he discovers the butterfly weed? What words or phrases suggest a change in his mood?
4. According to the poem, why did the mower not cut these flowers?
5. What image or phrases caught your attention, on a first reading? Why?

Second reading

6. In your opinion, what is the 'message from the dawn'?
7. What do you think the poet means when he says 'henceforth I worked no more alone'.

Third reading

8. Briefly outline the themes of this poem.
9. Shifts of mood and tone are marked by the word 'but'. Trace these changes in the poem.
10. The speaker describes the mower as a 'spirit kindred to my own'. In what sense is this true?

Fourth reading

11. Three times Frost introduces the concept of 'turning', in the poem. Examine the changes that occur with each of them.
12. Follow the development of the main ideas. Examine the images that convey these ideas and state whether or not you find them effective.
13. 'Frost rejects ornate, poetic diction preferring a language that is conversational and relaxed.' Examine Frost's use of language in the poem.
14. 'Frost's decision to write in conventional forms, using traditional rhythms and rhymes and syntax, reflects his belief that poetry should be accessible to the ordinary man.' Assess this poem in the light of the above statement.

Harvesting: painting by Julien Dupré (1851–1910)

Mending Wall

this poem is also prescribed for Ordinary Level exams in 2003 and 2004

Something there is that doesn't love a wall,
That sends the frozen-ground-swell under it,
And spills the upper boulders in the sun;
And makes gaps even two can pass abreast.
The work of hunters is another thing: 5
I have come after them and made repair
Where they have left not one stone on a stone,
But they would have the rabbit out of hiding,
To please the yelping dogs. The gaps I mean,
No one has seen them made or heard them made,   10
But at spring mending-time we find them there.
I let my neighbour know beyond the hill;
And on a day we meet to walk the line
And set the wall between us once again.
We keep the wall between us as we go.   15
To each the boulders that have fallen to each.
And some are loaves and some so nearly balls
We have to use a spell to make them balance:
'Stay where you are until our backs are turned!'
We wear our fingers rough with handling them.   20
Oh, just another kind of out-door game,
One on a side. It comes to little more:
There where it is we do not need the wall:
He is all pine and I am apple orchard.
My apple trees will never get across   25
And eat the cones under his pines, I tell him.
He only says, 'Good fences make good neighbours.'
Spring is the mischief in me, and I wonder
If I could put a notion in his head:
'*Why* do they make good neighbours? Isn't it   30
Where there are cows? But here there are no cows.
Before I built a wall I'd ask to know
What I was walling in or walling out,
And to whom I was like to give offence.
Something there is that doesn't love a wall,   35
That wants it down.' I could say 'Elves' to him,
But it's not elves exactly, and I'd rather
He said it for himself. I see him there

Bringing a stone grasped firmly by the top
In each hand, like an old-stone savage armed.   40
He moves in darkness as it seems to me,
Not of woods only and the shade of trees.
He will not go behind his father's saying,
And he likes having thought of it so well
He says again, 'Good fences make good neighbours.'   45

 # Explorations

First reading

1. You have been asked to paint a picture based on this poem. Where would you place the wall and the two men? What are the men doing? Are they looking at each other? Describe their postures and their facial expressions. What other details would you include?
2. How are the gaps in the wall created?
3. What do you think the poet means when he describes wall-building as 'just another kind of outdoor game'?
4. Outline the arguments Frost uses against building walls.

Second reading

5. In what sense is the neighbour 'all pine and I am apple orchard'?
6. 'He moves in darkness...' What forms of darkness overshadow the neighbour?
7. Describe as clearly as possible your image of the neighbour as Frost portrays him.

Third reading

8. Walls unite and divide. How is this illustrated within the poem?
9. 'Good fences make good neighbours'. Do you think the speaker agrees with this proverb? Explain your answer.
10. The neighbour repeats the proverb because 'he likes having thought of it so well'. Why is this comment ironic?
11. What do we learn about the narrator's personality in the poem?

Fourth reading

12. What themes and issues are raised in this poem?
13. How does Frost achieve a sense of mystery in the poem?

After Apple-Picking

My long two-pointed ladder's sticking through a tree
Toward heaven still,
And there's a barrel that I didn't fill
Beside it, and there may be two or three
Apples I didn't pick upon some bough.   5
But I am done with apple-picking now.
Essence of winter sleep is on the night,
The scent of apples: I am drowsing off.
I cannot rub the strangeness from my sight
I got from looking through a pane of glass   10
I skimmed this morning from the drinking trough
And held against the world of hoary grass.
It melted, and I let it fall and break.
But I was well
Upon my way to sleep before it fell,   15
And I could tell
What form my dreaming was about to take.
Magnified apples appear and disappear,
Stem end and blossom end,
And every fleck of russet showing clear.   20
My instep arch not only keeps the ache,
It keeps the pressure of a ladder-round.
I feel the ladder sway as the boughs bend.

Notes

[7] **Essence:** scent

[12] **hoary:** white with age (hoarfrost: white particles of frozen dew)

[40] **woodchuck:** a burrowing rodent or groundhog which hibernates for half the year

And I keep hearing from the cellar bin
The rumbling sound   25
Of load on load of apples coming in.
For I have had too much
Of apple-picking: I am overtired
Of the great harvest I myself desired.
There were ten thousand thousand fruit to touch,   30
Cherish in hand, lift down, and not let fall.
For all
That struck the earth,
No matter if not bruised or spiked with stubble,
Went surely to the cider-apple heap   35
As of no worth.
One can see what will trouble
This sleep of mine, whatever sleep it is.
Were he not gone,
The woodchuck could say whether it's like his   40
Long sleep, as I describe its coming on,
Or just some human sleep.

Apple Trees and Poplars in the setting sun: painting by Camille Pissaro (1831–1903)

Explorations

First reading

1. Imagine the orchard as Frost describes it in the opening lines. What details does he include? How would you describe the scene now the apple-picking is over?

2. Explain in your own words what happened at the drinking trough in the morning.

3. Why had the apple-picker to be so careful with the apples?

4. What connects the woodchuck and the harvester?

Second reading

5. The fruit has been harvested. How does the speaker feel now?

6. What is it that will trouble his sleep?

7. Select your favourite image in the poem and explain your choice.

8. Does the poet successfully capture the sensations of picking apples? Examine his use of images and the language used.

Third reading

9. There are moments of confusion in the poem. Is this deliberate? Why? Refer closely to the text in your answer.

10. In the poem, autumn is seen as a season of abundance rather than a time of decay. How does the poet recreate for the reader, the richness of the harvest?

11. A dream-like quality pervades the poem. How is this achieved? Consider the language used, the imagery, descriptions, metre and rhyme.

Fourth reading

12. Frost's language is sensuously evocative and rich in imagery. Discuss his use of tactile, visual and auditory imagery in the poem as a whole.

13. What part do sounds and rhythm play in the creation of the mood in the poem?

14. Briefly explain your personal reaction to 'After Apple-Picking'.

Birches

When I see birches bend to left and right
Across the lines of straighter darker trees,
I like to think some boy's been swinging them.
But swinging doesn't bend them down to stay.
Ice-storms do that. Often you must have seen them   5
Loaded with ice a sunny winter morning
After a rain. They click upon themselves
As the breeze rises, and turn many-colored
As the stir cracks and crazes their enamel.
Soon the sun's warmth makes them shed crystal shells   10
Shattering and avalanching on the snow-crust—
Such heaps of broken glass to sweep away
You'd think the inner dome of heaven had fallen.
They are dragged to the withered bracken by the load,
And they seem not to break; though once they are bowed   15
So low for long, they never right themselves:
You may see their trunks arching in the woods
Years afterwards, trailing their leaves on the ground
Like girls on hands and knees that throw their hair
Before them over their heads to dry in the sun.   20
But I was going to say when Truth broke in
With all her matter-of-fact about the ice-storm
I should prefer to have some boy bend them
As he went out and in to fetch the cows—
Some boy too far from town to learn baseball,   25
Whose only play was what he found himself,
Summer or winter, and could play alone.
One by one he subdued his father's trees
By riding them down over and over again
Until he took the stiffness out of them,   30
And not one but hung limp, not one was left
For him to conquer. He learned all there was
To learn about not launching out too soon
And so not carrying the tree away
Clear to the ground. He always kept his poise   35
To the top branches, climbing carefully
With the same pains you use to fill a cup
Up to the brim, and even above the brim.

Then he flung outward, feet first, with a swish,
Kicking his way down through the air to the ground.   40
So was I once myself a swinger of birches.
And so I dream of going back to be.
It's when I'm weary of considerations,
And life is too much like a pathless wood
Where your face burns and tickles with the cobwebs   45
Broken across it, and one eye is weeping
From a twig's having lashed across it open.
I'd like to get away from earth awhile
And then come back to it and begin over.
May no fate willfully misunderstand me   50
And half grant what I wish and snatch me away
Not to return. Earth's the right place for love:
I don't know where it's likely to go better.
I'd like to go by climbing a birch tree,
And climb black branches up a snow-white trunk   55
Toward heaven, till the tree could bear no more,
But dipped its top and set me down again.
That would be good both going and coming back.
One could do worse than be a swinger of birches.

A Road through Belvedere, Vermont:
painting by Thomas W. Whittredge
(1820–1910)

Explorations

Before reading

1. Have you ever climbed a tree? Discuss your experience, explaining where you were, how difficult it was and what skills you needed to climb up and down.

First reading

2. On a first reading, what do you see? Visualize the trees, the ice, the sky and the boy. What sounds can you hear? Are there any other details you should include?
3. What images caught your imagination?
4. How would you describe the general mood of the poem?

Second reading

5. Based on the details given by Frost, describe the character of the boy.
6. Would you agree that the boy is a skilled climber? What details support this point of view?
7. Do you think that the speaker really intends to climb trees again? What makes him long to be a 'swinger of birches' once more?
8. What do you understand by the line 'And life is too much like a pathless wood'?
9. Is the speaker's wish to escape from earth a death wish?

Explain your answer.

10. Explain clearly what you think Frost means in the last eight lines of the poem.

Third reading

11. Frost uses the image of girls drying their hair in the sun. Why? How effective is this image?
12. 'One could do worse than be a swinger of birches'. Does the poet present a convincing argument in support of this claim?
13. How does Frost achieve a conversational tone in the poem? Why does he adopt this voice?

Fourth reading

14. In what way do the boy's actions resemble those of a poet?
15. How does the music in the poem—sounds, metre etc.— contribute to the atmosphere?
16. Comment on the poet's contrasting use of light and darkness.
17. 'Though much of Frost's poetry is concerned with suffering, he is also capable of capturing moments of unearthly beauty and joy in his work.' Comment on the poem in the light of this statement.

'Out, Out—'

this poem is also prescribed for Ordinary Level exams in 2003 and 2004

The buzz-saw snarled and rattled in the yard
And made dust and dropped stove-length sticks of wood,
Sweet-scented stuff when the breeze drew across it.
And from there those that lifted eyes could count
Five mountain ranges one behind the other   5
Under the sunset far into Vermont.
And the saw snarled and rattled, snarled and rattled,
As it ran light, or had to bear a load.
And nothing happened: day was all but done.
Call it a day, I wish they might have said   10
To please the boy by giving him the half hour
That a boy counts so much when saved from work.
His sister stood beside them in her apron
To tell them 'Supper'. At the word, the saw,
As if to prove saws knew what supper meant,   15
Leaped out at the boy's hand, or seemed to leap—
He must have given the hand. However it was,
Neither refused the meeting. But the hand!
The boy's first outcry was a rueful laugh,
As he swung toward them holding up the hand   20
Half in appeal, but half as if to keep
The life from spilling. Then the boy saw all—
Since he was old enough to know, big boy
Doing a man's work, though a child at heart—
He saw all spoiled. 'Don't let him cut my hand off—   25
The doctor, when he comes. Don't let him, sister!'
So. But the hand was gone already.
The doctor put him in the dark of ether.
He lay and puffed him lips out with his breath.
And then—the watcher at his pulse took fright.   30
No one believed. They listened at his heart.
Little—less—nothing!—and that ended it.
No more to build on there. And they, since they
Were not the one dead, turned to their affairs.

Notes   **'Out, Out—':** The title is taken from William Shakespeare's famous tragedy *Macbeth*.
'Out, Out brief candle; life's but a walking shadow, a poor player that struts and
frets his hour upon the stage, and then is heard no more: it is a tale told by an
idiot, full of sound and fury, signifying nothing.'

[28] **ether:** an anaesthetic

Explorations

First reading

1. Read the poem aloud. What words and phrases made the greatest impact on your ear? What animals are suggested in the opening line? How are these animals evoked?

2. Why does Frost describe the scenery?

3. Frost refers repeatedly to 'they' and 'them'. Who do you think these people are? What is your impression of them?

4. The poem turns on the word 'supper'. What happens? Is it an appropriate word in the context?

5. 'He saw all spoiled'. In what sense is all spoiled?

6. What is the boy's immediate fear? Refer to the poem to support your answer.

Second reading

7. Trace the narrative line in this poem. Were you surprised by the ending? Do you think it is an effective conclusion?

8. Comment on the title. Is it a suitable one? Could you suggest another?

9. 'Little—less—nothing!' Read this line aloud and comment on the rhythm. What is the effect of the exclamation mark?

Third reading

10. How effectively does the poet evoke the terror felt by the boy? Examine the techniques used by Frost in your answer.

11. Would you describe the poet as a detached or a sympathetic observer? Is he angered by the incident? How do we know? Comment on the tone.

12. How does the poet engage the reader's sympathies for the boy? Examine the details given, the use of emotive language and the comments made throughout the poem.

Fourth reading

13. What themes and issues are explored in the poem?

14. Sound plays an important role in the poem. Examine the use of assonance, alliteration and onomatopoeia in 'Out, Out—'.

15. 'In his poetry, Frost confronts the reader with the harsh realities of life.' Discuss this statement, in the light of your reading of this poem.

16. Identify and discuss some of the distinctive qualities of Frost's style that are evident in this poem.

The Road Not Taken

this poem is also prescribed for Ordinary Level exams in 2003 and 2004

Two roads diverged in a yellow wood,
And sorry I could not travel both
And be one traveler, long I stood
And looked down one as far as I could
To where it bent in the undergrowth;   5

Then took the other, as just as fair,
And having perhaps the better claim,
Because it was grassy and wanted wear;
Though as for that the passing there
Had worn them really about the same,   10

And both that morning equally lay
In leaves no step had trodden black.
Oh, I kept the first for another day!
Yet knowing how way leads on to way,
I doubted if I should ever come back.   15

I shall be telling this with a sigh
Somewhere ages and ages hence:
Two roads diverged in a wood, and I—
I took the one less traveled by,
And that has made all the difference.   20

Explorations

First reading

1. On a first reading, what do you notice about the setting of the poem? What details made the deepest impression on you? Explain.
2. What is the main focus of the speaker's attention throughout the poem?
3. Why does he choose the second road? Are his reasons convincing?
4. Why will the speaker talk about this moment 'ages and ages hence'.
5. What is the difference referred to by Frost in the last line?

Second reading

6. Comment on the title of the poem. What does it lead you to expect? Does the poem fulfil your expectations?
7. On a surface level the speaker is faced with a choice between two paths. On a deeper level what do the roads symbolize?
8. What is the dominant mood of the poem? What words, phrases and images suggest this mood.

Third reading

9. What images create an autumnal atmosphere in the poem? Why did Frost choose this time of year?
10. What themes or issues can you identify in 'The Road Not Taken'?
11. Do you find the imagery in this poem effective in conveying the theme? Refer to specific images in your answer.
12. The poem opens and closes on a note of regret. Trace the development of thought and mood throughout the poem.

Fourth reading

13. Doubt is replaced by certainty in this poem. Examine the movement from one state to the other.
14. What appeals to you about this poem? Consider the theme, images, sounds, and particular words or phrases, in your answer.

Spring Pools

These pools that, though in forests, still reflect
The total sky almost without defect,
And like the flowers beside them, chill and shiver,
Will like the flowers beside them soon be gone,
And yet not out by any brook or river,   5
But up by roots to bring dark foliage on.

The trees that have it in their pent-up buds
To darken nature and be summer woods—
Let them think twice before they use their powers
To blot out and drink up and sweep away   10
These flowery waters and these watery flowers
From snow that melted only yesterday.

Note

[6] **foliage:** the leaves of a tree or plant

Explorations

First reading

1. What have the pools and the flowers got in common?
2. What do you notice about the trees? What characteristic of the trees does the poet focus on, especially in the second stanza? Why?
3. Why should the trees think twice before they drain the pools and overshadow the flowers?

Second reading

4. Outline the argument of the poem. Would you agree that it is condensed with considerable skill? What is the effect of this on the reader?
5. What image made the greatest impression on you? Explain your choice.
6. How important are the sounds of words in creating the atmosphere in this poem?

Third reading

7. What mood is evoked by this scene? How is this mood created?
8. The beauty of this poem lies in the aptness of the descriptions and the clarity of the language. Do you agree? Explain your answer.

Fourth reading

9. Fragility and strength are contrasted in the poem. Where is this contrast most evident? What is the effect? How is this effect achieved?
10. Discuss the techniques Frost uses in this poem to depict the changing nature of the world. Support your answer by quotation or reference.
11. 'Frost is a master of the lyric form, his images are sensuous, his language clear and his tone controlled.' Examine 'Spring Pools' in the light of this statement.
12. Give your personal reaction to the poem.

Acquainted With the Night

I have been one acquainted with the night.
I have walked out in rain—and back in rain.
I have outwalked the furthest city light.

I have looked down the saddest city lane.
I have passed by the watchman on his beat   5
And dropped my eyes, unwilling to explain.

I have stood still and stopped the sound of feet
When far away an interrupted cry
Came over houses from another street,

But not to call me back or say good-bye;   10
And further still at an unearthly height,
One luminary clock against the sky

Proclaimed the time was neither wrong nor right.
I have been one acquainted with the night.

Note

[12] **luminary:** something that gives light, especially a heavenly body

Explorations

First reading

1. Describe the scene in your own words.
2. Examine the images used. What have they got in common? Do they provide an insight as to the central idea of the poem?
3. How would you describe the poet's mood?

Second reading

4. What do you think is the main theme of the poem? Explain your answer.
5. Do you think the imagery used is effective in illustrating the theme? Which images are most appropriate, in your opinion?
6. What feelings does the poem arouse in you? How does it do this?

Third reading

7. What do you notice about the verbs in the poem? In what tense is it written? What purpose might this serve?
8. This poem can be read at more than one level. Suggest another reading of 'Acquainted With the Night'.

Fourth reading

9. Note the repetitions in the poem. What effect do they have?
10. How does Frost evoke the atmosphere of the urban landscape?
11. There is a deep sense of isolation in this poem. Do you agree? Where is it most evident, in your opinion?
12. ' 'Acquainted With the Night' is a tribute to the triumph of the human spirit in the face of adversity, rather than a record of the defeat of the soul at its darkest hour.' Discuss the poem in the light of this statement.

Design

I found a dimpled spider, fat and white,
On a white heal-all, holding up a moth
Like a white piece of rigid satin cloth—
Assorted characters of death and blight
Mixed ready to begin the morning right,   5
Like the ingredients of a witches' broth—
A snow-drop spider, a flower like a froth,
And dead wings carried like a paper kite.

What had that flower to do with being white,
The wayside blue and innocent heal-all?   10
What brought the kindred spider to that height,
Then steered the white moth thither in the night?
What but design of darkness to appall?—
If design govern in a thing so small.

Note

[2] **heal-all:** a common flower, used for medicinal purposes, usually blue or violet in
colour

Explorations

First reading

1. What do you normally associate with the word 'dimpled'?

2. What images in the octave captured your attention? What do they suggest about the subject matter of the poem?

3. The poet raises several issues in the sestet. What are these issues and what conclusion, if any does he reach?

4. Jot down the words or phrases that best describe your response to this poem, on a first reading.

Second reading

5. How does the octet-sestet division mark the development of thought in the poem.

6. Describe the poet's mood in the sestet.

7. What is the effect of the scene on the speaker? Does he find it repulsive, horrifying, interesting, puzzling? Refer to the text to support your answer.

Third reading

8. Briefly outline the main argument in this poem.

9. Discuss the poet's use of colour.

10. Would you describe this as a nature poem? Explain your answer.

Fourth reading

11. What view of life and death is expressed in the poem? Where is this most evident?

12. Comment on the way the imagery in the poem forges the link between evil and beauty, innocence and death.

13. What is your own reaction to 'Design'?

14. Briefly compare the portrayal of nature in this poem with its portrayal in another poem by Frost, on your course.

Provide, Provide

The witch that came (the withered hag)
To wash the steps with pail and rag
Was once the beauty Abishag,

The picture pride of Hollywood.
Too many fall from great and good   5
For you to doubt the likelihood.

Die early and avoid the fate.
Or if predestined to die late,
Make up your mind to die in state.

Make whole stock exchange your own!   10
If need be occupy a throne,
Where nobody can call *you* crone.

Some have relied on what they knew,
Others on being simply true.
What worked for them might work for you.   15

No memory of having starred
Atones for later disregard
Or keeps the end from being hard.

Better to go down dignified
With boughten friendship at your side   20
Than none at all. Provide, provide!

Notes

[1]   **hag:** an ugly old woman, a witch

[3]   **Abishag:** (1 Kings 1: 2–4) 'Having searched for a beautiful girl throughout the territory of Israel, they found Abishag of Shunem and brought her to the king. The girl was of great beauty. She looked after the king and waited on him...'

[12] **crone:** a withered old woman

Explorations

Before reading

1. Read the title only. Jot down what you imagine the poem is about before reading the poem itself.

First reading

2. The idea that youth rapidly fades is introduced in the opening stanza. What images convey this?

3. What advice does Frost offer as to how to avoid the worst aspects of old age?

4. How can one avoid being called a 'crone'?

5. Imagine you are the old woman in the poem. Write your response to 'Provide, Provide'.

Second reading

6. Can memories offer comfort to the old?

7. Has 'boughten friendship' any advantages according to the poet? What is his tone here?

8. What do you think is meant by the title of the poem?

Third reading

9. Is the poem intended to teach us a lesson? Comment on the moral.

10. Do you think Frost is being serious or humorous here? Examine the tone throughout the poem.

Fourth reading

11. Do your think there is an important theme in the poem? Explain your answer.

12. Examine the contrasts in the poem. State what they are and whether or not you think they are effective.

13. Did you enjoy this poem? Why?

14. 'Realism rather than pessimism is a hallmark of Frost's poetry.' Discuss this statement in the light of your reading of this poem.

8 T.S. ELIOT

prescribed for Higher Level exams in 2005 and 2006

Thomas Stearns Eliot was born on 26 September 1888, in St Louis, Missouri, US. He was the youngest of seven children. His father, Henry, was a brick manufacturer and his mother, Charlotte, was a teacher who also wrote poetry and supported social reform.

His father's ancestors had emigrated from East Coker, near Yeovil, in Somerset, England to Boston, Massachusetts in the late seventeenth century. T.S. Eliot's grandfather, William, moved to St Louis after he graduated from Harvard University in the 1830s. William became a prominent figure in St Louis, speaking out against slavery and promoting women's rights. There, he also established the first Unitarian Church. T.S. Eliot's mother encouraged her son's reverence for his grandfather and it is perhaps this influence which adds the almost missionary zeal to some of his poetry, seeking to bring a message to Western civilization, which he saw as a moral and cultural wasteland. The family's contact with Boston and the New England coast was maintained through summer visits. These were happy times for the young T.S. Eliot and it is not surprising that sea imagery and themes are prominent throughout his poetry.

1888–1965

Eliot entered Harvard University on 26 September 1906, his eighteenth birthday. There he published frequently in the *Harvard Advocate*, an undergraduate literary magazine, of which he also became editor. In Harvard, Professor Irving Babbit influenced Eliot through his classicism and emphasis upon tradition; George Santayana, the Spanish born philosopher awakened a love of philosophy in Eliot, which led to Eliot's own study of the British philosopher, Bradley, who exercised considerable influence on Eliot's thoughts. He also studied the Italian poet Dante, who remained a life-long source of inspiration. Eliot spent the academic year 1910–11 in Paris, where he studied in the

Sorbonne. During this time Eliot became fascinated with the sordid squalor of much of urban life. This was to become part of his poetic trademark. He also came under the influence of the French symbolist poets, in particular Baudelaire (1821–67). Intending to study in Germany in 1914, the outbreak of World War I forced him instead to go to England. There he met the American poet Ezra Pound, who would exert a considerable influence over his work and his literary career. At the insistence of Pound, the editor of the magazine *Poetry* agreed to publish 'The Love Song of J. Alfred Prufrock', from which one can date the beginning of modern poetry in English. This poem became the central piece of *Prufrock and other Observations*, published in 1917.

In 1915, Eliot married Vivienne Haigh-Wood. The marriage was to be difficult, leading to the nervous breakdown of both and the permanent illness of Vivienne. (In 1933 Eliot legally separated from her.) Eliot worked as a teacher for a year, 1915–16, leaving teaching to work in Lloyd's Bank until 1925 when he joined the publishing firm now known as Faber & Faber. 'The Wasteland' was published in 1922 and was immediately denounced as impenetrable and incoherent by conservative critics, but its depiction of a sordid society, empty of spiritual values appealed to the poetry reading public. The spiritual questing that informed this poem and others such as 'Journey of the

Magi' led in 1927 to Eliot's baptism into the Anglican Church, whose Anglo-Catholicism satisfied his spiritual and emotional needs. Religious themes became increasingly important to him leading to the publication of, among others, the poetic drama, 'Murder in the Cathedral' (1935), which deals with the assassination of St Thomas à Becket and to the 'Four Quartets', a philosophic sequence dealing with issues of spiritual renewal and of time. These sufficiently consolidated his reputation to the extent that he was awarded the Nobel Prize for Literature in 1948. Following his wife's death, Eliot married his secretary at Faber & Faber, which brought him great personal happiness. He died on 4 January 1965, after several years of declining health, from emphysema. His ashes are buried in East Coker, in Somerset, England.

Eliot's importance to twentieth-century poetry can hardly be overstated. Through his critical essays and especially through his own poetic practice he played a very considerable role in establishing the modern conception of poetry— impersonal but packed with powerful reserves of private emotions, learned, allusive and organized by associative connections. On a lighter note, his life-long love of cats lead to his publication of *Old Possum's Book of Practical Cats* (1939), which was the basis for *Cats*, a spectacular musical comedy of the 1980s.

The Love Song of J. Alfred Prufrock

S'io credessi che mia risposta fosse
a persona che mai tornasse al mondo,
questa fiamma staria senza più scosse.
Ma per ciò che giammai di questo fondo
non tornò vivo alcun, s'i'odo il vero,
senza tema d'infamia ti rispondo.

Let us go then, you and I,
When the evening is spread out against the sky
Like a patient etherised upon a table;
Let us go, through certain half-deserted streets,
The muttering retreats   5
Of restless nights in one-night cheap hotels
And sawdust restaurants with oyster-shells:
Streets that follow like a tedious argument
Of insidious intent
To lead you to an overwhelming question...   10
Oh, do not ask, 'What is it?'
Let us go and make our visit.

In the room the women come and go
Talking of Michelangelo.

The yellow fog that rubs its back upon the window-panes,   15
The yellow smoke that rubs its muzzle on the window-panes,
Licked its tongue into the corners of the evening,
Lingered upon the pools that stand in drains,
Let fall upon its back the soot that falls from chimneys,

Notes

S'io credessi...: from Dante (*Inferno* XXVII, 61–6), spoken by the warrior Count Guido da Montefeltro, in Hell for the false advice he gave to the Pope. It reads in English: 'If I believed that my reply would be to one who would return to the world, this flame would tremble no more; but as no-one ever returns alive from this depth, if what I hear is true, without fear of disgrace I answer you.'

[14] **Michelangelo:** the Italian painter and sculptor; a heroic contrast to Prufrock

Slipped by the terrace, made a sudden leap,   20
And seeing that it was a soft October night,
Curled once about the house, and fell asleep.

And indeed there will be time
For the yellow smoke that slides along the street
Rubbing its back upon the window-panes;   25
There will be time, there will be time
To prepare a face to meet the faces that you meet;
There will be time to murder and create,
And time for all the works and days of hands
That lift and drop a question on your plate;   30
Time for you and time for me,
And time yet for a hundred indecisions,
And for a hundred visions and revisions,
Before the taking of a toast and tea.

In the room the women come and go   35
Talking of Michelangelo.

And indeed there will be time
To wonder, 'Do I dare?' and, 'Do I dare?'
Time to turn back and descend the stair,
With a bald spot in the middle of my hair—   40
(They will say: 'How his hair is growing thin!')
My morning coat, my collar mounting firmly to the chin,
My necktie rich and modest, but asserted by a simple pin—
(They will say: 'But how his arms and legs are thin!')
Do I dare   45
Disturb the universe?
In a minute there is time
For decisions and revisions which a minute will reverse.

[23] **And indeed there will be time…:** echoes the Old Testament, Ecclesiastes 3: 1–8
[29] **works and days:** the title of a didactic poem by the Greek writer Hesiod, eighth century
    B.C.

For I have known them all already, known them all—
Have known the evenings, mornings, afternoons,   50
I have measured out my life with coffee spoons;
I know the voices dying with a dying fall
Beneath the music from a farther room.
So how should I presume?

And I have known the eyes already, known them all—   55
The eyes that fix you in a formulated phrase,
And when I am formulated, sprawling on a pin,
When I am pinned and wriggling on the wall,
Then how should I begin
To spit out all the butt-ends of my days and ways?   60
And how should I presume?

And I have known the arms already, known them all—
Arms that are braceleted and white and bare
(But in the lamplight, downed with light brown hair!)
Is it perfume from a dress   65
That makes me so digress?
Arms that lie along a table, or wrap about a shawl.
And should I then presume?
And how should I begin?

Shall I say, I have gone at dusk through narrow streets   70
And watched the smoke that rises from the pipes
Of lonely men in shirt-sleeves, leaning out of windows?...

I should have been a pair of ragged claws
Scuttling across the floors of silent seas.

And the afternoon, the evening, sleeps so peacefully!   75
Smoothed by long fingers,
Asleep...tired...or it malingers,
Stretched on the floor, here beside you and me.
Should I, after tea and cakes and ices,
Have the strength to force the moment to its crisis?   80

[52] **a dying fall:** the description of a piece of music by Duke Orsino in Shakespeare's *Twelfth Night*

But though I have wept and fasted, wept and prayed,
Though I have seen my head (grown slightly bald)
brought in upon a platter,
I am no prophet—and here's no great matter;
I have seen the moment of my greatness flicker,   85
And I have seen the eternal Footman hold my coat, and
snicker,
And in short, I was afraid.

And would it have been worth it, after all,
After the cups, the marmalade, the tea,   90
Among the porcelain, among some talk of you and me,
Would it have been worth while,
To have bitten off the matter with a smile,
To have squeezed the universe into a ball
To roll it towards some overwhelming question,   95
To say: 'I am Lazarus, come from the dead,
Come back to tell you all, I shall tell you all'—
If one, settling a pillow by her head,
Should say: 'That is not what I meant at all.
That is not it, at all.'   100
And would it have been worth it, after all,
Would it have been worth while,
After the sunsets and the dooryards and the sprinkled
streets,
After the novels, after the teacups, after the skirts that   105
trail along the floor—
And this, and so much more?—
It is impossible to say just what I mean!
But as if a magic lantern threw the nerves in patterns on a
screen: 110
Would it have been worth while

[82] **My head ... platter:** Matthew's Gospel 14: 3–11. The head of John the Baptist was
brought thus to Salome, as a reward for her dancing in front of Herod.

[86] **eternal Footman:** a personification of death; see John Bunyan's *The Pilgrim's Progress*
(1678)

[94] **squeezed...ball:** a reference to Andrew Marvell's (1621–78) poem of seduction 'To His
Coy Mistress'

[96] **Lazarus:** the dead man whom Jesus raised from the dead, see St John's Gospel 11: 1–44

If one, settling a pillow or throwing off a shawl,
And turning toward the window, should say:
'That is not it at all,
That is not what I meant at all.'   115

No! I am not Prince Hamlet, nor was meant to be;
Am an attendant lord, one that will do
To swell a progress, start a scene or two,
Advise the prince; no doubt, an easy tool,
Deferential, glad to be of use,   120
Politic, cautious, and meticulous;
Full of high sentence, but a bit obtuse;
At times, indeed, almost ridiculous—
Almost, at times, the Fool.

I grow old...I grow old...   125
I shall wear the bottoms of my trousers rolled.

Shall I part my hair behind? Do I dare to eat a peach?
I shall wear white flannel trousers, and walk upon the beach.
I have heard the mermaids singing, each to each.

I do not think that they will sing to me.   130

I have seen them riding seaward on the waves
Combing the white hair of the waves blown back
When the wind blows the water white and black.

We have lingered in the chambers of the sea
By sea-girls wreathed with seaweed red and brown   135
Till human voices wake us, and we drown.

[116] **Prince Hamlet:** in Shakespeare's play of the same name, Hamlet agonizes about being
indecisive

[118] **To swell a progress:** in Elizabethan times a state or royal journey

[122] **Full of high sentence:** a description of the talk of the Clerk in Chaucer's (1343–1400)
The Canterbury Tales

[124] **the Fool:** the court jester in Shakespeare's *King Lear*, a sort of idiot savant

[129] **mermaids singing:** A reference to John Donne's (1576–1631) poem 'Song'; also in
contrast to the sirens of Greek legend who lead sailors to their deaths.

Explorations

First reading

1. The 'J. Alfred Prufrock' of the title is the speaker in the poem. Knowing this, how do you visualize him? What words or phrases make images for you? Is he the sort of person you would expect to sing a love song?

2. What is the mood of the speaker in the poem? Anger, despair, regret or fear?

3. Would you agree that Prufrock is trying to come to some decision? What do you think this is? What, if anything, has Prufrock to look forward to?

Second reading

4. The Italian epigraph comes from Dante's *The Divine Comedy*. It is spoken by one of the damned souls in the Inferno. What sort of expectations does this arouse for you?

5. Who do you think is the 'you' of the first line? Is it the reader or is it another side of Prufrock's personality?

6. Would you agree that the dramatic scene outlined from lines 1–12 suggest some inner sickness or sordid lifestyle? How does the language used here add to this understanding?

7. In lines 13–14 what does the naming of Michelangelo mean to you? What do the rhythm and rhyme of these lines suggest to you? Why are they repeated later?

8. Would you agree that the image of the fog in lines 15–22 also suggests a cat? With what have cats been traditionally associated? What does the rhyming of 'leap' and 'sleep' suggest to you?

9. The motif of time is particularly strong in lines 23–4. Where else does it occur in the poem? What does 'To prepare a face to meet the faces that you meet,' mean to you?

10. Prufrock seems particularly self-conscious and indecisive in lines 37–48. Is there an incongruity between this and his apparent wish to 'disturb the universe'?

11. Would you agree that Prufrock is more disillusioned than angry at the meaninglessness of his life as described in lines 49–54?

12. What fears are expressed by Prufrock in lines 55–69? Does Prufrock show simultaneous attraction for and revulsion of women? How is this shown?

13. Do you agree that the question

The Balcony: painting by Edouard Manet (1832–1883)

raised in lines 70–74 adds to our understanding of Prufrock's predicament? What does the image of 'ragged claws scuttling' tell us about his state of mind? What is the tone here? Embarrassment? Distress? Self-irony? How does the language used add to the tone?

14. Some of the major themes of the poem come together in lines 75–88. What images suggest these themes? Would you agree that this section marks a turning point, where Prufrock accepts his inadequacy?

15. What does the reference to Lazarus in the lines 89–110 mean to you? Is it fear of rejection alone that makes Prufrock indecisive?

16. What does the line 'But as if a magic lantern threw the nerves in patterns on a screen' suggest to you?

17. How does Prufrock see himself in lines 111–19? Explain the references to 'Prince Hamlet' and 'the Fool'? Is there a tone of resignation here?

18. In lines 120–31, Prufrock seems to be making some decision at last. What is the quality of these decisions?

19. Would you agree that the reference to the sea and mermaids is an escape into a dream world? What brings him back to reality?

Third reading

20. What do you think is the 'overwhelming question' of the poem?

21. Show how the distrustful attitude of Prufrock toward others is seen in the ironical transitions in the poem.

22. Discuss the view that Prufrock's confusion and self-doubt are reflected in the apparent incoherence of the poem.

Fourth reading

23. 'Eliot's main concern in his poetry is the human condition in the modern world.' Discuss this view with references to both 'The Love Song of J. Alfred Prufrock' and 'A Game of Chess'.

24. The poet Ezra Pound called Prufrock a portrait of failure and futility. Would you agree?

25. Discuss the possibilities of dramatising this poem either on stage or on film. What difficulties would it present? How could these be overcome?

Preludes

this poem is also prescribed for Ordinary Level exams in 2005 and 2006

I

The winter evening settles down
With smell of steaks in passageways.
Six o'clock.
The burnt-out ends of smoky days.
And now a gusty shower wraps   5
The grimy scraps
Of withered leaves about your feet
And newspapers from vacant lots;
The showers beat
On broken blinds and chimney-pots,   10
And at the corner of the street
A lonely cab-horse steams and stamps.

And then the lighting of the lamps.

II

The morning comes to consciousness
Of faint stale smells of beer   15
From the sawdust-trampled street
With all its muddy feet that press
To early coffee-stands.

With the other masquerades
That time resumes,   20
One thinks of all the hands
That are raising dingy shades
In a thousand furnished rooms.

III

You tossed a blanket from the bed,
You lay upon your back, and waited;   25
You dozed, and watched the night revealing
The thousand sordid images
Of which your soul was constituted;
They flickered against the ceiling.
And when all the world came back   30
And the light crept up between the shutters,

And you heard the sparrows in the gutters,
You had such a vision of the street
As the street hardly understands;
Sitting along the bed's edge, where   35
You curled the papers from your hair,
Or clasped the yellow soles of feet
In the palms of both soiled hands.

IV

His soul stretched tight across the skies
That fade behind a city block,   40
Or trampled by insistent feet
At four and five and six o'clock;
And short square fingers stuffing pipes,
And evening newspapers, and eyes
Assured of certain certainties,   45
The conscience of a blackened street
Impatient to assume the world.

I am moved by fancies that are curled
Around these images, and cling:
The notion of some infinitely gentle   50
Infinitely suffering thing.

Wipe your hand across your mouth, and laugh;
The worlds revolve like ancient women
Gathering fuel in vacant lots.

Notes

[19] **masquerades:** false pretence, disguise

[22] **shades:** window blinds

[36] **curled the papers from your hair:** paper was used to curl hair before the arrival of manufactured curlers

[54] **vacant lots:** empty building sites

Explorations

First reading

1. The four poems here are snapshots of modern urban life, where the observer is like a camera moving through the streets. Imagine yourself as that observer, what do you see, hear and smell as you read the poem?

2. Did anything unexpected strike you?

Second reading

FIRST PRELUDE

3. In the First Prelude, would you agree that the image of 'The burnt-out ends of smoky days' (line 4) evokes a feeling of disgust at a useless end to a useless day? What other words and phrases emphasise the speaker's sense of staleness?

4. How is the sense of cramped conditions indoors evoked?

5. Lines 11–12 picture a lonely cab-horse, who is obviously also impatient and uncomfortable. Can this be seen as symbolic of urban life?

6. 'And then the lighting of the lamps' suggests perhaps an introduction to some dramatic events, but these possibilities are not fulfilled. Would you agree that the irony here contributes to the speaker's sense of aimless endurance?

SECOND PRELUDE

7. Would you agree that the atmosphere of the Second Prelude is oppressive and empty of charm? How is the morning rush hour conveyed?

8. The same sense of cramped indoor conditions seen in the First Prelude is continued here. What images suggest these?

9. For the speaker the rush of urban life is a 'masquerade'. It is a performance put on to give life an apparent meaning and purpose. Does anything lie behind this performance or is the speaker suggesting that the performance is all there is to life?

THIRD PRELUDE

10. The Third Prelude begins with the image of a woman whose sluggish half-conscious mind projects her interior being. What impression of the woman do we get here and later in this Prelude as she prepares for life's 'masquerade'? What vision of the street does she have? Can morning be seen almost as an intruder? Would you agree that the proper reaction to what is portrayed is disgust?

FOURTH PRELUDE

11. In the Fourth Prelude the street is personified. Its soul and the souls of the passers-by are

fused. How is the suffering of both conveyed? Is the speaker being ironic when he says? 'and eyes | Assured of certain certainties'?

12. The speaker is momentarily moved to pity in the face of human suffering when he says 'I am moved ... thing' Are you shocked by his immediate turn to cynicism when he says 'Wipe your hand across your mouth, and laugh'? Does he mean us to laugh at the plight of the 'ancient women gathering fuel'? Or is he suggesting that in face of the meaninglessness and suffering of life, pity is too easy an emotion?

Third reading

13. Discuss how Eliot depersonalises character by talking about bodily members in the poem. How does he depersonalise the observer/speaker?

14. What vital impulses, if any, animate the lives of the characters in the poems?

15. Compare the imagery Eliot uses here with that which he uses in 'The Love Song of J. Alfred Prufrock'.

16. In the art of music, a 'Prelude' is a short introductory piece. Examine the musical effects of the poems, particularly the use of rhythm and rhyme.

The Street: painting by George Grosz (1893–1959) representing the dysfunctional urban landscape described by Eliot

Aunt Helen

Miss Helen Slingsby was my maiden aunt,
And lived in a small house near a fashionable square
Cared for by servants to the number of four.
Now when she died there was silence in heaven
And silence at her end of the street.   5
The shutters were drawn and the undertaker wiped his feet—
He was aware that this sort of thing had occurred before.
The dogs were handsomely provided for,
But shortly afterwards the parrot died too.
The Dresden clock continued ticking on the mantelpiece,   10
And the footman sat upon the dining-table
Holding the second housemaid on his knees—
Who had always been so careful while her mistress lived.

Note

[10] **Dresden:** German city famous for its production of fine china

Explorations

First reading

1. What do you notice about the setting of the poem? List the things that made an immediate impression on you.

Second reading

2. What is the reaction to Aunt Helen's death? Does anyone mourn her? Does the poet mourn her?

3. Would the footman and housemaid have behaved as described in lines 11–12 when she was alive? Why are they behaving like this now?

4. Would you agree that Aunt Helen had a rather false sense of values? If so, how is this shown? Would you like her lifestyle?

Third reading

5. This poem is seen as a mockery of conventional middle-class life in the early twentieth century. Do you think Eliot is mocking the person of his aunt or is he rather satirising the external realities which surround her? Would you agree that her world is one of lifeless artifice, symbolised by a Dresden clock?

6. Eliot's poetic technique included presenting us with a gallery of comic types where (a) places and people are suggested in a few strokes but (b) gain their final tone and significance from the poem as a whole. Comment on his descriptions of the characters in the poem under these headings.

7. Do you find any trace of the personality or the feelings of the poet in this poem?

8. Do you think that there is anything in the structure of the poem which mimics the speech or tone of Aunt Helen?

A Game of Chess (extract from The Waste Land II)

The Chair she sat in, like a burnished throne,
Glowed on the marble, where the glass
Held up by standards wrought with fruited vines
From which a golden Cupidon peeped out
(Another hid his eyes behind his wing)   5
Doubled the names of sevenbranched candelabra
Reflecting light upon the table as
The glitter of her jewels rose to meet it,
From satin cases poured in rich profusion.
In vials of ivory and coloured glass   10
Unstoppered, lurked her strange synthetic perfumes,
Unguent, powdered, or liquid—troubled, confused
And drowned the sense in odours; stirred by the air
That freshened from the window, these ascended
In fattening the prolonged candle-flames,   15
Flung their smoke into the laquearia,
Stirring the pattern on the coffered ceiling.
Huge sea-wood fed with copper
Burned green and orange, framed by the coloured stone,
In which sad light a carvèd dolphin swam.   20

Notes

A Game of Chess: The title alludes to two plays by Thomas Middleton (1570–1627) i.e. *A Game of Chess* and *Women Beware Women*. Both of these involve sexual intrigue. In the latter play, a young woman is raped while her mother, quite unaware, plays a game of chess downstairs. The allusion refers to the theme of lust without love. The title could also refer to Shakespeare's play *The Tempest*, in which two lovers play a game of chess which is associated with fertility and genuine love. *The Tempest* is referred to again later in the poem.

[1] **The Chair she sat in, like a burnished throne:** This refers to Shakespeare's *Antony and Cleopatra*, Act II, Scene II, recalling Enorbarbus's long description of Cleopatra's first meeting with Antony.

[4] **Cupidon:** a 'beau' or 'Adonis', a handsome young man; also has echoes of Cupid

[12] **Unguent:** in ointment form

[16] **laquearia:** meaning a panelled ceiling; taken from the Roman poet Virgil's 'Aeneid' where he describes the banquet given by Dido, queen of Carthage, for Aeneas, with whom she fell in love

Above the antique mantel was displayed
As though a window gave upon the sylvan scene
The change of Philomel, by the barbarous king
So rudely forced; yet there the nightingale
Filled all the desert with inviolable voice   25
And still she cried, and still the world pursues,
'Jug Jug' to dirty ears.
And other withered stumps of time
Were told upon the walls; staring forms
Leaned out, leaning, hushing the room enclosed.   30
Footsteps shuffled on the stair.
Under the firelight, under the brush, her hair
Spread out in fiery points
Glowed into words, then would be savagely still.

'My nerves are bad to-night. Yes, bad. Stay with me. 35
Speak to me. Why do you never speak? Speak.
What are you thinking of? What thinking? What?
I never know what you are thinking. Think.'

I think we are in rats' alley
Where the dead men lost their bones.   40

'What is that noise?'
The wind under the door.
'What is that noise now? What is the wind doing?'
Nothing again nothing.

[22] **sylvan scene:** This is taken from Milton's *Paradise Lost*, IV, 140. The phrase occurs in the description of the Garden of Eden as Satan looks at it for the first time.

[23] **Philomel:** A Greek legend recalled in the Roman writer Ovid's *Metamorphoses VI*. Philomel was raped by her sister Procne's husband, Tereus, King of Thrace, who also cut off Philomel's tongue to prevent her telling. Philomel wove her story into a garment to inform Procne, who in revenge, killed Tereus's son and served him as a dish to Tereus at a banquet. The sisters fled pursued by Tereus, but the gods changed all three into birds; Tereus became a hawk, Procne a swallow and Philomel a nightingale. Poets often refer to a nightingale as 'Philomel'. The reference to the legend here may be to underscore secret or hidden lustful practices.

[42] **The wind under the door:** a reference to John Webster's (1578–1632) play *The Devil's Law Case*, a tragi-comedy

'Do   45
You know nothing? Do you see nothing? Do you remember
'Nothing? '

I remember
Those are pearls that were his eyes.
'Are you alive, or not? Is there nothing in your head?'   50
But
O O O O that Shakespeherian Rag—
It's so elegant
So intelligent
'What shall I do now? What shall 1 do?   55
I shall rush out as I am, and walk the street
With my hair down, so. What shall we do tomorrow?

What shall we ever do?'
The hot water at ten.
And if it rains, a closed car at four.   60
And we shall play a game of chess,
Pressing lidless eyes and waiting for a knock upon the door.

When Lil's husband got demobbed, I said—
I didn't mince my words, I said to her myself,
HURRY UP PLEASE ITS TIME   65
Now Albert's coming back, make yourself a bit smart.
He'll want to know what you done with that money he gave
you
To get yourself some teeth. He did, I was there.
You have them all out, Lil, and get a nice set,   70
He said, I swear, I can't bear to look at you.
And no more can't I, I said, and think of poor Albert,
He's been in the army four years, he wants a good time,
And if you don't give it him, there's others will, I said.
Oh is there, she said. Something o' that, I said.   75
Then I'll know who to thank, she said, and give me a straight
look.

[49] **Those are pearls that were his eyes:** from Shakespeare's *The Tempest*; Ariel's song that
speaks of drowning

[62] **Pressing lidless eyes...the door:** a reference to the game of chess in Middleton's play
Women Beware Women

HURRY UP PLEASE ITS TIME
If you don't like it you can get on with it, I said.
Others can pick and choose if you can't.   80
But if Albert makes off, it won't be for lack of telling.
You ought to be ashamed, I said, to look so antique.
(And her only thirty-one.)
I can't help it, she said, pulling a long face,
It's them pills I took, to bring it off, she said.   85
(She's had five already, and nearly died of young George.)
The chemist said it would be all right, but I've never been
the same.
You *are* a proper fool, I said.
Well, if Albert won't leave you alone, there it is, I said,   90
What you get married for if you don't want children?
HURRY UP PLEASE ITS TIME
Well, that Sunday Albert was home, they had a hot
gammon,
And they asked me in to dinner, to get the beauty of it hot—   95
HURRY UP PLEASE ITS TIME
HURRY UP PLEASE ITS TIME
Goonight Bill. Goonight Lou. Goonight May. Goonight.
Ta ta. Goonight. Goonight.
Good night, ladies, good night, sweet ladies, good night,   100
good night.

[100] **Good night, ladies...good night:** The last words spoken by Ophelia, heroine of
    Shakespeare's play *Hamlet*, who drowned, driven mad by love and by a time that is out of
    joint.

Background note

This poem is Section II of *The Waste Land*, published in 1922. *The Waste Land* summed up the
disillusionment and disgust of the post World War I generation, who saw the standardized
civilisation that was developing as barren and who saw twentieth-century man as condemned to a
living death. Such attitudes can also be seen in 'Preludes' and in 'The Love Song of J. Alfred
Prufrock'. At the centre of this living death lay an inability to love and a confusion between love and
lust. 'A Game of Chess' depicts the stunting effects of lust mistaken for love. In the poem we see
people as pawns moving about in two games that end not in checkmate but in stalemate.

Explorations

First reading

1. The first scene of the poem is set in a wealthy lady's boudoir (lines 1–62). What strikes you immediately about this scene?

2. The second scene (lines 63–101) is set in a public house. Try reading this scene aloud in a 'Cockney' or 'Scouser' accent. What impression of the women do you get?

Second reading

3. The opening section of the poem has been called a scene of splendid clutter. List some of these cluttering items. Would you find these attractive?

4. The immediate opening section, picturing the lady seated at her dressing table, is a reference to Cleopatra. Why do you think the poet makes this reference?

5. What does the description of the 'cupidons' suggest to you? Is there any hint of the lady's behaviour here?

6. Examine the description of the lady's perfumes. Is the poet suggesting her ability to seduce or is he describing by implication a deeply disturbed person? Look in particular at the choice of verbs.

7. Would you agree that the description of the ceiling adds a claustrophobic atmosphere to this decadent and sensuous scene?

8. Lines 21–24 refer to the Greek legend of Philomel who was changed into a nightingale, following her rape. How does this fit into the overall theme of the poem?

9. What does the description of the lady brushing her hair mean to you?

10. Lines 35–62 constitute a 'dialogue' between the lady and an apparently silent male protagonist. Would you agree that she is seen as quite neurotic here? What in the language used suggests this? Would you agree that his situation is as desperate as hers? Is the reference to Shakespeare elegant?

11. This setting closes with a deep feeling of purposelessness. What images particularly contribute to this theme of sterility?

12. The second scene (lines 63–101), narrated by an unidentified lower-class lady in a pub at closing time, is overheard by the protagonist. Tell the story narrated by the lady in your own words.

Would you regard this story as gossip?

13. In what ways are the themes of sterility, emptiness and lust continued here?

14. The barman's words have an immediate meaning but they also have longer-term implications. What are these, do you think?

15. The last line is taken from Shakespeare's Hamlet and is spoken by Ophelia, whom many see as having died for love. Why do you think it is included here?

Third reading

16. Examine the poem as a piece of social satire. What has it to teach us?

17. Discuss the interweaving of past and present in the poem. How do the references to classical literature, legend etc. add to our understanding of the poem?

18. Examine the use of rhythm and repetition in the poem. Would you describe the poem as musical?

19. Would you agree that both settings in the poem have all the elements of good drama?

Fourth reading

20. Explore the relationship between sensuality and culture in this poem.

21. 'Eliot is the poet of psychological turmoil, cultural decay and moral degeneracy.' Discuss this view in reference to this poem. Where else in Eliot's poetry can this be seen?

22. 'The lives of Eliot's characters are ultimately sterile.' Discuss this statement with reference to this poem and to others.

Journey of the Magi

'A cold coming we had of it,
Just the worst time of the year
For a journey, and such a long journey:
The ways deep and the weather sharp,
The very dead of winter.'   5
And the camels galled, sore-footed, refractory,
Lying down in the melting snow.
There were times we regretted
The summer palaces on slopes, the terraces,
And the silken girls bringing sherbet.   10
Then the camel men cursing and grumbling
And running away, and wanting their liquor and women,
And the night-fires going out, and the lack of shelters,
And the cities hostile and the towns unfriendly
And the villages dirty and charging high prices: 15
A hard time we had of it.
At the end we preferred to travel all night,
Sleeping in snatches,
With the voices singing in our ears, saying
That this was all folly.   20

Then at dawn we came down to a temperate valley,
Wet, below the snow line, smelling of vegetation,
With a running stream and a water-mill beating the dark-
ness,
And three trees on the low sky.   25
And an old white horse galloped away in the meadow.
Then we came to a tavern with vine-leaves over the lintel,
Six hands at an open door dicing for pieces of silver,
And feet kicking the empty wine-skins.
But there was no information, and so we continued   30
And arrived at evening, not a moment too soon
Finding the place; it was (you may say) satisfactory.

All this was a long time ago, I remember,
And I would do it again, but set down
This set down   35
This: were we led all that way for
Birth or Death? There was a Birth, certainly,

We had evidence and no doubt. I had seen birth and death,
But had thought they were different; this Birth was
Hard and bitter agony for us, like Death, our death.   40
We returned to our places, these Kingdoms,
But no longer at ease here, in the old dispensation,
With an alien people clutching their gods.
I should be glad of another death.

Notes

Magus: singular of Magi, the three wise men who brought gifts to the Infant Jesus

[1–5] **A cold ... of winter:** taken from the 1622 Christmas Day sermon of Bishop Launcelot Andrewes

[42] **the old dispensation:** life pre-Christ

 # Explorations

Before reading

1. The Magi are the Three Wise Men or Kings who visited the Infant Jesus at his birth in Bethlehem. Knowing this, what does the title of the poem lead you to expect?

First reading

2. Were any of your expectations met on reading the poem?

Second reading

3. The poem is the monologue of an old man reviewing the past. With what did he and the others have to struggle in making this journey? What forsaken luxuries did they still yearn for? Where does it suggest that they had deep doubts about their desire to witness a Birth?

4. At the end of the second section of the poem, the Magi arrive at Christ's birthplace after some fruitless searching. Could the imagery at the beginning of this section symbolise a birth or a new beginning? These are followed by symbols surrounding Christ's death. Can you identify these?

5. In the last book of the Bible, Revelations 19: 11, Christ is seen riding a white horse in glory. Is there anything

glorious about the image of the white horse here?

6. Would you agree that the last line of the second section is something of an anticlimax? Why is there no sense of awe or celebration?

7. In the final section the magus philosophically reflects on the significance of what he had seen. Birth (capitalised) is the birth of Christ which also brought a Death. What is this Death?—Christ's Death or the Death of an old way of life, or both? Is this why the Magi were no longer at ease in their own Kingdoms? Why should the magus be glad of another death?

Third reading

8. Eliot's theme is that death is the way to rebirth. Is this a paradox? Examine how the cycle of birth and death are suggested throughout the poem.

9. The poem can also be seen as representing Eliot's own spiritual journey from agnosticism to faith. He wrote it at the time of his baptism into the Anglican Church in 1927. Does the poem suggest a readiness to believe, an assertion of belief or indeed a sense of being conditioned by fate as much as faith?

10. How would you describe the tone of this poem?

Usk (extract from Landscapes III)

Do not suddenly break the branch, or
Hope to find
The white hart behind the white well.
Glance aside, not for lance, do not spell
Old enchantments. Let them sleep.   5
'Gently dip, but not too deep',
Lift your eyes
Where the roads dip and where the roads rise
Seek only there
Where the grey light meets the green air   10
The hermit's chapel, the pilgrim's prayer.

Notes

Usk: an area in Wales, about nine miles north of Newport

[3] **hart:** a male deer or stag

[6] **Gently dip, but not too deep:** from a song by George Peele (1558–96)—appropriate because of the song's suggestion of folk rituals

[11] **hermit:** one who chooses to live a life of isolation and prayer

[11] **pilgrim:** one who goes on a spiritual journey

 # Explorations

First reading

1. From a set of poems called *Landscapes*, Eliot wrote this following a holiday in Wales in 1935. In it, the poet evokes some images of the past. What are these images? To what period do they refer?

2. There is also a sense of movement in the poem. What images give the poem that sense?

Second reading

3. The first line exhorts the viewer not to break the peace of the scene, yet the next few lines forbid him to dwell on resurrecting the past. Is this a contradiction? Would you agree that the quoted line (line 6) shows the poet's true intention toward the past?

4. The last five lines suggest a more active journey. Toward what will it lead? What kind of journey is this for the poet?

5. 'Where the grey light meets the green air'. Examine this line. Could this symbolize a moment of clarification for the poet? What do the colours mean to you?

Third reading

6. Is there a sense of transition in this poem?

7. Comment on the use of colour in the poem. Does it help to enliven the atmosphere or indeed the sense of poet as painter?

8. Examine the lyrical qualities of the poem. How do they contribute to the energy which surrounds this poem?

9. Compare and contrast this poem with 'Rannoch, by Glencoe'.

Rannoch, by Glencoe (extract from Landscapes IV)

this poem is also prescribed for Ordinary Level exams in 2005 and 2006

Here the crow starves, here the patient stag
Breeds for the rifle. Between the soft moor
And the soft sky, scarcely room
To leap or soar. Substance crumbles, in the thin air
Moon cold or moon hot. The road winds in   5
Listlessness of ancient war,
Languor of broken steel,
Clamour of confused wrong, apt
In silence. Memory is strong
Beyond the bone. Pride snapped,   10
Shadow of pride is long, in the long pass
No concurrence of bone.

Note

Rannoch, by Glencoe: An area of the Scottish Highlands south of Fort William. This poem, like 'Usk', is from a set of poems called *Landscapes*.

Through Glencoe: painting by Louis B. Hurt (1856–1929)

Explorations

Before reading

1. What are your visions of the Scottish Highlands? What do they symbolize for you?

First reading

2. Were your views confirmed by this poem?
3. List the images of violence and death you see here. Are these images from the past or the present?
4. What sounds does the poet evoke?

Second reading

5. In the first few lines of the poem, how does Eliot suggest a sense of barrenness and oppressiveness?
6. The road appears to wander with no purpose. What words in particular evoke this lack of energy? Is the poet suggesting that a depressing sense of history is causing it? Compare the road here to that in 'Usk'.
7. The memory of past rivalries and wrongs are strong in this landscape. What is the poet's attitude to these? Is he suggesting that pride is that which keeps old rivalries from being resolved? Is this what he also means by 'no concurrence of bone'?

Third reading

8. Examine how Eliot creates a feeling of place in this poem. Would you agree that he creates a landscape which, paradoxically, is both austere and rich? How does he do this? What other paradoxes do you see in the poem?
9. We get little, if any, sense of the poet's presence in the poem. Why does he have this sense of detachment, do you think?
10. Discuss the feelings of constriction evident here. Examine where else in Eliot's poetry such feelings exist.
11. Would you consider this to be a lyrical poem?
12. Discuss this poem and 'Usk' under the heading 'Life and Death'.

East Coker IV (extract from The Four Quartets)

The wounded surgeon plies the steel
That questions the distempered part;
Beneath the bleeding hands we feel
The sharp compassion of the healer's art
Resolving the enigma of the fever chart.   5

Our only health is the disease
If we obey the dying nurse
Whose constant care is not to please
But to remind of our, and Adam's curse,
And that, to be restored, our sickness must grow worse.   10

The whole earth is our hospital
Endowed by the ruined millionaire,
Wherein, if we do well, we shall
Die of the absolute paternal care
That will not leave us, but prevents us everywhere.   15

The chill ascends from feet to knees,
The fever sings in mental wires.
If to be warmed, then I must freeze
And quake in frigid purgatorial fires
Of which the flame is roses, and the smoke is briars.   20

The dripping blood our only drink,
The bloody flesh our only food:
In spite of which we like to think
That we are sound, substantial flesh and blood—
Again, in spite of that, we call this Friday good.   25

Background note

'East Coker', from which this poem is taken, is in turn one of The Four Quartets written between 1935 and 1942. The main theme of 'East Coker' is that true wisdom is humility and that at a certain stage in its spiritual progress, the soul must put itself in the hands of God and die in order to be reborn. This is best exemplified by Jesus's death on the Cross. This theme of death and rebirth is also seen in 'The Journey of the Magi' and 'Usk'. In order to achieve one's rebirth, or full spiritual potential, one must first endure the 'Dark Night of the Soul', a time of emptiness and suffering but also of heightened awareness, so called by St John of the Cross, to whom Eliot is indebted.

Notes

East Coker: A village near Yeovil in Somerset, England, from which Eliot's direct ancestor, Andrew Eliot, left for the New World around 1699. T.S. Eliot's ashes were buried there after his death in 1965.

[1] **steel:** the surgeon's scalpel, similar to the 'dart of love' described by St John of the Cross in the 'Living Flame of Love'

[15] **prevents:** used here in the seventeeth-century sense of to go before with spiritual guidance or to predispose to repentance

[19] **purgatorial fires:** purgatory is a temporary state or place where the soul is purified by punishment

 # Explorations

First reading

1. Have you ever wondered why we call Good Friday 'good' when on that day Jesus was tortured horribly and killed? Is this a paradox? Think about this for a while.

2. The poem is full of paradoxes. List these. Do they help us to understand the notion of 'necessary evil', a perhaps temporary evil which will be to our ultimate good?

Second reading

3. The 'wounded surgeon' in the first stanza is Jesus. To what extent is He being compared to a physical surgeon? Why is His compassion 'sharp'? Why is the fever chart described as an 'enigma'?

4. The image of a hospital is continued in the second stanza,

where the nurse is the church. In what sense is she dying? What is her role? What was the curse put on Adam as he left the Garden of Eden?

5. The 'ruined millionaire' of the third stanza is Adam. Why is he called this? What was his legacy to the world? What is the desired outcome of doing well in this 'hospital'? If God is the provider of 'paternal care' what is His role?

6. The fourth stanza suggests a process of purgation. Is this the 'Dark Night of the Soul', i.e. a period of black despair before Life is rediscovered? How complete is this process? Is there any sense in which this purgation leads to healing?

7. The fifth stanza refers to both the Crucifixion and the Eucharist. In what ways is the imagery linked to the idea that suffering is the basis of our cure, seen throughout the poem? Is this why we call Good Friday good?

Third reading

8. Look again at Question 2 above and your list of paradoxes. Would you agree that physical suffering can lead to a spiritual good?

9. Examine the lyrical qualities of the poem. To what extent do these aid the devotional tone of the poem?

10. Would you consider this to be an emotional or intellectual poem?

11. The style of this poem reflects the style of seventeeth-century metaphysical poetry, such as that of Donne, Herbert or Marvell. Research the features of this style of poetry and indicate to what extent Eliot is using such a style here.

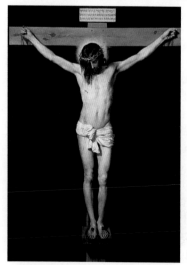

Crucifixion: painting by Diego Velásquez (1599–1660)

9 Patrick KAVANAGH

prescribed for Higher Level exams in 2004 and 2005

Patrick Kavanagh was born on 21 October 1904. He was the fourth child and the eldest son of James and Bridget (née Quinn) born in the townland of Mucker, Inniskeen parish, Co. Monaghan. From the age of twelve Kavanagh started writing verse and collected it in a copybook. His brother Peter later published this juvenilia in his *Collected Poems*. Kavanagh was keen to use the things around him in his poems no matter how mundane they may seem to others. Regular trips to Dundalk brought him into contact with literature especially with the literary journals of the time such as *Poetry*, and *The Irish Statesman*. He entered the joint trades of cobbler and small farmer like his father before him, but also began to see himself as someone different from the regular farmers. He now began to see himself as a poet.

His first volume of poetry *Ploughman and Other Poems* was published in 1936. It contained many of the ideas that would remain central to his poetry for the rest of his life. His poetry in this book examined not only his surrounding area but also poetry itself, *the nature of the poet and the creative act*. In 1939, Kavanagh made a major change to his life by giving up farming and decided to concentrate

1904–1967

on writing as a career, moving to live in Dublin in the process. He wrote a number of regular columns as well as book and film reviews at the time. As well as his poetry, he also produced a novel, *Tarry Flynn*. He also ventured into publishing a newspaper called *Kavanagh's Weekly* in 1952. Its stated purpose 'was to introduce the critical constructive note into Irish thought'. Kavanagh put every aspect of Irish life under scrutiny. It was either loved or hated at the time. Kavanagh himself was put under scrutiny later that year. An article in *The Leader* criticised his work. He sued *The Leader* for libel but lost. Soon after this period, he entered the Rialto hospital with lung cancer. Against great odds, he made a heroic recovery and spent the summer of 1955 regaining his strength on the banks of the Grand Canal in Dublin. He described this period as his 'rebirth'. Kavanagh's health began to decline again in the late 1950s. He returned to journalism. On 19 April 1967, he married Katherine Moloney whom he had known for a number of years;. on 30 November in that year he died at the age of sixty-three.

Inniskeen Road: July Evening

The bicycles go by in twos and threes—
There's a dance in Billy Brennan's barn tonight,
And there's the half-talk code of mysteries
And the wink-and-elbow language of delight.
Half-past eight and there is not a spot   5
Upon a mile of road, no shadow thrown
That might turn out a man or woman, not
A footfall tapping secrecies of stone.

I have what every poet hates in spite
Of all the solemn talk of contemplation.   10
Oh, Alexander Selkirk knew the plight
Of being king and government and nation.
A road, a mile of kingdom, I am king
Of banks and stones and every blooming thing.

Note   [11] **Alexander Selkirk:** A Scottish sailor who was
        abandoned on an uninhabited island. Daniel
        Defoe's *Robinson Crusoe* was based on his life.

Billy Brennan's barn, Inniskeen, Co. Monaghan

Explorations

First reading

1. What does the 'wink-and-elbow language of delight' mean? Do you think this is an appropriate phrase? Why?
2. Write a dialogue between some of the inhabitants of Billy Brennan's barn.
3. The poet names specific places and people in the poem. What effect does this have?
4. Who was Alexander Selkirk? Why does the poet compare himself to him?
5. Do you think that Kavanagh would forego being a poet in order to fit in with the crowd? Discuss this.

Second reading

6. The poet uses a good deal of alliteration in the first quatrain. What is the effect of this?
7. Do you see any changes in the language used in the three sections? Would you agree that there are different voices in the poem? Who is the focus of each section?
8. The word 'blooming' has two meanings in the poem. What are they?

Third reading

9. Compare the rhythm of the first quatrain with that of the second. Do you see any major changes? What effect does this have on the development of the poem?
10. Compare the rhythm of the first quatrain with that of the second. Do you see any major changes? How do the vowel sounds contribute to this?
11. Trace the development of thought in the poem over the first and second quatrains and the sestet.

Fourth reading

12. Imagine that the last line of this poem had never been written. How would it change your reading of the whole poem?
13. What is your image of the typical poet? Does Kavanagh, in this poem, fit this?
14. Would you agree with the assertion that 'Kavanagh is a whingeing self-pitying introvert who wants to have his cake and eat it'?

Epic

I have lived in important places, times
When great events were decided: who owned
That half a rood of rock, a no-man's land
Surrounded by our pitchfork-armed claims.
I heard the Duffys shouting 'Damn your soul'   5
And old McCabe stripped to the waist, seen
Step the plot defying blue cast-steel—
'Here is the march along these iron stones'
That was the year of the Munich bother. Which
Was most important? I inclined   10
To lose my faith in Ballyrush and Gortin
Till Homer's ghost came whispering to my mind
He said: I made the *Iliad* from such
A local row. Gods make their own importance.

Notes

[8] **march:** boundary
[9] **Munich bother:** 1939
[11] **Ballyrush and Gortin:** townlands in Co. Monaghan
[12] **Homer:** a Greek poet
[13] **Iliad:** an 'epic' poem by Homer

Patrick Kavanagh

Explorations

Before reading

1. Think about the title. What is an epic? What might you expect the poem to deal with?

First reading

2. What is the argument about? Does it seem important to you? Can you see how it could be important to others?

3. Do the people who are arguing seem to be reasonable. Describe what you imagine them to look like. Write a dialogue that either side might have among themselves.

4. Write a newspaper report on the argument.

5. What does Kavanagh mean by the 'Munich bother'? What does his attitude toward it seem to be?

6. What is his attitude toward the people of the village?

Second reading

7. The first line sounds very portentous. Do you think it is effective?

8. Examine the 'war' imagery that he uses. What does it suggest to you? Write about this.

9. The narrator changes his mind halfway through the poem. What do you notice about this change?

Third reading

10. Comment on the poet's use of irony.

Fourth reading

11. Do you think that the last line summarises the whole poem? In your own words, write about the theme.

12. In an epic poem there is often a hero. Is there one in this poem? Discuss this.

Shancoduff

this poem is also prescribed for Ordinary Level exams in 2004 and 2005

My black hills have never seen the sun rising,
Eternally they look north towards Armagh.
Lot's wife would not be salt if she had been
Incurious as my black hills that are happy
When dawn whitens Glassdrummond chapel.   5

My hills hoard the bright shillings of March
While the sun searches in every pocket.
They are my Alps and I have climbed the Matterhorn
With a sheaf of hay for three perishing calves
In the field under the Big Forth of Rocksavage.   10

The sleety winds fondle the rushy beards of Shancoduff
While the cattle-drovers sheltering in the Featherna Bush
Look up and say: 'Who owns them hungry hills
That the water-hen and snipe must have forsaken?
A poet? Then by heavens he must be poor.'   15
I hear and is my heart not badly shaken?

Notes   [10] **Rocksavage:** a place in Co. Monaghan near the poet's farm

[11] **Shancoduff:** a place in Co. Monaghan near the poet's farm

[12] **Featherna Bush:** a place in Co. Monaghan near the poet's farm

Explorations

First reading

1. The title of the poem is taken from the name of the place where Kavanagh's family had a farm. It is derived from two Irish words; 'Sean' and 'Dubh'. Do you know what these words mean? If not, find out. What sort of a place would you expect from such a name?

Second reading

2. How does Kavanagh describe this place? Draw a picture or describe the scene in your own words as you imagine it.
3. What is the cattle-drover's attitude to the hills?
4. What is the poet's reaction to this?

Third reading

5. He personifies the place. How does he do this? What effect does it have?
6. He names a lot of specific places in the poem e.g. Glassdrummond, Featherna, Rocksavage. Why does he do this?
7. He repeatedly uses the possessive 'my' when talking about the hills. What does it tell us about the narrator?
8. Do you think the cattle drovers have any value on poetry? Examine their words carefully.

Fourth reading

9. In an earlier version of the poem, Kavanagh used the word 'faith' instead of the word 'heart' in the last line of the poem. Why do you think he made that change? What effect does it have? Do you think that it was a good change to make?
10. In another poem Kavanagh says that 'Naming a thing is the love act and the pledge'. Relate that statement to 'Shancoduff'.
11. 'Shancoduff is a love poem.' Do you agree?

The Great Hunger

I

Clay is the word and clay is the flesh
Where the potato-gatherers like mechanized scare-crows
    move
Along the side-fall of the hill—Maguire and his men.
If we watch them an hour is there anything we can
    prove
Of life as it is broken-backed over the Book   5
Of Death? Here crows gabble over worms and frogs
And the gulls like old newspapers are blown clear of the
    hedges, luckily.
Is there some light of imagination in these wet clods?
Or why do we stand here shivering?
                        Which of these men   10
Loved the light and the queen
Too long virgin? Yesterday was summer. Who was it
    promised marriage to himself
Before apples were hung from the ceilings for Hallowe'en?
We will wait and watch the tragedy to the last curtain
Till the last soul passively like a bag of wet clay   15
Rolls down the side of the hill, diverted by the angles
Where the plough missed or a spade stands, straitening
    the way.

A dog lying on a torn jacket under a heeled-up cart,
A horse nosing along the posied headland, trailing
A rusty plough. Three heads hanging between wide-
    apart   20
Legs. October playing a symphony on a slack wire paling.
Maguire watches the drills flattened out
And the flints that lit a candle for him on a June altar
Flameless. The drills slipped by and the days slipped by
And he trembled his head away and ran free from the
    world's halter,   25
And thought himself wiser than any man in the townland
When he laughed over pints of porter
Of how he came free from every net spread
In the gaps of experience. He shook a knowing head
And pretended to his soul   30

That children are tedious in hurrying fields of April
Where men are spanging across wide furrows.
Lost in the passion that never needs a wife—
The pricks that pricked were the pointed pins of harrows.
Children scream so loud that the crows could bring   35
The seed of an acre away with crow-rude jeers.
Patrick Maguire, he called his dog and he flung a stone in
     the air
And hallooed the birds away that were the birds of the years.
Turn over the weedy clods and tease out the tangled skeins.
What is he looking for there?   40
He thinks it is a potato, but we know better
Than his mud-gloved fingers probe in this insensitive hair.

'Move forward the basket and balance it steady
In this hollow. Pull down the shafts of that cart, Joe,
And straddle the horse,' Maguire calls.   45
'The wind's over Brannagan's, now that means rain.
Graip up some withered stalks and see that no potato falls
Over the tail-board going down the ruckety pass—
And *that's* a job we'll have to do in December,
Gravel it and build a kerb on the bog-side. Is that
     Cassidy's ass   50
Out in my clover? Curse o' God—
Where is that dog?
Never where he's wanted.' Maguire grunts and spits
Through a clay-wattled moustache and stares about him
     from the height.
His dream changes again like the cloud-swung wind   55
And he is not so sure now if his mother was right
When she praised the man who made a field his bride.

Watch him, watch him, that man on a hill whose spirit
Is a wet sack flapping about the knees of time.
He lives that his little fields may stay fertile when his
     own body   60

Notes   [32] **spanging:** long fast steps
         [34] **harrows:** spiked frame for smoothing land

Is spread in the bottom of a ditch under two coulters
        crossed in Christ's Name.

He was suspicious in his youth as a rat near strange bread
When girls laughed; when they screamed he knew that
        meant
The cry of fillies in season. He could not walk
The easy road to his destiny. He dreamt   65
The innocence of young brambles to hooked treachery.

O the grip, O the grip of irregular fields! No man escapes.
It could not be that back of the hills love was free
And ditches straight.
No monster hand lifted up children and put down apes   70
As here
                                'O God if I had been wiser!'
That was his sigh like the brown breeze in the thistles.
He looks towards his house and haggard. 'O God if I
        had been wiser!'
But now a crumpled leaf from the whitethorn bushes   75
Darts like a frightened robin, and the fence
Shows the green of after-grass through a little window,
And he knows that his own heart is calling his mother a liar.
God's truth is life—even the grotesque shapes of its
        foulest fire.

The horse lifts its head and crashes   80
Through the whins and stones
To lip late passion in the crawling clover.
In the gap there's a bush weighted with boulders like
        morality,
The fools of life bleed if they climb over.

The wind leans from Brady's, and the coltsfoot leaves
        are holed with rust,   85
Rain fills the cart-tracks and the sole-plate grooves;
A yellow sun reflects in Donaghmoyne
The poignant light in light in puddles shaped by hooves.

Notes   [61] **coulter:** the iron cutter at the front of a ploughshare
          [87] **Donaghmoyne:** a townland in Co. Monaghan

Come with me, Imagination, into this iron house
And we will watch from the doorway the years run
    back,   90
And we will know that a peasant's left hand wrote on
    the page.
Be easy, October. No cackle hen, horse neigh, tree sough,
    duck quack.

Explorations

Before reading

1. What do you think of the title of the poem? Comment on the poet's use of the word 'Great'.

First reading

2. From reading the poem, how do you visualize Patrick Maguire? What age do you think he might be? What do you think he looks like? How does he live, etc.?

3. Write a diary for one day in the life of Patrick Maguire.

4. The poem describes a man and his physical environment. What is the relationship between the two? Describe his environment in your own words.

5. Can you find any indications in the poem of Maguire's attitude to women?

6. Maguire complains about children in the poem. Do you think that this represents his complete attitude toward children?

7. To what extent does Maguire attempt justification for his current position?

Second reading

8. What do you think of the poem's narrator? Is he sympathetic? Is he biased? Is he patronising, etc.?

9. In the fourth verse of the poem, Maguire speaks. Compare the impression that we get of him here with the impression we get from the narrator.

10. 'There is a difference between the life lived and the life wished for.' Do you think that this statement is true for Patrick Maguire? How is this conveyed to us?

Third reading

11. Late autumn is mentioned a number of times throughout the poem. What do you think is the significance of this image?

12. There are religious metaphors used in the poem—explain what each one refers to. What is their overall effect?

13. At the beginning of the poem, the sounds of the words are very harsh. Comment on some of the sounds and words used to give this harsh tone.

Fourth reading

14. Do you think that the poem as a whole could be an allegory for 1930s and 1940s Ireland? Explain your answer.

15. If a similar poem was being written about contemporary Ireland, do you think its concerns would be the same? What would its concerns be? What type of imagery would it use?

16. Do you think that the phrase 'God's truth is life' could be an apt summary of the whole poem?

17. Kavanagh paints a portrait of Patrick Maguire. It has been said that he does not paint a still life but rather uses a 'cinematic technique'. Using examples from the poem, explain what you think is meant by this.

Fifth reading

18. This is part one of a longer poem. Where do you think the poem will go from here?

A Christmas Childhood

this poem is also prescribed for Ordinary Level exams in 2004 and 2005

I

One side of the potato-pits was white with frost—
How wonderful that was, how wonderful!
And when we put our ears to the paling-post
The music that came out was magical.

The light between the ricks of hay and straw   5
Was a hole in Heaven's gable. An apple tree
With its December-glinting fruit we saw—
O you, Eve, were the world that tempted me

To eat the knowledge that grew in clay
And death the germ within it! Now and then   10
I can remember something of the gay
Garden that was childhood's. Again

The tracks of cattle to a drinking-place,
A green stone lying sideways in a ditch
Or any common sight the transfigured face   15
Of a beauty that the world did not touch.

II

My father played the melodion
Outside at our gate;
There were stars in the morning east
And they danced to his music.   20

Across the wild bogs his melodion called
To Lennons and Callans.
As I pulled on my trousers in a hurry
I knew some strange thing had happened.

Outside in the cow-house my mother   25
Made the music of milking;
The light of her stable-lamp was a star
And the frost of Bethlehem made it twinkle.

A water-hen screeched in the bog,
Mass-going feet   30
Crunched the wafer-ice on the pot holes,
Somebody wistfully twisted the bellows wheel.

My child poet picked out the letters
On the grey stone,
In silver the wonder of a Christmas townland,   35
The winking glitter of a frosty dawn.

Cassiopeia was over
Cassidy's hanging hill,
I looked and three whin bushes rode across
The horizon—the Three Wise Kings.   40
An old man passing said:
'Can't he make it talk'—
The melodion. I hid in the doorway
And tightened the belt of my box-pleated coat.

I nicked six nicks on the door-post   45
With my penknife's big blade—
There was a little one for cutting tobacco.
And I was six Christmases of age.

My father played the melodion,
My mother milked the cows,   50
And I had a prayer like a white rose pinned
On the Virgin Mary's blouse.

Notes

melodion: a small accordion
[37]   **Cassiopeia:** a northern constellation

Explorations

Before reading

1. The first part of the poem is an evocation of the poet's memories of his own childhood. What are your memories of Christmas-time when you were young?

First reading

2. Do you think that the narrator had a happy childhood? What are his happiest memories?

3. What type of a child do you think he was, according to the evidence in this poem? Discuss this.

4. Why does the narrator compare his village with Bethlehem?

5. What is the relationship between the narrator and nature?

Second reading

6. Show how Kavanagh uses religious imagery throughout the poem. What effect does it have? Does the imagery change as the poem progresses?

7. What type of voice does the narrator use: an adult voice, child voice or what? Read it aloud.

8. There is awe for the innocence of the past in this poem. Where and how is this conveyed?

Third reading

9. How does Kavanagh make the ordinary seem wondrous and extraordinary?

Fourth reading

10. What is the narrator's standing in relation to everybody else in the poem?

11. What does this poem say about childhood?

Advent

We have tested and tasted too much, lover—
Through a chink too wide there comes in no wonder.
But here in this Advent-darkened room
Where the dry black bread and the sugarless tea
Of penance will charm back the luxury   5
Of a child's soul, we'll return to Doom
The knowledge we stole but could not use.

And the newness that was in every stale thing
When we looked at it as children: the spirit-shocking
Wonder in a black slanting Ulster hill   10
Or the prophetic astonishment in the tedious talking
Of an old fool will awake for us and bring
You and me to the yard gate to watch the whins
And the bog-holes, cart-tracks, old stables where Time
        begins.

O after Christmas we'll have no need to go searching   15
For the difference that sets an old phrase burning—
We'll hear it in the whispered argument of a churning
Or in the streets where the village boys are lurching.
And we'll hear it among simple decent men too
Who barrow dung in gardens under trees,   20
Wherever life pours ordinary plenty.
Won't we be rich, my love and I, and please
God we shall not ask for reason's payment,
The why of heart-breaking strangeness in dreeping
        hedges
Nor analyse God's breath in common statement.   25
We have thrown into the dust-bin the clay-minted
        wages
Or pleasure, knowledge and the conscious hour—
And Christ comes with a January flower.

Explorations

Before reading

1. What do you know about 'Advent'? Share ideas.

First reading

2. The first line would suggest that the speaker has experienced a great many of the pleasures of the world. What is the disadvantage of this, as he outlines it in the second line? Explain this in your own words.

3. What is the speaker's personal plan for Advent and what is its purpose? Explore lines 2–6. What phrase do you think best sums up his goal? Discuss these?

4. What change does the speaker hope or expect will follow from this period of penance? Read the remainder of the poem again and list the main changes.

5. What is your understanding of the effect of 'penance'? Is the speaker's understanding different? Discuss this.

6. Who do you think the lover is? What leads you to this conclusion?

Second reading

7. Comment on the religious imagery used in the poem.

8. The poem is made up of two sonnets. Is the tone in each different? How?

9. The poet talks about money throughout the poem. What is wealth to him?

Third reading

10. What does the image of a January flower represent for you?

11. Write about the other images and sounds that the poet finds exciting. Do they have anything in common?

12. What is the poet's attitude to God?

Fourth reading

13. ' 'Advent' expresses a belief that poetry depends on the poet's attitude to the world.' Do you agree?

14. Picasso said that all artists should strive to reach a state of 'childlikeness'. Based on this poem, do you think Kavanagh would agree?

15. 'This poem is really Kavanagh's manifesto for his own poetry.' Do you agree? Where is this evident?

16. The poem was originally entitled 'Renewal'. Which title do you prefer? Which is the most appropriate?

On Raglan Road

(Air: 'The Dawning of the Day')

On Raglan Road on an autumn day I met her first and
    knew
That her dark hair would weave a snare that I might
    one day rue;
I saw the danger, yet I walked along the enchanted way,
And I said, let grief be a fallen leaf at the dawning of
    the day.

On Grafton Street in November we tripped lightly along
    the ledge   5
Of the deep ravine where can be seen the worth of
    passion's pledge,
The Queen of Hearts still making tarts and I not making
    hay—
O I loved too much and by such by such is happiness
    thrown away.   15

I gave her gifts of the mind I gave her the secret sign
    that's known
To the artists who have known the true gods of sound
    and stone   10
And word and tint. I did not stint for I gave her poems
    to say
With her own name there and her own dark hair like
    clouds over fields of May.

On a quiet street where old ghosts meet I see her walking
    now
Away from me so hurriedly my reason must allow
That I had wooed not as I should a creature made of
    clay—   15
When the angel woos the clay he'd lose his wings at the
    dawn of day.

Note   [1] **Raglan Road:** a street off Pembroke Street in Dublin

Explorations

First reading

1. What is the relationship between the poet and the dark-haired woman? What was their relationship?
2. What is the poet's attitude to love and courtship?
3. Was there an equal relationship?
4. How does he think he scared her off? What do you think?

Second reading

5. This poem is also a popular song. Are there any elements of the poem that make this obvious?

Third reading

6. Do you think that he's telling the truth when he says that he 'loved too much'?
7. Trace the images of nature in the poem.
8. What effect does he have by putting rhymes in the middle of lines?
9. What part does time play in the poem?

Fourth reading

10. Do you think that the phrase 'it takes two to tango' ever occurred to Kavanagh?
11. Is the poet a misogynist?

'On Raglan Road on an autumn day'

The Hospital

A year ago I fell in love with the functional ward
Of a chest hospital: square cubicles in a row
Plain concrete, wash basins—an art lover's woe,
Not counting how the fellow in the next bed snored.
But nothing whatever is by love debarred,   5
The common and banal her heat can know.
The corridor led to a stairway and below
Was the inexhaustible adventure of a gravelled yard.

This is what love does to things: the Rialto Bridge,
The main gate that was bent by a heavy lorry,   10
The seat at the back of a shed that was a suntrap.
Naming these things is the love-act and its pledge;
For we must record love's mystery without claptrap,
Snatch out of time the passionate transitory.

Note

[2] **hospital:** the Rialto Hospital, Dublin

Rialto Hospital

Explorations

Before reading

1. What feelings surface when you hear the word 'Hospital'? Now what is your immediate reaction to the first line and a half?

First reading

2. What does he find beautiful about the hospital?

3. Try to sketch out where things in the poem are in relation to each other physically.

4. The poet thinks that adventure in a 'gravelled yard' could be inexhaustible. Do you agree with him?

5. What do you think the poet means in lines 5 and 6? Discuss your interpretation.

Second reading

6. The tone of the poem is dominated by broad vowel sounds. What effect does this have?

7. What effect do the sounds at the end of the poem have? Describe these sounds.

Third reading

8. According to this poem, what does love do to things?

9. How does the poet use the conventions of the sonnet to make the points that he wants to make?

Fourth reading

10. Do you think that this poem actually does 'record love's mystery without claptrap'?

11. Is Kavanagh's poetic manifesto as shown in this poem put into practice in any of his other poems? If so, where?

12. Is the poet at ease with himself? Share your views on this.

Canal Bank Walk

Leafy-with-love banks and the green water of the canal
Pouring redemption for me, that I do
The will of God, wallow in the habitual, the banal
Grow with nature again as before I grew.
The bright stick trapped, the breeze adding a third   5
Party to the couple kissing on an old seat,
And a bird gathering materials for the nest for the Word
Eloquently new and abandoned to its delirious beat.
O unworn world enrapture me, encapture me in a web
Of fabulous grass and eternal voices by a beech,   10
Feed the gaping need of my senses, give me ad lib
To pray unselfconsciously with overflowing speech
For this soul needs to be honoured with a new dress
    woven
From green and blue things and arguments that cannot
    be proven.

Note   **Canal Bank Walk:** the Grand Canal near Baggot St. Bridge, Dublin

Walk by the Grand Canal: oil painting by Helen Mulkerns

Explorations

First reading

1. How does he set the scene?
2. What does Kavanagh want from God?

Second reading

3. How does Kavanagh use sound to express his mood in the first quatrain?
4. What is the relationship between nature and humans in the poem?
5. How important is the image of water in the poem?
6. What tense is the poem set in? Why is this important?
7. How does he use internal rhyme to set his mood and theme?
8. Go through the images by the canal bank; the twig, the couple etc. and show how they could relate to the poet's own state.

Third reading

9. The sestet has been described as a hymn. Explain how someone could come to this conclusion.
10. How does the narrator see himself?
11. In order to make sense the reader must often continue on from the end of one line into the next. What is the effect of these 'run-on' lines?
12. Where is God in the poem? How does the poet understand God and His place in the world?

Lines Written on a Seat on the Grand Canal, Dublin

'Erected to the Memory of Mrs Dermot O'Brien'

O commemorate me where there is water,
Canal water preferably, so stilly
Greeny at the heart of summer. Brother
Commemorate me thus beautifully
Where by a lock niagarously roars   5
The falls for those who sit in the tremendous silence
Of mid-July. No one will speak in prose
Who finds his way to these Parnassian islands.
A swan goes by head low with many apologies,
Fantastic light looks through the eyes of bridges—   10
And look! a barge comes bringing from Athy
And other far-flung towns mythologies.
O commemorate me with no hero-courageous
Tomb—just a canal-bank seat for the passer-by.

Notes

[8] **Parnassian:** of Parnassus; a mountain in Greece sacred to Apollo and the
muses

[11] **Athy:** a town in the Midlands

Patrick Kavanagh's Memorial Seat, Grand Canal, Dublin

Explorations

First reading

1. Where exactly is this poem situated? What kind of place do you think it is, from what we are shown in the poem? What makes it so attractive?

2. What mood is the poet in? What words or phrases suggest this?

Second reading

3. There is both movement and stillness in the poem. How does the poet reconcile these?

4. Do you think that Kavanagh is very much aware of his own mortality in this poem? Discuss this.

5. Why does he not want a tomb?

6. What does his preferred form of commemoration suggest about the poet?

Third reading

7. Where does the poet use alliteration and what is its effect?

8. Explore his use of hyperbole. What atmosphere does it help to create in this poem?

9. In the first quatrain he uses 'y' sounds frequently. What do you think is the effect of this?

10. Kavanagh tends to use half-rhymes rather than full rhymes in this poem. Examine these and say what you think is the effect of this technique.

Fourth reading

11. In the poem how does Kavanagh see the place and function of the poet?

12. Do poets deserve commemoration? Does Kavanagh?

10 *Elizabeth* BISHOP

prescribed for Higher Level exams in 2003 and 2006

Elizabeth Bishop was born on 8 February 1911 in Worcester, Massachusetts. Her father died when she was eight months old. Her mother never recovered from the shock and for the next five years was in and out of mental hospitals. In 1916 she was institutionalised and separated from her daughter, whom she was never to see again— she died in 1934. Elizabeth was reared for the most part by her grandparents in Great Village, Nova Scotia. The elegy 'First Death in Nova Scotia' draws on some childhood memories. 'Sestina' too evokes the sadness of this period. Yet her recollections of her Nova Scotia childhood were essentially positive and she had great affection for her maternal grandparents, aunts and uncles in this small agricultural village.

She went to boarding-school and then attended Vassar College, a private university, in New York, from 1930–34. She graduated in English literature (but also took Greek and music), always retaining a particular appreciation for Renaissance lyric poetry and for the works of Gerard Manley Hopkins. It was at Vassar that she first began to publish stories and poems in national magazines and where she met the poet Marianne Moore, who became an important influence on her career as a poet and with whom she maintained a lifelong friendship and correspondence. It was also at Vassar that she formed her first lesbian relationship, and here too, on her own admission, the lifelong problem with alcohol addiction began.

In 1939 she moved to Key West, Florida, a place she had fallen in love with over the previous years. 'The Fish' reflects her enjoyment of the sport of fishing at that time. Key West became a sort of refuge and

'Cabin with Porthole', a watercolour by Elizabeth Bishop

Elizabeth Bishop standing with a bicycle in Key West, Florida, c.1940

base for Bishop over the next fifteen years. In 1945 she won the Houghton Mifflin Poetry Award. In 1946 her first book of poetry, *North and South*, was published and was well received by the critics. 'The Fish' is among its thirty poems.

The years 1945–51, when her life was centred on New York, were very unsettled. She felt under extreme pressure in a very competitive literary circle and drank heavily. 'The Bight' and 'The Prodigal' reflect this dissolute period of her life.

In 1951 she left for South America on the first stage of a writer's trip round the world. She was fascinated by Brazil and by Lota Soares, on old acquaintance with whom she began a relationship that was to last until the latter's death in 1967. 'Questions of Travel' and 'The Armadillo' reflect this period of her life. In 1970 she was appointed poet in residence at Harvard, where she taught advanced verse writing and studies in modern poetry for her first year and, later, poets and their letters. She began to do a good many public readings of her poetry to earn a living. She continued to do public readings, punctuated by spells in hospital with asthma, alcoholism and depression. She died suddenly of a brain aneurysm on 6 October 1979.

The Fish

this poem is also prescribed for Ordinary Level exams in 2003 and 2006

I caught a tremendous fish
and held him beside the boat
half out of water, with my hook
fast in a corner of his mouth.
He didn't fight.   5
He hadn't fought at all.
He hung a grunting weight,
battered and venerable
and homely. Here and there
his brown skin hung in strips   10
like ancient wallpaper,
and its pattern of darker brown
was like wallpaper:
shapes like full-blown roses
stained and lost through age.   15
He was speckled with barnacles,
fine rosettes of lime,
and infested
with tiny white sea-lice,
and underneath two or three   20
rags of green weed hung down.
While his gills were breathing in
the terrible oxygen
—the frightening gills,
fresh and crisp with blood,   25
that can cut so badly—
I thought of the coarse white flesh
packed in like feathers,
the big bones and the little bones,
the dramatic reds and blacks   30
of his shiny entrails,
and the pink swim-bladder
like a big peony.
I looked into his eyes
which were far larger than mine   35
but shallower, and yellowed,
the irises backed and packed
with tarnished tinfoil

seen through the lenses
of old scratched isinglass.   40
They shifted a little, but not
to return my stare.
—It was more like the tipping
of an object toward the light.
I admired his sullen face,   45
the mechanism of his jaw,
and then I saw
that from his lower lip
—if you could call it a lip—
grim, wet, and weaponlike,   50
hung five old pieces of fish-line,
or four and a wire leader
with the swivel still attached,
with all their five big hooks
grown firmly in his mouth.   55
A green line, frayed at the end
where he broke it, two heavier lines,
and a fine black thread
still crimped from the strain and snap
when it broke and he got away.   60
Like medals with their ribbons
frayed and wavering,
a five-haired beard of wisdom
trailing from his aching jaw.
I stared and stared   65
and victory filled up
the little rented boat,
from the pool of bilge
where oil had spread a rainbow
around the rusted engine   70
to the bailer rusted orange,
the sun-cracked thwarts,
the oarlocks on their strings,
the gunnels—until everything
was rainbow, rainbow, rainbow!   75
And I let the fish go.

Note

[40] **isinglass:** a semi-transparent form of gelatine extracted from certain fish
and used in making jellies, glue, etc.

Explorations

First reading

1. How do you visualise the fish? Think of it as a painting or a picture. What details strike you on a first reading?
2. What is your initial impression of the speaker in this poem?

Second reading

3. Consider in detail the description of the fish. Which elements of the description could be considered objective or factual? Which elements could be seen as purely subjective on the part of the poet? Which are imagined or aesthetic elements in the description?
4. Do you think the poet's re-creation of the fish is a good one? Explain your views.

Third reading

5. Explore the attitude of the speaker toward the fish, over the entire length of the poem. What changes do you notice, and where?
6. Why do you think she released the fish? Explore the text for possible reasons.
7. Do you think this is an important moment for the poet? What does she learn or discover? Where, in the text, is this suggested?
8. Is the poet excited by this experience? Where, in the text, is this suggested? Comment on the tone of the poem.

Fourth reading

9. What issues does this poem raise? Consider what the poem has to say about:
   - our relationship with the natural world
   - the nature of creativity
   - moments of insight and decision
   - other themes hinted at.
10. Do you think the imagery is effective in getting across a real understanding of the fish and an awareness of the poet's mood? Explore any two relevant images and explain how they function.
11. This is quite a dramatic poem. Explain how the dramatic effect is created. Consider such elements as the way the narrative builds to a climax; the ending; the effect of the short enjambed lines; and the speaker's interior debate.
12. What did you like about this poem?

The Bight

(On my birthday)

At low tide like this how sheer the water is.
White, crumbling ribs of marl protrude and glare
and the boats are dry, the pilings dry as matches.
Absorbing, rather than being absorbed,
the water in the bight doesn't wet anything,   5
the color of the gas flame turned as low as possible.
One can smell it turning to gas; if one were Baudelaire
one could probably hear it turning to marimba music.
The little ocher dredge at work off the end of the dock
already plays the dry perfectly off-beat claves.   10
The birds are outsize. Pelicans crash
into this peculiar gas unnecessarily hard,
it seem to me, like pickaxes,
rarely coming up with anything to show for it,
and going off with humorous elbowings.   15
Black-and-white man-of-war birds soar
on impalpable drafts
and open their tails like scissors on the curves
or tense them like wishbones, till they tremble.
The frowsy sponge boats keep coming in   20
with the obliging air of retrievers,
bristling with jackstraw gaffs and hooks
and decorated with bobbles of sponges.
There is a fence of chicken wire along the dock
where, glinting like little plowshares,   25
the blue-gray shark tails are hung up to dry
for the Chinese-restaurant trade.
Some of the little white boats are still piled up
against each other, or lie on their sides, stove in,
and not yet salvaged, if they ever will be, from the last bad storm, 30
like torn-open, unanswered letters.
The bight is littered with old correspondences.
Click. Click. Goes the dredge,
and brings up a dripping jawful of marl.
All the untidy activity continues,   35
awful but cheerful.

Notes

Bight: recess of coast, bay

[2] **marl:** soil composed of clay and lime, sometimes used as fertiliser

[3] **pilings:** heavy beams driven into the sea-bed as support for a jetty or dock

[7] **Baudelaire:** Charles-Pierre Baudelaire (1821–67), French lyric poet, author of *Les Fleurs du Mal*

[8] **marimba:** type of xylophone used in African or South American music

[9] **ocher [ochre]:** orange-brown colour

[10] **claves [clefs?]:** symbols of musical notation; there are three clefs, C, G, and F, which, when placed on a particular line of a stave of music, show the pitch of the notes

[17] **impalpable:** not easily grasped; imperceptible to touch

[20] **frowsy:** slovenly, unkempt

 # Explorations

First reading

1. Think of the poem as a painting. Describe it as you see it laid out: background, foreground, centre, left side, right side.
2. What mood is suggested by the scene? Explain.

Second reading

3. In what ways do you think it differs from a chocolate-box painting?
4. Is the reader-viewer encouraged to view the scene in a new and fresh way? Where and how does this happen? Examine the details of the descriptions. What is unusual about them?

Third reading

5. What do you think is the impact of the subtitle, 'On my birthday'? Might it be significant that she marks her birthday in this way, viewing this scene? How might she identify with the scene? From the evidence of the text, what do you think her mood is?

Fourth reading

6. Consider the style of the versification. Concentrate on such aspects as metre, rhyme or the lack of it, the organisation of sentence or sense units, etc. What does the form of the poem contribute to its effectiveness?
7. Would you consider it accurate to suggest that the poem moves along in bursts of poetic intensity, punctuated by more prosaic reflections? Discuss.

At the Fishhouses

Although it is a cold evening,
down by one of the fishhouses
an old man sits netting,
his net, in the gloaming almost invisible,
a dark purple-brown,   5
and his shuttle worn and polished.
The air smells so strong of codfish
it makes one's nose run and one's eyes water.
The five fishhouses have steeply peaked roofs
and narrow, cleated gangplanks slant up   10
to storerooms in the gables
for the wheelbarrows to be pushed up and down on.
All is silver: the heavy surface of the sea,
swelling slowly as if considering spilling over,
is opaque, but the silver of the benches,   15
the lobster pots, and masts, scattered
among the wild jagged rocks,
is of an apparent translucence
like the small old buildings with an emerald moss
growing on their shoreward walls.   20
The big fish tubs are completely lined
with layers of beautiful herring scales
and the wheelbarrows are similarly plastered
with creamy iridescent coats of mail,
with small iridescent flies crawling on them.   25
Up on the little slope behind the houses,
set in the sparse bright sprinkle of grass,
is an ancient wooden capstan,
cracked, with two long bleached handles
and some melancholy stains, like dried blood,   30
where the ironwork has rusted.
The old man accepts a Lucky Strike.
He was a friend of my grandfather.
We talk of the decline in the population
and of codfish and herring   35
while he waits for a herring boat to come in.
There are sequins on his vest and on his thumb.

He has scraped the scales, the principal beauty,
from unnumbered fish with that black old knife,
the blade of which is almost worn away.   40

Down at the water's edge, at the place
where they haul up the boats, up the long ramp
descending into the water, thin silver
tree trunks are laid horizontally
across the gray stones, down and down   45
at intervals of four or five feet.

Cold dark deep and absolutely clear,
element bearable to no mortal,
to fish and to seals ... One seal particularly
I have seen here evening after evening.   50
He was curious about me. He was interested in music;
like me a believer in total immersion,
so I used to sing him Baptist hymns.
I also sang 'A Mighty Fortress Is Our God'.
He stood up in the water and regarded me   55
steadily, moving his head a little.
Then he would disappear, then suddenly emerge
almost in the same spot, with a sort of shrug
as if it were against his better judgment.
Cold dark deep and absolutely clear,   60
the clear gray icy water ... Back, behind us,
the dignified tall firs begin.
Bluish, associating with their shadows,
a million Christmas trees stand
waiting for Christmas. The water seems suspended   65
above the rounded gray and blue-gray stones.
I have seen it over and over, the same sea, the same,
slightly, indifferently swinging above the stones,
icily free above the stones,
above the stones and then the world.   70
If you should dip your hand in,
your wrist would ache immediately,
your bones would begin to ache and your hand would burn
as if the water were a transmutation of fire
that feeds on stones and burns with a dark gray flame.   75

If you tasted it, it would first taste bitter,
then briny, then surely burn your tongue.
It is like what we imagine knowledge to be:
dark, salt, clear, moving, utterly free,
drawn from the cold hard mouth   80
of the world, derived from the rocky breasts
forever, flowing and drawn, and since
our knowledge is historical, flowing, and flown.

'Nova Scotia Landscape', a watercolour by Elizabeth Bishop

Explorations

First reading

1. On a first reading, what do you notice about the setting of the poem? List the things that make an immediate impression on you.

2. Examine in detail what is being described in the first section. What is your impression of the atmosphere of the place?

3. What do you suppose is the writer's attitude to that scene in the first section? Does she find it repulsive, or awe-inspiring, or is she completely unaffected by it? Comment, with reference to the text.

4. What aspect of the scene draws the poet's main focus of attention during the entire poem?

Second reading

5. List all the characteristics or facets of the sea alluded to, or reflected on, by the poet throughout the poem.

6. Do you think she manages to evoke effectively the mysterious power of the sea? Comment.

Third reading

7. Bishop's poetic technique involved (a) detailed description and (b) making the familiar strange or unusual so that we see it afresh. Comment on her description of the sea, under these headings.

8. How would you assess the mood of this poem? Take into consideration both the landscape and the poet.

9. The poem is written in free verse. What does this contribute to the effect of the poem? What else do you notice about the technique of this poem?

Fourth reading

10. The poem builds to a moment of insight for the poet. Where is this, and what is the insight? Describe, in as much depth as you can, what she comes to learn from the sea.

11. Outline the main issues raised by this poem.

12. Do you find any trace of the personality or feelings of the poet in this poem? Comment.

The Prodigal

The brown enormous odor he lived by
was too close, with its breathing and thick hair,
for him to judge. The floor was rotten; the sty
was plastered halfway up with glass-smooth dung.
Light-lashed, self-righteous, above moving snouts,   5
the pigs' eyes followed him, a cheerful stare—
even to the sow that always ate her young—
till, sickening, he leaned to scratch her head.
But sometimes mornings after drinking bouts
(he hid the pints behind a two-by-four),   10
the sunrise glazed the barnyard mud with red;
the burning puddles seemed to reassure.
And then he thought he almost might endure
his exile yet another year or more.

But evenings the first star came to warn.   15
The farmer whom he worked for came at dark
to shut the cows and horses in the barn
beneath their overhanging clouds of hay,
with pitchforks, faint forked lightnings, catching light,
safe and companionable as in the Ark.   20
The pigs stuck out their little feet and snored.
The lantern—like the sun, going away—
laid on the mud a pacing aureole.
Carrying a bucket along a slimy board,
he felt the bats' uncertain staggering flight,   25
his shuddering insights, beyond his control,
touching him. But it took him a long time
finally to make his mind up to go home.

Note

[23] **aureole:** a halo of light around the sun or moon

Explorations

Before reading

1. What does the title of the poem lead you to expect?

First reading

2. Were any of your expectations met on reading the poem?
3. How do you see the character in this poem?
   - What is he doing? How does he live?
   - Why is he there?
   - Does he find any satisfaction in his work?
   - What helps him endure his exile?
4. What details of the scene affected you most?

Second reading

5. Examine the final five lines. What do you think the 'shuddering insights, beyond his control' might be? Re-create his thoughts as you imagine them here.
6. Bishop appeals to a range of senses—smell, sight, sound, touch—to re-create the atmosphere of the place. Examine a sample of each type of image and discuss the effect.
7. How would you describe the atmosphere of the place? Is it one of unrelieved misery, or is there some contentment in it? Refer to the text.
8. Examine the poet's attitude to the prodigal. Do you think she is condemnatory, sympathetic, or neutral? Discuss, with reference to the text.
9. What is your own attitude to the prodigal?

Third reading

10. What are the main human issues raised by this poem?
11. Briefly express the theme of the poem.
12. Bishop's poetic technique involved really looking at the detail of her subject matter. Where do you think this works best in 'The Prodigal'?

Questions of Travel

There are too many waterfalls here; the crowded streams
hurry too rapidly down to the sea,
and the pressure of so many clouds on the mountaintops
makes them spill over the sides in soft slow-motion,
turning to waterfalls under our very eyes.   5
—For if those streaks, those mile-long, shiny, tearstains,
aren't waterfalls yet,
in a quick age or so, as ages go here,
they probably will be.
But if the streams and clouds keep travelling, travelling,   10
the mountains look like the hulls of capsized ships,
slime-hung and barnacled.

Think of the long trip home.
Should we have stayed at home and thought of here?
Where should we be today?   15
Is it right to be watching strangers in a play
in this strangest of theatres?
What childishness is it that while there's a breath of life
in our bodies, we are determined to rush
to see the sun the other way around?   20
The tiniest green hummingbird in the world?
To stare at some inexplicable old stonework,
inexplicable and impenetrable,
at any view,
instantly seen and always, always delightful?   25
Oh, must we dream our dreams
and have them, too?
And have we room
for one more folded sunset, still quite warm?

But surely it would have been a pity   30
not to have seen the trees along this road,
really exaggerated in their beauty,
not to have seen them gesturing
like noble pantomimists, robed in pink.
—Not to have had to stop for gas and heard   35
the sad, two-noted, wooden tune

of disparate wooden clogs
carelessly clacking over
a grease-stained filling-station floor.
(In another country the clogs would all be tested.   40
Each pair there would have identical pitch.)
—A pity not to have heard
the other, less primitive music of the fat brown bird
who sings above the broken gasoline pump
in a bamboo church of Jesuit baroque: 45
three towers, five silver crosses.
—Yes, a pity not to have pondered,
blurr'dly and inconclusively,
on what connection can exist for centuries
between the crudest wooden footwear   50
and, careful and finicky,
the whittled fantasies of wooden cages.
—Never to have studied history in
the weak calligraphy of songbirds' cages.
—And never to have had to listen to rain   55
so much like politicians' speeches:
two hours of unrelenting oratory
and then a sudden golden silence
in which the traveller takes a notebook, writes:

'Is it lack of imagination that makes us come   60
to imagined places, not just stay at home?
Or could Pascal have been not entirely right
about just sitting quietly in one's room?

Continent, city, country, society:
the choice is never wide and never free.   65
And here, or there ... No. Should we have stayed at home,
wherever that may be?'

Notes

[45] **baroque:** the style of art that developed in the seventeenth century after the
Renaissance, characterised by massive, complex and ornate design

[62] **Pascal:** Blaise Pascal (1623–62), French mathematician, physicist and
philosopher, author of *Pensées*, who commented: 'I have discovered that all human
evil comes from this, man's being unable to sit still in a room.'

Explorations

First reading

1. This is a travel poem with a difference. What are the elements found here that one would normally expect of a travel poem, and what elements do you find different or unusual?

2. Follow the traveller's eye. What does she notice in particular about the geography and culture of Brazil?

3. What impression of Brazilian culture do you get? Examine the references in detail.

Second reading

4. Do you think the poet feels comfortable in this place? What is her attitude to what she sees? Do you think she is just the usual tired, grumpy traveller, or what?

5. One critic has said that Bishop is essentially a poet of the domestic, because she feels estranged in the greater world. Comment on that statement, in the light of your reading of this poem.

6. What bothers her about travel? Jot down your ideas on this.

Third reading

7. List the main issues raised in this poem.

8. What do you notice about the style in which the poem is written? Comment critically on it.

'Brazilian Landscape', a watercolour by Elizabeth Bishop

The Armadillo

For Robert Lowell

This is the time of year
when almost every night
the frail, illegal fire balloons appear.
Climbing the mountain height,

rising toward a saint   5
still honored in these parts,
the paper chambers flush and fill with light
that comes and goes, like hearts.

Once up against the sky it's hard
to tell them from the stars—   10
planets, that is—the tinted ones:
Venus going down, or Mars,

or the pale green one. With a wind,
they flare and falter, wobble and toss;
but if it's still they steer between   15
the kite sticks of the Southern Cross,

receding, dwindling, solemnly
and steadily forsaking us,
or, in the downdraft from a peak,
suddenly turning dangerous.   20

Last night another big one fell.
It splattered like an egg of fire
against the cliff behind the house.
The flame ran down. We saw the pair

of owls who nest there flying up   25
and up, their whirling black-and-white
stained bright pink underneath, until
they shrieked up out of sight.

The ancient owls' nest must have burned.
Hastily, all alone,   30

Notes

[3] **fire balloons:** St John's Day (24 June) was celebrated by releasing these fire balloons in a type of local religious worship. Air currents took them up the mountainside, where they sometimes became a hazard to houses. Bishop's partner, Lota Soares, had a sprinkler system installed on the roof to counter the danger.

[16] **Southern Cross:** a constellation of stars in the Southern Hemisphere

a glistening armadillo left the scene,
rose-flecked, head down, tail down,

and then a baby rabbit jumped out,
short-eared, to our surprise.
So soft!—a handful of intangible ash   35
with fixed, ignited eyes.

Too pretty, dreamlike mimicry!
O falling fire and piercing cry
and panic, and a weak mailed fist
clenched ignorant against the sky!   40

 # Explorations

First reading

1. Trace the sequence of events in the poem.
2. What images strike you most forcibly?
3. What is your first impression of the location in this poem? How do you imagine it?

Second reading

4. Do you think it would be correct to say that the poet is ambivalent in her attitude to the fire balloons? Discuss.
5. Trace the development of the fire imagery throughout the poem. How does the poet link it with the natural world?
6. Where do you think the poet's sympathies lie in this poem? Explain.

Third reading

7. Examine the poet's outlook on life here. What image of the local people is presented? What view of humanity in general informs this poem? Can you discern a philosophy of life behind it? Note your impressions, however tentative. Then formulate your thoughts in a more organised way.
8. Would you say the poet is uncharacteristically emotional here? Explain your views.
9. What else do you notice about the style of this poem?

Fourth reading

10. Why do you think this might be considered an important poem?

Sestina

September rain falls on the house.
In the failing light, the old grandmother
sits in the kitchen with the child
beside the Little Marvel Stove,
reading the jokes from the almanac,   5
laughing and talking to hide her tears.

She thinks that her equinoctial tears
and the rain that beats on the roof of the house
were both foretold by the almanac,
but only known to a grandmother.   10
The iron kettle sings on the stove.
She cuts some bread and says to the child,

It's time for tea now; but the child
is watching the teakettle's small hard tears
dance like mad on the hot black stove,   15
the way the rain must dance on the house.
Tidying up, the old grandmother
hangs up the clever almanac

on its string. Birdlike, the almanac
hovers half open above the child,   20
hovers above the old grandmother
and her teacup full of dark brown tears.
She shivers and says she thinks the house
feels chilly, and puts more wood in the stove.

It was to be, says the Marvel Stove.   25
I know what I know, says the almanac.
With crayons the child draws a rigid house
and a winding pathway. Then the child
puts in a man with buttons like tears
and shows it proudly to the grandmother   30

But secretly, while the grandmother
busies herself about the stove,
the little moons fall down like tears
from between the pages of the almanac

into the flower bed the child   35
has carefully placed in the front of the house.

Time to plant tears, says the almanac.
The grandmother sings to the marvellous stove
and the child draws another inscrutable house.

 # Explorations

First reading

1. What is the prevailing atmosphere in this poem? What elements chiefly contribute to this?
2. What are the recurring elements in this poem?

Second reading

3. How do you see the grandmother?
4. How do you see the child here?
5. Is the child completely unhappy? Are there any alleviating soft elements in her life?
6. What do you think is absent from the child's picture of life?

Third reading

7. Do you understand how the poem is constructed? Explain briefly.
8. Trace the progression of the tear imagery throughout the poem, from the reference to September rain in the first stanza. How do you interpret this, in the context of the statement the poet is making about her childhood?
9. Examine the references to her drawings of the house. What do they suggest to you about the child and her environment?

Fourth reading

10. What thoughts does this poem spark off about childhood and about domestic relationships?
11. Do you think Bishop has made a successful re-creation of a child's world? Examine, in particular, the actions and the diction.
12. Would you consider this to be a sentimental poem? The term 'sentimental' can be read neutrally as 'emotional thought expressed in literature' or more negatively as 'showing emotional weakness, mawkish tenderness'. Which, if either, description applies? Discuss.

First Death in Nova Scotia

In the cold, cold parlor
my mother laid out Arthur
beneath the chromographs:
Edward, Prince of Wales,
with Princess Alexandra,   5
and King George with Queen Mary.
Below them on the table
stood a stuffed loon
shot and stuffed by Uncle
Arthur, Arthur's father.   10

Since Uncle Arthur fired
a bullet into him,
he hadn't said a word.
He kept his own counsel
on his white, frozen lake,   15
the marble-topped table.
His breast was deep and white,
cold and caressable;
his eyes were red glass,
much to be desired.   20

'Come,' said my mother,
'Come and say good-bye
to your little cousin Arthur.'
I was lifted up and given
one lily of the valley   25
to put in Arthur's hand.
Arthur's coffin was
a little frosted cake,
and the red-eyed loon eyed it
from his white, frozen lake.   30

Arthur was very small.
He was all white, like a doll
that hadn't been painted yet.
Jack Frost had started to paint him

Notes

[3] **chromograph:** printed reproduction of a colour photograph

[8] **loon:** a diver, a kind of bird, noted for its clumsy gait on land

[36] **Maple Leaf:** national emblem of Canada

[42] **ermine:** white fur with black spots, from a type of stoat, used in monarchs' robes

the way he always painted   35
the Maple Leaf (Forever).
He had just begun on his hair,
a few red strokes, and then
Jack Frost had dropped the brush
and left him white, forever.   40

The gracious royal couples
were warm in red and ermine;
their feet were well wrapped up
in the ladies' ermine trains.
They invited Arthur to be   45
the smallest page at court.
But how could Arthur go,
clutching his tiny lily,
with his eyes shut up so tight
and the roads deep in snow?   50

 # Explorations

First reading

1. First decide who is speaking. Where and when was the event depicted, and what age is the speaker?
2. What do you find unusual or confusing on a first reading?
3. If we consider the speaker to be a young child, does this help you come to grips with the poem? Re-read.

Second reading

4. What is most noticeable about the scene here?
5. What is the atmosphere in the parlour?
6. How do you think the child speaker feels? Discuss.

Third reading

7. Examine the title. Why 'first death'? Discuss the many possible connotations of this.
8. Comment on the use of colour in the poem.
9. Comment on the versification.

Fourth reading

10. Do you think the poet has managed to re-create successfully the young child's experience?
11. Contrast this poem with Séamus Heaney's 'Mid-Term Break'.
12. What did you learn about Elizabeth Bishop from a reading of this poem?

Filling Station

this poem is also prescribed for Ordinary Level exams in 2003 and 2006

Oh, but it is dirty!
—this little filling station,
oil-soaked, oil-permeated
to a disturbing, over-all
black translucency.   5
Be careful with that match!

Father wears a dirty,
oil-soaked monkey suit
that cuts him under the arms,
and several quick and saucy   10
and greasy sons assist him
(it's a family filling station),
all quite thoroughly dirty.

Do they live in the station?
It has a cement porch   15
behind the pumps, and on it
a set of crushed and grease-
impregnated wickerwork;
on the wicker sofa
a dirty dog, quite comfy.   20

Some comic books provide
the only note of color—
of certain color. They lie
upon a big dim doily
draping a taboret   25
(part of the set), beside
a big hirsute begonia.

Why the extraneous plant?
Why the taboret?
Why, oh why, the doily?   30
(Embroidered in daisy stitch
with marguerites, I think,
and heavy with gray crochet.)

Somebody embroidered the doily.

Notes

[24] **doily:** small ornamental table-napkin

[25] **taboret:** a type of stool

[32] **marguerites:** daisies

Somebody waters the plant,   35
or oils it, maybe. Somebody
arranges the rows of cans
so that they softly say:
ESSO—SO—SO—SO
to high-strung automobiles.   40
Somebody loves us all.

 # Explorations

Before reading

1. Think about the title. What do you see?

First reading

2. Describe the atmosphere this poem creates for you. What details appear to you to be significant in creating this? Discuss them.

Second reading

3. Plan the shots you would use if you were making a film of this scene. Describe what you see in each shot, and explain your choice of detail.

4. Is there any progression, development of complexity etc. in this film? How do you understand it?

5. What do the doily, the taboret and the begonia add to the atmosphere?

Third reading

6. What is it about this scene that fascinates the poet: the forecourt, the domestic details, or something else? Discuss.

7. How do you understand the 'somebody' in stanza 6?

Fourth reading

8. Do you think the poet is discovering a truth, and making a statement about life? If so, what? Discuss this.

9. Write up your own notes on the theme of the poem, the poet's philosophy of life, her poetic method, and the style and tone of the poem.

10. 'The details of Bishop's poems are always compelling but never the whole point.' Discuss, with reference to the text.

11. 'This is a poem that manages to create poignancy and wit simultaneously.' Discuss.

In the Waiting Room

In Worcester, Massachusetts,
I went with Aunt Consuelo
to keep her dentist's appointment
and sat and waited for her
in the dentist's waiting room.   5
It was winter. It got dark
early. The waiting room
was full of grown-up people,
arctics and overcoats,
lamps and magazines.   10
My aunt was inside
what seemed like a long time
and while I waited I read
the *National Geographic*
(I could read) and carefully   15
studied the photographs:
the inside of a volcano,
black, and full of ashes;
then it was spilling over
in rivulets of fire.   20
Osa and Martin Johnson
dressed in riding breeches,
laced boots, and pith helmets.
A dead man slung on a pole
—'Long Pig', the caption said.   25
Babies with pointed heads
wound round and round with string;
black, naked women with necks
wound round and round with wire
like the necks of light bulbs.   30
Their breasts were horrifying.
I read it right straight through.
I was too shy to stop.
And then I looked at the cover:
the yellow margins, the date.   35

Suddenly, from inside,
came an *oh!* of pain
—Aunt Consuelo's voice—

Note

[21] **Osa and Martin Johnson:** American photographers and explorers; Bishop first saw the Johnsons' jungle film *Baboons* in the winter of 1935

not very loud or long.
I wasn't at all surprised;   40
even then I knew she was
a foolish, timid woman.
I might have been embarrassed,
but wasn't. What took me
completely by surprise   45
was that it was *me*:
my voice, in my mouth.
Without thinking at all
I was my foolish aunt,
I—we—were falling, falling,   50
our eyes glued to the cover
of the *National Geographic*,
February, 1918.

I said to myself: three days
and you'll be seven years old.   55
I was saying it to stop
the sensation of falling off
the round, turning world
into cold, blue-black space.
But I felt: you are an I,   60
you are an *Elizabeth*,
you are one of *them*.
Why should you be one, too?
I scarcely dared to look
to see what it was I was.   65
I gave a sidelong glance
—I couldn't look any higher—
at shadowy gray knees,
trousers and skirts and boots
and different pairs of hands   70
lying under the lamps.
I knew that nothing stranger
had ever happened, that nothing
stranger could ever happen.
Why should I be my aunt,   75
or me, or anyone?
What similarities—
boots, hands, the family voice

I felt in my throat, or even
the *National Geographic*   80
and those awful hanging breasts—
held us all together
or made us all just one?
How—I didn't know any
word for it—how 'unlikely' ...   85
How had I come to be here,
like them, and overhear
a cry of pain that could have
got loud and worse but hadn't?

The waiting room was bright   90
and too hot. It was sliding
beneath a big black wave,
another, and another.

Then I was back in it.
The War was on. Outside,   95
in Worcester, Massachusetts,
were night and slush and cold,
and it was still the fifth
of February, 1918.

Date of the poem

It was probably written about 1970 and was published in the *New Yorker* on 17 July 1971. It is the opening poem of her collection *Geography III*, published in 1976.

Explorations

Before reading

1. What might you expect from this title?
2. Do you remember what it was like as a child to sit in a dentist's waiting-room? Re-create such an experience. Make brief notes for yourself.

First reading

3. In the poem, what elements of the waiting-room experience are all too familiar to you?
4. Who is the speaker in this poem? Assemble as much information, factual and impressionistic, as you can.

Second reading

5. After the familiar, what is encountered by the child?
6. Which event most unnerves her? Can you suggest why she is unnerved?
7. What is the child's reaction to this experience?

Third reading

8. What is your understanding of the experience described in this poem? Comment briefly.
9. What view of woman does Bishop project in this poem?

10. Comment on the experience of childhood reflected here.

Fourth reading

11. What themes or issues are raised by this poem? Explain how the poet deals with some of the following:
   - a child's realisation of selfhood
   - the poet's uncomfortable connection with the rest of humanity
   - the variety and strangeness of the world of which one is a part
   - that we are always at risk of being ambushed by the unfamiliar, even in the security of the domestic
   - that the chief lessons of childhood are learning to deal with pain and mortality, and accepting unity in spite of difference
   - any others?
12. What is your own reaction to this poem? Structure your thoughts in the form of questions.
13. Comment on the structure of the poem (five sections) and the type of verse used.

11 Sylvia PLATH

prescribed for Higher Level exams in 2003, 2004 and 2006

Sylvia Plath was born in Boston, Massachusetts on 27 October 1932, to Aurelia Schober Plath and Otto Plath, professor of Biology and German at Boston University. In 1940 Otto died after a long illness, a tragedy which haunted Sylvia throughout her life. From a young age, Sylvia wanted above all else to be a writer. Already writing at the age of five, she had her first poem published in the children's section of the *Boston Herald* at the age of eight. She was a brilliant High School student, consistently earning A grades and also led a busy social life. She had a number of stories and poems published—and also got many rejection slips; this pattern recurred throughout her writing life. In 1950 she entered the prestigious Women's University, Smith College, Massachusetts.

In 1952 Plath was selected to work as one of twenty 'guest editors' with *Mademoiselle* magazine in New York City. On her return to Wellesley, she suffered a serious bout of depression for which she was given electric shock treatment. However, this seems to have deepened her depression and she attempted suicide in August, leading to a four-month spell in a psychiatric hospital. She resumed

1932–1963

her studies in Smith College in January 1953, graduating with honours in 1955, and winning a Fulbright scholarship to study in Cambridge, England. There she met Ted Hughes, a young English poet, whom she married in June 1956.

Sylvia and Ted worked and wrote in the US for two years and returned to London in December 1959. 'Black Rook in Rainy Weather' and 'The Times Are Tidy' date from this period. Her first book, *The Colossus and Other Poems*, was published in February 1960, but received disappointing reviews. April 1960 saw the birth of their daughter, Frieda. The following year they moved to Devon where their son, Nicholas, was born in January 1962. Throughout this time, Sylvia was writing poetry, (including 'Morning Song', 'Finisterre', 'Mirror', 'Pheasant' and 'Elm') some of which was published in magazines in Britain and the US. Her semi-autobiographical novel, *The Bell Jar,* was published in 1963.

Shortly after Nicholas's birth, Ted and Sylvia separated. She remained in Devon, caring for her children and writing, despite poor

Sylvia Plath

health and recurring depression. She completed most of the poems which made up her second book, *Ariel* (published posthumously), among them 'Poppies in July' and 'The Arrival of the Bee Box'. In mid-December 1962, she moved to London with her children. The poems she wrote at this time include 'Child', written on 28 January 1963. However, unable to cope with the many difficulties facing her, she took her own life on 11 February 1963. Since her death, her writing has received wide acclaim, including the prestigious Pulitzer Prize, an award rarely bestowed posthumously.

Black Rook in Rainy Weather

On the stiff twig up there
Hunches a wet black rook
Arranging and rearranging its feathers in the rain.
I do not expect a miracle
Or an accident   5

To set the sight on fire
In my eye, nor seek
Any more in the desultory weather some design,
But let spotted leaves fall as they fall,
Without ceremony, or portent.   10

Although, I admit, I desire,
Occasionally, some backtalk
From the mute sky, I can't honestly complain:
A certain minor light may still
Lean incandescent   15

Out of kitchen table or chair
As if a celestial burning took
Possession of the most obtuse objects now and then—
Thus hallowing an interval
Otherwise inconsequent   20

By bestowing largesse, honour,
One might say love. At any rate, I now walk
Wary (for it could happen
Even in this dull, ruinous landscape); sceptical,
Yet politic; ignorant   25

Of whatever angel may choose to flare
Suddenly at my elbow. I only know that a rook
Ordering its black feathers can so shine
As to seize my senses, haul
My eyelids up, and grant   30

A brief respite from fear
Of total neutrality. With luck,
Trekking stubborn through this season
Of fatigue, I shall
Patch together a content   35

Of sorts. Miracles occur,
If you care to call those spasmodic
Tricks of radiance miracles. The wait's begun again
The long wait for the angel,
For that rare, random descent.   40

Notes

[2] **rook:** crow

[8] **desultory:** without method, disjointed

[10] **portent:** omen of some possibly calamitous event

[15] **incandescent:** glowing, brilliant

[19] **hallowing:** making sacred

[21] **largesse:** generously given present

[25] **politic:** prudent

[31] **respite:** brief period of relief

Explorations

Before reading

1. What picture does the title create for you? Does it suggest a particular mood?

First reading

2. The poem is set against a very definite landscape: read the poem and describe the scene as accurately as you can. Build your picture from the poet's words and phrases.

3. What does the narrator seem to be doing in this poem? What thoughts does this lead to?

4. Describe the atmosphere the poem creates for you. What details are most important in setting this atmosphere?

Second reading

5. There is an abrupt change between lines 3 and 4. What is it?

6. The narrator claims that 'I do not expect ... nor seek ...'. What does she neither expect nor seek? (Lines 4–10.)

7. What does she 'admit' to desiring? How does she convey the idea that it may not be possible to get what she desires?

8. Can you find other places in the poem where she makes a statement, and then qualifies it—'neutralises' it? What do

such statements tell us about the narrator's frame of mind?

9. The 'minor light' of line 14 'may' have an extraordinary effect: read lines 14–22 carefully and explain this effect in your own words.

10. Can you explain how the 'rook | Ordering its black feathers can ... grant | A brief respite' to the speaker? A brief respite from what?

11. In the final lines, she is waiting for the 'rare, random descent' of the angel. What might the angel bring? What examples of this has she already given?

12. The angel's 'rare, random descent' is a metaphor: what do you think it represents? Look at references to other heavenly phenomena before answering.

Third reading

13. Comment on the effect of the repetition of the sound 'rain' in line 3.

14. Look through the poem again, and pick out words connected with darkness and light. Compare the images or words used. Can you find any pattern?

15. The narrator does not 'seek ... design' in things around her. How does the language reflect that lack of design, the

accidental nature of what happens? A good starting point might be to identify the words associated with time or chance.

16. There is a mixture of the everyday/earthly and the extraordinary/miraculous here. How is this effect achieved? You might find it helpful to contrast concrete descriptions with references to the sacred.

Fourth reading

17. Examine the rhyme scheme. What pattern do you find? What is the effect of this careful sound pattern?

18. Write a note on the style of the poem, looking at tone, language, imagery, structure.

19. Throughout her life, Plath was preoccupied with the conflict between her ambitions to be a poet and the expectations of a society which defined women as home-makers. Re-read this poem with this in mind. Would you agree that this could be one theme of the poem? Are there other possibilities? Write about what you consider to be the main themes of this poem.

The Times Are Tidy

Unlucky the hero born
In this province of the stuck record
Where the most watchful cooks go jobless
And the mayor's rôtisserie turns
Round of its own accord.   5

There's no career in the venture
Of riding against the lizard,
Himself withered these latter-days
To leaf-size from lack of action:
History's beaten the hazard.   10

The last crone got burnt up
More than eight decades back
With the love-hot herb, the talking cat,
But the children are better for it
The cow milks cream an inch thick.   15

Notes

[4] **rôtisserie:** A rotating spit, traditionally used to roast whole animals.
Often a communal service used by peasants who would not own an oven
or a spit.

[11] **crone:** witch

Explorations

Before reading

1. Think back to folk-tales or legends you have read or heard involving knights in armour, witches and monsters. What can you remember about their world, the adventures described?

2. Jot down whatever comes into your mind when you hear the word 'tidy'.

First reading

3. The poem puts two eras side by side. What can you learn from the poem about each of them?

4. Which era sounds more appealing to you? Why? Which does the author seem to favour? Refer to the poem to support your impression.

Second reading

5. Try to mentally recapture the effect of listening to a stuck record. What do you think the poet is telling you about 'this province' when she uses this image? Do you think this links in any way with 'tidy'?

6. The poem was written about a particular phase in American political life. Suggest then what the 'mayor's rôtisserie' might represent? Who might the 'cooks' be?

7. We are told that the jobless cooks are the 'most watchful': why then are they jobless? By choice? Because they have been sacked?

8. What mythical creature does the lizard resemble? Think of medieval knights and the creatures they did battle with. What is there in this stanza to show that the poet intends this connection to be made?

9. In what way has 'history' beaten the hazard?

10. What association exists between the crone and the 'love-hot herb', the 'talking cat' and the 'cream an inch thick'?

11. What do the crone, the hero and the lizard have in common? How does their absence affect the 'times'?

12. Most of the poem focuses on what this age has lost: the last two lines suggest a gain. What is this? Do you think the poet is being serious here, or is she being ironic? Explain your answer.

Third reading

13. Two eras are contrasted in the poem. How do they differ? Be precise—refer to the text for each point you make.

14. Choose the image(s) you consider to be most effective. Explain your choice.

15. Keeping in mind the title, the images used and the comparisons made, write a note on the tone of the poem.

General question

16. 'This poem is an ironic commentary on an era of smug, self-satisfied complacency in American life.' Discuss this statement, referring to imagery, language and tone.

Morning Song

Love set you going like a fat gold watch.
The midwife slapped your footsoles, and your bald cry
Took its place among the elements.

Our voices echo, magnifying your arrival. New statue.
In a drafty museum, your nakedness   5
Shadows our safety. We stand round blankly as walls.

I'm no more your mother
Than the cloud that distils a mirror to reflect its own slow
Effacement at the wind's hand.

All night your moth-breath   10
Flickers among the flat pink roses. I wake to listen:
A far sea moves in my ear.

One cry, and I stumble from bed, cow-heavy and floral
In my Victorian nightgown.
Your mouth opens clean as a cat's. The window square   15

Whitens and swallows its dull stars. And now you try
Your handful of notes;
The clear vowels rise like balloons.

Explorations

Before reading

1. Look at the title of this poem: jot down the ideas you associate with both words. What mood do they evoke?

First reading

2. Stanzas 1–3 centre on the infant taking her place in the world: how do others respond to her? Which emotions come across most clearly?

3. How do you understand the image of the baby as a 'New statue' taking its place in a 'drafty museum'? How does nakedness 'shadow' the safety of the onlookers? (There are a number of possibilities.)

4. Explain in your own words what happens in stanzas 4–6. Do you find the description realistic?

Second reading

5. What emotions does the opening line suggest to you? Look at the first word, the image, the rhythm. Do you think it is an effective opening line? Why?

6. Identify the noises named in the poem. Name the source of each sound. Who is listening to them? What impression do they create? How do they contribute to the texture of the poem?

Third reading

7. This poem is rich in vivid imagery and word-pictures. Identify these.

8. Say what each image or word-picture suggests about the baby, about the mother, about the world they inhabit. How is this suggested? Refer to the language, the juxtaposition of images, the associations implied.

9. Explain the cloud/mirror/wind image used in stanza 3. What does the comparison suggest about the narrator's feelings about motherhood?

General questions

10. 'Morning Song' is a tender evocation of a simple, daily event. Examine how the writer conveys the mood of tenderness, while avoiding sentimentality.

11. Compare this poem with 'Child' in terms of theme, tone, language and imagery. Which of the two poems do you prefer? Why?

Finisterre

This was the land's end: the last fingers, knuckled and rheumatic,
Cramped on nothing. Black
Admonitory cliffs, and the sea exploding
With no bottom, or anything on the other side of it,
Whitened by the faces of the drowned.   5
Now it is only gloomy, a dump of rocks—
Leftover soldiers from old, messy wars.
The sea cannons into their ear, but they don't budge.
Other rocks hide their grudges under the water.

The cliffs are edged with trefoils, stars and bells   10
Such as fingers might embroider, close to death,
Almost too small for the mists to bother with.
The mists are part of the ancient paraphernalia—
Souls, rolled in the doom-noise of the sea.
They bruise the rocks out of existence, then resurrect them.   15
They go up without hope, like sighs.
I walk among them, and they stuff my mouth with cotton.
When they free me, I am beaded with tears.

Our Lady of the Shipwrecked is striding toward the horizon,
Her marble skirts blown back in two pink wings.   20
A marble sailor kneels at her foot distractedly, and at his foot
A peasant woman in black
Is praying to the monument of the sailor praying.
Our Lady of the Shipwrecked is three times life size,
Her lips sweet with divinity.   25
She does not hear what the sailor or the peasant is saying—
She is in love with the beautiful formlessness of the sea.

Gull-colored laces flap in the sea drafts
Beside the postcard stalls.
The peasants anchor them with conches. One is told: 30
'These are the pretty trinkets the sea hides,
Little shells made up into necklaces and toy ladies.
They do not come from the Bay of the Dead down there,
But from another place, tropical and blue,
We have never been to.   35
These are our crêpes. Eat them before they blow cold.'

Finisterre: the westernmost tip of Brittany—literally 'land's end'

[3] **Admonitory:** giving a warning

[10] **trefoils:** three-leaved plants

[13] **paraphernalia:** belongings, bits and pieces, ornaments

[14] **doom:** judgement, punishment

[30] **conches:** spiral shells

[36] **crêpes:** light, lacy, crispy pancakes—specialty of Brittany

 # Explorations

Before reading

1. What kind of landscape/ seascape do the place names 'Finisterre' and 'land's end' suggest? How do you visualize it—colours, shapes, sounds, weather…?

First reading

Stanza 1

2. Read stanza 1. What overall picture do you form of the scene? What words or images do you find most striking? Is the personification effective?

3. How is language used to create the impression of an attack, a battle? Does this description of a headland create a familiar picture for you?

Stanza 2

4. What does stanza 2 describe? How does it connect with stanza 1? Notice how language and imagery are used to create links.

5. What qualities do you usually associate with mist? Which of these qualities does this mist share? What other qualities does the narrator attribute to it? Do these add anything new?

6. What is your impression of the atmosphere in this place? How is it created?

Second reading

Stanza 3

7. Describe in your own words the scene depicted in stanza 3. What connection is there with the first two stanzas?

8. The perspective in this stanza has changed: the poet is showing us things from a different angle. How is this indicated?

9. This stanza tells a little story within the poem. Tell it in your own words.

Stanza 4

10. The stalls in stanza 4 are suggested through a few precise details: look at the description—can you picture them?

11. This stanza differs remarkably from the preceding stanzas. In what way?

12. Identify the ideas/words/images which link stanza 4 with the earlier stanzas. Explain the connection.

13. We now learn that the bay is named the 'Bay of the Dead': does the name fit, in your opinion? Why do you think the poet did not name it until the end of the poem?

Third reading

14. Comment on the effect of the image in the lines 1 and 2. How is this image developed in the rest of this stanza and in stanza 2?

15. Stanza 3 opens with a description of the monument. Contrast the 'I' of stanza 2 with Our Lady of the Shipwrecked. What is the impact of the contrast? What is the narrator's attitude to Our Lady?

16. Comment on the language used to describe the scene—the details given, the intentions or qualities attributed to each figure. Where does the narrator fit into this scene? What does she seem to be saying about prayer?

17. The author broadens the scope of the poem through the stall-keeper's comments, which reflect quite a different response to the bay. How? What is the effect of the wider canvas?

18. How does the final line strike you? Would you agree that there is a slightly ironic note here? What effect does this have on your reading of the poem?

General questions

19. Write a note on the tone of the poem. Be aware of the gradual change in tone, reflected in the language and imagery; note the differences between the narrator's attitude, and that of the other figures in the poem.

20. Trace the progress of thought from the opening line to the end of the poem. Focus on how the author moves from the inner thoughts of the narrator to a more objective view. Note where the changes occur.

21. Plath once commented: '…a poem, by its own system of illusions, can set up a rich and apparently living world within its particular limits.' Write about 'Finisterre' in the light of this comment, looking at her choice of words, images, sound effects and point of view.

Coastal landscape of Finisterre

Mirror

I am silver and exact. I have no preconceptions.
Whatever I see I swallow immediately
Just as it is, unmisted by love or dislike.
I am not cruel, only truthful—
The eye of a little god, four-cornered.   5
Most of the time I meditate on the opposite wall.
It is pink, with speckles. I have looked at it so long
I think it is a part of my heart. But it flickers.
Faces and darkness separate us over and over.

Now I am a lake. A woman bends over me,   10
Searching my reaches for what she really is.
Then she turns to those liars, the candles or the moon.
I see her back, and reflect it faithfully.
She rewards me with tears and an agitation of hands.
I am important to her. She comes and goes.   15
Each morning it is her face that replaces the darkness.
In me she has drowned a young girl, and in me an old woman
Rises toward her day after day, like a terrible fish.

Note

[11] **reaches:** stretch of water, depths

Explorations

Before reading

1. Think for a minute about a mirror. Write down quickly all the words, ideas and associations that come to mind.

First reading

2. Listen to this poem a number of times. What is it saying?

3. Write a note on the form of the poem: number of stanzas, number of lines etc.

4. Pick out all the 'I' statements. How many are there? What effect do they have?

5. Identify the qualities the mirror claims to possess. What overall impression is created by these attributes?

6. Notice the position of the words 'a little god': they are at the exact centre of stanza 1. Can you suggest why the poet placed them just there?

7. What impression is created by the description of 'the opposite wall'?

8. In stanza 2, the mirror states that it is now 'a lake': what similarities are there between a lake and a mirror? What differences are there? How does this new image expand the mirror image?

9. Why do you think the narrator describes the candles and the moon as 'liars'?

10. What might cause the woman's tears and agitation? How does this point broaden the scope of the poem?

11. The mirror/lake contains three phases of the woman's life: what are these?

Second reading

12. The focus—the point of view—changes between stanzas 1 and 2. How has the centre of consciousness changed? What is the effect of this?

13. Write a note about what you think the 'terrible fish' may be.

14. 'I am important to her': this is a very strong statement. How could a mirror be important to her? What do you think the mirror may represent to the narrator? (Try to move beyond the most obvious points.)

Third reading

15. Compare the opening lines (1–3) with the final lines. Trace the progress of thought through the poem, showing how the narrator moves from the opening statement to the conclusion. Note the changes in tone which occur.

16. The poem concludes on a note of desperation. How is this prepared for in the poem as a whole?

17. Do you agree that the narrator

has 'no preconceptions' as stated in line 1? What evidence can you find to support your opinion? Look especially at phrases like 'I think', 'those liars' etc.

18. While the poem is unrhymed, Plath uses a variety of sound effects. Identify some of these, and say what effect they create.

General questions

19. Many writers and artists use the mirror as a symbol—for example, of the self, the alter ego, the 'dark side of the soul'. Re-read the poem with this idea in mind. How does it colour your reading of the poem? Does it fit the poem?

20. It has been argued that in this poem Plath is addressing the conflict between what a woman was expected to be (smooth, unruffled, reflecting the image the world wanted to see), and her true nature struggling to be heard, seen for what it is (the 'terrible fish'). Re-read the poem in the light of this comment, and write your response.

Pheasant

You said you would kill it this morning.
Do not kill it. It startles me still,
The jut of that odd, dark head, pacing

Through the uncut grass on the elm's hill.
It is something to own a pheasant,   5
Or just to be visited at all.

I am not mystical: it isn't
As if I thought it had a spirit.
It is simply in its element.

That gives it a kingliness, a right.   10
The print of its big foot last winter,
The tail-track, on the snow in our court—

The wonder of it, in that pallor,
Through crosshatch of sparrow and starling.
Is it its rareness, then? It is rare.   15

But a dozen would be worth having,
A hundred, on that hill—green and red,
Crossing and recrossing: a fine thing!

It is such a good shape, so vivid.
It's a little cornucopia.   20
It unclaps, brown as a leaf, and loud,

Settles in the elm, and is easy.
It was sunning in the narcissi.
I trespass stupidly. Let be, let be.

Notes   [14] **crosshatch:** criss-cross pattern

          [20] **cornucopia:** A mythical horn, always full of flowers and
               fruit. A symbol of plenty.

 # Explorations

First reading

1. The poem opens very abruptly: it plunges the reader right into the narrator's preoccupation. What is this? Why do you think she repeats the word 'kill'?

2. Lines 3 and 4 present a graphic picture. What scene is evoked?

3. The speaker's attitude toward the pheasant is clearly signalled in lines 5 and 6. What is it? Can you find any further echo of this feeling in the poem?

4. In stanzas 4 and 5 the poet pictures the pheasant: how does she underline its difference to the other birds that visit her yard?

5. Stanza 7 moves back to the present: the pheasant's 'clap' draws her attention. What was it doing before it flew up into the elm?

6. She loves the colour, the shape, the sound of the pheasant. Identify where each of these is praised.

Second reading

7. In verse 3 the narrator explains why she feels so honoured by the visit of the pheasant: identify what 'it is' and what 'it isn't' that touches her. Why do you think she tells us that she is 'not mystical'?

8. In what sense is she trespassing? What does this

word suggest about her attitude to the pheasant?

9. How do the final words link back to the opening statement and request? Do you feel the narrator has got her way at the end? Explain.

10. What is the tone/mood of the poem? Use the text to support your points, paying attention to the narrator's relationship with 'you'.

General question

11. Plath describes the pheasant as 'vivid'. The same word could apply to this poem: it is strong, vigorous and sinewy. Write about this quality of the poem. Look at language—verbs, nouns, adjectives—as well as imagery, structure, rhythm and rhyme.

Elm

For Ruth Fainlight

I know the bottom, she says. I know it with my great tap root:
It is what you fear.
I do not fear it: I have been there.

Is it the sea you hear in me,
Its dissatisfactions?   5
Or the voice of nothing, that was your madness?

Love is a shadow.
How you lie and cry after it
Listen: these are its hooves: it has gone off, like a horse.

All night I shall gallop thus, impetuously,   10
Till your head is a stone, your pillow a little turf,
Echoing, echoing.

Or shall I bring you the sound of poisons?
This is rain now, this big hush.
And this is the fruit of it: tin-white, like arsenic.   15

I have suffered the atrocity of sunsets.
Scorched to the root
My red filaments burn and stand, a hand of wires.

Now I break up in pieces that fly about like clubs
A wind of such violence   20
Will tolerate no bystanding: I must shriek.

The moon, also, is merciless: she would drag me
Cruelly, being barren.
Her radiance scathes me. Or perhaps I have caught her.

I let her go. I let her go   25
Diminished and flat, as after radical surgery.
How your bad dreams possess and endow me.

I am inhabited by a cry.
Nightly it flaps out
Looking, with its hooks, for something to love.   30

I am terrified by this dark thing
That sleeps in me;
All day I feel its soft, feathery turnings, its malignity.

Clouds pass and disperse.
Are those the faces of love, those pale irretrievables?   35
Is it for such I agitate my heart?

I am incapable of more knowledge.
What is this, this face
So murderous in its strangle of branches?—

Its snaky acids hiss.   40
It petrifies the will. These are the isolate, slow faults
That kill, that kill, that kill.

Notes

[15] **arsenic:** lethal poison

[18] **filaments:** thread-like conductors of electrical current

[24] **scathe:** to hurt or injure, especially by scorching

[35] **irretrievables:** cannot be recovered or won back

Explorations

First reading

1. Listen to the poem a number of times. What sounds are most striking? Which words stay in your mind? Jot down your impressions.
2. What attitude does 'I' seem to adopt toward 'you' in stanza 3?
3. Stanzas 5–8 introduce rain, sunset, wind and moon: how is each one presented? How do they affect 'I'?
4. What change seems to occur in 'I' in stanzas 9–14? Can you identify at what point the change began?
5. Would you agree that the latter half of the poem powerfully conveys a nightmare world? Which images and phrases are most effective in building this impression?

Second reading

6. 'Elm' opens on a confident, objective note, as if the narrator is quite detached from 'you'. How is this achieved?
7. Trace the references to love in the poem. How does the narrator view love? Is it important to her?
8. There are several references to violence, both physical and mental. Select those you consider most powerful. What is the source of the violence?
9. Compare the force of love with the force of evil. Which comes across as the more powerful? Explain how this is achieved.

Third reading

10. Plath uses many rich and powerful images. The central image is the elm, the 'I' persona. (*a*) Trace the elm's feelings, mood through the poem. (*b*) What do you think the elm may symbolise to the poet? In answering this, reflect on the tone, the utter weariness, the feelings of anguish, the growing terror and the role 'you' plays in generating these feelings.
11. The moon is another important image in the poem. Re-read the stanzas describing it (8, 9, 13). What qualities are attributed to it? What do you think it symbolises? Can you explain the seeming contradictions?

Fourth reading

12. The poet uses rich sound effects throughout the poem. Note where she uses rhyme, assonance, repetition, cacophony and soft sounds. How do these affect the reader/listener?

13. The poem opens with a calm
    confident voice, a sense of
    control: 'I know... | I do not
    fear...'. It closes on a note of
    hysterical despair, total loss of
    control: 'It petrifies the will.
    These are the isolate, slow
    faults | That kill, that kill, that
    kill.' Trace the change through
    the poem. Describe how this
    transformation is achieved.

General questions

14. 'Plath infuses this poem with a
    strong sense of vulnerability
    pitted against destructive
    energy.' What is your response
    to this statement? Use detailed
    reference to the poem in
    support of each point you
    make.

15. ' 'Elm' is a powerful urgent
    statement spoken by a narrator
    who has been abandoned by
    the person she loves.' Discuss
    this view of the poem.

16. 'This poem has the surreal
    quality of a nightmare in
    which the smallest objects
    seem fraught with hidden
    significance.' Discuss how this
    effect is achieved, basing each
    point you make on specific
    reference to the poem.

Poppies in July

Little poppies, little hell flames,
Do you do no harm?

You flicker. I cannot touch you.
I put my hands among the flames. Nothing burns.

And it exhausts me to watch you   5
Flickering like that, wrinkly and clear red, like the skin of a mouth.

A mouth just bloodied.
Little bloody skirts!

There are fumes that I cannot touch.
Where are your opiates, your nauseous capsules?   10

If I could bleed, or sleep!—
If my mouth could marry a hurt like that!

Or your liquors seep to me, in this glass capsule,
Dulling and stilling.

But colorless. Colorless.   15

Notes   [10] **opiates:** narcotics, drugs which induce sleep, dull feelings
            [10] **nauseous:** causing vomiting or illness

 # Explorations

Before reading

1. Imagine a poppy: what
    qualities do you associate with
    it? Think of colour, texture
    and shape.

First reading

2. The poem opens with a
    question. What does it suggest
    to you?
3. Describe what the narrator is
    doing in this poem. What

thoughts are triggered by her actions?

4. Identify the words associated with fire in lines 1–6. What is the narrator's feeling about this fire/these poppies? What does fire symbolize? Do you see any of these qualities reflected here?

5. Which qualities of the poppies might make the narrator think of a mouth?

6. What could 'bloody' a mouth? Do any of the other words suggest violence?

7. Lines 9–13 focus on another aspect of poppies: what is this?

8. Looking at the various descriptions of the poppies, try to explain the author's attitude to them.

Second reading

9. What feelings does the narrator convey in this poem? Say how each feeling is suggested, referring to specific words and images.

10. There is a strong contrast between lines 1–8 and lines 9–15. How is this effected? Look at how words, images and tone contribute to the contrast.

11. The narrator seems to imply an answer to the question posed in stanza 1. How does she answer it?

Third reading

12. While there is no end rhyme in this poem, the poet uses quite intricate sound effects, including repetition. Trace these, noting the effect they have.

13. Write a paragraph about the poet's use of colour in the poem, noting how she moves from the vividness of the early stanzas to the final repeated 'colorless'. What might the loss of colour say about the narrator's feelings?

14. The poem moves from the outside world to the inner world of the narrator. Chart this movement through the poem. How does she connect one to the other?

Fourth reading

15. Do you consider the intensity of the feeling conveyed is consistent with a simple description of poppies? What underlying emotion do you think might cause such intense anguish? Discuss this point, referring to the text in support of your arguments.

16. In both 'Poppies in July' and 'Elm', Plath takes a simple natural object and invests it with intense feelings, creating a metaphor for personal suffering—the inner struggle to come to terms with an overwhelming problem. Write a comparison of the two poems.

The Arrival of the Bee Box

this poem is also prescribed for Ordinary Level exams in 2003, 2004 and 2006

I ordered this, this clean wood box
Square as a chair and almost too heavy to lift.
I would say it was the coffin of a midget
Or a square baby
Were there not such a din in it.   5

The box is locked, it is dangerous.
I have to live with it overnight
And I can't keep away from it.
There are no windows, so I can't see what is in there.
There is only a little grid, no exit.   10

I put my eye to the grid.
It is dark, dark,
With the swarmy feeling of African hands
Minute and shrunk for export,
Black on black, angrily clambering.   15

How can I let them out?
It is the noise that appals me most of all,
The unintelligible syllables.
It is like a Roman mob,
Small, taken one by one, but my god, together!   20

I lay my ear to furious Latin.
I am not a Caesar.
I have simply ordered a box of maniacs.
They can be sent back.
They can die, I need feed them nothing, I am the owner.   25

I wonder how hungry they are.
I wonder if they would forget me
If I just undid the locks and stood back and turned into a tree.
There is the laburnum, its blond colonnades,
And the petticoats of the cherry.   30

They might ignore me immediately
In my moon suit and funeral veil.
I am no source of honey

So why should they turn on me?
Tomorrow I will be sweet God, I will set them free.   35

The box is only temporary.

Explorations

First reading

1. Stanza 1 gives the background to the arrival of the bee box and the narrator's reaction. Which feeling is most obvious? Have you ever felt this way about bees, wasps…?

2. How does she seem to relate to the bees in stanzas 3–5?

3. Stanza 5 concludes with the statement 'They can die'. Do you actually believe she means this? How does she undermine her statement? Be precise.

4. How does she propose to escape the bees' wrath if she releases them?

5. She describes her clothing as a 'moon suit': what ideas does this image suggest?

6. Comment on the contradiction between 'I am no source of honey' and 'I will be sweet God'. Note the play on words—what is the tone of these lines? How can she be 'sweet God' to the bees?

7. What happens in this poem? What part does the 'I' of the poem play in the event?

Second reading

8. The language used to describe the bee box is strong, suggesting something sinister and dangerous. Select the words or images that help to create this impression.

9. There is a contradiction between the image of a coffin and the intense life within the box. Which idea—death or life—is implied with more strength in the rest of the poem? Be precise.

10. In stanza 3, the writer creates a graphic metaphor for the bees

and their sound. Identify these and note the common link between them. What do they tell us about the narrator?

11. In stanzas 4 and 5, the bees have become a metaphor for the narrator's words. Explain the image, trying to convey some of the feeling she captures. What relationship is suggested between the narrator and her words in these two stanzas?

12. The image of turning into a tree is associated with the Greek myth of the god Apollo and Daphne: she turned into a tree to escape his attentions. What does this association say about the narrator's attitude to the bees?

13. Write a detailed description of the changes in the narrator's attitude between stanza 1 and stanza 7.

14. The final line stands alone, separated from the rest of the poem which is arranged in five-line stanzas. What does the line suggest? How does it colour the reader's response to the poem as a whole?

Third reading

15. Plath makes extensive use of internal rhyme, assonance and word play. One example is 'square as a chair'. Here, 'chair' suggests the homely and ordinary, while 'square' implies honest, straightforward, exact. The rhyme almost echoes the box's shape—its regularity and squareness. Identify other examples of sound effects and word-play in the poem. Comment on their use.

16. This poem moves between the real and familiar world, and the symbolic. Can you identify what is real and ordinary, what happens on the surface?

17. On the symbolic level, what is suggested by the poem? Look at the metaphors used for the bee box, the bees, the 'I' persona. Be aware of the feelings conveyed throughout.

18. There is a touch of dark humour, self-mockery, running through the poem. Where is this most obvious? What effect does it have on the reader?

General question

19. What do you consider to be the central theme of the poem? In answering, refer to the writer's tone and the images used. Look also at your answers to questions 16 and 17.

Child

this poem is also prescribed for Ordinary Level exams in 2003, 2004 and 2006

Your clear eye is the one absolutely beautiful thing.
I want to fill it with color and ducks,
The zoo of the new

Whose names you meditate—
April snowdrop, Indian pipe,   5
Little

Stalk without wrinkle,
Pool in which images
Should be grand and classical

Not this troublous   10
Wringing of hands, this dark
Ceiling without a star.

Explorations

First reading

1. Read this poem aloud and listen to its lyrical tone. What is your first impression of the speaker's feeling for her child? Try to imagine the speaker and child—what image do you see?
2. What pictures does she create for the child's 'eye'?
3. Which words here remind you of childlike things? What mood is usually associated with these?
4. How do you interpret the final stanza? Does it affect your reading of the rest of the poem?

Second reading

5. What feelings does the narrator display toward the child in the opening stanzas?
6. Does the narrator's focus remain consistent through the poem? Where do you think the change occurs? Look at the verb tenses used when answering this.
7. How is the adult/narrator/mother contrasted with the child?

Third reading

8. What is the effect of line 1 on the reader? Examine how this is achieved.
9. Write a paragraph showing how this contrasts with the final lines. Look at language, imagery, tone.
10. The language of the poem is fresh, clear and simple. What is the effect of this?
11. Write a note about the impressions created by this poem for you.

12 Séamus HEANEY

prescribed for Higher Level exams in 2003, 2004 and 2005

Séamus Heaney was born on 13
April 1939 on the family farm at
Mossbawn, near Bellaghy, Co.
Derry. During 1945–51 he attended
Anahorish primary school; in the
period 1951–57 he was educated at
St Columb's College in Derry and
during the period 1957–61 at
Queen's University, Belfast, where he
got a first-class degree in English
language and literature. In 1961 and
1962 he took a teacher training
diploma at St Joseph's College of
Education in Belfast. In 1966 he was
appointed lecturer in English at
Queen's University.

Heaney's first volume of poetry,
Death of a Naturalist, was
published in 1966. Filled mostly
with the characters, scenes, customs,
flora and fauna of the countryside
that formed him, this volume
explores Heaney's cultural and
poetic origins, it includes 'Twice
Shy' and 'Valediction'. *Door in the
Dark*, Heaney's second volume, was
published in 1969. While the first
collection dealt mainly with
childhood, coming of age, and the
poet's relationship with the
somewhat heroic figure of his father;
Door in the Dark deals with more
adult relationships. A few poems,
such as 'The Forge', hark back to
the style of the first volume in the
celebration of local skills and in the

1939–

poet's discovery in them of
metaphors for his own craft. But the
poet's Irish focus broadens out from
local considerations to a more
general awareness of geography,
history and archaeology in such
poems as 'Bogland'.

Heaney's third volume of poetry
was published in 1972. The year
1969 had seen riots, bombs and
sectarian killings. The provisional
IRA became a powerful force and
the British army was deployed on
the streets. Yet Heaney hardly ever
addresses these contemporary
political issues directly; instead he
makes a journey back into the past
of prehistoric humankind. In 'The

Tollund Man' Heaney finds an oblique way of examining the sacrificial killings, the power of religion and the deadly demands of myth in our society. Heaney spent the academic year 1970–71 as guest lecturer at the University of California in Berkeley and found it difficult to settle back into life in Northern Ireland when he returned, a transition he described as 'like putting an old dirty glove on again'. He found the daily ritual of roadblocks, arrests, vigilante patrols, explosions and killings deeply disturbing. Heaney decided that it was time to leave Belfast and devote himself entirely to his writing. He resigned his post as lecturer in English at Queen's University and moved with his family to a cottage at Glanmore, Co. Wicklow, during the summer of 1972, determined to go it alone as a poet and freelance writer.

Heaney's fourth volume of poetry, *North*, was published in 1975: in Part I he ranges over three thousand years of European civilisation, from the myths of Classical Greece to nineteenth-century Irish history—examining stories of conquest, cultural conflict and deeds of violence. A sequence of six poems entitled *Singing School* was published in 1972. The year 1969 had seen marked milestones in his development as a poet and member of his tribe: the Northern Catholic. 'A Constable Calls' is part of the *Singing School* sequence. Here he recalls, from a child's perspective, his fear of an alien law. This collection of conflict poems is prefaced by two totally different poems: two peaceful poems outside the stream of history and time recalling the security of childhood, the holistic nature of the old ways of life, the peacefulness of the countryside, and the stability and certainty provided by family love and values. These two poems are 'Mossbawn: Two Poems in Dedication', of which the first is 'Sunlight'.

Field Work, Heaney's fifth collection, was published in 1979. It includes 'The Skunk' and 'The Harvest Bow'. *Seeing Things*, published in 1991, in some ways sees a return to the concerns of the early Heaney. It deals with personal vision and personal history rather than with politics or historical issues. 'Field of Vision' and 'Lightenings VIII' were published in this collection. The final poem by Heaney in this anthology is 'St Kevin and the Blackbird' from *The Spirit Level* published in 1996.

In 1988 Heaney was elected professor of poetry at the University of Oxford, and in 1995 his lectures were published as *The Redress of Poetry*. In 1995 he was awarded the Nobel Prize for Literature.

Twice Shy

Her scarf à la Bardot,
In suede flats for the walk,
She came with me one evening
For air and friendly talk.
We crossed the quiet river,   5
Took the embankment walk.

Traffic holding its breath,
Sky a tense diaphragm:
Dusk hung like a backcloth
That shook where a swan swam,   10
Tremulous as a hawk
Hanging deadly, calm.

A vacuum of need
Collapsed each hunting heart
But tremulously we held   15
As hawk and prey apart,
Preserved classic decorum,
Deployed our talk with art.

Our juvenilia
Had taught us both to wait,   20
Not to publish feeling
And regret it all too late—
Mushroom loves already
Had puffed and burst in hate.

So, chary and excited   25
As a thrush linked on a hawk,
We thrilled to the March twilight
With nervous childish talk:
Still waters running deep
Along the embankment walk.   30

Explorations

First reading

1. Picture the scene of this poem in your mind. (*a*) Trace the couple's journey across the landscape. (*b*) What does he notice about her? (*c*) What does he notice about the scene around them?

2. What do these details tell us about the nature of the relationship?

Second reading

3. Compose a diary entry as the poet might have written it later that day. Structure it as a psychological diary, recording the emotions and feelings noticed on the walk. Keep it true to the text.

Third reading

4. What exactly is the poet describing here?

5. What do we learn about the object of the poet's love? Discuss the implications of this.

6. Do you think there is a delicate balance of feelings in this poem? Explain.

7. What does this poem contribute to our understanding of love?

Fourth reading

8. Do you find the imagery effective in conveying the theme? Discuss, with reference to particular images.

9. In contrast, do you think the language might be considered tired, even clichéd? Examine phrases such as 'twice shy' and 'still waters running deep.' Do you think the need to rhyme has introduced a certain artificiality?

10. From your intuition or experience, would you consider this poem to have captured something of the truth of human relationships? Discuss.

Valediction

Lady with the frilled blouse,
And simple tartan skirt,
Since you have left the house
Its emptiness has hurt
All thought. In your presence   5
Time rode easy, anchored
On a smile; but absence
Rocked love's balance, unmoored
The days. They buck and bound
Across the calendar   10
Pitched from the quiet sound
Of your flower-tender
Voice. Need breaks on my strand;
You've gone, I am at sea.
Until you resume command   15
Self is in mutiny.

 # Explorations

First reading

1. 'Valediction' means words of farewell. (*a*) How has his lover's departure affected the poet? (*b*) What do we discover about her from this poem?

2. Do you think this poem marks a permanent rift, or a mere interlude? Refer to the text.

Second reading

3. List all the unanswered questions lurking in your mind about the two people featured here, or the nature of their relationship. Refer to the text. Do we know very much at all about the relationship?

4. The poet uses the extended metaphor of a ship at sea to communicate his feelings. (*a*) Trace the suggestions about the poet's state of mind that are communicated by this metaphor. (*b*) Comment on the effectiveness of this metaphor in the context. (*c*) Do you think this technique of extended metaphor limits the depth of feelings expressed? Discuss, with reference to the text.

Third reading

5. Briefly express the theme dealt with in this poem.

The Forge

All I know is a door into the dark.
Outside, old axles and iron hoops rusting;
Inside, the hammered anvil's short-pitched ring,
The unpredictable fantail of sparks
Or hiss when a new shoe toughens in water.   5
The anvil must be somewhere in the centre,
Horned as a unicorn, at one end square,
Set there immovable: an altar
Where he expends himself in shape and music.
Sometimes, leather-aproned, hairs in his nose,   10
He leans out on the jamb, recalls a clatter
Of hoofs where traffic is flashing in rows;
Then grunts and goes in, with a slam and flick
To beat real iron out, to work the bellows.

CD Track 3

 # Explorations

Before reading

1. Read the title only. Jot down all the images that come into your head of what you might expect to see in the forge.

First reading

2. What do you actually see in this picture of the forge?
3. Where is the speaker standing in this poem? Do you think this might be significant? Why? What can he see? What can he not see?

Second reading

4. What can we say about the smith from his appearance and manner? Refer to the text.
5. How do you think the smith views his work? Read again lines 13 and 14.

6. How does the poet view the smith's work? Read again lines 6–9.

Third reading

7. What do you think is the poet's theme here?
8. Could the poem be read in a symbolic way, i.e. as dealing with a subject other than the surface one of the work of a blacksmith? If so, how?
9. Comment on the appropriateness of the imagery in this poem.
10. Would you agree with the following criticism by James Simmons?
    ' 'The Forge', from which the title of the book is taken, is shapely and vivid at first but fails to stand as a metaphor for the creative act. It becomes a cliché portrait of the village smithy. The smith has hairs in his nose and remembers better times. He retreats from the sight of modern traffic to beat real iron out, to work the bellows.'
    Give your opinion on both the metaphor and the portrait of the village forge.

Fourth reading

11. Comment on the style of language used. Is it poetic, prosaic, conversational, or what?
12. Do you think Heaney brings a sense of concrete realism to his art? Comment, with reference to the text.
13. What elements of the poem do not work very well for you? Explain, with reference to the text.

Bogland

For T.P. Flanagan

We have no prairies
To slice a big sun at evening—
Everywhere the eye concedes to
Encroaching horizon,

Is wooed into the cyclops' eye   5
Of a tarn. Our unfenced country
Is bog that keeps crusting
Between the sights of the sun.

They've taken the skeleton
Of the Great Irish Elk   10
Out of the peat, set it up
An astounding crate full of air.

Butter sunk under
More than a hundred years
Was recovered salty and white.   15
The ground itself is kind, black butter

Melting and opening underfoot,
Missing its last definition
By millions of years.
They'll never dig coal here,   20

Only the waterlogged trunks
Of great firs, soft as pulp.
Our pioneers keep striking
Inwards and downwards,

Every layer they strip   25
Seems camped on before.
The bogholes might be Atlantic seepage.

CD Track 4

Notes

[5] **cyclops:** In Greek mythology a Cyclops was one of a race of one-eyed giants.

[6] **tarn:** a small mountain lake

Explorations

First reading

1. Explain the contrast between the prairies and the Irish landscape, as described in the first two stanzas.
2. Where else in the poem is this cultural contrast referred to?
3. What properties of bogland are dwelt on in stanzas 3–6?
4. Who do you see as the speaking voice in this poem?

Second reading

5. What queries are raised in your mind by a further reading? List at least three.
6. What do you think this poem is about?

Third reading

7. If we accept that the bog is a metaphor for Irishness, what is the poet saying on this theme? Refer to the text to substantiate your views.
8. Comment on the tone of this poem. Do you think the poet is pessimistic, excited, neutral, nostalgic, or what? Refer to the text.
9. Do you think this poem asks you to think in a different way about what it means to be Irish? Explain.
10. Consider the following critical comment made by another poet, James Simmons: 'As a man and poet in his life and philosophy Heaney is not geared to progress and reform. He wants to wallow and look back. He is going through a door into the dark, inward and downward, a kind of Jungian ground he will call it.' Which elements of this criticism do you think are justified? Do you think any element is unwarranted? Justify your comments with reference to the text.

Fourth reading

11. What questions would you like to ask Séamus Heaney about this poem?
12. In the form of headings, or a flow chart, or a spider diagram, bring together your ideas on the theme and imagery of this poem.

'Boglands' (for Séamus Heaney), an oil painting by T.P. Flanagan

The Tollund Man

I

Some day I will go to Aarhus
To see his peat-brown head,
The mild pods of his eye-lids,
His pointed skin cap.

In the flat country nearby   5
Where they dug him out,
His last gruel of winter seeds
Caked in his stomach,

Naked except for
The cap, noose and girdle,   10
I will stand a long time.
Bridegroom to the goddess,

She tightened her torc on him
And opened her fen,
Those dark juices working   15
Him to a saint's kept body,

Trove of the turfcutters'
Honeycombed workings.
Now his stained face
Reposes at Aarhus.   20

II

I could risk blasphemy,
Consecrate the cauldron bog
Our holy ground and pray
Him to make germinate

The scattered, ambushed   25
Flesh of labourers,
Stockinged corpses
Laid out in the farmyards,

Tell-tale skin and teeth
Flecking the sleepers   30

Of four young brothers, trailed
For miles along the lines.

III

Something of his sad freedom
As he rode the tumbril
Should come to me, driving,   35
Saying the names

Tollund, Grauballe, Nebelgard,
Watching the pointing hands
Of country people,
Not knowing their tongue.   40

Out there in Jutland
In the old man-killing parishes
I will feel lost,
Unhappy and at home.

The head of Tollund Man

Explorations

First reading

1. Listen to a reading of part I. What do you see? What words or phrases make images for you?

2. Now read it. Describe the poet's subject. What details do you find most interesting? Why?

3. Identify the speaker in the poem. Identify the 'he' and 'she' referred to.

4. Explain the incident described. What do you think happened?

Second reading

5. Now read part I again. What is still unclear?

6. Read part II. What is the poet writing about here, and when do you think it occurred?

7. What do you think is the connection between part II and part I?

Third reading

8. What is happening in part III?

9. How does the poet feel? Read the second-last stanza aloud. Listen to the sounds of the words. Picture the scene in your mind.

10. Explain why you think the poet feels 'lost, unhappy and at home.'

Fourth reading

11. Examine the parallels and contrasts between Tollund Man and modern people as Heaney pictures them in this poem.

12. Is the poem making a political statement? If so, what?

13. Discuss the political imagery in this poem.

14. Make brief notes on the themes dealt with in this poem.

15. Comment on the variety of imagery used throughout the poem.

16. Do you think Heaney manages to create a feeling of sympathy for Tollund Man? How does he manage to achieve this?

17. Michael Parker described this poem as 'a potent combination of historical analogy and myth and intense emotion which exhibits the depth of Heaney's religious nature.' Discuss this analysis, substantiating your view by reference to the text.

Sunlight

There was a sunlit absence.
The helmeted pump in the yard
heated its iron,
water honeyed

in the slung bucket   5
and the sun stood
like a griddle cooling
against the wall

of each long afternoon.
So, her hands scuffled   10
over the bakeboard,
the reddening stove

sent its plaque of heat
against her where she stood
in a floury apron   15
by the window.

Now she dusts the board
with a goose's wing,
now sits, broad-lapped,
with whitened nails   20

and measling shins:
here is a space
again, the scone rising
to the tick of two clocks.

And here is love   25
like a tinsmith's scoop
sunk past its gleam
in the meal-bin.

Explorations

First reading

1. What is described here?
2. What details stand out on a first reading?

Second reading

3. Think of the poem as a picture in two panels: the yard and the kitchen. (*a*) Study the detail of each scene, and discuss the significance of each piece of detail. What era is evoked by the detail? (*b*) Examine the portrait of Mary Heaney. What kind of person is she? (*c*) Describe the atmosphere created in each scene, and explain how it is created.

Third reading

4. This is the opening poem in a volume that deals for the most part with violence, conflict, and conquest. Does this surprise you? Explain.
5. In that context, what do you think is the significance of the poem? What does this poem suggest about the poet's values and attitudes to living?
6. Do you think there is any significance in the change from past tense to present tense that occurs from stanza 5 onwards?
7. Explain your own reaction to this poem.

A Constable Calls

this poem is also prescribed for Ordinary Level exams in 2003, 2004 and 2005

His bicycle stood at the window-sill,
The rubber cowl of a mud-splasher
Skirting the front mudguard,
Its fat black handlegrips

Heating in sunlight, the 'spud'   5
Of the dynamo gleaming and cocked back,
The pedal treads hanging relieved
Of the boot of the law.

His cap was upside down
On the floor, next his chair.   10
The line of its pressure ran like a bevel
In his slightly sweating hair.

He had unstrapped
The heavy ledger, and my father
Was making tillage returns   15
In acres, roods, and perches.

Arithmetic and fear.
I sat staring at the polished holster
With its buttoned flap, the braid cord
Looped into the revolver butt.   20

'Any other root crops?
Mangolds? Marrowstems? Anything like that?'
'No.' But was there not a line
Of turnips where the seed ran out

In the potato field? I assumed   25
Small guilts and sat
Imagining the black hole in the barracks.
He stood up, shifted the baton-case

Further round on his belt,
Closed the domesday book,   30
Fitted his cap back with two hands,

And looked at me as he said goodbye.

A shadow bobbed in the window.
He was snapping the carrier spring
Over the ledger. His boot pushed off   35
And the bicycle ticked, ticked, ticked.

 # Explorations

First reading

1. What descriptive details of the bicycle did you notice as you read this poem? Did they seem to you in any way significant?

2. What details of the policeman's description did you think significant? What type of character is suggested by these details?

Second reading

3. What do you think is the boy's attitude to the bicycle, as described in the poem? Where and how is this attitude communicated to the reader?

4. What is the relationship between the participants in this encounter: the policeman, the boy and his father? Examine the imagery and dialogue and the actions of those involved.

Third reading

5. Can you understand how the boy feels? Explain.

6. Do you think the poem faithfully represents how a child might actually feel in this situation? Examine your own experiences to test the truth of the poem.

7. Outline the main themes of this poem, as you understand them.

8. From your reading of this poem, would you agree that one of Heaney's strengths as a poet is his ability to create realistic descriptions in minute detail?

Fourth reading

9. What is your evaluation of this poem's truth and significance?

The Skunk

this poem is also prescribed for Ordinary Level exams in 2003, 2004 and 2005

Up, black, striped and damasked like the chasuble
At a funeral mass, the skunk's tail
Paraded the skunk. Night after night
I expected her like a visitor.

The refrigerator whinnied into silence.   5
My desk light softened beyond the verandah.
Small oranges loomed in the orange tree.
I began to be tense as a voyeur.

After eleven years I was composing
Love-letters again, broaching the word 'wife'   10
Like a stored cask, as if its slender vowel
Had mutated into the night earth and air

Of California. The beautiful, useless
Tang of eucalyptus spelt your absence.
The aftermath of a mouthful of wine   15
Was like inhaling you off a cold pillow.

And there she was, the intent and glamorous,
Ordinary, mysterious skunk,
Mythologized, demythologized,
Snuffing the boards five feet beyond me.   20

It all came back to me last night, stirred
By the sootfall of your things at bedtime,
Your head-down, tail-up hunt in a bottom drawer
For the black plunge-line nightdress.

CD Track 8

Explorations

First reading

1. What images do you notice in particular? What sounds or smells? How would you describe the atmosphere?

2. The poem is set in two separate places, at two different times. Where is that division reflected in the stanzas? What are the two distinct times and places?

3. What image is associated with both locations? Explain the connection.

Second reading

4. How would you describe the poet's mood or state of mind in the first five stanzas?

5. What part does the skunk play here? What are your reactions to this analogy?

6. What is the poet saying in stanza 5?

Third reading

7. Examine the nature of the poet's relationship with his wife, as it comes across in this poem.

Fourth reading

8. Examine the sensuous language in this poem.

9. What does the imagery contribute to the effectiveness of the poem?

10. Do you think the transmutation of wife and skunk works well?

11. What exactly is the poet saying about love and relationships?

Fifth reading

12. Give a considered response to the following evaluation of the poem by the critic Neil Corcoran:
' 'The Skunk' is characteristic of these marriage poems, which are one of the highest points of Heaney's career: tender without being cosy, personal without being embarrassingly self-revealing. They are poems of a deeply disinterested maturity, managing an intensely difficult tone: honest and quite without self-regard.'
Deal separately with each point.

The Harvest Bow

As you plaited the harvest bow
You implicated the mellowed silence in you
In wheat that does not rust
But brightens as it tightens twist by twist
Into a knowable corona,   5
A throwaway love-knot of straw.

Hands that aged round ashplants and cane sticks
And lapped the spurs on a lifetime of game cocks
Harked to their gift and worked with fine intent
Until your fingers moved somnambulant: 10
I tell and finger it like braille,
Gleaning the unsaid off the palpable.

And if I spy into its golden loops
I see us walk between the railway slopes
Into an evening of long grass and midges,   15
Blue smoke straight up, old beds and ploughs in hedges,
An auction notice on an outhouse wall—
You with a harvest bow in your lapel,

Me with the fishing rod, already homesick
For the big lift of these evenings, as your stick   20
Whacking the tips off weeds and bushes
Beats out of time, and beats, but flushes
Nothing: that original townland
Still tongue-tied in the straw tied by your hand.

The end of art is peace   25
Could be the motto of this frail device
That I have pinned up on our deal dresser—
Like a drawn snare
Slipped lately by the spirit of the corn
Yet burnished by its passage, and still warm.   30

CD Track 9

Notes

Harvest Bow: a knot woven from wheat straw, a symbol of a fruitful harvest, embodying the spirit of the corn

[5] **corona:** halo of light round the sun

[10] **somnambulant:** sleep-walking (here, performing unconsciously, as in sleep)

[12] **palpable:** capable of being touched, felt, or readily perceived

A harvest bow from Ulster

Explorations

First reading

1. As you read, visualise the poem in your mind's eye. What colours predominate? Which images strike you in particular? How do you imagine the setting?

Second reading

2. 'As you plaited the harvest bow'—who do you think is the 'you' addressed in the poem: a person older or younger than the poet, living in the town or in the country? What type of person?

3. Where is the poem set? Are there a number of settings in it? Examine the imagery again.

4. Examine the time frames in the poem. Is it set in the present or the past, or both? Read the verses in the order 5, 1, 2, 3, 4. Does this help to clarify which is the present, which is the recent past, and which are distant memories?

5. In your own words, briefly reconstruct the narrative.

Third reading

6. Trace the various references to the harvest bow that are scattered throughout the poem. Examine each image and say what it suggests to you about the significance of the bow.

7. How does the poet regard the bow? Is it important to him? What does it enable him to do?

8. How do you think the father viewed the bow?

9. How does the poet regard his father? Examine the images used about him and the tone of the utterances referring to him.

10. If the father was a better communicator, what do you think he might have said in stanza 4?

Fourth reading

11. What do you imagine he might mean by the motto 'The end of art is peace'?

12. What lines, phrases or images are still unclear to you? Discuss interpretations.

13. What does the poem reveal about Heaney's attitude to his rural heritage?

14. What does the poet feel about the value of art and poetry in society?

Fifth reading

15. What is your own reaction to 'The Harvest Bow'? Does it say anything of significance to you?

16. What questions would you like to ask the poet if you could?

Field of Vision

this poem is also prescribed for Ordinary Level exams in 2003, 2004 and 2005

I remember this woman who sat for years
In a wheelchair, looking straight ahead
Out the window at sycamore trees unleafing
And leafing at the far end of the lane.

Straight out past the TV in the corner,   5
The stunted, agitated hawthorn bush,
The same small calves with their backs to wind and rain,
The same acre of ragwort, the same mountain.

She was steadfast as the big window itself.
Her brow was clear as the chrome bits of the chair.   10
She never lamented once and she never
Carried a spare ounce of emotional weight.

Face to face with her was an education
Of the sort you got across a well-braced gate—
One of those lean, clean, iron, roadside ones   15
Between two whitewashed pillars, where you could see

Deeper into the country than you expected
And discovered that the field behind the hedge
Grew more distinctly strange as you kept standing
Focused and drawn in by what barred the way.   20

CD Track 10

Explorations

First reading

1. Read only stanzas 1–3. What exactly do you see? Describe the woman. Describe the view from the window.
2. What kind of person do you think this woman was? Refer to the text.

Second reading

Still on stanzas 1–3,

3. How do you think the poem will end?
4. Why do you think Heaney is concentrating on this woman?

Why is she important for him?

Third reading

5. Read the two final verses. How does the poet actually see the significance of this woman?
6. What is he writing about? In your own words, briefly express the theme of this poem.

Fourth reading

7. Comment on the poem under the headings 'Structure', 'Language', and 'Imagery'.

Lightenings VIII

The annals say: when the monks of Clonmacnoise
Were all at prayers inside the oratory
A ship appeared above them in the air.

The anchor dragged along behind so deep
It hooked itself into the altar rails   5
And then, as the big hull rocked to a standstill,

A crewman shinned and grappled down the rope
And struggled to release it. But in vain.
'This man can't bear our life here and will drown,'

The abbot said, 'unless we help him.' So   10
They did, the freed ship sailed, and the man climbed back
Out of the marvellous as he had known it.

CD Track 11

 Explorations

St Kevin and the Blackbird

And then there was St Kevin and the blackbird.
The saint is kneeling, arms stretched out, inside
His cell, but the cell is narrow, so

One turned-up palm is out the window, stiff
As a crossbeam, when a blackbird lands   5
And lays in it and settles down to nest.

Kevin feels the warm eggs, the small breast, the tucked
Neat head and claws and, finding himself linked
Into the network of eternal life,

Is moved to pity: now he must hold his hand   10
Like a branch out in the sun and rain for weeks
Until the young are hatched and fledged and flown.

And since the whole thing's imagined anyhow,
Imagine being Kevin. Which is he?
Self-forgetful or in agony all the time   15

From the neck on out down through his hurting fore-arms?
Are his fingers sleeping? Does he still feel his knees?
Or has the shut-eyed blank of underearth

Crept up through him? Is there distance in his head?
Alone and mirrored clear in love's deep river,   20
'To labour and not to seek reward,' he prays,

A prayer his body makes entirely
For he has forgotten self, forgotten bird
And on the riverbank forgotten the river's name.

CD Track 12

Notes

    [1] **St Kevin:** St Kevin was the founder of a monastic settlement at Glendalough,
        Co. Wicklow, in the seventh century, known for extraordinary self-discipline. It
        was his practice during Lent to live separate from the community, as a hermit.
        This story has its origins in such a time of prayer in his tiny cell. Such was his
        fame that Glendalough became an important place of pilgrimage.

    [3] **cell:** a hermit's small, one-roomed dwelling

Explorations

First reading

1. Read stanzas 1–4. What was your first reaction on reading these? Jot down or share your thoughts orally.
2. How do you think we might be expected to react to this narrative—as a factual piece or as sheer fantasy, as religious myth, as a parable, or what? Does the first line give us a clue—'And then there was…'? With what context do we usually associate this type of opening phrase?
3. From the evidence here, what can we say about St Kevin? Explore the following:
   • What kind of person is he? What qualities has he?
   • What are his values? What is important to him?
   • What is his attitutde to nature, and why is this experience significant for him?

Second reading

4. Despite the poem's playfulness and sense of fun there are elements of serious religious atmosphere in these first four stanzas: 'kneeling, arms stretched out'; 'the cell is narrow'; 'stiff | As a crossbeam'. Consider each image in detail and explore what is suggested about the religious way of life.
5. 'Linked | Into the network of eternal life'—how was this important for St Kevin, and what significance has it for the poem as a whole?
6. What else do you notice about these four stanzas?

Third reading

Read the entire poem through.

7. As the poet invites us, imagine being St Kevin. Write your thoughts and feelings.
8. Which do you think he is, 'self-forgetful' or 'in agony'? Could 'self-forgetful' be read in more than one way?
9. Which understanding of St Kevin does the poet opt for? Read stanzas 7 and 8 in detail and explain the poet's view.
10. Is there a shift in tone and in the poet's attitude in these last stanzas? What is it, and how is it conveyed in the language? Do you think the poet admires the saint's philosophy of life?

Fourth reading

11. What notion of prayer and of religious contemplation comes across from this poem?
12. Explore Heaney's use of natural imagery to convey his theme. Do you find it effective?
13. 'There is a strong sensuous quality to this poem.' Comment.
14. Do you find this an unusual poem? Comment.

13 *Michael* LONGLEY

prescribed for Higher Level exams in 2005 and 2006

Michael Longley was born in Belfast on 27 July 1939, of English parents. His father, Richard, who features in the poems 'Wounds', 'Wreaths' and 'Last Requests', fought in the trenches in the First World War and was gassed, wounded, decorated, and promoted to the rank of captain. In *Tuppenny Stung*, a short collection of autobiographical chapters published in 1994, Longley describes his family, primary and secondary education and the forces of his early cultural formation: Protestant schoolboys' fears of the dark savageries supposedly practised by Catholics, an English education system dismissive of Irish culture and history, and Protestant Belfast's fear and resentment of the Republic. His early education and local socialisation made him aware of conflicting classes and religions, and of the duality of Irish identity.

Later he was educated at the Royal Belfast Academical Institution. In 1958 he went to Trinity College, Dublin, where the student population at the time consisted mainly of southern and northern Protestants, middle- and upper-class English, and a scattering of southern Catholics. He studied classics and wrote poetry but felt very under-read in English literature

1939–

until taken in hand by his friend and young fellow-poet Derek Mahon.

Longley worked for the Arts Council of Northern Ireland in the period 1970–91, when he took early retirement. His work for the arts was driven by a number of guiding principles, among which were the nurturing of indigenous talent; support for the artists, not just the arts; allied to the need to transcend class barriers and bring the arts, at an affordable price, to the working class. He was a champion of cultural pluralism, fostering the artistic expression of both sides of the religious and political divide. His vision of Ulster culture has always sought to include its many different strands and influences and so to encourage a unique hybrid rather than separate, antagonistic cultures.

No Continuing City (1969), Longley's first collection, is known for its technically accomplished and learned poetry—among its concerns are poets, poetry and nature. It is best known for the erudite, witty and sophisticated love poetry, almost in the metaphysical tradition. *An Exploded View* (1973) continues to deal with poetry and poetic issues. Nature is also a major preoccupation. ('Badger' is from this volume.) The collection does respond briefly to the upsurge of violence in Northern Ireland around this time. In 'Wounds' the violence is seen in the broad perspective of international conflict. A great number of the poems focus on an alternative life in the west of Ireland. 'Carrigskeewaun' and 'Poteen' are among these.

The Echo Gate (1979) demonstrates Longley's now-established bifocal view: on Belfast and Mayo. He confronts the political violence in its stark everyday settings in 'Wreaths' and explores the war experiences of his father as a perspective on this violence in 'Last Requests'. He also explores the folklore, ethos and culture of the west of Ireland and finds a bleak unconscious parallel between its crude violence and that of Belfast in 'Self-Heal'. *Gorse Fires* (1991) is centred on Longley's adopted second home of Carrigskeewaun in Co. Mayo; but it also includes poems on the Holocaust, the Second World War and the Spanish Civil War. Interspersed with these are some free translations from Homer's *Odyssey*, focusing on Odysseus's return to his home and interpreted by some critics as having strong (if oblique) relevance to Longley's own home province. 'Laertes' is from this sequence.

Michael Longley is a fellow of the Royal Society of Literature and a member of Aosdána. He is married to the critic and academic Edna Longley.

Badger

For Raymond Piper

I

Pushing the wedge of his body
Between cromlech and stone circle,
He excavates down mine shafts
And back into the depths of the hill.

His path straight and narrow   5
And not like the fox's zig-zags,
The arc of the hare who leaves
A silhouette on the sky line.

Night's silence around his shoulders,
His face lit by the moon, he   10
Manages the earth with his paws,
Returns underground to die.

II

An intestine taking in
patches of dog's-mercury,
brambles, the bluebell wood;   15
a heel revolving acorns;
a head with a price on it
brushing cuckoo-spit, goose-grass;
a name that parishes borrow.

III

For the digger, the earth-dog   20
It is a difficult delivery
Once the tongs take hold,
Vulnerable his pig's snout
That lifted cow-pats for beetles,
Hedgehogs for the soft meat,   25

His limbs dragging after them
So many stones turned over,
The trees they tilted.

Notes

[2] **cromlech:** a name
formerly used for the
remains of a portal tomb;
here the poet uses it to
mean the horizontal slab
on top of the upright
stones

[14] **dog's mercury:** a
herbaceous woodland
plant, usually regarded as
toxic

[19] **a name that
parishes borrow:** the
poet refers to *broc*, the
Irish for 'badger' (in fact
the element Broc found in
place-names—for example
Domhnach Broc,
anglicised Donnybrook—
is the man's name Broc)

Explorations

First reading: section I

1. Think of section I as a picture or painting. What do you see? Consider the setting described, the background, the lighting, and the main subject.

2. What do you notice about the badger? How do you visualise the animal? Examine the connotations of descriptive words and phrases, such as 'the wedge of his body'; 'Night's silence around his shoulders'; 'he | Manages the earth'. How do the badgers' paths differ from those of other animals, and what might this suggest about the nature of the badger?

3. What is suggested here about the animal's relationship with the earth? Consider his association with cromlech and stone circle; how he 'manages' the earth; how he 'Returns underground to die.'

4. Do you think the badger has particular significance for the poet? Explain.

5. How would you describe the atmosphere of section I? What words or phrases help to create it?

Second reading: section II

6. What do you notice about the badger's diet?

7. What other aspects of the badger's environmental function are referred to in section II?

8. 'a head with a price on it ... a name that parishes borrow.' What do these lines suggest about human attitudes to the badger?

Third reading: section III

9. What do you think is happening in section III?

10. Contrast the humans' treatment of the environment in section III with the badger's management of the earth in sections I and II.

11. Do you think the poet has some sympathy for the animal in this section? Which phrases or images might suggest this?

12. Explore the ironies in the first stanza of this section.

Fourth reading

13. What point is the poet making about humankind's interaction with the environment?

14. What other themes do you notice in the poem?

15. Would you agree that 'Longley displays the scientific assurance of a naturalist'?

16. 'Longley's view of the west of Ireland is a realistic rather than a romantic one.' On the evidence of the poem 'Badger' would you agree with this

statement? Refer to the text to support your argument.

17. Summarise your thoughts and feelings on this poem.

Wounds

CD Track 14

Here are two pictures from my father's head—
I have kept them like secrets until now:
First, the Ulster Division at the Somme
Going over the top with 'Fuck the Pope!'
'No Surrender!': a boy about to die,   5
Screaming 'Give 'em one for the Shankill!'
'Wilder than Gurkhas' were my father's words
Of admiration and bewilderment.
Next comes the London-Scottish padre
Resettling kilts with his swagger-stick,   10
With a stylish backhand and a prayer.
Over a landscape of dead buttocks
My father followed him for fifty years.
At last, a belated casualty,
He said—lead traces flaring till they hurt—   15
'I am dying for King and Country, slowly.'
I touched his hand, his thin head I touched.

Now, with military honours of a kind,
With his badges, his medals like rainbows,
His spinning compass, I bury beside him   20
Three teenage soldiers, bellies full of
Bullets and Irish beer, their flies undone.
A packet of Woodbines I throw in,
A lucifer, the Sacred Heart of Jesus
Paralysed as heavy guns put out   25
The night-light in a nursery for ever;
Also a bus-conductor's uniform—
He collapsed beside his carpet-slippers
Without a murmur, shot through the head
By a shivering boy who wandered in   30
Before they could turn the television down
Or tidy away the supper dishes.
To the children, to a bewildered wife,
I think 'Sorry Missus' was what he said.

Notes

[3] **Ulster Division:** a division of the British army in the First World War

[3] **Somme:** a river in north-eastern France, the scene of continuous heavy fighting during the First World War, particularly from July to November 1916

[4] **Going over the top:** an infantry attack, with soldiers climbing out of the trenches

[6] **Shankill:** an area of west Belfast around the Shankill Road, inhabited mainly by Protestants

[9] **London-Scottish padre:** the regimental chaplain; 'London-Scottish' refers to his father's regiment. He seems preoccupied with flicking down the dead soldiers' kilts in order to allow them some dignity in death.

[24] **lucifer:** an old name for a match

 # Explorations

First reading

(Focus on the first half of the poem.)

1. The first part of the poem is taken up with the 'two pictures from my father's head'. Explore the first picture—lines 3–8. What are your thoughts about this?

2. Interpret the father's reaction—lines 7–8.

Or

3. Compose a brief diary extract that the father might have written on the evening following the attack.

4. Explore the second picture—lines 9–11. What are your thoughts on this?

5. Reflect on the two images. What do they suggest to you about people at war? Jot down all the ideas suggested by these pictures.

6. Read lines 12–15. What do you discover about the effects of war on the father?

7. From a reading of the first part of this poem, what do you discover about Longley's father?

8. Comment on the relationship between father and son. Refer to specific words and phrases.

Second reading

(Focus on the second half of the poem.)

9. What is happening in the second part of this poem? Read it a number of times. If you are still confused, examine the first three lines very carefully.

10. At this surreal burial ceremony the poet interns an odd collection of objects and images. (*a*) Comment on the significance of the objects directly connected with the father. What is revealed about the father and about the

relationship between father and son? (*b*) Explore the images of violence. What do you see? What do they suggest to you about the society?

11. 'A shivering boy who wandered in': compose an interior monologue of the imagined thoughts of this boy.

Third reading

12. Examine the structure or division of this poem into two parts. How do the two parts relate? What point is the poet making here?

13. Comment on the themes explored in this poem. What view of life is presented?

14. Do you think the poet is angry, saddened, depressed or what by these happenings? Refer to specific phrases and lines.

15. Would you agree that this poem shows the ordinary human being as insignificant and powerless in the face of violence? Refer to specific incidents in the text.

16. Comment on any feature of the poet's style you consider significant. You might consider the impact of the imagery; the humour; the tone of the piece; the surreal nightmarish effects; the realism; or any other.

Soldiers from the Royal Irish Rifles during a break from fighting at the Battle of the Somme in 1916

Poteen

Enough running water
To cool the copper worm,
The veins at the wrist,
Vitriol to scorch the throat—

And the brimming hogshead,   5
Reduced by one noggin-full
Sprinkled on the ground,
Becomes an affair of

Remembered souterrains,
Sunk workshops, out-backs,   10
The back of the mind—
The whole bog an outhouse

Where, alongside cudgels,
Guns, the informer's ear
We have buried it—   15
Blood-money, treasure-trove.

Notes

Poteen: illegally produced alcohol, [poitín]

[2] **copper worm:** a spiral of copper piping, part of the equipment used in the still that produces alcohol

[4] **vitriol:** sulphuric acid; used metaphorically it means caustic speech or criticism

[5] **hogshead:** a large cask or barrel

[6] **noggin:** a measure of spirits

[9] **souterrains:** underground chambers

Explorations

First reading

1. What is happening in the first two stanzas? What do you see? Which words and phrases create the most striking images for you? What particular quality of the poitín is emphasised?

2. Why do you think they might sprinkle 'one noggin-full … on the ground'? Explore all possibilities, both practical and symbolic.

Second reading

3. If we interpret the sprinkling as a superstitious gesture and agree that this primitive action casts the speaker's mind back in time, what does he recall or imagine? Explore stanzas 3 and 4.

4. What have these imagined locations in common with the setting of the present activity?

5. What is suggested to you by the line 'The whole bog an

outhouse'?

6. What atmosphere is conjured up by this catalogue of images in the two final stanzas?

7. How are they connected to 'the back of the mind'?

Third reading

8. How would you describe the culture or way of life that is imaginatively unearthed by the speaker?

9. What statement about Irishness is made by the poem?

10. What part does the imagery play in the impact of the poem? Refer to specific examples.

11. Consider the shape of the poem, the length of the lines and the number of sentences used. Do these enhance and complement the subject matter and activity in the poem? Explain how the form contributes to this poem.

Carrigskeewaun

For Penny and David Cabot

The Mountain
This is ravens' territory, skulls, bones,
The marrow of these boulders supervised
From the upper air: I stand alone here
And seem to gather children about me,
A collection of picnic things, my voice   5
Filling the district as I call their names.

The Path
With my first step I dislodge the mallards
Whose necks strain over the bog to where
Kittiwakes scrape the waves: then, the circle
Widening, lapwings, curlews, snipe until   10
I am left with only one swan to nudge
To the far side of its gradual disdain.

The Strand
I discover, remaindered from yesterday,
Cattle tracks, a sanderling's tiny trail,
The footprints of the children and my own   15
Linking the dunes to the water's edge,
Reducing to sand the dry shells, the toe-
And fingernail parings of the sea.

The Wall
I join all the men who have squatted here
This lichened side of the dry-stone wall   20
And notice how smoke from our turf fire
Recalls in the cool air above the lake
Steam from a kettle, a tablecloth and
A table she might have already set.

The Lake
Though it will duplicate at any time   25
The sheep and cattle that wander there,
For a few minutes every evening
Its surface seems tilted to receive
The sun perfectly, the mare and her foal,
The heron, all such special visitors.   30

Carrigskeewaun: a townland in the parish of Kilgeever, Co. Mayo; the name means 'rock of the wall ferns'

[1] **raven:** a large black bird that feeds chiefly on carrion

[7] **mallard:** a wild duck

[9] **Kittiwake:** small marine gull

[10] **lapwing:** bird of the plover family

[10, 14] **curlew, snipe, sanderling:** types of wading bird, usually found in marshy places or by the seashore

 # Explorations

First reading

The Mountain

1. What is the poet's first impression of this landscape? Of what does it remind him? What is the significance of the raven?

2. How does the speaker react to the bleak landscape? Explore the contrast between his thoughts and the nature of the terrain.

The Path

3. What is happening in this section? What do you see? How do you picture the poet in the scene?

4. How would you describe the poet's relationship with the local fauna? Where is this indicated in the language?

Second reading

The Strand

5. What absorbs the poet's attention here?

6. What aspects of the cycle of nature does he find fascinating?

7. How would you describe the atmosphere of this section? How is this achieved by the language and imagery?

The Wall

8. How does he portray his feelings of a sense of continuity?

9. Do you think he feels at all lonely here? Explain.

The Lake

10. If this were a painting, what would it show? What colours would you use?

11. What aspects of nature are emphasised in this section?

Third reading

12. In general, how do you think Longley feels about Carrigskeewaun? Explore the evidence for this.

13. Explain how the imagery

Whooper swans on the lake at Carrigskeewaun, a drawing by Michael Viney

conveys the atmosphere of the place.

14. What particular significance do you think Carrigskeewaun might have for Longley? Explain your views, with reference to this and other poems by Longley.

Fourth reading

15. Alan Peacock writes about the notion of escape to elemental places found among some urban writers: 'The dangers of course in this view of writing are well-known: sentimentality, a penchant for the picturesque and a tendency towards idealisation which masks realities.' Examine 'Carrig-skeewaun' from the point of view of his general reservations on this type of poem.

16. Peacock also mentions Longley's 'genuinely sympathetic and at the same time coolly scientific engagement with the particularities of the environment'. Do you think this statement could be applied to 'Carrigskeewaun'? Explain, with reference to the text.

17. Do you think this poem shows 'a man at ease with himself and his fellows' (Brown)?

18. What did you discover about the poet from a reading of this poem?

Wreaths

The Civil Servant
He was preparing an Ulster fry for breakfast
When someone walked into the kitchen and shot him:
A bullet entered his mouth and pierced his skull,
The books he had read, the music he could play.

He lay in his dressing gown and pyjamas   5
While they dusted the dresser for fingerprints
And then shuffled backwards across the garden
With notebooks, cameras and measuring tapes.

They rolled him up like a red carpet and left
Only a bullet hole in the cutlery drawer: 10
Later his widow took a hammer and chisel
And removed the black keys from his piano.

The Greengrocer
He ran a good shop, and he died
Serving even the death-dealers
Who found him busy as usual   15
Behind the counter, organised
With holly wreaths for Christmas,
Fir trees on the pavement outside.

Astrologers or three wise men
Who may shortly be setting out   20
For a small house up the Shankill
Or the Falls, should pause on their way
To buy gifts at Jim Gibson's shop,
Dates and chestnuts and tangerines.

The Linen Workers
Christ's teeth ascended with him into heaven: 25
Through a cavity in one of his molars
The wind whistles: he is fastened for ever
By his exposed canines to a wintry sky.

I am blinded by the blaze of that smile
And by the memory of my father's false teeth   30

Brimming in their tumbler: they wore bubbles
And, outside of his body, a deadly grin.

When they massacred the ten linen workers
There fell on the road beside them spectacles,
Wallets, small change, and a set of dentures:⁣   35
Blood, food particles, the bread, the wine.

Before I can bury my father once again
I must polish the spectacles, balance them
Upon his nose, fill his pockets with money
And into his dead mouth slip the set of teeth.⁣   40

 # Explorations

The Civil Servant

First reading

1. What do you notice about the incident?
2. Ponder the description of the killing: 'A bullet entered his mouth and pierced his skull'. How do you think the line should be read? Explain the tone you would employ.
3. What kind of man was the victim? Examine the details.
4. What is your reaction to the treatment of the victim after death?

Second reading

5. What does the poem say to you about violence and about the value and significance of human life?
6. Comment on the tone of the writing. Examine the descriptions, the choice of words, the style of speech. Is there any evidence of emotional reaction to this killing?

The Greengrocer

First reading

7. What do you find most incongruous about this killing?
8. What is your understanding of the reference to 'Astrologers or three wise men'?
9. How do you read the tone of this piece?

The Linen Workers

First reading

10. Explore each of the three main images developed here—the Christ figure, the father and the massacre—in stanzas 1, 2, 3. (*a*) How are they linked? What have the Christ figure

---

and the father to do with the massacre? (*b*) Comment on the quality and nature of the images. Are they everyday, realistic, unusual, or what?

11. In what ways does the treatment of violence here differ from that in the other poems?

Overall reading

12. Record your thoughts on a final reading of the three pieces.

13. What aspects of violence engage Longley's imagination?

14. Comment on the poet's style of imagery and on the tone of the narration.

15. 'Violence is unblinkingly looked at in its graphic, but strangely intimate, everyday actuality' (Alan Peacock). Do you think Peacock's view of Longley's work could be applied to this poem? Explain, with reference to the detail of the poem.

Last Requests

this poem is also prescribed for Ordinary Level exams in 2005 and 2006

I

Your batman thought you were buried alive,
Left you for dead and stole your pocket watch
And cigarette case, all he could salvage
From the grave you so nearly had to share
With an unexploded shell. But your lungs   5
Surfaced to take a long remembered drag,
Heart contradicting as an epitaph
The two initials you had scratched on gold.

II

I thought you blew a kiss before you died,
But the bony fingers that waved to and fro   10
Were asking for a Woodbine, the last request
Of many soldiers in your company,
The brand you chose to smoke for forty years
Thoughtfully, each one like a sacrament.
I who brought peppermints and grapes only   15
Couldn't reach you through the oxygen tent.

CD Track 18

Explorations

First reading: part I

1. What do you notice about the episode described here?
2. What does it convey of the poet's view of war? Explain, with reference to the text.
3. Is there a certain light-heartedness about this, despite the topic? Explain.

Second reading: part II

4. In your own words, describe the death-bed scene as you see it from a reading of this section.
5. Is the scene as you imagine a death-bed scene might be?

6. Is there a sense of sadness behind the humour? Where?
7. Write about the poet's view of his father. (*a*) What are his significant memories of him? (*b*) Do you suppose father and son were close? Explain.
8. Which lines created most impact for you? Explain.

Third reading

9. What impression of the poet did you form from reading this poem? Refer to the text.
10. What view of life informs or inspires this poem? Refer to the text.

Mayo Monologues—
Self-Heal

I wanted to teach him the names of flowers,
Self-heal and centaury; on the long acre
Where cattle never graze, bog asphodel.
Could I love someone so gone in the head
And, as they say, was I leading him on?   5
He'd slept in the cot until he was twelve
Because of his babyish ways, I suppose,
Or the lack of a bed: hadn't his father
Gambled away all but rushy pasture?
His skull seemed to be hammered like a wedge   10
Into his shoulders, and his back was hunched,
Which gave him an almost scholarly air.
But he couldn't remember the things I taught:
Each name would hover above its flower
Like a butterfly unable to alight.   15
That day I pulled a cuckoo-pint apart
To release the giddy insects from their cell.
Gently he slipped his hand between my thighs.
I wasn't frightened; and still I don't know why,
But I ran from him in tears to tell them.   20
I heard how every day for one whole week
He was flogged with a blackthorn, then tethered
In the hayfield. I might have been the cow
Whose tail he would later dock with shears,
And he the ram tangled in barbed wire   25
That he stoned to death when they set him free.

Notes

[2] **Self-heal:** any of various plants believed to have healing properties

[2] **centaury:** a plant said to have been discovered by Chiron the centaur

[3] **bog asphodel:** asphodel is a lily-type plant, common on moorlands, considered an immortal flower in mythology and said to cover the Elysian meadows (Homer's *Odyssey*)

[16] **cuckoo-pint:** a plant commonly called 'lords and ladies'; it has sexual connotations because of its appearance

Explorations

First reading: lines 1–15

1. 'I wanted to teach him'. Who are the two people involved?
2. What do we learn of 'him' in the first fifteen lines? Consider physical appearance, mental ability and the manner of his treatment. Why do you think he is not named?
3. Explore the speaker's motivation in this. Is it clear-cut? Is she herself clear about it?

Second reading: lines 16 to end

4. Explore the speaker's reaction to the incident—lines 16–20. Can she explain it? Can you understand her reaction
5. Examine the consequent treatment of the man. Can you understand any possible reasons for it? What are the long-term consequences?

Third reading

6. What are your thoughts on finishing this poem? What are your feelings?
7. Who is the victim here? Could this be read as a poem on victims?
8. What view of society is advanced by this poem?
9. 'Beauty and violence and sexuality are reflected in the imagery.' Comment, with reference to the text.
10. Do you think Longley is angered by this episode? Comment on the tone of the poem.

An Amish Rug

this poem is also prescribed for Ordinary Level exams in 2005 and 2006

As if a one-room schoolhouse were all we knew
And our clothes were black, our underclothes black,
Marriage a horse and buggy going to church
And the children silhouettes in a snowy field,

I bring you this patchwork like a smallholding   5
Where I served as the hired boy behind the harrow,
Its threads the colour of cantaloupe and cherry
Securing hay bales, corn cobs, tobacco leaves.

You may hang it on the wall, a cathedral window,
Or lay it out on the floor beside our bed   10
So that whenever we undress for sleep or love
We shall step over it as over a flowerbed.

Notes

Amish: A group of conservative Mennonite Christians in the United States characterised by distinctive dress (plain black clothes, no jewellery) and non-conformist way of life (agriculture, simple living, shunning motor vehicles); plainness and naturalness characterise their architecture and artwork. In stark contrast, this colourful rug was made for tourists.

[6] **harrow:** agricultural implement consisting of a frame with downward-pointing spikes dragged over a field to break up the earth

[7] **cantaloupe:** small, delicately flavoured melon with red and orange flesh

Explorations

First reading

1. What did you learn of the Amish way of life from a reading of this poem?
2. Describe the rug from the clues provided in the second stanza.
3. How might it be displayed? Refer to the text.

Second reading

4. What do you think is the poet's attitude to the Amish values and way of life? Refer to specific words and phrases.
5. Do you think the poet is happy in his relationship?
6. What do you consider to be the main theme of this poem?

Third reading

7. Comment on the significance of colours in the poem.
8. Do you think the poem displays a naïve romantic view of life?
9. Consider this as a love poem. Do you like it? Outline your thinking.

Fourth reading

10. 'Longley's international perspective lends depth to his poetry.' Examine 'An Amish Rug' from the point of view of this statement.

Laertes

When he found Laertes alone on the tidy terrace, hoeing
Around a vine, disreputable in his gardening duds,
Patched and grubby, leather gaiters protecting his shins
Against brambles, gloves as well, and to cap it all,
Sure sign of his deep depression, a goatskin duncher,   5
Odysseus sobbed in the shade of a pear-tree for his father
So old and pathetic that all he wanted then and there
Was to kiss him and hug him and blurt out the whole story,
But the whole story is one catalogue and then another,
So he waited for images from that formal garden,   10
Evidence of a childhood spent traipsing after his father
And asking for everything he saw, the thirteen pear-trees,
Ten apple-trees, forty fig-trees, the fifty rows of vines
Ripening at different times for a continuous supply,
Until Laertes recognised his son and, weak at the knees,   15
Dizzy, flung his arms around the neck of great Odysseus
Who drew the old man fainting to his breast and held him there
And cradled like driftwood the bones of his dwindling father.

CD Track 21

Note [5] **duncher:** dialect term for a hat or cap

 # Explorations

First reading

1. Examine the portrait of Laertes
    in the first five lines of this poem.
    What do you notice about
    him? What is his state of mind?
2. What is Odysseus's first
    reaction on seeing his father?
3. What does he actually do?
    Explore lines 10–14. Why do
    you think he acts in this way?

Second reading

4. Explore in detail the
    relationship between father and
    son depicted in this poem.

5. What other themes do you find
    submerged in the poem?
    Explain.
6. Do you think Longley's eye for
    detail contributes to the success
    of the poem?
7. Is there a sense of dramatic
    excitement in the poem? How
    is it created? Examine the
    sentence structure of the poem.

Third reading

8. Do you think this poem
    communicates any significant
    truths? Comment.

Ceasefire

I

Put in mind of his own father and moved to tears
Achilles took him by the hand and pushed the old king
Gently away, but Priam curled up at his feet and
Wept with him until their sadness filled the building.

II

Taking Hector's corpse into his hands Achilles   5
Made sure it was washed and, for the old king's sake,
Laid out in uniform, ready for Priam to carry
Wrapped like a present home to Troy at daybreak.

III

When they had eaten together, it pleased them both
To stare at each other's beauty as lovers might,   10
Achilles built like a god, Priam good-looking still
And full of conversation, who earlier had sighed:

IV

'I get down on my knees and do what must be done
And kiss Achilles' hand, the killer of my son.'

Notes

[2] **Achilles:** one of the legendary Greek heroes

[3] **Priam:** King Priam of Troy was father of the princes Hector and Paris; it was Paris who brought about the war by abducting Helen from Sparta in Greece

[5] **Hector:** see above

Explorations

First reading

1. Examine the first stanza. What is happening here? What do you see? Describe the scene. If you are unclear, read also stanza 4.
2. In the first stanza, what detail did you find most moving? Explain.
3. Why does Achilles relent?
4. In the first stanza, what do the postures reveal of the different roles of the two men?
5. How would you describe the mood of the first stanza? What words or images help to create this?
6. What do his actions in the second stanza reveal about Achilles?
7. Comment on the description 'to carry | Wrapped like a present home to Troy'?

Second reading

8. What do you think is the significance of the fact that they 'had eaten together'? Do you think there is a change of mood in the third stanza? Is there a noticeable shift in power between the two characters?
9. The third stanza reflects a growing respect and mutual admiration. How is this communicated? Do you find this unexpected, even uncomfortable? What is the effect here?
10. What does the third stanza reveal of classical Greek culture? What qualities were valued in the society?

Third reading

11. Briefly outline the theme of this piece as you understand it.
12. Do you think that Homer's themes are of universal significance? Explain.
13. Could you read this as one of Longley's father-son poems? What does it add to that theme?
14. Could you read this as a 'political' poem? Explore that aspect of it.

14 Derek MAHON

prescribed for Higher Level exams in 2003 and 2004

Mahon is a retiring man who shuns publicity and literary politics. Born in 1941, he was the only child of a Church of Ireland family. He grew up in Glengormley, a north-side suburb of Belfast. His father worked in the Harland and Wolff shipyard, where the *Titanic* was built, and his mother in the Flax Spinning Company. His earliest memories are of the bomb raids of Belfast during the Second World War. He spent much of his school holidays cycling, often to the seaside town of Portrush and sometimes even to Donegal. He was a choirboy in St Peter's Church, and says that this experience fostered his interest in language. While at school he discovered poetry but that did not deter him from being, in his own words, a 'fairly nifty' scrum half. Cinema also attracted him, especially war movies and *A Night to Remember*, a film about the *Titanic*. He attended Royal Belfast Academical Institution, a grammar school. When he failed the eyesight test for the Merchant Navy he entered Trinity College, Dublin, where he studied French, English and Philosophy, and began writing poetry in earnest. Later he studied at the Sorbonne in Paris. On leaving university Mahon earned a living from freelance journalism and

1941–

teaching as well as radio and television work. For years his humorous, insightful literary reviews in *The Irish Times* attracted a regular following. In addition to Dylan Thomas, the first modern poets he encountered were Robert Graves, W.B. Yeats and Louis MacNeice (another Northern Irish poet). He claims a cultural affinity with Dublin-born writer Samuel Beckett that relates to their shared Protestantism and mordant humour. Other poets whom he admires include the Americans, Robert Lowell, Elizabeth Bishop and Hart Crane. French and Russian poetry also interests him, and he has been awarded numerous prizes for his translations.

He has lived in Canada, the US, London, Kinsale Co. Cork and briefly in Northern Ireland. His relationship with his home place is complex. He found it impossible to settle there, yet admits to feelings of guilt for having abandoned it. He recognises that his middle class, urban background is uninspiring and unlike its rural counterpart, has little mythology or symbolism to nurture his imagination. His raw materials are the unresolved tensions and ironies of harsh, intolerant Belfast. If he does have a hidden myth, it is what Terence Brown describes as 'the Protestant Planter's historical myth of conquest, and careful, puritan self-dependence frozen to vicious, stupid bigotry'. Mahon has rejected the idea that poetry should be socially or politically relevant. Poetry 'may appear to be about history or politics or autobiography, but [it] is essentially an artistic activity', he writes. He believes that it is about shape and form, about taking the formless and making it interesting. Notice the spareness of his poems: the few, precise details; the limited palette of colour; the controlled tone; the unyielding landscape; all fastidiously chosen. That technical virtuosity is matched by inspiration. 'You need soul, song and formal necessity,' he has written. Yet he recognises that a life spent pursuing perfect form and technique carries the danger of isolating the poet from fellow humans. His interest in form is evident in his versions of classic dramas. He has adapted French plays by Molière and Racine as well as Euripides' *The Bacchae*. You will encounter Mahon's early poetry in the selection here—the most recent poem included was published in 1985. In later poems he has adopted a less tense and less minimalist style, using a more relaxed and contemporary conversational idiom—characterised by an informal candour, longer lines and playful lists. The autobiographical, intimate form of the verse letter, in particular, attracts him. Nowadays Mahon lives in Dublin and is a member of Aosdána, an elected group of Irish artists who receive pensions from the state. He has two adult children.

Derek Mahon

Grandfather

this poem is also prescribed for Ordinary Level exams in 2003 and 2004

They brought him in on a stretcher from the world,
Wounded but humorous; and he soon recovered.
Boiler-rooms, row upon row of gantries rolled
Away to reveal the landscape of a childhood
Only he can recapture. Even on cold   5
Mornings he is up at six with a block of wood
Or a box of nails, discreetly up to no good
Or banging round the house like a four-year-old—

Never there when you call. But after dark
You hear his great boots thumping in the hall   10
And in he comes, as cute as they come. Each night
His shrewd eyes bolt the door and set the clock
Against the future, then his light goes out.
Nothing escapes him; he escapes us all.

Notes

[3] **gantries:** overhead structures with a platform supporting a travelling
crane, an essential tool of shipbuilding

[11] **cute:** the word means attractive and also shrewd, cunning or crafty

Explorations

First reading

1. Who is the subject of the poem?
2. Where did grandfather work?
3. Describe grandfather's working life and contrast it with his present-day activities.

Second reading

4. Describe grandfather's conduct.
5. Do you think that the members of his community would approve of his behaviour?
6. Note the adjectives used to

describe grandfather. What do they suggest about his personality?

7. Outline his bedtime ritual.
8. What do the first two lines of the poem tell us about the old man?

Third reading

9. How does he relate to the outside world?
10. What is the speaker's attitude toward grandfather? What evidence is there to support your view?
11. Why do you think that grandfather is described as 'cute'?
12. What is revealed about his attitude to the future?
13. Describe the mood of the poem. Is it serious, playful, dark, or a combination of these and other moods?
14. Look at the three prepositions in the first line, 'in', 'on' and 'from'. What do they convey about grandfather's relationship with the world?
15. Comment on the diction of the poem.

Fourth reading

16. Would you consider this a nostalgic poem? Why?
17. What is the effect of the repetition in the poem? Examine these examples: 'row upon row of gantries rolled'; '...he is up at six with a block of wood | Or a box of nails, discreetly up to no good'; 'You hear his great boots thumping in the hall | And in he comes, as cute as they come.'
18. In what ways might grandfather be a role model for the speaker of the poem?
19. What values are underwritten and questioned in this poem?
20. What characteristics of the sonnet do you discern in this poem? How does it differ from the Shakespearean sonnet? You might take account of the rhyming scheme, the irregular use of the iambic pentameter (the metre most common to the sonnet), the 'turn' or volta.
21. Examine the treatment of time in this poem. Consider, for example, the implicit contrast between the old man and the speaker, two generations younger. Think about the childhood memories to which only he has access. Note the poem's treatment of seasonal change and the ebb and flow of days. What does the future hold for grandfather?

Day Trip to Donegal

We reached the sea in early afternoon,
Climbed stiffly out; there were things to be done,
Clothes to be picked up, friends to be seen.
As ever, the nearby hills were a deeper green
Than anywhere in the world, and the grave   5
Grey of the sea the grimmer in that enclave.

Down at the pier the boats gave up their catch,
A writhing glimmer of fish; they fetch
Ten times as much in the city as here,
And still the fish come in year after year—   10
Herring and mackerel, flopping about the deck
In attitudes of agony and heartbreak.

We left at eight, drove back the way we came,
The sea receding down each muddy lane.
Around midnight we changed-down into suburbs   15
Sunk in a sleep no gale-force wind disturbs.
The time of year had left its mark
On frosty pavements glistening in the dark.

Give me a ring, goodnight, and so to bed…
That night the slow sea washed against my head,   20
Performing its immeasurable erosions—
Spilling into the skull, marbling the stones
That spine the very harbour wall,
Muttering its threat to villages of landfall.

At dawn I was alone far out at sea   25
Without skill or reassurance—nobody
To show me how, no promise of rescue—
Cursing my constant failure to take due
Forethought for this; contriving vain
Overtures to the vindictive wind and rain.   30

Notes

[6] **enclave:** a part of one state surrounded by another, but viewed by the surrounding territory. It can also mean a group of people who are culturally, intellectually or socially distinct from those surrounding them.

[29] **vain:** both meanings, proud and conceited, and worthless and futile, apply here

[30] **vindictive:** vengeful, spiteful, unforgiving

Explorations

First reading

1. Generally, what kind of experiences are day trips?
2. Discuss the significance of the title of this poem.
3. What does the speaker see on the pier?
4. Where does the speaker go in stanza three?
5. Briefly paraphrase each stanza.

Second reading

6. The encounter with the sea has a profound effect on the speaker. What is it about the sea that makes it so profoundly different from the land?
7. What is the most telling image in the poem for you?
8. Note where the plural 'we' gives way to the singular 'I'. What does this shift convey?
9. Discuss the contrasts that abound in this poem. In addition to the oppositions of land and sea already mentioned, you might consider the antitheses of suburban and rural landscape, isolation and camaraderie, night and day. Note the contrast in stanza four between the desultory goodbyes and the experience that follows.
10. Having read the poem, do you detect an irony in the term 'day trip'?

Third reading

11. How is the speaker's thinking and feeling altered by the sight of the dying fish?
12. Describe the movement in the poem.
13. Alliteration is widely used in this poem—for example, in stanza one there is an

accumulation of 'gr' sounds: 'green | ...grave | Grey...grimmer'. Find other examples of alliteration in the poem. Why is this and how effective is it?

14. Consider some of the distinctive features of stanza three. Comment on sentence length, the change of setting, the pace of the third line and how this is achieved.

15. What does the speaker mean when he says he is 'far out to sea'?

Fourth reading

16. In what ways could the erosion of the sea be compared to the effects of history?

17. What change is brought about in the speaker as a result of his day trip?

18. What political significance might be read into the greenness of Donegal, the fact that the speaker sees it as an enclave, and the grim, greyness of its sea?

After the Titanic

this poem is also prescribed for Ordinary Level exams in 2003 and 2004

They said I got away in a boat
And humbled me at the inquiry. I tell you
   I sank as far that night as any
Hero. As I sat shivering on the dark water
   I turned to ice to hear my costly   5
Life go thundering down in a pandemonium of
   Prams, pianos, sideboards, winches,
Boilers bursting and shredded ragtime. Now I hide
   In a lonely house behind the sea
Where the tide leaves broken toys and hatboxes   10
   Silently at my door. The showers of
April, flowers of May mean nothing to me, nor the
   Late light of June, when my gardener
Describes to strangers how the old man stays in bed
   On seaward mornings after nights of   15
Wind, takes his cocaine and will see no one. Then it is
   I drown again with all those dim
Lost faces I never understood, my poor soul
   Screams out in the starlight, heart
Breaks loose and rolls down like a stone.   20
   Include me in your lamentations.

Notes

Titanic: The *Titanic* was a ship built in Belfast. It was completed in 1912 and was described as 'the latest thing in the art of shipbuilding'. The word 'titanic' has come to mean colossal, and indeed, the ship was immense. That it was built in Belfast placed the city at the very leading edge of the Industrial Revolution. However, it sank dramatically when it collided with an iceberg on its maiden voyage to America, with the loss of 1,500 lives, the greatest tragedy in maritime history. This catastrophe has entered the global imagination as a major disaster, and was a mortal blow to the self-confidence of the age.

[1] **They said I got away in a boat:** The speaker of the poem is Bruce Ismay (1892–1937), manager of the White Star Line for which the *Titanic* sailed. He was one of the relatively few men to have escaped from the sinking *Titanic*, and he was strongly criticised for failing to help the drowning passengers.

[6] **pandemonium:** meaning chaos, confusion, turmoil. In John Milton's poem, 'Paradise Lost', it is the place of all demons.

[7] **winches:** plural of a windlass, the crank of a wheel or axle (singular is 'winch')

[8] **ragtime:** a type of jazz music, a syncopated musical rhythm developed by American black musicians in the 1890s and usually played on the piano

[15] **seaward:** going or facing toward the sea

[16] **cocaine:** a drug used both as a local anaesthetic and a stimulant

[21] **lamentations:** At one level, 'Include me in your lamentations' is the plea of the poem's speaker, Bruce Ismay, for inclusion in the community's mourning of the victims of the *Titanic* disaster. However, it is also a reference to the Old Testament book containing five poems that constitute the 'Lamentations of Jeremiah'.

 # Explorations

Workers leaving the Belfast Shipyard in 1911 with the half-finished *Titanic* in the background

Ecclesiastes

CD Track 26

God, you could grow to love it, God-fearing, God-
    chosen purist little puritan that,
for all your wiles and smiles, you are (the
    dank churches, the empty streets,
the shipyard silence, the tied-up swings) and   5
    shelter your cold heart from the heat
of the world, from woman-inquisition, from the
    bright eyes of children. Yes, you could
wear black, drink water, nourish a fierce zeal
    with locusts and wild honey, and not   10
feel called upon to understand and forgive
    but only to speak with a bleak
afflatus, and love the January rains when they
    darken the dark doors and sink hard
into the Antrim hills, the bog meadows, the heaped   15
    graves of your fathers. Bury that red
bandana and stick, that banjo; this is your
    country, close one eye and be king.
Your people await you, their heavy washing
    flaps for you in the housing estates —   20
a credulous people. God, you could do it, God
    help you, stand on a corner stiff
with rhetoric, promising nothing under the sun.

Notes

Ecclesiastes: the title of an Old Testament book of the Bible, but also a person who addresses an assembly, a preacher

[2] **purist:** a person who scrupulously advocates rigid precision and formality, especially in the field of language or art

[2] **puritan:** In its historical meaning, the term refers to a member of a group of English protestants who regarded the Reformation as incomplete and refused to subscribe to the established church, that is, the Church of Ireland or the Church of England. They sought to simplify and regulate forms of worship. However, a puritan is also a distinct character type, a person who practises extreme strictness in matters of religion and morals. The term could be applied in both senses to the person addressed in the poem.

[5] **the tied-up swings:** It was customary for many local authorities in Northern Ireland to close public parks on Sundays.

[9] **zeal:** fervour and earnestness in furthering a cause; uncompromising partisanship; fanaticism; indefatigable enthusiasm

[10] **locusts and wild honey:** In the Bible, this was often the only food available to penitents who fasted in the desert.

[13] **afflatus:** a divine creative impulse; inspiration

[16–17] **red | bandana...stick...banjo:** emblems of non-conformity, wanderlust and art

[18] **close one eye:** closing one eye may sharpen the focus, but it restricts the range of vision and is a metaphor for narrow-mindedness

[21] **credulous:** gullible

[23] **rhetoric:** The discipline, or art, of persuasive writing or speaking. It often implies exaggeration or insincerity.

 # Explorations

First reading

1. What does the word 'Ecclesiastes' mean?
2. Where is the poem set?
3. Who is the speaker in this poem?
4. Describe the ecclesiastes to whom this poem is addressed. What kind of person is he or she?
5. Describe the place in which this preacher's community lives.

Second reading

6. Is the title a good one? Why?
7. What does the preacher promise his or her people?
8. Find some positive and negative images of Belfast in this poem.
9. Find some references to the Bible and to religion in this poem.
10. Are the speaker and the ecclesiastes one and the same person? Why do you think that?
11. What colours predominate in this poem?
12. What kind of atmosphere pervades the place described?
13. What groups of people tend to wear black and why?

Third reading

14. Discuss the mood of the poem.
15. What tone does the speaker use?
16. Why must the ecclesiastes leave behind the 'red | bandana...stick...banjo'?
17. What is the effect of the repetition of the word 'God'?
18. In what does the preacher take pleasure?

Fourth reading

19. Explore some of the rhetorical devices employed in the poem. These might include the declamatory tone, the fluency and formality, the repetitions of sentence structure and the amplitude of the first two sentences.
20. Discuss the irony of this poem. At whom is it directed?
21. Can you identify any parallels between the preacher depicted here and the poet-speaker?
22. Show how the first and last sentences of the poem are similar. Consider the sentence structure, the sentiments expressed and the repetition of words. What purpose does this form serve?

As It Should Be

We hunted the mad bastard
Through bog, moorland, rock, to the starlit west
And gunned him down in a blind yard
Between ten sleeping lorries
And an electricity generator.   5

Let us hear no idle talk
Of the moon in the Yellow River;
The air blows softer since his departure.

Since his tide-burial during school hours
Our children have known no bad dreams.   10
Their cries echo lightly along the coast.

This is as it should be.
They will thank us for it when they grow up
To a world with method in it.

Notes

[1] **We hunted the mad bastard:** The persona of the poem is a spokesman for the Irish Free State, which condones the murder of the revolutionary, the dreamer.

[3] **blind:** in this case, walled up, closed at one end; also lacking foresight and understanding

[5] **an electricity generator:** a machine for converting mechanical energy into electrical energy

[7] **the moon in the Yellow River:** This is the title of a play by Denis Johnston written in 1931. Johnston took the phrase from Ezra Pound's image of a drunken poet, Li-Po, who grasped at illusory ideals and was drowned while trying 'to embrace the moon in the yellow river'. The play's story is set in Ireland in 1927, and one of the new Irish State's projects intended to modernise the country is a hydroelectric scheme. When a revolutionary called Blake tries to blow up its generator, Lanigan, an officer of the Free State, shoots him. In this poem, a revolutionary is shot among lorries beside an electricity generator, monuments to progress. Material improvement comes at a price, in this case brutal murder.

[9] **tide-burial:** the body is cast into the water and carried away on the tide

[14] **method:** implies orderliness, regular habits, procedure, pattern, system

Explorations

First reading

1. On what incident is this poem based?
2. In what part of the country was the fugitive pursued?
3. Would it be easy to hide in bog, moorland or rock?
4. Where was he found?
5. What did his pursuers do when they found him?

Second reading

6. How did they dispose of his body?
7. Whom does the 'we' of the poem represent?
8. Why does the speaker say that the children no longer have bad dreams?

Third reading

9. What is the effect of the obscenity in the first line?
10. What image of themselves do the speakers present in the first stanza?
11. What values do the speakers wish to pass on to their children?
12. Show how the poem suggests that violence is implicated in the fabric of the state from its foundation.
13. Describe the speaker's tone.

Fourth reading

14. Comment on the variations in line and stanza length.
15. What is it that the speakers wish to suppress? With what will they replace it?
16. Compare the ironic tone of this poem with that of other poems by Mahon.
17. In what sense are the speakers making history?
18. Examine this poem's links to other literary works.

A Disused Shed in Co. Wexford

Notes

Let them not forget us, the weak souls among the asphodels.
— Seferis, *Mythistorema*

(for J.G. Farrell)

Even now there are places where a thought might grow —
Peruvian mines, worked out and abandoned
To a slow clock of condensation,
An echo trapped for ever, and a flutter
Of wild flowers in the lift-shaft,   5
Indian compounds where the wind dances
And a door bangs with diminished confidence,
Lime crevices behind rippling rain-barrels,
Dog corners for bone burials;
And in a disused shed in Co. Wexford,   10

Deep in the grounds of a burnt-out hotel,
Among the bathtubs and washbasins
A thousand mushrooms crowd to a keyhole.
This is the one star in their firmament
Or frames a star within a star.   15
What should they do there but desire?
So many days beyond the rhododendrons
With the world waltzing in its bowl of cloud,
They have learnt patience and silence
Listening to the rooks querulous in the high wood.   20

They have been waiting for us in a foetor
Of vegetable sweat since civil war days,
Since the gravel-crunching, interminable departure
Of the expropriated mycologist.
He never came back, and light since then   25
Is a keyhole rusting gently after rain.
Spiders have spun, flies dusted to mildew
And once a day, perhaps, they have heard something —
A trickle of masonry, a shout from the blue
Or a lorry changing gear at the end of the lane.   30

asphodels: A
type of lily. It
has been
represented in
literature as
an immortal
flower
growing in
the fields of
Elysium, the
place where,
in Greek
mythology,
the blessed
go after
death.

Seferis: George
Seferis
(1900–71),
a Greek poet
and
ambassador
to Britain,
whose poetry
draws on
Greek
mythology.

There have been deaths, the pale flesh flaking
Into the earth that nourished it;
And nightmares, born of these and the grim
Dominion of stale air and rank moisture.
Those nearest the door grow strong —   35
'Elbow room! Elbow room!'
The rest, dim in a twilight of crumbling
Utensils and broken pitchers, groaning
For their deliverance, have been so long
Expectant that there is left only the posture.   40

A half century, without visitors, in the dark —
Poor preparation for the cracking lock
And creak of hinges; magi, moonmen,
Powdery prisoners of the old regime,
Web-throated, stalked like triffids, racked by drought   45
And insomnia, only the ghost of a scream
At the flash-bulb firing-squad we wake them with
Shows there is life yet in their feverish forms.
Grown beyond nature now, soft food for worms,
They lift frail heads in gravity and good faith.   50

They are begging us, you see, in their wordless way,
To do something, to speak on their behalf
Or at least not to close the door again.
Lost people of Treblinka and Pompeii!
'Save us, save us,' they seem to say,   55
'Let the god not abandon us
Who have come so far in darkness and in pain.
We too had our lives to live.
You with your light meter and relaxed itinerary,
Let not our naive labours have been in vain!'   60

Notes *continued*

   J.G. Farrell: This poem had its source in Farrell's novel *Troubles*. Farrell, a good friend of
   Mahon, was drowned while fishing in 1979. 'I'd read *Troubles* and I was convinced that there
   was a shed in it, with mushrooms', Mahon has written. 'But when I went back and re-read it,
   the shed with the mushrooms was missing. I must have imagined it.'

[6] **compounds:** large open enclosures for housing workers

[14] **firmament:** the sky

[17] **rhododendrons:** evergreen shrubs with large flowers that grow profusely in some parts of
   Ireland

[20] **querulous:** complaining, fractious

[21] **foetor:** stench

[22] **civil war days:** This is probably a reference to the civil war fought in Ireland in 1922–23. It began when some members of nationalist movements rejected the treaty that brought an end to the War of Independence fought with Britain. Although the actual death toll was not high, it left a legacy of bitterness and a lasting influence on the shape of party politics in Ireland. J.G. Farrell's novel *Troubles*, which inspired this poem, is set in civil war Ireland.

[24] **expropriated mycologist:** an expert on fungi or mushrooms who has been dispossessed, especially one whose property has been taken away by the state

[43] **magi:** the 'wise men' who brought gifts to the infant Jesus; the plural of 'magus', a word that means a sorcerer; also priests in ancient Persia

[43] **moonmen:** They are moonmen because they have been denied the light of the sun for so long.

[45] **triffids:** These are monstrous, lethal plants from outer space that can propel themselves about, originally in John Wyndham's science fiction novel, *The Day of the Triffids*. This book describes the contrast between a comfortable setting and a sudden invasion that is a metaphysical catastrophe. The term has now come to describe any hostile plant.

[45] **racked by drought:** tortured by thirst

[46] **insomnia:** sleeplessness

[54] **Treblinka:** a Nazi concentration camp in Poland where Jews were put to death during the Second World War

[54] **Pompeii:** a city in south-east Italy which was buried after Mount Vesuvius erupted in 79 B.C.

[59] **itinerary:** a detailed route, often mapped out for tourists by travel consultants

 # Explorations

First reading

1. Name some of the places where 'a thought might grow'.
2. Describe in detail the mushrooms' surroundings.
3. How have they spent their existence?
4. Describe the horrors endured by the forgotten mushrooms in stanza four.
5. How long have they been behind locks?
6. Describe the effect of their confinement on the mushrooms.
7. How do they respond to the garish light of 'the flash-bulb firing-squad'?

Second reading

8. What is distinctive about the places 'where a thought might grow'?
9. What is the mushrooms' plea?

10. How do the mushrooms communicate?
11. Discuss the title of the poem.

Third reading

12. What is the significance of the opening phrase 'Even now'?
13. Describe the tone, or range of tones, of this poem. How does the poem represent the strong emotions aroused by the plight of the abandoned?
14. Why do you think Mahon chose to nominate mushrooms as his central characters?
15. Why does the poet delay before introducing the mushrooms, around which the poem is centred?
16. What is the effect of the rhetorical question 'What should they do there but desire'?
17. What does the poet mean when he writes 'the world waltzing in its bowl of cloud'?
18. Discuss who or what you think the 'expropriated mycologist' represents.

Fourth reading

19. How does Mahon achieve the effect of time passing in stanzas two and three?
20. Identify the specific historic references in the poem and discuss their significance.
21. What is the speaker's reaction to the plight of the mushrooms?
22. Would the liberation of the mushrooms resolve all their difficulties? Does being part of history offer a solution to the agonies described in the poem?
23. In what way is this poem a meditation on the legacy of war?
24. What difficulties confront the speaker of this poem? You might refer to the problem of speaking on behalf of the voiceless, representing them rather than enabling them to speak for themselves.
25. Show how this poem depicts the manner in which the powerful abandon and ignore the helpless.
26. What in your opinion, is significant about the epigram and dedication?
27. How do the themes of this poem relate to those in other poems by Mahon that you have read?
28. Consider the use of the past tense in 'We too had our lives to live' (stanza six).
29. Does this poem suggest that Mahon is 'through with history', as he has twice suggested in other poems? What evidence is there to support your opinion?
30. In what ways is the speaker of the poem involved in the present exploitation of the victims of history?
31. Show how Mahon achieves a local and global context. What does this double focus suggest?

The Chinese Restaurant in Portrush

Before the first visitor comes the spring
Softening the sharp air of the coast
In time for the first seasonal 'invasion'.
Today the place is as it might have been,
Gentle and almost hospitable. A girl   5
Strides past the Northern Counties Hotel,
Light-footed, swinging a book-bag,
And the doors that were shut all winter
Against the north wind and the sea-mist
Lie open to the street, where one   10
By one the gulls go window-shopping
And an old wolfhound dozes in the sun.

While I sit with my paper and prawn chow mein
Under a framed photograph of Hong Kong
The proprietor of the Chinese restaurant   15
Stands at the door as if the world were young,
Watching the first yacht hoist a sail
— An ideogram on sea-cloud — and the light
Of heaven upon the hills of Donegal;
And whistles a little tune, dreaming of home.   20

Notes

Portrush: a seaside town in north Antrim, to which the young Mahon would cycle at weekends

[12] **wolfhound:** This is perhaps an oblique reference to the bloody Ulster cycle of heroic tales. When the young mythical champion Cuculann killed a wolfhound owned by Culann, a blacksmith, he replaced the animal as Culann's guardian, and became known as the hound of Ulster. In one of his exploits, he single-handedly defended Ulster from the army of Queen Maeve of Connaught. Here the hound is sleeping, suggesting that ancient aggressions are temporarily laid aside.

[18] **ideogram:** a character symbolising or representing the idea of a thing without indicating the sequence of sounds in its name. Ideograms are used in Chinese writing.

Explorations

First reading

1. To what 'invasion' does the poem's persona refer?
2. Why is the word 'invasion' placed in quotation marks?
3. What is meant by 'the gulls go window-shopping'?
4. What does the speaker find attractive about Portrush on this particular day?
5. Where is the restaurateur's home?
6. How is Donegal depicted?

Second reading

7. In stanza two, what does the speaker see and what does the restaurateur see?
8. Put yourself in the persona's position in stanza two, seated in the restaurant. Sketch the scene described in that stanza.
9. How do the seasons affect Portrush?

Third reading

10. How does the poet achieve the optimistic, upbeat tone of the first stanza?
11. Comment on the humour in this poem. You might refer to the title, the name of the hotel, the 'almost hospitable' place, the 'invasion', and the dozing wolfhound. You might also consider the humorous rhyming of 'Hong Kong' with 'restaurant' and 'young'. What is the effect of this humour?

Fourth reading

12. What does the poet mean by 'as if the world was young'? You might relate the statement to Mahon's preoccupation with the horrors perpetrated by humans throughout history.
13. What statement does the poem make about the nature of home?
14. In what ways is this a visual poem?

Rathlin

A long time since the last scream cut short —
Then an unnatural silence; and then
A natural silence, slowly broken
By the shearwater, by the sporadic
Conversation of crickets, the bleak   5
Reminder of a metaphysical wind.
Ages of this, till the report
Of an outboard motor at the pier
Shatters the dream-time and we land
As if we were the first visitors here.   10

The whole island a sanctuary where amazed
Oneiric species whistle and chatter,
Evacuating rock-face and cliff-top.
Cerulean distance, an oceanic haze —
Nothing but sea-smoke to the ice-cap   15
And the odd somnolent freighter.
Bombs doze in the housing estates
But here they are through with history —
Custodians of a lone light which repeats ·
One simple statement to the turbulent sea.   20

A long time since the unspeakable violence —
Since Somhairle Buí, powerless on the mainland,
Heard the screams of the Rathlin women
Borne to him, seconds later, upon the wind.
Only the cry of the shearwater   25
And the roar of the outboard motor
Disturb the singular peace. Spray-blind,
We leave here the infancy of the race,
Unsure among the pitching surfaces
Whether the future lies before us or behind.   30

Notes

Rathlin: Rathlin is an island off the north Antrim coast. It attracted settlers from the Bronze Age through the Middle Ages. Its landscape is magnificent, with masses of basalt columns, similar to those in the Giant's Causeway, contrasting with chalk cliffs. It contained a fortified castle in the late Middle Ages. Robert the Bruce hid there in 1306, in a cave, and learnt persistence and patience from the spiders he saw ceaselessly repairing their webs. There is now a national nature reserve on the island.

[4] **shearwater:** a long-winged seabird of the puffin family

[4] **sporadic:** intermittent, occasional

[6] **metaphysical wind:** The term 'metaphysical' relates to the philosophy of being and knowing, the philosophy of mind, abstract or subtle talk. The sounds of Rathlin are reminders or echoes of speech. There is a pun on the word 'wind'. The wind creates a sound on Rathlin that is reminiscent of human conversation, but 'wind' can also mean idle, pointless talk.

[9] **dream-time:** In Australian aboriginal mythology, dream-time is also called the 'alcheringa', the golden age when the first ancestors were created.

[12] **Oneiric:** relating to dreams

[14] **Cerulean:** deep blue like a clear sky

[16] **somnolent:** sleepy, drowsy

[18] **through with history:** This phrase also occurs in another poem by Mahon, 'The Last of the Fire Kings'.

[19] **a lone light:** There is a lighthouse on the nature reserve in the east of the island.

[22–23] **Somhairle Buí... I ...Rathlin women:** Probably refers to Sorley Boy MacDonnell (1505?–1590). He was a Scots-Irish chieftain whose lands stretched from the glens of Antrim across the Mull of Kintyre to include Islay and Kintyre in Scotland. Queen Elizabeth's marshal in Ireland, the eighteenth Earl of Essex, was determined to subdue him in 1575. Expecting a battle, Somhairle 'put most of his plate [silver], most of his children, and the most of the children of his gentlemen with their wives' in a fortified castle on the island of Rathlin. On Essex's orders, they were all massacred, with Somhairle, almost frantic with despair, witnessing the carnage from the mainland. In all, five or six hundred people perished (not only women, as Mahon suggests, but men and children too), either in the castle or hunted down and butchered as they sought shelter on the rugged island.

[29] **pitching:** sloping; intense; in motion; unstable

 # Explorations

First reading

1. What kind of place is Rathlin?
2. How does the speaker arrive on the island?
3. What does the first line suggest to you about Rathlin's past?
4. Why was the silence first 'unnatural' and then 'natural'?
5. Who or what inhabits the island now?

6. What effect does the arrival of the speaker's boat have on the island?
7. Paraphrase the description of Rathlin and its setting found in the first six lines of stanza two.

Second reading

8. What does the speaker mean by 'dream-time' in stanza one?

---

9. Why is the violence done to Somhairle MacDonnell's family described as 'unspeakable'?

10. What is the 'one simple statement' that the birds repeat to the sea?

11. Why, in your opinion, is the opening phrase 'A long time' repeated at the beginning of the last stanza?

Third reading

12. Explain the phrase 'here they are through with history'.

13. What is the effect of the accumulation of terms such as 'oneiric', 'haze', 'sea-smoke' and 'somnolent' in stanza two?

14. Comment on the juxtaposition of the 'somnolent freighter' and the 'dozing bombs' at the centre of stanza two.

Fourth reading

15. What link does the speaker forge between the brutal murder of the MacDonnell tribe in Elizabethan times and the troubles raging in Northern Ireland as the poem was written?

16. Explore the treatment of time in this poem. You might refer to dream-time, historical time and the future. You might compare and contrast the timescale of Rathlin with that of the inhabitants of the housing estates.

17. Examine Mahon's use of rhyme, partial or slant rhyme, feminine rhyme and half-rhyme in this poem.

18. What might the speaker mean when he claims he is 'Unsure... I Whether the future lies before us or behind'?

Church Bay, Rathlin Island

Antarctica

(for Richard Ryan)

'I am just going outside and may be some time.'
The others nod, pretending not to know.
At the heart of the ridiculous, the sublime.

He leaves them reading and begins to climb,
Goading his ghost into the howling snow;   5
He is just going outside and may be some time.

The tent recedes beneath its crust of rime
And frostbite is replaced by vertigo:
At the heart of the ridiculous, the sublime.

Need we consider it some sort of crime,   10
This numb self-sacrifice of the weakest? No,
He is just going outside and may be some time —

In fact, for ever. Solitary enzyme,
Though the night yield no glimmer there will glow,
At the heart of the ridiculous, the sublime.   15

He takes leave of the earthly pantomime
Quietly, knowing it is time to go.
'I am just going outside and may be some time.'
At the heart of the ridiculous, the sublime.

Background note

Antarctica: The Antarctic is the south polar region. This poem relates to an incident that took place during Captain Robert Scott's expedition to Antarctica in 1911–12. His plan was to be the first to reach the South Pole. After much hardship and mismanagement, he and three others, including Captain Lawrence Oates (1880–1912), attained their goal, only to find that an expedition led by a Norwegian, Roald Amundsen, had succeeded just three weeks before them. Scott's return journey was dogged by misfortune. One member suffered a bad fall and died a fortnight later. Oates's frostbitten feet became gangrenous and he begged the others to abandon him. They refused. To avoid being a burden he walked out into the night, to his certain death, with the words 'I am just going outside and may be some time.' The other three struggled to within a mere eleven miles of their base camp, but then a blizzard struck. Their bodies were found in a tent eight months later.

Richard Ryan: an Irish diplomat and poet, author of a poem on the American army's massacre of Vietnamese people at My Lai.

Notes

[3] **sublime:** exalted, grand, noble, awe-inspiring, lofty, majestic

[5] **Goading:** urging on

[7] **rime:** frost formed from cloud or fog; poets sometime use the word 'rime' to describe the glittery frost often seen on plants on clear, still days

[8] **frostbite:** damage to body tissue exposed to freezing temperatures. Severe cases lead to gangrene and the body tissue dies

[8] **vertigo:** dizziness, a whirling sensation, a tendency to lose one's balance

[13] **enzyme:** An enzyme causes a living organism to change but is not changed itself. In scientific terms, it is a protein that acts as a catalyst in a specific biochemical reaction.

 # Explorations

First reading

1. Why do you think the poem is called 'Antarctica'? What images does Antarctica conjure up?

2. Who is the speaker of the first line?

3. Who are 'The others' referred to in the second line?

Second reading

4. Summarise the story told in the first three stanzas.

5. Why does the persona in the poem 'go outside'?

6. What will happen to him when he leaves the tent?

7. What is the rhyming pattern in this poem?

Third reading

8. How does the speaker of the poem view Oates's act?

9. What conclusion does the speaker come to about Oates's action?

10. How would you describe the tone?

11. How does Mahon achieve this tone?

12. Consider the last line of each stanza. What pattern do you notice?

Fourth reading

13. What is the effect of the caesura after 'for ever' in stanza five?

14. In what ways do the last three stanzas differ from the first three? How does the last stanza differ from the others?

15. The persona of the poem calls Oates a 'solitary enzyme'. What is the effect of using a scientific term to describe a human being?

16. What is meant by 'the earthly pantomime'?

17. Discuss the run-on line or enjambment in the last stanza.

18. Do you agree with the speaker that Oates's suicidal act is both ridiculous and sublime? Why?

Scott and his team finding Amundsen's tent at the South Pole, 18 January 1912

Captain Lawrence Oates

Kinsale

CD Track 32

The kind of rain we knew is a thing of the past —
deep-delving, dark, deliberate you would say,
browsing on spire and bogland; but today
our sky-blue slates are steaming in the sun,
our yachts tinkling and dancing in the bay   5
like racehorses. We contemplate at last
shining windows, a future forbidden to no one.

Notes

Kinsale: a town situated in Co. Cork, nowadays a thriving seaside
tourist resort and a fishing port. Kinsale is important from the point of
view of the history of Ulster and Ireland because in the battle fought
there in 1601, Queen Elizabeth's soldier, Mountjoy, routed the Ulster
chieftains Hugh O'Neill and Hugh O'Donnell. This defeat signalled the
end of Gaelic rule in Ireland. Ulster, which had been the province most
resistant to English rule, was colonised by Scots and English settlers and
became eventually the most anglicised. Kinsale is therefore the site of
failure, a post-historical place.

[3] **browsing on:** feeding on; also randomly surveying or skimming

Explorations

First reading

1. Describe Kinsale as depicted in this poem.
2. Describe the rain.
3. When the rain stops, how does the landscape change?

Second reading

4. Here the rain has negative implications. With what is it associated, do you think?
5. The yachts are described as 'tinkling and dancing... I like racehorses'. Compare and contrast this image with the description of the rain.
6. Do you think the imagery is effective in getting across an awareness of the poet's mood?
7. 'Tinkling' is an unusual verb to describe the sound of yachts. Why do you think Mahon uses it?

Third reading

8. Notice that 'past' rhymes with 'at last'. Does this echo reinforce the sense of relief that the past is over?

9. What events from the past might the poet have in mind in this poem? The title of the poem points us in a particular direction.
10. The first person plural 'we' is used twice in the poem. Is that significant?
11. In what ways are the rain and the past alike?
12. Why do you think that Mahon set this poem in Kinsale and not in any other seaside town in Ireland?

Fourth reading

13. How would looking through shining windows affect the way we see the world?
14. How does the poet suggest that while he is optimistic, there is no certainty about the future?
15. The speaker contemplates shining windows, but does not look through them or see reflections in them. Is that significant?

15 Eavan BOLAND

Eavan Boland was born in Dublin in 1944, daughter of the painter Frances Kelly and the diplomat Frederick Boland. She was educated at Holy Child Convent, Killiney, and Trinity College, Dublin. For some years she lectured at Trinity College in the English Department, before becoming a literary journalist, chiefly with the *Irish Times* but also with RTE, where she produced award-winning poetry programmes for radio. She married the novelist Kevin Casey; exchanging the Dublin literary scene for family life in the suburbs where she wrote prolifically.

New Territory (1967) was her first volume of poetry. Her second volume, *The War Horse* (1975), deals with the Northern Ireland 'troubles' and with the way violence encroaches on our domestic lives. The poem 'Child of Our Time' is taken from this volume. Her third volume, *In Her Own Image* (1980), explores the darker side of female identity, 'woman's secret history'; it deals with real but taboo issues such as anorexia, infanticide, mastectomy, menstruation and domestic violence. The fourth collection, *Night Feed* (1982), celebrates the ordinary, everyday domestic aspect of woman's identity. The fifth volume,

1944–

The Journey (1986), and the sixth volume, *Outside History* (1990), consider the image of woman in Irish history as illustrated in painting and in literature—a tale of exploitation and repression, of being marginalised and kept from the centre of influence. The seventh collection, *In a Time of Violence* (1994), deals specifically with Irish national and historical issues; such as the famine, agrarian violence and the Easter Rising. It also focuses on the theme of women as mothers and the relationship between mothers and daughters. The poem 'This Moment' is taken from this volume.

The place of the woman writer in Irish literature, mythology and history is a prominent theme in Boland's poetry and other writings. Her pamphlet *A Kind of Scar* (1989) examines this issue. Her collection of autobiographical prose, published in 1995, is entitled *Object Lessons: The Life of the Woman and the Poet in Our Time*. In 1980 she was joint founder of Arlen House, a feminist publishing company.

Eavan Boland

The War Horse

This dry night, nothing unusual
About the clip, clop, casual

Iron of his shoes as he stamps death
Like a mint on the innocent coinage of earth.

I lift the window, watch the ambling feather   5
Of hock and fetlock, loosed from its daily tether

In the tinker camp on the Enniskerry Road,
Pass, his breath hissing, his snuffling head

Down. He is gone. No great harm is done.
Only a leaf of our laurel hedge is torn—   10

Of distant interest like a maimed limb,
Only a rose which now will never climb

The stone of our house, expendable, a mere
Line of defence against him, a volunteer

You might say, only a crocus, its bulbous head   15
Blown from growth, one of the screamless dead.

But we, we are safe, our unformed fear
Of fierce commitment gone; why should we care

If a rose, a hedge, a crocus are uprooted
Like corpses, remote, crushed, mutilated?   20

He stumbles on like a rumour of war, huge
Threatening. Neighbours use the subterfuge

Of curtains. He stumbles down our short street
Thankfully passing us. I pause, wait,

Then to breathe relief lean on the sill   25
And for a second only my blood is still

With atavism. That rose he smashed frays
Ribboned across our hedge, recalling days

Of burned countryside, illicit braid:
A cause ruined before, a world betrayed.   30

Notes

[4] **mint:** place where money is coined

[6] **hock:** joint on horse's leg corresponding to the human ankle

[6] **fetlock:** tuft of hair above and behind the horse's hoof

[27] **atavism:** resemblance to remote ancestors; in this instance the horse's violation of the domestic garden stirs race memories of English colonial violence and the destruction of Irish homesteads

[29] **braid:** anything plaited or interwoven, such as hair or ribbon, or the gold and silver thread decoration on uniforms; it might refer to rebel uniforms

 # Explorations

Genesis of the poem

This poem stems from an incident when the front garden of Boland's new house in the suburbs was invaded a number of times by a stray horse, presumed to belong to local travellers. Perhaps the horse had lived there when the site was open fields.

First reading

1. On a first reading, what do you see? Visualise the night, the garden, the atmosphere, the animal. What sounds are there in this scene?

2. At one level, this horse is made real to the reader. How is this realised? What words best convey the shape, size, movement etc. of the animal to us? Explore sounds of words as well as visual images. What is your first impression of the horse?

3. Do you think this horse carries a sense of menace or threat? Examine the first four couplets especially. Explore the imagery, the sounds of words and the rhythm of the piece in coming to a conclusion.

4. How is the fragility of the domestic garden conveyed to us? What words or images suggest this?

Second reading

5. What do you notice about the speaker's reactions to this intrusion? Do they change as the poem progresses? Make specific references to the text.

6. (a) Could this piece be read as a political poem, with the horse as a symbol of violence? What evidence do you find in the poem for this reading? (b) At a symbolic level, what is being suggested here about the nature of violence?

Third reading

7. How do you read the poem? What themes do you find it deals with, and what levels of meaning do you notice?

The Famine Road

'Idle as trout in light Colonel Jones
these Irish, give them no coins at all; their bones
need toil, their characters no less.' Trevelyan's
seal blooded the deal table. The Relief
Committee deliberated: 'Might it be safe,   5
Colonel, to give them roads, roads to force
from nowhere, going nowhere of course?'

   one out of every ten and then
   another third of those again
   women—in a case like yours.   10

Sick, directionless they worked; fork, stick
were iron years away; after all could
they not blood their knuckles on rock, suck
April hailstones for water and for food?
Why for that, cunning as housewives, each eyed—   15
as if at a corner butcher—the other's buttock.

   anything may have caused it, spores,
   a childhood accident; one sees
   day after day these mysteries.

Dusk: they will work tomorrow without him.   20
They know it and walk clear. He has become
a typhoid pariah, his blood tainted, although
he shares it with some there. No more than snow
attends its own flakes where they settle
and melt, will they pray by his death rattle.   25

   You never will, never you know
   but take it well woman, grow
   your garden, keep house, good-bye.

'It has gone better than we expected, Lord
Trevelyan, sedition, idleness, cured   30
in one; from parish to parish, field to field;
the wretches work till they are quite worn,
then fester by their work; we march the corn
to the ships in peace. This Tuesday I saw bones
out of my carriage window. Your servant Jones.'   35

> *Barren, never to know the load*
> *of his child in you, what is your body*
> *now if not a famine road?*

Notes

Famine Road: In the Great Famine of 1845–48 the potato crop failed and the people were left destitute and starving. Among the relief works organised to allow the hungry to earn money was road construction; but these roads were rarely meant to be used and often ended uselessly in bog or field. So the famine road might be read as a symbol of unfulfilled lives that go nowhere.

[1] **Colonel Jones:** Lieutenant-Colonel Jones was one of the officers in charge of relief works around Newry. There exists a letter from him to Trevelyan reporting on work carried out during the winter of 1846; this may be the source of the exchange here.

[3] **Trevelyan:** Charles Trevelyan was a senior British civil servant, Assistant Secretary to the Treasury, in charge of relief works in Ireland at the outbreak of the Great Famine in 1845. At first his approach was dominated by the laissez-faire (non-intervention) policy popular at the time, and he was concerned that the Irish might be demoralised by receiving too much government help. Later he came to realise that they would not survive without it; but he never really warmed to the Irish, speaking of 'the selfish, perverse and turbulent character of the people'.

[4] **Relief Committee:** committees that organised local schemes to try to alleviate the starvation

[22] **pariah:** outcast

[30] **sedition:** conduct or language directed towards the overthrow of the state

[33] **corn to the ships:** Despite the starvation, normal commerce was carried on, and corn was exported as usual, though grain carts now needed protection against the local population.

 # Explorations

First reading

1. Read aloud Trevelyan's letter in the first three lines of the poem. How do you think it should sound? Consider the tone. What is Trevelyan's attitude? What words or phrases convey his attitude particularly well? What do Trevelyan's gestures add to the tone of this? Read it as you think he would say it.

2. Read aloud the Relief Committee's speech to Colonel Jones, as you imagine it said. Pay attention to the tone of

'might it be safe' and 'going nowhere of course.'

3. Read stanzas 3 and 5 (beginning 'Sick' and 'Dusk', respectively). What do you notice about the relief work and the condition of the people?

4. Consider Colonel Jones's letter to Trevelyan ('It has gone better...'). What does it reveal about the writer—his priorities, his attitude to the Irish, his awareness of the famine, etc.? Is there evidence of sympathy, or of superiority and indifference? Consider phrases such as 'the wretches...', 'fester by their work', 'march ... in peace.' What is the effect of the hollow rhyme 'bones—Jones'? Read the letter aloud as you think he might say it.

Second reading

5. In the third stanza, how is the desperate bleakness of the people's situation conveyed? What image in particular conveys the depth of their degradation? Explain your thinking.

6. Illness isolates and degrades human beings. How is this portrayed in the fifth stanza? Consider the effect of the imagery and the sounds of words.

Third reading

7. Now explore the woman's story (stanzas 2, 4, 6, and 8). (a) Who is speaking in the first three stanzas? Which words suggest that? (b) Consider the tone, and read these three aloud. (c) Who speaks the last stanza? How does the speaker feel? Which words best convey the feelings?

8. Write an extract from that woman's diary, as she might compose it, following that meeting. Fill it with the thoughts you imagine going through her head as she listened to the consultant.

Fourth reading

9. What statement do you think this poem makes on the status of women?

10. Explain the comparisons implied in the poem between the experience of women and the treatment of the famine people. Do you find it enlightening? Explain.

11. In her writings, Boland has often expressed concern that history is sometimes simplified into myth.
'Irish poets of the nineteenth century, and indeed their heirs in this century, coped with their sense of historical injury by writing of Ireland as an abandoned queen or an old mother. My objections to this are ethical. If you consistently

simplify women by making them national icons in poetry or drama you silence a great deal of the actual women in that past, whose sufferings and complexities are part of that past, who intimately depend on us, as writers, not to simplify them in this present.' [From the interview in *Sleeping with Monsters*.]

Do you think 'The Famine Road' shows an awareness of the real complexity of actual lives from history? Explain, with reference to the text.

12. What sense of national identity or Irishness comes across from 'The Famine Road'?

Child of Our Time

For Aengus

this poem is also prescribed for the Ordinary Level exam in 2005

Yesterday I knew no lullaby
But you have taught me overnight to order
This song, which takes from your final cry
Its tune, from your unreasoned end its reason;
Its rhythm from the discord of your murder   5
Its motive from the fact you cannot listen.

We who should have known how to instruct
With rhymes for your waking, rhythms for your sleep,
Names for the animals you took to bed,
Tales to distract, legends to protect   10
Later an idiom for you to keep
And living, learn, must learn from you dead,

To make our broken images, rebuild
Themselves around your limbs, your broken
Image, find for your sake whose life our idle   15
Talk has cost, a new language. Child
Of our time, our times have robbed your cradle.
Sleep in a world your final sleep has woken.

Background Note

This poem was inspired by a press photograph showing a firefighter carrying a dead child out of the wreckage of the Dublin bombings in May 1974.

Explorations

First reading

1. If you hadn't read the title or the last three lines, what might suggest to you that the poem was written to a child? Examine stanzas 1 and 2.

2. The speaker acknowledges that it was the child's death that prompted her to compose this poem ('you have taught me overnight to order | This song'). How does she feel about the child's death in the first stanza? Examine the words and phrases describing the death: 'your final cry', 'your unreasoned end', and 'the discord of your murder'. What do these phrases tell us about the way the poet views the death?

3. In the second stanza notice that the main clause consists of the first word and the final five words in the stanza: 'We ... must learn from you dead'. The rest of the stanza is in parenthesis and relates to 'we', presumably the adult society. (a) In what way has adult society failed, according to the poet? (b) What particular aspect of childbearing and education does she focus on? (c) 'Later an idiom for you to keep | And living, learn'. In your own words, what do you think is meant by this? ('Idiom' here means style of expression.)

4. In the third stanza the child's body is described poetically as 'your broken image'. What does this picture suggest to you?

5. What do you think she has in mind when she says that we need to (a) rebuild 'our broken images ... around your limbs' and (b) 'find ... a new language'?

6. Does the speaker find any ray of hope for the society in which this calamity occurred? Refer to the text of the third stanza.

Second reading

7. Consider this poem as an elegy, a meditation on death. What ideas on that subject are explored or suggested?

8. Can this be read as a public or political poem? Explain, with reference to the text.

9. Concerning the poet's feelings, do you find here a sense of personal sorrow or community guilt and sorrow? Explain your thinking.

Third reading

10. The poem might be seen as a mixture of dirge and lullaby. What elements of dirge or of lullaby do you find? Consider the theme, the choice of language, the imagery, the repetitions, etc.

The Black Lace Fan My Mother Gave Me

It was the first gift he ever gave her,
buying it for five francs in the Galeries
in pre-war Paris. It was stifling.
A starless drought made the nights stormy.

They stayed in the city for the summer.   5
They met in cafés. She was always early.
He was late. That evening he was later.
They wrapped the fan. He looked at his watch.
She looked down the Boulevard des Capucines.
She ordered more coffee. She stood up.   10
The streets were emptying. The heat was killing.
She thought the distance smelled of rain and lightning.

These are wild roses, appliquéd on silk by hand,
darkly picked, stitched boldly, quickly.
The rest is tortoiseshell and has the reticent,   15
clear patience of its element. It is

a worn-out, underwater bullion and it keeps,
even now, an inference of its violation.
The lace is overcast as if the weather
it opened for and offset had entered it.   20

The past is an empty café terrace.
An airless dusk before thunder. A man running.
And no way now to know what happened then—
none at all—unless, of course, you improvise:

The blackbird on this first sultry morning,   25
in summer, finding buds, worms, fruit,
feels the heat. Suddenly she puts out her wing—
the whole, full, flirtatious span of it.

CD Track 36 ⊙

Explorations

First reading

1. The black lace fan was a present from the poet's father to her mother and was passed on later to the speaker. How do you visualise the fan? What assistance does the poem give us? Examine the details in stanza 4.

2. How do you visualise the scene, the background, the atmosphere of the evening as the woman waits? Look at the details.

3. What do you notice about the man in the poem? What else would you like to know about him: why is he always late? Is the gift a peace offering or a genuine love token? What does he really feel for her? Can any of these questions be answered from the poem?

4. What do you notice about the woman? Examine the details. What do they suggest about how she is feeling, etc.? While remaining faithful to the text, jot down what you imagine are the thoughts inside her head as she waits.

5. Do you think this was a perfectly matched and idyllic relationship? What is suggested by the poem? Explain.

Second reading

6. How does the poet think of the fan? Does she see it as more than just the usual love token, a symbol in the sensual ritual? Explore in detail her imaginative apprehension of the fan in stanza 5. For example, what is meant by 'it keeps … an inference of its violation' and 'the lace is overcast as if the weather … had entered it'?

7. How do you think the final stanza relates to the rest of the poem? Does the mating display of the blackbird add anything to the connotations of the keepsake?

8. How do you think you would regard the first present from a lover? Were you at all surprised by the fact that the mother in this poem gave away the fan? Explain your thinking.

9. Do you think the poet views the keepsake solely in a romantic or in an erotic way? How do you think she sees it?

10. Examine what the poet herself says (in *Object Lessons*) about the symbol. What does this add to your own thinking on the subject?

'I make these remarks as a preliminary to a poem I wrote about a black lace fan my mother had given me, which my father had given her in a heat wave in Paris in the thirties. It would be wrong to say I was clear, when I wrote this poem, about disassembling an erotic politic. I was not. But I was aware of my own sense of the traditional erotic object—in this case the black fan—as a sign not for triumph and acquisition but for suffering itself. And without having words for it, I was conscious of trying to divide it from its usual source of generation: the sexualised perspective of the poet. To that extent I was writing a sign which might bring me close to those emblems of the body I had seen in those visionary years, when ordinary objects seemed to warn me that the body might share the world but could not own it. And if I was not conscious of taking apart something I had been taught to leave well alone, nevertheless, I had a clear sense of—at last—writing the poem away from the traditional erotic object towards something which spoke of the violations of love, while still shadowing the old context of its power. In other words, a back-to-front love poem.'

Third reading

11. What does the poem say to you about love and time?
12. In your own words, outline the themes you find in this poem.
13. What images appeal to you particularly? Explain why you find them effective.
14. Comment on the use of symbolism in this poem.

Fourth reading

15. 'The past is an empty café terrace.
    An airless dusk before thunder.
    A man running.
    And no way now to know what happened then—
    none at all—unless, of course, you improvise:'
    In a brief written description, improvise the sequel to the 'empty café terrace' and 'A man running' as you imagine it. Keep faith with the spirit of the poem.

The Shadow Doll

They stitched blooms from the ivory tulle
to hem the oyster gleam of the veil.
They made hoops for the crinoline.

Now, in summary and neatly sewn—
a porcelain bride in an airless glamour—   5
the shadow doll survives its occasion.

Under glass, under wraps, it stays
even now, after all, discreet about
visits, fevers, quickenings and lusts

and just how, when she looked at   10
the shell-tone spray of seed pearls,
the bisque features, she could see herself

inside it all, holding less than real
stephanotis, rose petals, never feeling
satin rise and fall with the vows   15

I kept repeating on the night before—
astray among the cards and wedding gifts—
the coffee pots and the clocks and

the battered tan case full of cotton
lace and tissue-paper, pressing down, then   20
pressing down again. And then, locks.

Notes

Shadow Doll: this refers to the porcelain doll modelling the proposed
wedding dress, under a dome of glass, sent to the nineteenth-century bride by
her dressmaker

[1] **tulle:** soft, fine silk netting used for dresses and veils

[2] **oyster:** off-white colour

[12] **bisque:** unglazed white porcelain used for these models

[14] **stephanotis:** tropical climbing plant with fragrant white flowers

Explorations

First reading

1. The function of the doll is explained above; but what does the title 'shadow doll' suggest to you?
2. What do you notice about the model dress?
3. 'A porcelain bride in an airless glamour'—what does this suggest to you about the poet's view of the doll?
4. Do you think the poet understands the doll's significance in more general terms, as an image of something, a symbol? If so, of what?

Second reading

5. What image of woman is portrayed by the doll? Explore stanza 3 in particular.

6. How does this image contrast with the poet's experience of her own wedding? Explore stanzas 5, 6, and 7.
7. The speaker's reality is more appealing, despite the clutter; but has she anything in common with the 'shadow doll'?

Third reading

8. What does the poem say to you about the image of woman? Refer to the text to substantiate your ideas.
9. Explore the significance of colour in this poem.
10. 'In the main, symbol and image carry the main themes of this poem.' Comment, with reference to the text.

A porcelain dress doll in satin and lace (England, c.1887)

White Hawthorn in the West of Ireland

I drove West
in the season between seasons.
I left behind suburban gardens.
Lawnmowers. Small talk.

Under low skies, past splashes of coltsfoot,   5
I assumed
the hard shyness of Atlantic light
and the superstitious aura of hawthorn.

All I wanted then was to fill my arms with
sharp flowers,   10
to seem, from a distance, to be part of
that ivory, downhill rush. But I knew,

I had always known
the custom was
not to touch hawthorn.   15
Not to bring it indoors for the sake of

the luck
such constraint would forfeit—
a child might die, perhaps, or an unexplained
fever speckle heifers. So I left it   20

stirring on those hills
with a fluency
only water has. And, like water, able
to re-define land. And free to seem to be—

for anglers,   25
and for travellers astray in
the unmarked lights of a May dusk—
the only language spoken in those parts.

Note

[5] **coltsfoot:** wild plant with yellow flowers

Explorations

First reading

1. In this migration, what is the speaker leaving behind her? From what little is said in the first stanza, what do you understand of her attitude to life in suburbia?

2. How does her state of mind alter as she drives west? Explore stanzas 2 and 3. How does this experience contrast with life in suburbia?

3. According to the poem, what is the significance of hawthorn in folklore?

4. Water too is a deceptive source of hidden energies. What is the poet's thinking on this? Explore stanzas 6 and 7.

Second reading

5. 'The speaker's attitude to the hawthorn is a combination of passionate, sensuous attraction balanced by a degree of nervous respect.' Would you agree? Substantiate your views with reference to the text.

6. What do you think this poem reveals about the speaker?

7. What statement is the poet making about our modern way of life?

Third reading

8. List the themes or issues raised by this poem.

9. What is your personal reaction to this poem?

'Hawthorn Hedge in Summer', a watercolour by T.P. Flanagan

Outside History

There are outsiders, always. These stars—
these iron inklings of an Irish January,
whose light happened

thousands of years before
our pain did: they are, they have always been   5
outside history.

They keep their distance. Under them remains
a place where you found
you were human, and

a landscape in which you know you are mortal.   10
And a time to choose between them.
I have chosen:

out of myth into history I move to be
part of that ordeal
whose darkness is   15

only now reaching me from those fields,
those rivers, those roads clotted as
firmaments with the dead.

How slowly they die
as we kneel beside them, whisper in their ear.   20
And we are too late. We are always too late

Explorations

First reading

1. Boland's argument is that Irish history has been turned into myth and therefore rendered false and remote from real lives. Do you think the image of the stars is an effective metaphor for historical myths? Examine the attributes of the stars as suggested in the first two stanzas.

2. In contrast, what aspects of real, lived history are emphasised in this poem?

Second reading

3. The poet chooses to turn her back on myth, and this choice brings her, and the reader, face to face with the unburied dead of history. Does she find this an easy choice? Explore her feelings on this. What words, phrases, gestures etc. indicate her feelings?

4. What do you think she means by the last line of the poem? Explore possible interpretations.

Third reading

5. On the evidence of this poem as a whole, what is the poet's attitude to the historical past?

6. Comment on the effectiveness of the imagery.

This Moment

this poem is also prescribed for the Ordinary Level exam in 2005

A neighbourhood.
At dusk.

Things are getting ready
to happen
out of sight. 5

Stars and moths.
And rinds slanting around fruit.

But not yet.

One tree is black.
One window is yellow as butter. 10

A woman leans down to catch a child
who runs into her arms
this moment.

Stars rise.
Moths flutter. 15
Apples sweeten in the dark.

Explorations

First reading

1. What do you see in this scene? List the items.
2. What senses, other than sight, are involved, or hinted at?
3. Do you think this scene unusual or very ordinary? Explain. What do you think the poet is celebrating here?
4. Yet there is a hint of the mysterious about the scene. Where and what do you think is suggested?

Second reading

5. What do you think is the most significant image in the poem? How does the poet draw attention to its importance?

6. Do you notice any sense of dramatic build-up in the poem? Examine the sequence of ideas and images.
7. Explore the imagery. What do the images contribute to the atmosphere? What is suggested, for example, by 'one window is yellow as butter' and by 'apples sweeten in the dark'?

Third reading

8. What is the key moment in this poem all about?
9. What do you think the poem is saying about nature?
10. Do you think it is making a statement about the experience of women? Explain your ideas.

Love

Dark falls on this mid-western town
where we once lived when myths collided.
Dusk has hidden the bridge in the river
which slides and deepens
to become the water   5
the hero crossed on his way to hell.

Not far from here is our old apartment.
We had a kitchen and an Amish table.
We had a view. And we discovered there
love had the feather and muscle of wings   10
and had come to live with us,
a brother of fire and air.

We had two infant children one of whom
was touched by death in this town
and spared; and when the hero   15
was hailed by his comrades in hell
their mouths opened and their voices failed and
there is no knowing what they would have asked
about a life they had shared and lost.

I am your wife.   20
It was years ago.
Our child is healed. We love each other still.
Across our day-to-day and ordinary distances
we speak plainly. We hear each other clearly.

And yet I want to return to you   25
on the bridge of the Iowa river as you were,
with snow on the shoulders of your coat
and a car passing with its headlights on:

I see you as a hero in a text—
the image blazing and the edges gilded—   30
and I long to cry out the epic question
my dear companion:
Will we ever live so intensely again?
Will love come to us again and be

so formidable at rest it offered us ascension   35
even to look at him?

But the words are shadows and you cannot hear me.
You walk away and I cannot follow.

 # Explorations

First reading

1. The poem is occasioned by a return visit to 'this mid-western town' in America where they had once lived. Which lines refer to present time and which refer to that earlier stay?
2. 'When myths collided'—what do you think this might refer to?
3. Explore the mood of the opening stanza. How is it created, and does it fit in with the mythical allusions? Explain.
4. On a first reading, what issues do you notice that preoccupy the poet?

Second reading

5. The second stanza contains some memories of the speaker's previous visit. What was important to her?
6. What insights about love are communicated in the second stanza? What is your opinion of the effectiveness of the imagery used?
7. The poet uses allusions from myth to create an awareness of death in the third stanza. What insights on death are communicated to you by this very visual presentation? Do you think this is an effective way of recording the speaker's feelings? Explain your view.
8. Explore the speaker's feelings for her husband at the present time, and contrast them with past emotions. Is she content? What does she yearn for?

Third reading

9. Overall, what does this poem have to say about love? What does she think is important?
10. What other themes do you find are dealt with?
11. What has the poem to say about women's experience?
12. What do the mythical allusions contribute to the poem?
13. Comment on the effectiveness of the imagery.

Fourth reading

14. What did you discover from reading this poem?

The Pomegranate

The only legend I have ever loved is
the story of a daughter lost in hell.
And found and rescued there.
Love and blackmail are the gist of it.
Ceres and Persephone the names.   5
And the best thing about the legend is
I can enter it anywhere. And have.
As a child in exile in
a city of fogs and strange consonants,
I read it first and at first I was   10
an exiled child in the crackling dusk of
the underworld, the stars blighted. Later
I walked out in a summer twilight
searching for my daughter at bed-time.
When she came running I was ready   15
to make any bargain to keep her.
I carried her back past whitebeams
and wasps and honey-scented buddleias.
But I was Ceres then and I knew
winter was in store for every leaf   20
on every tree on that road.
Was inescapable for each one we passed.
And for me.
                It is winter
and the stars are hidden.   25
I climb the stairs and stand where I can see
my child asleep beside her teen magazines,
her can of Coke, her plate of uncut fruit.
The pomegranate! How did I forget it?
She could have come home and been safe   30
and ended the story and all
our heart-broken searching but she reached
out a hand and plucked a pomegranate.
She put out her hand and pulled down
the French sound for apple and   35
the noise of stone and the proof
that even in the place of death,
at the heart of legend, in the midst
of rocks full of unshed tears

ready to be diamonds by the time   40
the story was told, a child can be
hungry. I could warn her. There is still a chance.
The rain is cold. The road is flint-coloured.
The suburb has cars and cable television.
The veiled stars are above ground.   45
It is another world. But what else
can a mother give her daughter but such
beautiful rifts in time?
If I defer the grief I will diminish the gift.
The legend will be hers as well as mine.   50
She will enter it. As I have.
She will wake up. She will hold
the papery flushed skin in her hand.
And to her lips. I will say nothing.

Notes

Pomegranate: the fruit of a North African tree, the size and colour of an
orange. In classical mythology it was associated with the underworld.

[5] **Ceres and Persephone:** Ceres in Roman mythology (identified with
Demeter in Greek mythology) was the goddess of corn and growing
vegetation, an earth goddess. Her daughter by Zeus, Persephone, was
carried off to the underworld by Hades. Ceres wandered over the earth in
mourning, vainly searching. In grief she made the earth barren for a year.
She resisted all entreaties by the gods to allow the earth back to fertility.
Eventually Zeus sent his messenger to persuade Hades to release
Persephone, which he did, but not before he had given her a pomegranate
seed to eat. This fruit was sacred to the underworld, and so Persephone
was condemned to spend one third of each year there with Hades, only
appearing back on earth each spring, with the first fertility.

Explorations

First reading

1. The poet says: '...the best thing about the legend is | I can enter it anywhere.' When did she first encounter it and why did she find it relevant to her life?
2. At what other times and in what ways did the legend run parallel to her own situation?
3. How closely do you think the poet identifies with the myth? What evidence is there for this?

Second reading

4. What does the poem tell us about the poet's relationship with her daughter?
5. What does the legend contribute to that relationship?
6. What do you think the poet has in common with Ceres?

Third reading

7. Where and how do the time zones of past and present fuse and mingle? What does this suggest about the importance of myth in our lives?
8. What statement do you think this poem is making about the significance of legend to ordinary lives? Refer to the text.
9. What truths about human relationships are discovered in this poem?

Fourth reading

10. Examine the different motifs in the imagery—fruit, darkness, stars, stone, etc. What do these strands of imagery contribute to the atmosphere and the themes?
11. What effect did reading this poem have on you?

Ordinary Level
Explanatory Note

Candidates taking the Ordinary (Pass) Level examination have a choice of questions when dealing with prescribed poems.

Ordinary Level candidates can answer either:
1. A question on one of the poems by a Higher Level poet prescribed for that year, or
2. A question from a list of other prescribed poems.

1. The poems by Higher Level poets, which may also be studied by Ordinary Level candidates, are listed below. Candidates are advised to check which of these poems are prescribed for the year in which they are sitting their examination. (See Course Overview pages iv–vii)

2. The alternative poems which Ordinary Level candidates may choose are contained on pages 427–547. Candidates should check which of these poems are prescribed for the year in which they are sitting their examination. (See Course Overview pages iv–vii)

Ordinary Level:
ALTERNATIVE POEMS

Anonymous

Sir Patrick Spens

prescribed for the Ordinary Level exam in 2004

I. THE SAILING

The king sits in Dunfermline town
Drinking the blude-red wine,
'O whare will I get a skeely skipper
To sail this new ship o'mine?'

O up and spak an eldern knight,　　　　　　5
Sat at the king's right knee;
'Sir Patrick Spens is the best sailor
That ever sailed the sea.'

Our king has written a braid letter,
And seal'd it with his hand,　　　　　　10
And sent it to Sir Patrick Spens,
Was walking on the strand.

'To Noroway, to Noroway,
To Noroway o'er the faem;
The king's daughter o' Noroway,　　　　　15
'Tis thou must bring her hame.'

The first word that Sir Patrick read
So loud, loud laugh'd he;
The neist word that Sir Patrick read
The tear blinded his e'e.　　　　　　20

'O wha is this has done this deed
And tauld the king o' me
To send us out, at this time o' year,
To sail upon the sea?

Notes

Sir Patrick Spens: is
　a fine example of
　the 'border
　ballads' which
　flourished in
　northern England
　and Scotland in
　the fourteenth and
　fifteenth centuries
[3] **skeely:** skilful
[9] **braid:** broad, i.e.
　plain, outspoken
[19] **neist:** next
[20] **e'e:** eye, plural
　'eyen'
[21] **wha:** who

'Be it wind, be it weet, be it hail, be it sleet,   25
Our ship must sail the faem;
The king's daughter o' Noroway,
'Tis we must fetch her hame.'

They hoysed their sails on Monenday morn
Wi' a' the speed they may;   30
They hae landed in Noroway
Upon a Wodensday.

II. THE RETURN

'Mak' ready, mak' ready, my merry men a'!
Our gude ship sails the morn.'
'Now ever alack, my master dear   35
I fear a deadly storm.

'I saw the new moon late yestreen
Wi' the auld moon in her arm;
And if we gang to sea, master,
I fear we'll come to harm.'   40

They hadna sail'd a league, a league,
A league but barely three,
When the lift grew dark, and the wind blew loud,
And gurly grew the sea.

The ankers brak, and the topmast lap,   45
It was sic a deadly storm:
And the waves cam owre the broken ship
Till a' her sides were torn.

'Go fetch a web o' the silken claith,
Another o' the twine,   50
And wap them into our ship's side,
And let nae the sea come in.'

They fetch'd a web o' the silken claith,
Another o' the twine,
And they wapp'd them round that gude ship's side, 55
But still the sea cam in.

Notes

[29] **hoysed:** hoisted
[37] **yestreen:** yesterday evening
[43] **lift:** sky
[44] **gurly:** rough, stormy
[45] **ankers brak:** anchors broke
[45] **lap:** sprang, broke
[46] **sic:** such
[47] **owre:** over
[49] **web:** roll
[51] **wap:** wrap, bind

O laith, laith were our gude Scots lords
To wet their cork-heel'd shoon;
But lang or a' the play was play'd
They wat their hats aboon.   60

And mony was the feather bed
That flatter'd on the faem;
And mony was the gude lord's son
That never mair cam hame.

O lang, lang may the ladies sit,   65
Wi' their fans into their hand,
Before they see Sir Patrick Spens
Come sailing to the strand!

And lang, lang may the maidens sit
Wi' their gowd kames in their hair,   70
A-waiting for their ain dear loves!
For them they'll see nae mair.

Half-owre, half-owre to Aberdour,
'Tis fifty fathoms deep;
And there lies gude Sir Patrick Spens,   75
Wi' the Scots lords at his feet!

Notes

[57] **laith:** loath
[58] **shoon:** shoes
[59] **lang or:** long
     before
[60] **wat:** wet
[60] **aboon:** above
[62] **flatter'd:**
     fluttered, floated
[64] **mair:** more
[70] **gowd kames:**
     good combs

 # Explorations

First reading

1. Why did the king write to Sir Patrick Spens?
2. How does Sir Patrick react to the mission from the king in stanzas 5 and 6?
3. What omens are seen prior to the return journey? Why does the sailor 'fear we'll come to harm'?
4. Describe how the weather deteriorates in stanzas 11 and 12. What damage is inflicted on the ship? Do you find the descriptions effective and dramatic?
5. What desperate efforts are made to save the ship in stanzas 13 and 14? Was there really any chance that these measures might be successful?
6. Irony is used regarding the reluctance of the 'Scots lords'

to get their shoes wet. Explain.

7. 'For them they'll see nae mair'
   How are the ladies and
   maidens presented in the
   poem? How do you imagine
   them? Think about how they
   might look and the kind of
   people they are.

8. 'And there lies gude Sir Patrick
   Spens,
   Wi' the Scots lords at his feet!'
   What point is the poet making
   in the final two lines?

Second reading

9. Read the poem aloud. What
   do you notice about its
   vocabulary, sounds and
   rhythms? What sort of accent
   should you adopt? Are there
   any lines or phrases that
   particularly appeal to you?

10. What do we learn in the poem
    about Sir Patrick Spens? Could
    you say what the poet's
    attitude to him is? How do
    you visualise him?

11. Is the poet sympathetic to the
    Scots lords? Explain your
    answer.

12. Write out your favourite
    stanza from the poem in
    standard English. Compare the
    result to the original. What
    conclusions have you come to
    as a result of this exercise?

13. How is the special atmosphere
    of the poem built up? You
    might consider the language,
    the imagery, the use of nautical
    detail, the use of dialogue and

sound effects?

14. Does the poem strike you as
    being especially gripping at
    any point? Describe the scene.
    Can you suggest why?

15. Compose a diary entry from
    the viewpoint of 'The king's
    daughter o' Noroway' or from
    the perspective of one of the
    Scots lords.

Third reading

16. Ballads often use broken
    narrative, what events in the
    story are suggested rather than
    described? Is the story-telling
    technique effective?

17. Analyse how dialogue is used
    in the poem? What effects are
    achieved by using direct
    speech?

18. What phrases are repeated in
    the poem? Does this repetition
    have any thing to do with the
    fact that ballads are sung from
    memory? Does the repetition
    have any other purpose?

Fourth reading

19. Did you enjoy reading this
    poem? How do you feel about
    the story and the language in
    which it is told?

20. ' 'Sir Patrick Spens' is a poem
    that must be read aloud.'
    Discuss. Choose three
    examples of lines or phrases
    from the poem to support your
    answer.

Robert Herrick (1591–1674)

Herrick came from a London family and was less than three days old when his father committed suicide. No records show that Herrick went to school but at sixteen we know he was an apprentice goldsmith to his uncle. He had a university education and at the age of thirty-two was ordained a minister. Most of his best poetry was written on his appointment as a Dean in Devon. With the death of Charles I and the arrival of Cromwell, he fell out of favour, lost his deanery and returned to London. He returned to Devon at the restoration of Charles II. He died there fourteen years later.

Whenas in silks my Julia goes

prescribed for Ordinary Level exams in 2005 and 2006

Whenas in silks my Julia goes,
Then, then, methinks, how sweetly flows
The liquifaction of her clothes!

Next, when I cast mine eyes and see
That brave vibration each way free,   5
— O how that glittering taketh me!

Notes

[2] **methinks:** I think
[3] **liquifaction:** to make into a liquid
[6] **taketh:** attracts, charms

Explorations

First reading

1. Can you imagine the incident that might have led to the poet writing this poem?

2. How does the poet use the actual sounds of the words to suggest the texture of the 'silks' in the first three lines of the poem? Pay particular attention to his use of 's' and 'l' sounds.

3. '...how sweetly flows
   The liquifaction of her clothes!'
   What quality of the 'silks' is suggested by these lines? Do you think that the words chosen by the poet work

----

successfully to suggest this
quality? Why?

4. In lines 4–6, the poet
describes another quality of
the 'silks'. Choose two words
from these lines that you feel
clearly suggest what this
quality is.

Second reading

5. Examine the senses that the
poet appeals to in this poem.
Does this emphasis on sensory
description tell you anything
about the nature of his feelings
for Julia? What effect does she
have on him?

6. Is it important that Julia is
wearing 'silks'? Why? Discuss
how the poem would be
altered if, for instance, Julia
was wearing 'denim' or
'tweed'.

Third reading

7. The poet uses rather odd
language, such as 'Whenas',
'methinks', 'cast mine eyes'
and 'taketh'. Does it remind
you of any other sort of
writing you may have read or
heard?

8. Is there a sense of tension in
this poem? How and where is
it suggested?

9. Do you think that the poet is
really concerned with the
quality and texture of the
'silks' or is he, perhaps, only
interested in them because of
what lies beneath? Use the
poem to support your view.

10. How do you think Julia would
have felt when she read this
poem?

George Herbert (1593–1633)

George Herbert was born in Montgomery, Wales, and educated at Cambridge where he held the prestigious post of public orator. He had been involved in life at the royal court and sat as a member of parliament in 1624 and 1625. After the death of King James I he became disillusioned with public life and embarked on a career in the Church, he became a deacon in 1626 and was ordained four years later. As rector of Bemerton near Salisbury he composed a series of sacred poems which were published posthumously as *The Temple* and a prose work *A Priest to the Temple*. He died from consumption in 1633.

Love

prescribed for Ordinary Level exams in 2003 and 2004

Love bade me welcome: yet my soul drew back,
        Guiltie of dust and sinne.
But quick-ey'd Love, observing me grow slack
        From my first entrance in,
Drew nearer to me, sweetly questioning,   5
        If I lack'd any thing.

A guest, I answer'd, worthy to be here:
        Love said, You shall be he.
I the unkinde, ungratefull? Ah my deare,
        I cannot look on thee.   10
Love took my hand, and smiling did reply
        Who made the eyes but I?

Truth Lord, but I have marr'd them: let my shame
        Go where it doth deserve.
And know you not, sayes Love, who bore the blame?   15
        My deare, then I will serve.
You must sit down, sayes Love, and taste my meat:
        So I did sit and eat.

Explorations

Before reading

1. Have you ever been in a situation where you had to face a parent, teacher or figure in authority, to account for your actions? Everyone has; describe how you felt. What emotions did you go through?

First reading

2. How do you visualise the character of 'Love' in the first stanza? Where do you see the setting of the poem?

3. What kind of mental picture do you have of the narrator?

4. What obstacles to Love's invitation does the narrator mention in the second stanza? How does Love reply?

5. How does Love persuade the speaker to accept the invitation in the final stanza? What does the narrator offer to do?

Second reading

6. 'Guiltie of dust and sinne' Is this an effective image for conveying the poet's sense of unworthiness?

7. Is Love a good host? Support your answer from the text.

8. What effect is achieved in the poem by conversational phrases such as: 'Ah my deare' and 'My deare'?

9. What do you think is symbolised by 'and taste my meat'?

Third reading

10. 'And know you not, sayes Love, who bore the blame?' What is this line saying about the Christian doctrine of Redemption?

11. This poem has been described as a dramatic parable. Do you think this is an accurate summing up of how the poem works?

John Milton (1608–1674)

John Milton was born in London of well-to-do parents who appear to have given him a good basic education, especially in music and literature. He attended St Paul's School and graduated with BA and MA degrees from Cambridge. Milton was appointed 'Latin secretary of the council of state' by Oliver Cromwell in 1649, because of his fluency in Latin, the language of diplomacy at that time. He wrote extensively on religious and political matters as well as writing poetry in Latin and English. His eyesight which had been failing for some time, failed him completely when he was aged forty-four. From then on he dictated his work to his secretaries and family members. Milton's masterpiece, the epic *Paradise Lost*, was published in 1667 in which he attempted 'to justify the ways of God to men'. The restoration of the monarchy briefly threatened Milton with execution for regicide, and brought an end to

his political career in 1660. Having been granted a royal pardon he retired to concentrate on writing and published the sequel to *Paradise Lost*, called *Paradise Regained*, as well as a drama called *Samson Agonistes* in 1671. A revised volume of his collected poetry appeared the following year. Milton died of gout in 1674.

When I Consider

prescribed for the Ordinary Level exam in 2005

When I consider how my light is spent,
E're half my days, in this dark world and wide,
And that one Talent which is death to hide,
Lodg'd with me useless, though my Soul more bent
To serve therewith my Maker, and present   5
My true account, least he returning chide,
Doth God exact day-labour, light deny'd,
I fondly ask; But patience to prevent
That murmur, soon replies, God doth not need
Either man's work or his own gifts, who best   10
Bear his milde yoak, they serve him best, his State
Is Kingly. Thousands at his bidding speed
And post o're Land and Ocean without rest:
They also serve who only stand and waite.

Notes

[3] **Talent:** gift, faculty, also a unit of currency in New Testament times

[4] **bent:** determined

[8] **fondly:** foolishly

[11] **yoak:** yoke, burden

 # Explorations

First reading

1. What is Milton saying about his blindness in the opening three lines? How do you imagine 'this dark world'?

2. Does Milton take the parable of the Talents seriously? What is the implication of 'which is death to hide'?

3. What does Milton's soul incline to do? What does this tell us about him?

4. 'Doth God exact day-labour, light deny'd'
   What is your understanding of this line? What does the question tell us about Milton's attitude to God?

5. What does 'Patience' reply to the question posed in the first eight lines? According to Milton, does God need man's work? Does he need man's gifts?

6. According to Milton, how do people best serve God? How can God be served passively?

Second reading

7. Read the poem aloud. What do you notice about its sounds and rhythm? How many full stops appear in the text? Does this affect how you read the poem? What tone of voice should you adopt?

8. Comment on the financial terminology, 'spent'; 'Talent';

'Lodg'd'; 'account'. What is Milton saying with this choice of words?

9. How do you see John Milton on the evidence of the poem? What kind of person do you think he was? Does he display any self-pity or sense of injustice? What comment would you make on how he deals with his disability?

10. How would you summarise the octet?

11. Describe how Milton resolves his difficulties in the sestet. Do you find his conclusion convincing?

12. How does Milton feel toward God in the poem? What words and images convey his emotions?

Third reading

13. Examine how images of light and darkness are used in the first eight lines. Do you consider such imagery to be appropriate?

14. How is the majesty of God conveyed in the final six lines?

15. Would you agree that this poem's language has a biblical quality? What words or phrases would you highlight for comment?

16. What do you think of Milton's portrayal of God? Is this interpretation of God one you are comfortable with?

17. How would you describe the mood of the final line? Has the conclusion been anticipated in the poem?

18. Write a paragraph giving your personal response to the poem.

Henry Vaughan (1622–1695)

Henry Vaughan was born in Wales. He studied in Oxford but left without taking a degree, he went on to study law and later medicine. Vaughan practised as a doctor in Breconshire, after fighting in The English Civil War on the royalist side. His first poems were secular in nature and dealt with love and the fashionable concerns of the age. Some profound spiritual experience prompted him to more sacred and serious themes and he repudiated frivolous verse. He was influenced by George Herbert 'whose holy life and verse gained many pious Converts, (of whom I am the least)' and Platonic philosophy. Vaughán's best religious poetry in *Silex Scintillans* has a mystical quality which is quite distinctive.

Peace

prescribed for the Ordinary Level exam in 2006

My Soul, there is a Countrie
Far beyond the stars,
Where stands a winged Centrie
All skilfull in the wars,
There above noise, and danger   5
Sweet peace sits crown'd with smiles,
And one born in a Manger
Commands the Beauteous files,
He is thy gracious friend,
And (O my Soul awake!)   10
Did in pure love descend
To die here for thy sake,
If thou canst get but thither,
There growes the flowre of peace,
The Rose that cannot wither,   15
Thy fortresse, and thy ease;
Leave then thy foolish ranges;
For none can thee secure,
But one, who never changes,
Thy God, thy life, thy Cure.   20

Notes

[3] **Centrie:** sentry
[8] **files:** ranks, as in soldiers
[17] **ranges:** wanderings

Explorations

First reading

1. How do you visualise the 'Countrie | Far beyond the stars'? What kind of heaven is suggested by Vaughan's description?

2. 'And one born in a Manger Commands the Beauteous files' What is your impression of Christ from these lines? Are you surprised by the image of Christ as a military commander?

3. According to the speaker, how is the flower of peace to be grasped? Look at line 13 carefully.

4. What do you understand by 'Thy fortresse, and thy ease'? What qualities are highlighted here?

5. Why must the listener 'Leave then thy foolish ranges'? What reward is on offer?

Second reading

6. Read the poem aloud. What do you notice about the sound and rhythm of the poem? Note how Vaughan punctuates the poem. Read the last two lines again, pay particular attention to the pauses after the commas. What effect is achieved?

7. Make a list of the military vocabulary used in the poem. How are such warlike terms appropriate in a poem about peace?

8. What is the tone of this poem? What words and images convey the tone?

Third reading

9. 'The Rose that cannot wither' Do you think this is an effective image? Does this metaphor blend with the other patterns of imagery that Vaughan explores?

10. What do you think was the writer's intention in writing this poem? Discuss this in your group or class.

11. Do you find this poem convincing? Explore your personal response to the text.

12. 'The search for permanence in a changing world is characteristic of Henry Vaughan.' Discuss this statement with reference to 'Peace'.

13. How would you describe Vaughan's concept of peace? Would your personal view of peace be different?

William Blake (1757–1827)

William Blake was one of the foremost English poets of the Romantic period. A visionary, he was particularly interested in the emotional, psychological and spiritual side of the human being. His most well-known writings are the short lyrical poems of the volumes *Songs of Innocence* (1789) and *Songs of Experience* (1794), which Blake himself described as 'showing the two contrary states of the human soul.' 'A Poison Tree' is taken from *Songs of Experience*.

A Poison Tree

prescribed for the Ordinary Level exam in 2003

I was angry with my friend:
I told my wrath, my wrath did end.
I was angry with my foe:
I told it not, my wrath did grow.

And I water'd it in fears,   5
Night and morning with my tears;
And I sunned it with smiles,
And with soft deceitful wiles.

And it grew both day and night,
Till it bore an apple bright;   10
And my foe beheld it shine,
And he knew that it was mine,

And into my garden stole
When the night had veil'd the pole:
In the morning glad I see   15
My foe outstretch'd beneath the tree.

Notes

A Poison Tree: the poison tree of Java, so noxious that even a touch is fatal

[10] **an apple bright:** symbol of temptation, from the Garden of Eden story

[14] **night had veil'd the pole:** the North Pole, which Blake sometimes used as an image of evil; here night has covered the northern hemisphere in darkness

Explorations

Before reading

1. Are you the kind of person who can tell people straight out if they annoy you, or do you suffer in silence and bear a grudge?
   (a) Think about a time when you had to tell some 'home truths' to a friend. What happened? (b) Think about a time when you really resented someone or something but didn't voice your anger or other feelings. Describe it.

First reading

2. In the first two stanzas, how does Blake deal with his anger?
3. What image of the speaker do you form from this?
4. Stanzas 3 and 4 employ symbolism to continue the story. Explain the significance of the apple, the garden, and the 'foe outstretch'd beneath the tree.'

Second reading

5. What insights into human nature does this poem provide for you? Would you agree that Blake is completely honest in confronting the unpleasant side of life?
6. Do you find this poem depressing, uplifting, instructive, or what? Explain your reaction to it.

Third reading

7. Briefly express what you understand as the theme or moral of the poem.
8. Do you think the poem is effective? Consider, for example, whether you think the imagery appropriate to this kind of poem; whether the rhymes might mislead us and so conceal the dark philosophy of the poem; whether the simplicity of the piece is powerfully effective or off-putting.

Samuel Taylor Coleridge (1772–1834)

Samuel Taylor Coleridge was born the youngest of fourteen children and was a precocious, lonely child. After the death of his father, when he was aged nine, he attended Christ's Hospital school in London. Coleridge went on to Cambridge but was unsuited to the academic life— he left briefly to join a cavalry regiment but later returned. He gave up his studies finally in 1794. He married Sara Fricker as part of an abortive scheme to establish a 'pantisocratic' colony (a utopian community where all rule equally) in Pennsylvania. As this marriage got into difficulty, he turned for support to Wordsworth whom he met in 1795, and collaborated to produce a highly influential volume of poetry *Lyrical Ballads* (1798). Coleridge left the Wordsworths to go to Germany but his health began to fail—he returned to England in 1799 and developed a dependency on laudanum, a form of liquid opium taken for pain relief.

His later poetry was far inferior to his earlier work, and he began a new career as a lecturer, editor, critic and philosopher. From 1816 Coleridge was a permanent guest of Dr James Gillman and was saved from destitution and total mental collapse. His literary autobiography, *Biographia Literaria*, was published in 1817. Samuel Taylor Coleridge died on 25 July 1834 at Highgate in London.

A summary of 'The Rime of the Ancient Mariner'

The Ancient Mariner meets three guests on their way to a wedding, he detains one of them in order to tell his story. He tells how his ship was driven toward the South Pole by a storm. When the ship is surrounded by ice an albatross flies through the fog and is received with joy by the crew. The ice splits and the bird moves on with the ship; then inexplicably the mariner shoots it with a crossbow. For this act of cruelty a curse falls on the ship. She is driven north to the Equator and is becalmed under burning sun in a rotting sea. The albatross is hung around the neck of the hated mariner. A skeleton ship approaches, on which Death and Life-in-Death are playing dice, and when it vanishes all the crew die except the mariner. Suddenly, watching the beauty of the watersnakes in the moonlight, he blesses them—and the albatross falls from his neck. The ship sails home and the mariner is saved, but for a penance he is condemned to travel from land to land and to teach by his example love and reverence for all God's creatures. The activities of a parallel spirit world are described in marginal notes to the poem. (Based on a synopsis from *The Oxford Companion to English Literature*.)

The Rime of the Ancient Mariner

prescribed for Ordinary Level exams in 2005 and 2006

PART IV

'I fear thee, ancient Mariner!
I fear thy skinny hand!
And thou art long, and lank, and brown,
As is the ribbed sea-sand.

> The wedding guest feareth that a spirit is talking to him.

I fear thee and thy glittering eye,   220
And thy skinny hand, so brown.'—
Fear not, fear not, thou wedding-guest!
This body dropt not down.
Alone, alone, all, all alone,
Alone on a wide wide sea!   225
And never a saint took pity on
My soul in agony.

> But the ancient Mariner assureth him of his bodily life, and proceedeth to relate his horrible penance.

That many men, so beautiful!
And they all dead did lie:
And a thousand thousand slimy things   230
Lived on; and so did I.

> He despiseth the creatures of the calm.

I looked upon the rotting sea,
And drew my eyes away;
I looked upon the rotting deck,
And there the dead men lay.   235

> And envieth that they should live and so many lie dead.

I looked to heaven, and tried to pray;
But or ever a prayer had gusht,
A wicked whisper came, and made
My heart as dry as dust.

I closed my lids, and kept them close,   240
And the balls like pulses beat;
For the sky and the sea, and the sea and the sky
Lay like a load on my weary eye,
And the dead were at my feet.

But the curse liveth
for him in the eye of
the dead men.

The cold sweat melted from their limbs,   245
Nor rot nor reek did they:
The look with which they looked on me
Had never passed away.

An orphan's curse would drag to hell
A spirit from on high;   250
But oh! more horrible than that
Is the curse in a dead man's eye!
Seven days, seven nights, I saw that curse,
And yet I could not die.

The moving Moon went up the sky,   255
And no where did abide;
Softly she was going up,
And a star or two beside—

In his loneliness and
fixedness he yearneth
towards the
journeying Moon, and
the stars that still
sojourn, yet still move
onward; and every
where the blue sky
belongs to them, and
is their appointed rest,
and their native
country and their own
natural homes, which
they enter
unannounced, as lords
that are certainly
expected and yet there
is a silent joy at their
arrival.

Her beams bemocked the sultry main,
Like April hoar-frost spread;   260
But where the ship's huge shadow lay,
The charmed water burnt alway
A still and awful red.

Beyond the shadow of the ship,
I watched the water-snakes: 265
They moved in tracks of shining white,
And when they reared, the elfish light
Fell off in hoary flakes.

By the light of the
Moon he beholdeth
God's creatures of the
great calm.

Within the shadow of the ship
I watched their rich attire: 270

Blue, glossy green, and velvet black,
They coiled and swam; and every track
Was a flash of golden fire.

O happy living things! no tongue
Their beauty might declare: 275
A spring of love gushed from my heart,
And I blessed them unaware:
Sure my kind saint took pity on me,
And I blessed them unaware.

The selfsame moment I could pray;   280
And from my neck so free
The Albatross fell off, and sank
Like lead into the sea.

Their beauty and their happiness.

He blesseth them in his heart.

The spell begins to break.

He prayeth best, who loveth best
All thing both great and small;   615
For the dear God who loveth us,
He made and loveth all.

The Mariner whose eye is bright,
Whose beard with age is hoar,
Is gone: and now the Wedding-Guest   620
Turned from the bridegroom's door.

He went like one that hath been stunned,
And is of sense forlorn:
A sadder and a wiser man,
He rose the morrow morn.   625

Notes

[218] **lank:** slender, thin

[246] **reek:** to smell badly or to stink

[259] **bemocked:** an archaic form of 'mocked'

[259] **sultry:** hot and humid

[260] **hoar:** grey-white

[267] **elfish:** fairylike

[270] **attire:** dress

Explorations

First reading

1. Why does the wedding guest fear the Ancient Mariner? What picture have you formed of the Mariner's appearance?

2. Visualise the scene described in stanzas 3–5. Describe what you see. What sights would you find particularly shocking? How do you imagine the setting?

3. How does the Mariner feel in stanzas 6–9? Why does he want to die?

4. How does the mood change as 'The moving Moon went up the sky'? Why does the Mariner want to be like the moon and stars? Read the commentary in the marginal text.

5. How does the Mariner react to the water snakes in stanzas 12 and 13? Why does he feel as he does toward the creatures? What do you think his normal reaction to snakes might be?

6. What is the effect of 'I blessed them unaware'? What do you think motivated the Mariner? Does his action have a special significance in the light of his experiences?

7. Do you think there might be a link between the Mariner being able to pray and the albatross falling from his neck?

Second reading

8. Read the poem aloud. What do you notice about its sounds and rhythm? Does the ballad style help the narrative? Do any lines appeal to you because of how they sound?

9. What kind of a mental picture do you have of the ancient Mariner? How do you think he looks and speaks? What kind of person is he?

10. How would you describe the atmosphere in stanzas 3–7? What words and images are used to convey the atmosphere?

11. How do you react to the description of the dead men in lines 253–6? What details make it effective?

12. 'But where the ship's huge shadow lay,
The charmed water burnt alway
A still and awful red.'
Why do you think there is such a contrast between the effects of the moonlight and the shadow of the ship? What does 'burning red' suggest to you?

Third reading

13. What do you think the albatross symbolises?

14. How does the Mariner feel toward his shipmates? What

emotion underlies his attitude?

15. Does the motionlessness of the ship reflect the Mariner's state of mind? Explain.

16. Coleridge wrote that the moral of the Ancient Mariner is 'to teach, by his own example, love and reverence to all things that God made and loveth'. Does this statement contribute to your understanding of the poem?

Fourth reading

17. Can you trace the beginnings of the Mariner's spiritual regeneration in the poem?

18. What can you glean from the poem about the poet? How do you see him? Do you think he might be an interesting person?

19. Give your personal evaluation of the poem. How do you feel about it? Is there anything in the poem you would like to question Coleridge about?

20. What role does the supernatural play in Part IV of 'The Rime of the Ancient Mariner'? Is the supernatural entirely distinct from nature in the poem?

Percy Bysshe Shelley (1792–1822)

The son of an English country gentleman, Shelley was educated at Eton and Oxford, where he spent a rebellious and unhappy youth. Revolutionary in thought, he was anti-religious and anti-monarchy and wrote and spoke publicly on the need for radical social and political reforms. He felt it was the role of the poet to be prophetic and visionary. He lived a fairly

unconventional family life, much of it in Italy, where the Shelleys seemed dogged by illness and death. It was here that he wrote some of his best-known poems, such as 'Stanzas Written in Dejection Near Naples', 'Ode to the West Wind', 'Ode to a Skylark', and 'Prometheus Unbound'.

Ozymandias

prescribed for the Ordinary Level exam in 2003

I met a traveller from an antique land
Who said: Two vast and trunkless legs of stone
Stand in the desert ... Near them, on the sand,
Half sunk, a shattered visage lies, whose frown,
And wrinkled lip, and sneer of cold command,   5
Tell that its sculptor well those passions read
Which yet survive, stamped on these lifeless things,
The hand that mocked them, and the heart that fed:
And on the pedestal these words appear:
'My name is Ozymandias, king of kings: 10
Look on my works, ye Mighty, and despair!'
Nothing beside remains. Round the decay
Of that colossal wreck, boundless and bare
The lone and level sands stretch far away.

Notes

Ozymandias: another name for the Pharaoh Rameses II of Egypt (thirteenth century B.C.), whose great tomb at Thebes was shaped like a sphinx. It was the great historian Diodorus the Sicilian who first referred to it as the tomb of Ozymandias
[1] **antique:** ancient
[4] **visage:** face
[8] **The hand that mocked:** the hand that imitated, referring to the hand of the sculptor
[8] **the heart that fed:** the king's heart which gave life to these qualities and passions that were captured in stone by the sculptor

Explorations

First reading

1. The poem is in the form of a narrative or story told by a traveller who had been to 'an antique land'. What suggestions and pictures does this phrase conjure up for you?
2. What did the traveller actually see, as reported in lines 2–4? What is your first reaction to this scene: interesting, pathetic, grotesque, or what? Why do you think he might consider this worth reporting?
3. Where is this scene? What impressions of the land do we get?
4. Does the poet tell us the name of the place? Why do you think this is?

Second reading

5. What do we learn of the king from this sculpture: qualities, character traits, etc.?
6. Do you think Shelley appreciates the sculptor's skill? Explain.
7. Relate lines 4–8 in your own words and as simply as possible.

Third reading: the sestet etc.

8. What was your own reflection on reading the words on the pedestal?
9. Explore the final two and-a-half lines. What do you see? Really look. What atmosphere is created here? What statement do you think is being made?
10. What do you think this poem is saying about human endeavour and about power? Explain with reference to specific phrases etc.
11. Consider the imagery. Do you think the imagery appropriate to the theme? Explain. What pictures do you find most effective?

Fourth reading

12. How does the poet make use of irony to communicate his theme? Do you find this effective?
13. Would you agree that this poem embodies Shelley's view that the poet should really be a kind of prophet or wise person in society? Discuss this with reference to the text.
14. What features of the sonnet do you notice in the poem? Do you think it is a good sonnet?
15. Do you think this poem was worth reading? Why, or why not?

Edward Thomas (1878–1917)

At the outbreak of the First World War, Thomas was thirty-six-years old, married with two children. His decision to enlist came from a sense of idealism. He was killed on Easter Monday 1917. The encouragement of his friend, the American poet Robert Frost, brought him to write poetry and his war poems reflect not just his experience of war, but his love of the English countryside. His language shows a deceptive strength and his work artistic integrity.

Adlestrop

prescribed for the Ordinary Level exam in 2006

Yes, I remember Adlestrop—
The name, because one afternoon
Of heat the express-train drew up there
Unwontedly. It was late June.

The steam hissed. Someone cleared his throat.   5
No one left and no one came
On the bare platform. What I saw
Was Adlestrop—only the name

And willows, willow-herb, and grass,
And meadowsweet, and haycocks dry,   10
No whit less still and lonely fair
Than the high cloudlets in the sky.

And for that minute a blackbird sang
Close by, and round him, mistier,
Farther and farther, all the birds   15
Of Oxfordshire and Gloucestershire.

Notes

[4] **Unwontedly:** unusually

[10] **haycocks:** small haystacks

[11] **whit:** the least possible amount

Explorations

First reading

1. Have you ever stopped briefly on a car or train journey? Can you describe the scene you saw? Are there any similarities between your experience and the one described in this poem?

2. What does the poet notice about Adlestrop in the first two stanzas?

3. 'No one left and no one came On the bare platform.' Can you find the word in the poem that explains why this happened?

4. Describe in your own words the picture that the poet creates in the third and fourth stanzas of the poem. Is it a pleasant one?

5. How is the scene in stanzas 1 and 2 different to the scene in stanzas 3 and 4? Can you explain why this change takes place?

Second reading

6. Consider the senses that the poet appeals to in this poem. How do they contribute to the overall effect?

7. What sort of mood do you think the poet was trying to create? Are there any words that are especially important in suggesting this mood?

8. How does the poet suggest a sense of distance in the poem? Choose two phrases that you feel are important in creating this effect.

Third reading

9. Do you think that the poet was on his own or travelling with a friend? Use the poem to support your opinion.

10. Why do you think the poet remembers this scene? Was it because he spent a long time looking at it or can you suggest another reason?

William Carlos Williams (1883–1963)

The early poetic work of William Carlos Williams shows the influence of two of the major poets of the twentieth century, Ezra Pound and T.S. Eliot. However, he eventually felt limited by this, and searched for an authentic American expression in poetry. He found this in writing about commonplace objects and the lives of ordinary people. In this way, he managed to bring out the significance of people and things we might otherwise take for granted. He has proved an inspiration for accepted major poets, in particular Ginsberg. His output  includes stories and plays besides his five well-known books of poetry.

The Red Wheelbarrow

prescribed for Ordinary Level exams in 2004 and 2005

so much depends
upon

a red wheel
barrow

glazed with rain   5
water

beside the white
chickens

Explorations

First reading

1. Write down three words to describe your first reaction to this poem. Discuss these in your group or class. Is it possible to agree on three words to describe the reaction of the whole class or are there a number of different reactions in the group?

2. Where do you think this poem is set, in the city or in the country? What words in the poem support your view?

3. In your own words, write down what this poem is about. Did you find it easy or difficult to do this? Why?

Second reading

4. Can you suggest a connection between the wheelbarrow and the chickens?

5. How do you feel when it rains? Is the fact that it is raining important in the poem? Why?

6. Do the first four words of the poem tell you anything about the poet's reaction to what he sees? Do you empathise with his feelings? Why?

Third reading

7. Does this poem create a mood? How would you describe it? Use the piece to support your view.

8. Consider which is more important in the poem, what the poet sees or what he feels. Is it more than just a simple description?

9. In your own words, write down what you now think this poem is about. Compare it with your answer to Question 3. Has your opinion changed in any way?

10. Is it the way that words are arranged, or how they sound, or the feelings they express, that turns them into poetry? What do you expect to see in a poem? How does this piece go against your expectations? Can sixteen words be classed as a poem? Why? Discuss these issues in your group or class.

David Herbert Lawrence (1885–1930)

David Herbert Lawrence, poet and novelist, was born in Nottinghamshire, the son of a coalminer and an ex-schoolteacher. His parents quarrelled frequently and Lawrence formed a passionate bond with his mother. She was determined to keep him out of the mines and encouraged his education. He won a scholarship to the local High School and attended Nottingham University after working as a clerk in a surgical goods factory to raise money. After qualifying as a teacher, he went to work in London but was advised to give up teaching because of his poor health.

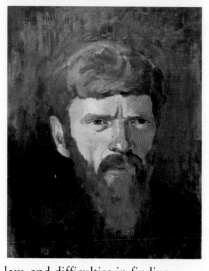

He took up writing professionally and his third novel *Sons and Lovers* (1913) established his reputation as a novelist. Lawrence eloped with the wife of his old professor in Nottingham, Frieda Weekly (née von Richtofen) and lived a nomadic existence, travelling extensively. His frankness on sexual matters and use of four-letter words in his books led to trouble with the law, and difficulties in finding publishers. Lawrence thought that civilisation had failed and found himself drawn to the cultures of primitive peoples; he felt that instinct should be exalted over reason and body over mind. He published six volumes of poetry and three volumes of short stories, his novels include: *The Rainbow, The Lost Girl, Women in Love, Lady Chatterley's Lover* and *Aaron's Rod*. D.H. Lawrence died from tuberculosis in 1930.

Piano

prescribed for Ordinary Level exams in 2005 and 2006

Softly, in the dusk, a woman is singing to me:
Taking me back down the vista of years, till I see
A child sitting under the piano, in the boom of the tingling strings
And pressing the small, poised feet of a mother who smiles as she sings.

In spite of myself, the insidious mastery of song   5
Betrays me back, till the heart of me weeps to belong
To the old Sunday evenings at home, with winter outside
And hymns in the cosy parlour, the tinkling piano our guide.

So now it is vain for the singer to burst into clamour
With the great black piano appassionato. The glamour   10
Of childish days is upon me, my manhood is cast
Down in the flood of remembrance. I weep like a child for the past.

Notes

[5] **insidious:** treacherous, seductive or having a subtle effect

[9] **clamour:** loud, continuous noise

[10] **appassionato:** a directive to a performer to play a certain passage passionately, or with
intense emotion or feeling; impassioned

 # Explorations

Before reading

1. Shelley wrote that 'our sweetest songs are those that tell our saddest thoughts'. Is this statement true? To test Shelley's theory, list your three favourite songs and discuss them with your classmates.

First reading

2. How do you imagine the scene described in the first line? What details come to mind? Where do you think the song is being performed?

3. What impression do you get of the mother in the first stanza? How does the child feel about her?

4. 'The insidious mastery of song' What power does the singing hold over the speaker in the second stanza?

5. Describe the 'Sunday evenings' as the speaker remembers them. What kind of atmosphere was there? How do you imagine the setting? Why is 'winter' mentioned?

6. Why is it 'vain' for the singer to burst into song? Why do you think the speaker describes the singing as 'clamour'?

7. Why does the speaker 'weep like a child'?

Second reading

8. What feelings are present in the poem? What words or images convey the emotions?

9. How do you imagine the speaker? What kind of person do you think he is? If you could speak to Lawrence, what questions would you ask him?

10. List the different sound images you notice in the poem and say what each contributes to the atmosphere.

11. On the evidence of the poem, does the speaker want to be taken 'back down the vista of years'? Why do you think this is so?

Third reading

12. Select two examples from the poem where you think the poet's choice of words is particularly effective in describing a scene or conveying a feeling. Explain your selection.

13. Do you find this poem moving? How do you feel about what it has to say?

14. D.H. Lawrence was a successful novelist, can you see any evidence of his narrative skills in the poem? Is he good at describing scenes and capturing atmosphere? Would you be encouraged or discouraged to read one of his novels after reading the poem?

15. 'The poetry of D.H. Lawrence has an immediate and personal quality.' Does your reading of 'Piano' support this view? Write a paragraph exploring your analysis.

Siegfried Sassoon (1886–1967)

Sassoon enlisted in the British army on the first day of the First World War and was one of the few poets to survive the fighting. He is best known for his satirical poems of disillusionment with the war, such as 'The Hero', 'Base Details' and 'The General'. 'Everyone Sang' celebrates the sense of freedom and escape felt at the end of the war. In 1919 Sassoon became literary editor of the *Daily Herald* and achieved notice for his semi-autobiographical writings, beginning with *Memoirs of a Fox-Hunting Man* (1928) and *Memories of an Infantry Officer* (1930).

Everyone Sang

prescribed for the Ordinary Level exam in 2003

Everyone suddenly burst out singing;
And I was filled with such delight
As prisoned birds must find in freedom
Winging wildly across the white
Orchards and dark green fields; on; on; and out of sight.   5

Everyone's voice was suddenly lifted,
And beauty came like the setting sun.
My heart was shaken with tears and horror
Drifted away ... O but every one
Was a bird; and the song was wordless; the singing will never be done. 10

Explorations

First reading

1. 'Everyone suddenly burst out singing.' What circumstances, do you imagine, might give rise to such a spontaneous outburst of joy? You do not need to confine yourself to the circumstances of this particular poem.
2. In this poem, how do you think the poet feels? Indicate three phases or images that lead you to this conclusion.
3. On a first reading, what do you see? Indicate two images that come to your attention most strongly.
4. Which similes or metaphors do you think convey the sense of freedom most effectively? Give a reason for each choice.

Second reading

5. Do you think this is an emotional moment for the poet? Describe the emotions he is conveying here. Support your answer with reference to the text.
6. How does the poet convey the sense of excitement? Think of the choice of language, the imagery, and the structure of the lines.

Third reading

7. Do you think this poem makes a valuable contribution to the body of war poetry? Comment.

Edwin Muir (1887–1959)

Muir was born in the Orkneys but later moved to Glasgow. His broad and strongly held ideas seemed to have crystallised after the First World War. He is noted most of all as a poet, although he was also a novelist, journalist and university lecturer in his time. The breadth of his interests and vision is shown in his active promotion and translation of major European writers into English. His output is considerable, ranges wide over the field of writing, and his poetry—which shows a concentrated integrity of purpose—was edited by no less a poet than T.S. Eliot.

The Horses

prescribed for Ordinary Level exams in 2005 and 2006

Barely a twelvemonth after
The seven days war that put the world to sleep,
Late in the evening the strange horses came.
By then we had made our covenant with silence,
But in the first few days it was so still   5
We listened to our breathing and were afraid.
On the second day
The radios failed; we turned the knobs; no answer.
On the third day a warship passed us, heading north,
Dead bodies piled on the deck. On the sixth day   10
A plane plunged over us into the sea. Thereafter
Nothing. The radios dumb;
And still they stand in corners of our kitchens,
And stand, perhaps, turned on, in a million rooms
All over the world. But now if they should speak,   15
If on a sudden they should speak again,
If on the stroke of noon a voice should speak,
We would not listen, we would not let it bring
That old bad world that swallowed its children quick

At one great gulp. We would not have it again.   20
Sometimes we think of the nations lying asleep,
Curled blindly in impenetrable sorrow,
And then the thought confounds us with its strangeness.
The tractors lie about our fields; at evening
They look like dank sea-monsters couched and waiting.   25
We leave them where they are and let them rust:
'They'll moulder away and be like other loam'.
We make our oxen drag our rusty ploughs,
Long laid aside. We have gone back
Far past our fathers' land.   30

                              And then, that evening
Late in the summer the strange horses came.
We heard a distant tapping on the road,
A deepening drumming; it stopped, went on again
And at the corner changed to hollow thunder.   35
We saw the heads
Like a wild wave charging and were afraid.
We had sold our horses in our fathers' time
To buy new tractors. Now they were strange to us
As fabulous steeds set on an ancient shield   40
Or illustrations in a book of knights.
We did not dare go near them. Yet they waited,
Stubborn and shy, as if they had been sent
By an old command to find our whereabouts
And that long-lost archaic companionship.   45
In the first moment we had never a thought
That they were creatures to be owned and used.
Among them were some half-a-dozen colts
Dropped in some wilderness of the broken world,
Yet new as if they had come from their own Eden.   50
Since then they have pulled our ploughs and borne our loads,
But that free servitude still can pierce our hearts.
Our life is changed; their coming our beginning.

Notes

[4] **covenant:** an agreement or a contract

[22] **impenetrable:** cannot be penetrated or broken through

[23] **confounds:** confuses, puzzles

[25] **dank:** unpleasantly damp and cold

[27] **moulder:** decay

[40] **steeds:** horses

[45] **archaic:** primitive, of an ancient time

[48] **colts:** young male horses

[52] **servitude:** slavery

Explorations

First reading

1. Imagine that a World War broke out tomorrow and Ireland was involved in it. How do you think your life would be changed? Discuss what might happen to your family, your home and the normal routine of everyday life. If you know someone who was alive during the First World War or the Second World War ask them what they remember about those times.

2. What images does the poet use to suggest the ways in which the 'seven days war' gradually affected people's lives? Can you explain why these things happened as a result of the war?

3. How did people react to the war? Choose two phrases that express their feelings. Do you find these feelings understandable? Why?

4. Why do you think the poet uses sound to describe the arrival of the horses? What effect do you think he was trying to achieve?

5. What was the first reaction of the people to the horses? Why do you think they felt like this? Trace how their reaction changes over time.

Second reading

6. Choose one image from the poem that you feel captures the terrible effect that war has on people and explain why you chose it.

7. Radios play an important part in this poem. Can you explain why they went dead? Why do you think people would not listen to the radios if they did start to work again? Does it have anything to do with the lasting effects of the 'seven day war'? Consider how and why governments often control the media of a country.

8. In what ways do the horses help people cope with life after the war?

Third reading

9. 'Our life is changed; their coming our beginning.' What tone of voice do you think should be used to read this line? Does the tone of the poem change as the piece develops. Read the poem aloud, then try to pick out exactly where these changes of tone occur.

10. Do you think this poem was written recently? Support your opinion by referring to the poem. Is the poem relevant in today's world? Try looking at newspapers or magazines to see if there are any stories that remind you of this poem.

Edna St Vincent Millay (1892–1950)

Edna St Vincent Millay was born in Maine, US, in 1892 and came from a professional background. Her remarkable gifts were recognised while she was still a teenager and her education at Vassar College was funded by Caroline Dow. She was both beautiful and intelligent, with a strongly developed sense of justice and a remarkable insight into the dangers of fascism. She won the Pulitzer Prize for Poetry in 1923—the first woman to do so. Her work continued to be published regularly and her *Collected Sonnets* appeared in 1941. Her *Collected*

Poems were published posthumously in 1952. Her work combines the sensitivity of her feminine side and the rigour of her undoubted intellect.

What Lips My Lips Have Kissed

prescribed for Ordinary Level exams in 2003 and 2004

What lips my lips have kissed, and where, and why,
I have forgotten, and what arms have lain
Under my head till morning; but the rain
Is full of ghosts tonight, that tap and sigh
Upon the glass and listen for reply,   5
And in my heart there stirs a quiet pain
For unremembered lads that not again
Will turn to me at midnight with a cry.
Thus in winter stands the lonely tree,
Nor knows what birds have vanished one by one,   10
Yet knows its boughs more silent than before:
I cannot say what loves have come and gone,
I only know that summer sang in me
A little while, that in me sings no more.

Explorations

First reading

1. The idea that sounds can call up memories from the past is important in this poem. Are there any sounds that trigger certain memories for you? Perhaps you have a piece of music that reminds you of an incident from your past?

2. Imagine this poem is a scene on television. Can you describe what it would look like? What words in the poem help you to picture this setting?

3. What types of 'love' can people experience? What kind of 'love' do you think the poet is remembering in the first three lines of the poem? Choose two images from the poem that support your view.

4. How would you describe the poet's mood in lines 1–8 of this poem? Can you find one line that clearly expresses this mood?

Second reading

5. What do you think the poet has in common with the 'lonely tree' in line 9? How do the first eight lines of the poem help you to understand why she sees herself like this?

6. Explain in your own words how the 'lads' might be connected to the 'birds' in line 10.

7. Write down five words that you think of when you hear the word 'summer'. Consider the words that the class comes up with. Do they have anything in common? Why do you think the poet uses 'summer' to describe the time when she was loving and being loved?

Third reading

8. Was the poet young or old when she wrote this poem? What evidence is there in the poem to support your view?

9. What impression do you get of the poet's attitude to 'love' from this poem? What is your reaction to this attitude? Are you surprised that this poem was written by a woman? Why?

10. This poem is written in the 'sonnet' form, with an octet (lines 1–8) and a sestet (lines 9–14). Consider whether the poet was successful in fitting what she wanted to say into this structure.

Robert Graves (1895–1985)

The descendant of a distinguished Anglo-Irish family but born and educated in England, Robert Graves is probably better known for his autobiography, *Goodbye to All That* (1929), and for his historical novels *I, Claudius* and *Claudius the God* than his poetry, of which he produced a great many volumes. 'Hedges Freaked with Snow' is a section of 'Three Songs for the Lute' in *New Poems, 1962*. The volume features some very bleak love poems.

Hedges Freaked with Snow

prescribed for the Ordinary Level exam in 2003

No argument, no anger, no remorse,
No dividing of blame.
There was poison in the cup—why should we ask
From whose hand it came?

No grief for our dead love, no howling gales   5
That through darkness blow,
But the smile of sorrow, a wan winter landscape,
Hedges freaked with snow.

Notes

Freaked: 'freak' can mean (a) to fleck or streak with colour or (b) a sudden causeless change of mind, a capricious humour

[7] **wan:** pale, of sickly complexion

Explorations

Before reading

1. Have you ever broken off with a friend (or boyfriend or girlfriend)? Were you full of hurt or anger, or could you be detached about it? Think about it.

First reading

2. What is your first impression of the poet's attitude here?

3. 'There was poison in the cup.' What does this suggest to you about how the relationship ended? What might have happened? Imagine a scenario.

4. 'Why should we ask | From whose hand it came?' Why do you think he doesn't want to talk about it? Is he callous or afraid, or what?

5. 'No grief for our dead love...' How do you think the speaker feels here? Does this fit in easily with the reading of the speaker as callous and unconcerned? How do you understand the speaker's feelings?

Second reading

6. 'The smile of sorrow': imagine where you yourself might need to put on a smile of sorrow. Describe what it feels like to put on such a front. What does this image suggest about the speaker's feelings here?

7. Think about the images of nature in this poem. What atmosphere do they create? What do they suggest about the relationship?

Third reading

8. What does this poem reveal to you about love?

9. What does it say about human beings? Does it leave you with a bleak or a dignified view of humanity? Explain briefly.

10. How do you imagine his former lover might have reacted when she read this poem? Compose a letter she might have written to the poet, setting out her feelings.

11. Outline your feelings for the speaker of this poem. Do you feel sorry for him, angry with him, or what? Explain.

Stevie Smith (1902–1971)

Florence Margaret (Stevie) Smith was born in Yorkshire but reared by her mother and aunt in London in what she described as 'a house of female habitation'. She worked all her life as secretary to the chairman of a publishing firm, where she wrote her famous first novel, *Novel on Yellow Paper* (1936). But she is best known for her witty and strange verse, of which there are eight volumes; 'she came to be recognised as a very special poet of strangeness, loneliness and quirky humour,' as the critic Anthony Thwaite said. 'Deeply Morbid' is taken from the collection *Harold's Leap* (1950).

Deeply Morbid

prescribed for the Ordinary Level exam in 2003

Deeply morbid deeply morbid was the girl who typed the letters
Always out of office hours running with her social betters
But when daylight and the darkness of the office closed about her
Not for this ah not for this her office colleagues came to doubt her
It was that look within her eye   5
Why did it always seem to say goodbye?

Joan her name was and at lunchtime
Solitary solitary
She would go and watch the pictures
In the National Gallery   10
All alone all alone
This time with no friend beside her

She would go and watch the pictures
All alone.

Will she leave her office colleagues   15
Will she leave her evening pleasures
Toil within a friendly bureau
Running later in her leisure?
All alone all alone
Before the pictures she seems turned to stone.   20

Close upon the Turner pictures
Closer than a thought may go
Hangs her eye and all the colours
Leap into a special glow
All for her, all alone   25
All for her, all for Joan.

First the canvas where the ocean
Like a mighty animal
With a really wicked motion
Leaps for sailors' funeral   30

Holds her panting. Oh the creature
Oh the wicked virile thing
With its skin of fleck and shadow
Stretching tightening over him.
Wild yet captured wild yet captured   35
By the painter, Joan is quite enraptured.

Now she edges from the canvas
To another loved more dearly
Where the awful light of purest
Sunshine falls across the spray,   40
There the burning coasts of fancy
Open to her pleasure lay.
All alone, all alone
Come away, come away
All alone.   45

Lady Mary, Lady Kitty
The Honourable Featherstonehaugh

Polly Tommy from the office
Which of these shall hold her now?
Come away, come away   50
All alone.

The spray reached out and sucked her in
It was a hardly noticed thing
That Joan was there and is not now
(Oh go and tell young Featherstonehaugh)   55
Gone away, gone away
All alone.

She stood up straight
The sun fell down
There was no more of London Town   60
She went upon the painted shore
And there she walks for ever more
Happy quite
Beaming bright
In a happy happy light   65
All alone.

They say she was a morbid girl, no doubt of it
And what befell her clearly grew out of it
But I say she's a lucky one
To walk for ever in that sun   70
And as I bless sweet Turner's name
I wish that I could do the same.

 # Explorations

First reading: stanzas 1–3

1. From a reading of the first stanza, what are your first impressions of Joan? Consider the evidence of friends, her habits, her looks, etc.

2. Is there anything that would indicate that she is 'deeply morbid'? Is she strange in any way?

3. Explore stanzas 2 and 3. What does she do in her lunchtime? What do you notice about this

activity, as described in the poem? What words indicate her state of mind or humour, and what is suggested?

Second reading: stanzas 4–6

4. What do you notice about the Turner pictures Joan is viewing?
5. How is the ocean portrayed? Comment on the relationship between humankind and the ocean here.
6. What are Joan's feelings for the paintings? Comment on her attitude to Turner's art.
7. In stanza 7 Joan moves from the first Turner canvas 'to another loved more dearly'. What features of this does she appreciate in particular? What does she mean by 'the burning coasts of fancy'? How does the painting affect her?

Third reading

8. Explain what happens in stanzas 8, 9, and 10. Are we to take this literally or do you think it is metaphorical? If so, what is the significance?
9. Here, for the first time, we are conscious of the personal voice of the poet. What is revealed of her attitude to and feelings about the happening? Do you think this is an important point in the poem? Why?

Fourth reading

10. Explain your general reaction to this poem. Did you find it strange, odd, weird, daft or silly, or had it a serious point? If so, what?
11. What impression of city life and work do we get from this poem?
12. Comment on the view of life or philosophy behind this poem.
13. Outline the main themes it deals with.
14. What do you notice about the style of writing? Comment on two of the following: choice of language; the form of the lines and stanzas; the imagery; the metre or rhythms; the sounds of words.

W.H. Auden (1907–1973)

Wystan Hugh Auden was born at York on 21 February 1907 and educated at Oxford and Berlin. He is considered one of the most important English poets of the 1930s, writing on political and social themes. A prolific poet, he wrote in a variety of verse forms, composing both humorous and serious poetry. 'Funeral Blues', originally a song in one of his plays, is taken from the volume *Another Time* (1940), which contains many of his best-known poems, such as 'September 1939' and 'Lullaby'. Auden spent much of his life in the United States, becoming an

American citizen in 1946.

Funeral Blues

prescribed for the Ordinary Level exam in 2003

Stop all the clocks, cut off the telephone,
Prevent the dog from barking with a juicy bone,
Silence the pianos and with muffled drum
Bring out the coffin, let the mourners come.

Let aeroplanes circle moaning overhead   5
Scribbling on the sky the message He Is Dead,
Put the crêpe bows round the white necks of the public doves,
Let the traffic policemen wear black cotton gloves.

He was my North, my South, my East and West,
My working week and my Sunday rest,   10
My noon, my midnight, my talk, my song;
I thought that love would last for ever: I was wrong.

The stars are not wanted now: put out every one;
Pack up the moon and dismantle the sun;
Pour away the ocean and sweep up the wood.   15
For nothing now can ever come to any good.

Explorations

First reading

1. What images grab your attention?
2. What do you think is happening in this poem?
3. Do you find it unusual in any way? Explain.

Second reading

4. The first two stanzas create the atmosphere of a funeral. What sights and sounds of a funeral do you notice?
5. It used to be a custom that clocks were stopped in a house where a death had occurred: as well as marking the time of death, this signified that time stood still for the grieving family. Do you think that the signs of mourning have been carried to extremes in the first two stanzas? Examine the actions called for.
6. How do you think the first stanza should be read: in a low, defeated tone, or semi-hysterical, or what? Read it aloud.
7. Read the second stanza aloud.
8. Do you think there might be a change of tone from the third stanza on? Read aloud stanzas 3 and 4.
9. Are you sympathetic to the speaker in this poem?

Third reading

10. What does the third stanza suggest about the relationship between the speaker and the person mourned? Examine each line in detail for the kernel of truth behind the clichés.
11. How do you understand the speaker's state of mind, particularly in the last verse?
12. Do you take this poem to be a serious statement about loss and bereavement, or do you find it exaggerated and 'over the top'? Explain your opinion. Do you think it could be read as a satire, that is, a poem ridiculing, in this case, the public outpouring of emotion at the funerals of famous people? Read the poem again.

Fourth reading

13. What do you think the poem is saying?
14. Look at the imagery again. How does it fit in with what the poem is saying?
15. Find out what you can about blues music and lyrics. What elements of a blues song do you find in the poem?
16. What do you like about this poem?

Louis MacNeice (1907–1963)

Louis MacNeice was born in Belfast in 1907 to parents who were originally from the West of Ireland. His father was a Church of Ireland rector and later became a Bishop. His mother died when he was quite young having previously suffered from mental illness. He was educated in England at Sherborne Preparatory School and later at Merton College, Oxford. He was married twice. Firstly to Mary Ezra in 1930 and then to Heidi Anderson in 1942. He had one child by each of them, a boy and a girl respectively. In the 1930s he became associated with Auden, Spender and others and they formed a poetry movement which was to have an influence on poetry in England for much of the rest of the century.

In 1941 he joined the BBC and spent the rest of his life working there. He wrote many radio plays at the BBC. He also published twelve volumes of poetry, three books of criticism and an autobiography called *The Strings are False*. MacNeice wrote a lot of long poems such as the brilliant *Autumn Journal*

but is best remembered for his lyric poetry such as 'Snow', 'Carrickfergus' and 'Prayer before Birth'. He has been a major influence on many Irish and English poets especially people like Derek Mahon and Michael Longley who edited his *Selected Poems*.

Autobiography

prescribed for Ordinary Level exams in 2004 and 2005

In my childhood trees were green
And there was plenty to be seen.

Come back early or never come.

My father made the walls resound,
He wore his collar the wrong way round.   5

Come back early or never come.

My mother wore a yellow dress;
Gently, gently, gentleness.

Come back early or never come.

When I was five the black dreams came;   10
Nothing after was quite the same.

Come back early or never come.

The dark was talking to the dead;
The lamp was dark beside my bed.

Come back early or never come.   15

When I woke they did not care;
Nobody, nobody was there.

Come back early or never come.

When my silent terror cried,
Nobody, nobody replied.   20

Come back early or never come.

I got up; the chilly sun
Saw me walk away alone.

Come back early or never come.

Explorations

First reading

1. What do you think his father's occupation was? What particular details does the speaker remember about his father?

2. What particular quality of his mother's remains in his memory?

Second reading

3. What changed at five?

4. What words or phrases in the poem do you think best convey the atmosphere of the nightmares?

5. In your own words suggest how you imagine the boy must have felt at those times?

6. What words or phrases in the poem express the sense of loneliness and isolation experienced by the boy? What word is much repeated and what is the effect of that?

7. What colours does the writer use throughout the poem? What do you think each might represent? How and where do they change?

Third reading

8. Who is speaking in the chorus line? Who do you think is being addressed? What do you think the poet wants to convey in this line?

9. The simple rhyme sounds, and the light, tripping rhythm or beat is usually associated with a happy children's poem or a nursery rhyme. Is there a contrast here between the rhymes and rhythms and the nature of the thoughts and feelings conveyed? What is the effect of this?

10. Where and how does the tone change as the poem develops?

Fourth reading

11. Which section of the poem made the most impact on you? Write a paragraph about your reaction to it.

12. In two paragraphs, explain the main themes of this poem.

13. MacNeice called this poem 'a naïve-seeming kind of little ballad'. Would you agree with his assessment?

John Hewitt (1907–1987)

John Hewitt was born in Belfast and educated at Methodist College and Queen's University. He considered himself to be of a liberal Protestant mind in religion but radical in social policy. He worked in the Belfast Museum and Art Gallery from 1930 until 1957. Above all else he was devoted to Ulster, and his poems deal with the culture and heritage of the province and its political and religious divisions. He also wrote about childhood memories and personal themes; but he is most famous for his nature poems capturing the life of the Glens of Antrim.

The Green Shoot

prescribed for the Ordinary Level exam in 2003

In my harsh city, when a Catholic priest,
known by his collar, padded down our street,
I'd trot beside him, pull my schoolcap off
and fling it on the ground and stamp on it.

I'd catch my enemy, that errand-boy,   5
grip his torn jersey and admonish him
first to admit his faith, and when he did,
repeatedly to curse the Pope of Rome;

schooled in such duties by my bolder friends;
yet not so many hurried years before,   10
when I slipped in from play one Christmas Eve
my mother bathed me at the kitchen fire,

and wrapped me in a blanket for the climb
up the long stairs; and suddenly we heard
the carol-singers somewhere in the dark, 15
their voices sharper, for the frost was hard.

My mother carried me through the dim hall
into the parlour, where the only light
upon the patterned wall and furniture
came from the iron lamp across the street; 20

and there looped round the lamp the singers stood,
but not on snow in grocers' calendars,
singing a song I liked until I saw
my mother's lashes were all bright with tears.

Out of this mulch of ready sentiment, 25
gritty with threads of flinty violence,
I am the green shoot asking for the flower,
soft as the feathers of the snow's cold swans.

 # Explorations

Before reading

1. How would you describe the culture of your own locality and environment? What do you notice about the dominant attitudes in your school, housing estate, class or family? It might help to:
   - list three things your community values
   - list three things your community is strongly against
   - describe how important or regular customs are practised
   - say whether any group of people is badly treated. Discuss these questions.

First reading: lines 1–9

2. Visualise the incident in the first stanza. Notice the different styles of walking: 'padded', 'trot'. What is suggested here about the different attitudes of each of the participants? What do you think might be the significance of the gesture with the school cap?

3. What does the gesture reveal about the attitude to the

priest? What does it reveal of the mentality of those who thought it a proper thing to do?

4. What was your own reaction to it?

5. Imagine the feelings of the priest. Write a diary entry for the incident as he might have written it.

6. Do you think that class as well as religious difference plays a part in the conflict in the second stanza? Where is this indicated?

7. What might be the thoughts of the errand-boy?

Second reading: stanzas 3–6

8. Describe the atmosphere in the house on Christmas Eve. How is this created?

9. What does this episode reveal about the relationship between the boy and his mother? What do we learn about the character of the boy? Does it accord at all with the youth of the first two stanzas?

10. In what way is the incident significant? How does the poet read it, and why does he think it significant? Read the last stanza.

Third reading

11. What do you think Hewitt means by the last two lines? Put the idea in your own words.

12. Do you think the poet has a good eye for detail? Explain.

13. In general, what is the poet saying about his cultural background?

14. Do you think people can overcome and outgrow their upbringing and the culture of their particular environment? Discuss this.

15. What insights did the poem give you into the culture of Northern Ireland?

Dylan Thomas (1914–1953)

Dylan Thomas was born in Swansea where his father was an English teacher. After attending the local grammar school he went to work as a journalist on a local newspaper, *The South Wales Daily Post*. In 1934 he went to London where he worked as a journalist and reviewer, as well as doing other jobs for newspapers and magazines. During the Second World War he came to work as a scriptwriter for the BBC and a number of film companies. In the postwar years he began broadcasting, featuring his own poems and stories. Thomas published four volumes of poetry and two prose works. His 'play for voices' *Under Milk Wood*, which evokes the spirit of a Welsh village from early morning to night, was published after his death. Thomas said of his poetry 'I wrote my poems for the glory of God and the love of man'.

He married Caitlin Macnamara in 1937, and after much wandering eventually settled in Wales in 1949. He went to America on a lecture and poetry-reading tour the following year and made a great deal of money. Unfortunately Thomas found life as a literary celebrity a strain, which he relieved by heavy drinking. In 1953 he died in America after a heavy drinking bout.

Do Not Go Gentle Into That Good Night

prescribed for Ordinary Level exams in 2005 and 2006

Do not go gentle into that good night,
Old age should burn and rave at close of day;
Rage, rage against the dying of the light.

Though wise men at their end know dark is right,
Because their words have forked no lightning they   5
Do not go gentle into that good night.

Good men, the last wave by, crying how bright
Their frail deeds might have danced in a green bay,
Rage, rage against the dying of the light.
Wild men who caught and sang the sun in flight,   10
And learn, too late, they grieved it on its way,
Do not go gentle into that good night.

Grave men, near death, who see with blinding sight
Blind eyes could blaze like meteors and be gay,
Rage, rage against the dying of the light.   15

And you, my father, there on the sad height,
Curse, bless, me now with your fierce tears, I pray.
Do not go gentle into that good night.
Rage, rage against the dying of the light.

Background note

Dylan Thomas's father was blind when he died.

 # Explorations

Before reading

1. Imagine how you would feel if someone you care about was critically ill. Try to describe the thoughts that would go through your mind as you waited by their bedside.

First reading

2. What do you think the poet means by 'that good night'? Does it mean the same as 'the dying of the light' or do you feel this might be a reference to the father's blindness?

3. How, according to Thomas, should 'Old age' react 'at close of day'?

4. What do 'wise' men know in stanza 2? Do they act according to their knowledge? Critics have interpreted 'forked no lightning' as meaning: 'were not inspired by the words'. Does this make sense to you?

5. How do 'Good men' react in the third stanza? Has 'the last wave' something to do with a last wave of the hand or the last wave in the sea?

6. What is the poem saying about how 'Wild men' lived their lives?

7. There is paradox in seeing with 'blinding sight' as the 'Grave men, near death' do. What do you think the poet is trying to suggest here? If you are unsure, leave the question and come back to it later. Did you notice the pun in 'Grave men'?

8. What is Thomas asking his father to do in the final stanza? Have you any idea of what he means by 'fierce tears'?

Second reading

9. Read the poem aloud. What tone of voice should you adopt? What is the effect of the refrain in the final line of each stanza? How for example should 'Rage, rage' be read? Does the sound give you an idea of how the poet feels? Should the poem be read at a brisk or slow pace? Why?
10. Do you get a sense from the poem about how life should be lived according to the poet?
11. How does the poet feel about his father?
12. Why do you think the final stanza is four lines long when the other stanzas contain three?

Third reading

13. Look at the images of light and darkness that run through the poem? What does light symbolise for the poet? What does darkness represent?
14. What emotions does the poet feel in the poem? What words or images suggest how he feels?
15. How do you imagine the poet's father? What kind of a person was he? How do you think he lived his life?
16. State briefly what the theme of this poem is? Can you sum up your understanding of the text in one or two sentences?

17. Do you find the poet's language unusual or difficult? Write about any two features of the writer's style?
18. Is the poet sincere in what he has to say about his father? Justify your answer?

Fourth reading

19. Does this poem build up to a climax? Can you see any structure in how the poem is developed?
20. Do you think the effort involved in understanding this poem was worthwhile? Do you think that critics who complained about the obscurity of Dylan Thomas's poems were justified? Does any line or phrase from the poem stick in your mind? Can you relate to the poet's feelings?
21. 'No paraphrase will ever do justice to the verse of Dylan Thomas.' Would you agree with this statement? Consider how sound, sense and imagery combine to produce the overall impact.
22. 'Dylan Thomas is intense and passionate.' Comment on the poem's emotional atmosphere. How do you react to Thomas's portrayal of feelings? Are you moved by the poem?
23. What is the poet's attitude to death as displayed in the poem?

Judith Wright (1915–)

Judith Wright is one of the most important Australian poets of the twentieth century. Her first volume of poetry, *The Moving Image* (1946), dealt with the Aboriginal and convict history of Australia and made an immediate impact. She also writes about the Australian landscape and the solitary figures of Australian rural life, and she is interested in conservationist issues. She also explores the theme of love, and particularly maternal experience, in *Woman to Man* (1949). Her *Collected Poems, 1942–1970* was published in 1972.

Request to a Year

prescribed for the Ordinary Level exam in 2003

If the year is meditating a suitable gift,
I should like it to be the attitude
of my great-great-grandmother,
legendary devotee of the arts,

who, having had eight children   5
and little opportunity for painting pictures,
sat one day on a high rock
beside a river in Switzerland

and from a difficult distance viewed
her second son, balanced on a small ice-floe,   10
drift down the current towards a waterfall
that struck rock-bottom eighty feet below,

while her second daughter, impeded,
no doubt, by the petticoats of the day,

stretched out a last-hope alpenstock   15
(which luckily later caught him on his way).

Nothing, it was evident, could be done;
and with the artist's isolating eye
my great-great-grandmother hastily sketched the scene.
The sketch survives to prove the story by.   20

Year, if you have no Mother's day present planned;
reach back and bring me the firmness of her hand.

 # Explorations

First reading

1. Picture the drama in this scene.
    What do you see? Roughly
    sketch the outline of the scene
    and describe what you see.
    What is happening? Where is
    each character? Imagine the
    expression on the face of each.
2. What was the reaction of the
    great-great-grandmother to the
    incident? Can you explain her
    reaction? What is your
    impression of her?
3. Do you think this poem is
    meant to be taken seriously?
    Explain your view.

Second reading

4. Does the poet realise that this
    scenario is incredible? Where is
    this indicated?

5. Explore the poet's reaction to
    the great-great-grandmother. Is
    it one of horror, indifference,
    admiration, or what? What
    quality of the great-great-
    grandmother's does she
    respect?
6. Explain the title of the poem.

Third reading

7. How is the humour created?
    Explore the effect of
    exaggeration, unexpected
    behaviour, the language used,
    and irony. Do you consider
    this light humour or bleak
    humour? Why?
8. What statements do you think
    the poem is making about
    motherhood, about art, or
    about childhood?

Edwin Morgan (1920–)

Morgan was born in Glasgow, was first published in 1952 and was still being published in 1996. Such a long career is marked by an ability and vision to write poetry inspired by a wide and varied list of subjects, from space travel to mythological goddesses. His prolific output includes libretti, plays, criticism and translations from Anglo-Saxon and Russian. His poems are as varied in form as they are in material, showing, for example, similarities to mediaeval Latin writing on the one hand and e. e. cummings on the other.

Strawberries

prescribed for the Ordinary Level exam in 2006

There were never strawberries
like the ones we had
that sultry afternoon
sitting on the step
of the open french window   5
facing each other
your knees held in mine
the blue plates in our laps
the strawberries glistening
in the hot sunlight   10
we dipped them in sugar
looking at each other
not hurrying the feast
for one to come
the empty plates   15
laid on the stone together
with the two forks crossed
and I bent towards you
sweet in that air
in my arms   20
abandoned like a child
from your eager mouth
the taste of strawberries
in my memory
lean back again let me love you   25

let the sun beat
on our forgetfulness
one hour of all
the heat intense
and summer lightening   30
on the Kilpatrick hills

let the storm wash the plates

Explorations

First reading

1. The poet suggests that food connected with special moments has a special taste. Would you agree with him? Have you any special memories where the food seemed to taste especially good?

2. What impression do you get of the setting for this poem? Do you find it a surprising setting for a poem? Why?

3. What sort of a relationship do you think these two people have? Choose two phrases from the poem to support your view.

Second reading

4. What is the weather like as the couple eat the strawberries? Does it tell you anything about their feelings?

5. 'the empty plates
   laid on the stone together
   with the two forks crossed'
   Why do you think the poet introduces this image into the poem at this point? Does it have any connection with the couple?

6. How does the poet use the weather to suggest the intensifying of their emotions? Do you think that this is a

successful device or is it rather over-dramatic?

Third reading

7. 'not hurrying the feast
   for one to come'
   Eating is a sensual experience. Can the 'feast' of strawberries be seen as a preparation for another equally sensual 'feast'? What is your reaction to this connection of ideas?

8. Eating is also an important social activity. Can you think of occasions where sharing food has a special significance perhaps even suggesting a change in the nature of a relationship? How would you feel if you had to share a table in a restaurant with a stranger, or if you were invited to a friend's home for a meal?

9. Why do you think the poet chose to write this poem without any punctuation? Was he trying to suggest something about the moment, or perhaps about the way that he remembers the moment?

10. This is a remembered moment. Do you think that this affects the way in which the poet views the scene? Can memories be trusted? Does it matter if they are unreliable?

Denise Levertov (1923–1997)

Denise Levertov was born in Essex in England. Her father had converted from Judaism to become an Anglican parson. She was educated completely at home and at five years old decided that she would become a writer. At the age of twelve she sent her poetry to T.S. Eliot who responded very positively to her work. She published her first poem at seventeen and her first collection in 1946. During World War Two she worked as a civilian nurse during the bombing of London.

In 1947, she married an American and soon after moved to the US with him. By 1956 she had become an American citizen. Her poetry became much less formal and she was heavily influenced by poets such as William Carlos Williams. Her second American volume, *With Eyes at the Back of Our Heads*, in 1959 established her as one of the great American poets and her British roots were by now a thing of the past. During the 1960s she became very involved in activism and feminism. She was strongly opposed to the Vietnam War. *The Sorrow Dance*, which emphasised her feelings to the Vietnam War and to the death of her sister, was a passionate angry collection. In all she published more than twenty volumes of poetry. She died in December 1997.

What Were They Like?

prescribed for Ordinary Level exams in 2004 and 2005

1. Did the people of Vietnam
   use lanterns of stone?
2. Did they hold ceremonies
   to reverence the opening of buds?
3. Were they inclined to laughter?   5
4. Did they use bone and ivory,
   jade and silver, for ornament?
5. Had they an epic poem?
6. Did they distinguish between speech and singing?

1. Sir, their light hearts turned to stone.   10
   It is not remembered whether in gardens
   stone lanterns illumined pleasant ways.
2. Perhaps they gathered once to delight in blossom,
   but after the children were killed
   there were no more buds.   15
3. Sir, laughter is bitter to the burned mouth.
4. A dream ago, perhaps. Ornament is for joy.
   All the bones were charred.
5. It is not remembered. Remember,
   most were peasants; their life   20
   was in rice and bamboo.
   When peaceful clouds were reflected in the paddies
   and the water buffalo stepped surely along terraces,
   maybe fathers told their sons old tales.
   When bombs smashed those mirrors   25
   there was time only to scream.
6. There is an echo yet
   of their speech which was like a song.
   It was reported their singing resembled
   the flight of moths in moonlight.   30
   Who can say? It is silent now.

Explorations

Before reading

1. What do you know about the Vietnam War? Find out about it and discuss it.

First reading (lines 1–9)

2. Read the questions. What does the questioner want to find out?

3. What do these questions tell us about the questioner—for example: what preconceptions does s/he have about the Vietnamese; what is his/her profession—journalist, historian, archaeologist or what?

4. Read the questions aloud in the tone of voice you would expect the questioner to ask them. Discuss the tone and manner of the questioning.

5. What responses would you expect to each of these questions? Suggest sample answers.

Second reading (lines 10–31)

6. Are the answers as you expected? What do you find surprising or unexpected? Do you think the answers might have surprised the questioner? Why?

7. From the answers, what do we learn about the way of life of the Vietnamese?

8. What is the chief preoccu- pation of the person who replies—what preys on his/her mind and colours all the replies?

9. Do you think the tone of the answers differs from that of the questions? Explain your views on this and discuss them in your group or class.

Third reading

10. What is your favourite image or phrase in the poem?

11. Examine each of the metaphors individually: the light, the bud, laughter, decoration, heritage and culture. What is suggested by each metaphor? What do they contribute to the atmosphere of the poem?

12. What impression is given of the attitude to life of Vietnamese people after the war? Where is this suggested?

13. Are there any signs of hope for the future in this poem?

Fourth reading

14. Were you moved by the poem? Discuss your reaction with your group or class.

15. What do you think the poem is saying? Write two or three paragraphs on this.

16. Have you previously read a poem that took the format of a 'question and answer' sequence? What do you think of this format? Is it effective in this case? Explain your views.

Patricia Beer (1924–1999)

Patricia Beer was born in Exmouth, Devon, into a Plymouth Brethren family. Her father was a railway clerk and her mother a teacher, Beer wrote a vivid account of her stern upbringing in *Mrs Beer's House* (1968). Patricia won a scholarship to Exmouth Grammar School and achieved a first-class honours degree at Exeter University. She went on to St Hugh's College, Oxford, and lived in Italy teaching English during the period 1947–53. After a succession of temporary jobs Beer was appointed lecturer in English at Goldsmiths' College in London in 1962, where she remained for six years. In 1964 she married an architect, John Damien Parsons with whom she refurbished a Tudor farmhouse in Up Ottery, Devon, where she lived the rest of her life. Patricia Beer left teaching to become a full-time writer four years later.

In all, Beer published nine volumes of poetry, one novel and an academic study *Reader I Married Him*—an analysis of the major nineteenth-century women novelists and their female characters. Patricia Beer makes her poems out of the ordinary events of daily life with a wry humour and a sharp eye for detail.

The Voice

prescribed for the Ordinary Level exam in 2006

When God took my aunt's baby boy, a merciful neighbour
Gave her a parrot. She could not have afforded one
But now bought a new cage as brilliant as the bird,
And turned her back on the idea of other babies.

He looked unlikely. In her house his scarlet feathers   5
Stuck out like a jungle, though his blue ones blended
With the local pottery which carried messages
Like 'Du ee help yerself to crame, me handsome.'

He said nothing when he arrived, not a quotation
From pet-shop gossip or a sailor's oath, no sound   10
From someone's home: the telephone or car-door slamming,
And none from his: tom-tom, war-cry or wild beast roaring.

He came from silence but was ready to become noise.
My aunt taught him nursery rhymes morning after morning.
He learnt Miss Muffett, Jack and Jill, Little Jack Horner,   15
Including her jokes; she used to say turds and whey.

A genuine Devon accent is not easy. Actors
Cannot do it. He could though. In his court clothes
He sounded like a farmer, as her son might have.
He sounded like our family. He fitted in.   20

Years went by. We came and went. A day or two
Before he died, he got confused, and muddled up
His rhymes. Jack Horner ate his pail of water.
The spider said what a good boy he was. I wept.

He had never seemed puzzled by the bizarre events   25
He spoke of. But that last day he turned his head towards us
With the bewilderment of death upon him. Said
'Broke his crown' and 'Christmas pie'. And tumbled after.

My aunt died the next winter, widowed, childless, pitied
And patronised. I cannot summon up her voice at all.   30
She would not have expected it to be remembered
After so long. But I can still hear his.

 # Explorations

First reading

1. What impression of the aunt do you get from the first stanza? How do you visualise her?

2. 'He looked unlikely.' What do you think the author means by this?

3. How do you imagine the aunt's home looked? Examine the

detail in the two opening stanzas.

4. Why do you think the aunt taught the parrot nursery rhymes? Is there a connection with the loss of her baby son?
5. 'He fitted in.' How did the parrot fit in?
6. Why do you think the author 'wept'? How does she feel about the parrot?
7. What do you think the poet means by 'pitied | And patronised'? What does this tell us about how people perceived the aunt?

Second reading

8. Read the poem aloud. Jot down what you notice about its sounds and rhythms.
9. How do you react to the first sentence? Is it an effective opening?
10. Comment on the 'jungle' simile in the second stanza.
11. Do you get a sense of place from the references to Devon and the local pottery? Does this enrich the poem?
12. 'With the bewilderment of death upon him. Said | 'Broke his crown' and 'Christmas pie.' And tumbled after.'
    Comment on these lines. Do you think the lines work well? Can you detect some humour in the clever phrasing?

13. What evidence is there in the poem that the parrot was regarded more as a family member than as a mere household pet?
14. How do you feel about the aunt's life? Can you suggest why we are not told her name?

Third reading

15. Briefly state what the theme of the poem is?
16. Would you agree that there is genuine warmth of feeling in this poem?
17. How do you react to the style in which the poem is written? Comment on any three features. You might consider the poet's conversational language, her wry humour, her eye for detail and her use of imagery.
18. What is the mood of this poem? What choice of words and images suggest the mood? Look closely at the final stanza.
19. What have you learned about the character of the author from reading the poem?

Fourth reading

20. Write a paragraph giving your personal reaction to 'The Voice'. Would you recommend it?

Elizabeth Jennings (1926–)

Elizabeth Jennings was born in Lincolnshire, England and was educated at Oxford University. In the famous poetry anthology *The New Lines* she was the only woman poet. This placed her alongside many of the writers of 'The Movement' which included Kingsley Amis, Philip Larkin and others. Her poetry is often interested in finding order in experience. It often searches for answers rather than giving a message. It concerns itself with the chase as much as the beast.

One Flesh

prescribed for Ordinary Level exams in 2004 and 2005

Lying apart now, each in a separate bed,
He with a book, keeping the light on late,
She like a girl dreaming of childhood,
All men elsewhere—it is as if they wait
Some new event: the book he holds unread,   5
Her eyes fixed on the shadows overhead.

Tossed up like flotsam from a former passion,
How cool they lie. They hardly ever touch,
Or if they do it is like a confession
Of having little feeling—or too much.   10
Chastity faces them, a destination
For which their whole lives were a preparation.

Strangely apart, yet strangely close together,
Silence between them like a thread to hold
And not wind in. And time itself's a feather   15
Touching them gently. Do they know they're old,
These two who are my father and my mother
Whose fire from which I came, has now grown cold?

Explorations

First reading
Stanza 1

1. The scene is described with all the clarity of a photograph. What do you notice about the picture? Describe the scene exactly.

2. Write out three questions you would like to ask the couple.

3. 'It is as if they wait | Some new event'. What does this suggest? Explore possible meanings.

Second reading
Stanza 2

4. Their relationship now is different to their former one. Explain the difference as we learn about it from the second stanza.

5. 'Tossed up like flotsam from a former passion'. What does this suggest about the condition of their lives? Explore all the possible. connotations of this image.

6. What do you imagine they are thinking, as they lie there? Draft a 'thoughts-inside-the-head' sequence for each person.

Third reading
Entire poem

7. 'Strangely apart, yet strangely close together'. How can this be?

8. There is a sense in this poem that neither parent can be complete without the other. Do you agree? Where is this evident?

9. Do you think they know that they are old?

10. If you had only read the first two verses, would you have known that the poem was about the poet's parents? What effect did this information have on you?

11. How do you think the poet feels about her parents?

Fourth reading

12. What particular images do you think contribute most to the atmosphere in this poem? Explain.

13. Explain the 'thread' simile.

14. Trace the rhyming scheme the poet uses. What is the effect of the sounds of these words?

15. What is the poem saying about age, love and families? Write three paragraphs on this.

16. Read Louis MacNeice's poem 'Autobiography' on page 473. In what ways are the attitudes of the speakers different?

Richard Murphy (1927–)

Richard Murphy was born in Mayo in 1927. His poetry collections include: *The Archaeology of Love* (Dolmen, 1955); *Sailing to an Island* (Faber, 1963); *The Battle of Aughrim* (Knopf and Faber, 1968; LP recording 1969); *High Island* (Faber, 1974); *High Island: New and Selected Poems* (Harper and Row, 1975); *Selected Poems* (Faber, 1979); *The Price of Stone* (Faber, 1985); *The Price of Stone and Earlier Poems* (Wake Forrest, 1985); *New Selected Poems* (Faber, 1989); *The Mirror Wall* (Bloodaxe, 1989) and *In the Heart of the Country: Collected Poems*, (Oldcastle, Co. Meath, Gallery Press, 2000). His awards include the Æ Memorial Award (1951); first prize, Guinness Awards, Cheltenham (1962); British Arts Council Awards (1967 and 1976); Marten Toonder Award (1980); Fellow of the Royal Society

of Literature (1969); American-Irish Foundation Award (1983). He lives in Co. Dublin.

His poetry is often concerned with issues of history. He is renowned as a crafter of poems who has been overlooked in recent years because of the fascination with Northern poetry.

The Reading Lesson

prescribed for the Ordinary Level exam in 2006

Fourteen years old, learning the alphabet,
He finds letters harder to catch than hares
Without a greyhound. Can't I give him a dog
To track them down, or put them in a cage?
He's caught in a trap, until I let him go,   5
Pinioned by 'Don't you want to learn to read?'
'I'll be the same man whatever I do.'

He looks at a page as a mule balks at a gap
From which a goat may hobble out and bleat.
His eyes jink from a sentence like flushed snipe   10
Escaping shot. A sharp word, and he'll mooch
Back to his piebald mare and bantam cock.
Our purpose is as tricky to retrieve
As mercury from a smashed thermometer.

'I'll not read anymore.' Should I give up?   15
His hands, long-fingered as a Celtic scribe's,
Will grow callous, gathering sticks or scrap;
Exploring pockets of the horny drunk
Loiterers at the fairs, giving them lice.
A neighbour chuckles. 'You can never tame   20
The wild duck: when his wings grow, he'll fly off.'

If books resembled roads, he'd quickly read:
But they're small farms to him, fenced by the page,
Ploughed into lines with letters drilled like oats:
A field of tasks he'll always be outside.   25
If words were bank-notes, he would filch a wad;
If they were pheasants, they'd be in his pot
For breakfast, or if wrens he'd make them king.

 # Explorations

First reading

1. What's the boy's background? Can you tell from the evidence in the poem?
2. Does the boy fit a stereotype?
3. What is the relationship between the two in the poem? Is it equal?

Second reading

4. Do you think the boy will give up?

5. Do you think the narrator will give up?
6. Will learning to read really change his life?
7. How does the narrator feel about the exercise?

Third reading

8. Why do you think the poet uses so many nature-related metaphors in the poem? Suggest a possible reason.

9. What do you think of the dialogue that is used in the poem? Is it realistic? Explain your thinking.
10. How does the last verse change the tone of the poem?
11. In the second verse the boy's reactions are compared to 'animals'. Do you think these descriptions are delivered well?

Are they fair?

Fourth reading
12. Do you think the neighbour is right?
13. Do you think a wild duck should be tamed?
14. With whom of the two main characters in the poem do you empathise most? Why?

Thomas Kinsella (1928–)

Thomas Kinsella was born in Dublin in 1928 and was educated at O'Connell Schools and University College, Dublin. He worked in the civil service for nineteen years before going to the University of Illinois in 1965. He returned to Ireland in 1992 and now lives in Wicklow. Kinsella has been a prolific poet and has translated extensively from Irish and edited *The New Oxford Book of Irish Verse*. His collections of poetry include: *Poems* (1956), *Another September* (1958), *Downstream* (1962), *Nightwalker and Other Poems* (1968), *Butcher's Dozen* (1972), *One and Other Poems* (1979), *Peppercanister Poems 1972–1978* (1979), *St Catherine's Clock* (1987), *Poems From City Centre* (1994). Kinsella's

translation of the epic *Tain Bo Cuailgne* was published as *The Tain* in 1969. He has been awarded the Gugenheim Fellowship twice and the Denis Devlin award on three occasions.

Mirror in February

prescribed for Ordinary Level exams in 2004 and 2005

The day dawns with scent of must and rain,
Of opened soil, dark trees, dry bedroom air.
Under the fading lamp, half dressed—my brain
Idling on some compulsive fantasy—
I towel my shaven jaw and stop, and stare,   5
Riveted by a dark exhausted eye,
A dry downturning mouth.

It seems again that it is time to learn,
In this untiring, crumbling place of growth
To which, for the time being, I return.   10
Now plainly in the mirror of my soul
I read that I have looked my last on youth
And little more; for they are not made whole
That reach the age of Christ.

Below my window the awakening trees,   15
Hacked clean for better bearing, stand defaced
Suffering their brute necessities,
And how should the flesh not quail that span for span
Is mutilated more? In slow distaste
I fold my towel with what grace I can,   20
Not young and not renewable, but man.

Note

[18] **quail:** flinch

 Explorations

Before reading

1. What are your plans for the future when you leave school? How do you see yourself in ten years' time? Do you think you will have changed as a person? Are there personal goals you would like to achieve? How do you see yourself in twenty years' time? Will you see life differently? Will your priorities change? Do you expect to be happier with your life? Write a paragraph which explores these issues.

First reading

2. How do you visualise the scene

---

in the opening two lines? What details stand out for you?

3. How do you see the speaker in the opening stanza? What does the 'dark exhausted eye' and 'dry downturning mouth' suggest to you? Can you detect the speaker's mood?

4. In the second stanza what does the speaker see 'plainly in the mirror of my soul'?

5. What does the speaker see when he looks out the window in the final stanza? Note the key details.

6. What do you think the speaker means by 'the flesh ... is mutilated more'?

7. 'In slow distaste'. What does the speaker feel distaste for?

8. How does the poet feel at the end of the poem? Is there anger and disgust, or acceptance and resignation? Can you detect any other emotion in the poem's ending?

Second reading

9. What details establish the atmosphere in the first three lines? List the key words.

10. Why do you think the first stanza is in the present tense? If, for instance, the verbs were in the past tense would the scene be as dramatic and immediate?

11. '...this untiring, crumbling place of growth'
Can you explain the paradox in this line?

12. What does the reference to Christ in the second stanza suggest to you?

13. Examine the emotional associations of Kinsella's choice of the following words: 'hacked', 'defaced', 'brute necessities', 'mutilated'. What is Kinsella saying about the process of ageing by using these words?

14. Comment on the possible meanings for 'grace' in line 20.

Third reading

15. Do you think the 'mirror of my soul' is an effective metaphor for mental reflection? Explain your answer.

16. Is this a dramatic poem? Look at the opening, the representative gestures, the use of the present tense and the language? Is a state of mind being dramatised?

17. Describe the poet's mood. How is the mood of the poem conveyed?

18. How do you react to this poem? Write a paragraph giving your response to the text.

19. Compose a diary entry that the poet might have written that February morning.

20. Do you like the way Kinsella uses language? Choose two lines or phrases that illustrate your view.

John Montague (1929–)

Born in New York of Irish parents, John Montague returned as a boy to what remained of the family farm at Garvaghy, Co. Tyrone. He was educated at St Patrick's College, Armagh; University College, Dublin and has been a university lecturer in America, France and Ireland. A prolific poet, he is probably most famous for his volume *The Rough Field* (1972), in which he investigates his personal and historical experience of Northern Ireland. John Montague was the first holder of the Ireland Chair of Poetry.

The Cage

prescribed for the Ordinary Level exam in 2003

My father, the least happy
man I have known. His face
retained the pallor
of those who work underground:
the lost years in Brooklyn   5
listening to a subway
shudder the earth.

But a traditional Irishman
who (released from his grille
in the Clark St I.R.T.)   10
drank neat whiskey until
he reached the only element
he felt at home in any longer: brute oblivion.

And yet picked himself
up, most mornings,   15
to march down the street

Notes

[1] **My father:** James Montague sold his farm to raise money for a business venture that proved unsuccessful; he failed to find work and, after involvement in republican activities in Co. Tyrone, emigrated to the United States in 1925; so perhaps he had reason to be unhappy

extending his smile
to all sides of the good,
all-white neighbourhood
belled by St Teresa's church.   20

When he came back
we walked together
across fields of Garvaghy
to see hawthorn on the summer
hedges, as though   25
he had never left;
a bend of the road

which still sheltered
primroses. But we
did not smile in   30
the shared complicity
of a dream, for when
weary Odysseus returns
Telemachus should leave.

Often as I descend   35
into subway or underground
I see his bald head behind
the bars of the small booth;
the mark of an old car
accident beating on his   40
ghostly forehead.

[33] **Odysseus:**
king of Ithaca
and legendary
Greek hero of
Homer's epic
poem The
Odyssey; he
survived the
Trojan War, but
for ten years the
sea god
Poseidon
prevented him
from returning
home;
Montague sees
his father's long
exile in terms of
the trials of
Odysseus
[34] **Telemachus:**
in The Odyssey,
the son of
Odysseus and
his wife,
Penelope

Background note

In 1952 John Montague accepted a scholarship to study in the United States and
intended to visit his father in New York. But, coincidentally, the father returned home and
they were able to spend some time together before John went to postgraduate school at
Yale University in 1953; hence the reference to Telemachus leaving after Odysseus'
return.

Explorations

First reading

1. On a first reading of the poem, did you notice any reasons that might account for the father being 'the least happy man'?

2. Consult the notes above on the father and on Odysseus and Telemachus. What do they add to your understanding of the father's situation?

3. How many different locations or scenes do you notice in this poem?

Second reading: stanzas 1–3

4. Consider the atmosphere of New York as portrayed in the poem. What sounds do you hear? What do we discover of the people, the environment, etc.? Do you think the poet manages to make it real for the reader? What image made you think?

5. Examine the portrayal of the father. What physical descriptions are given, and what might they suggest about the man? What do you notice about his working conditions? Do you think he is happy in his job? Why, according to the poet, does he drink so much? Has he any redeeming qualities? Refer to phrases or lines to support your answers.

6. The poem is entitled 'The Cage'. Where does this image occur, and what does it refer to? What does it suggest about the father's attitude?

7. Do you think the portrait of the father is a totally depressing one? Explain your views with reference to the poem.

Third reading

8. What is the poet's attitude to his father? Does he resent his father's drinking, admire him, feel sorry for him, remember him with affection, or what? Refer to lines or images in your answer.

9. Briefly, what do you consider to be the theme of the poem?

10. Would you consider this to be a powerful portrayal of the Irish emigrant? Explain your view with reference to the text.

11. What features of the poem do you find to be most successful? Consider effective characterisation; clear, concrete imagery; simple narrative structure; the ability to evoke sympathy without overdoing it; painful honesty; or any other feature.

U.A. Fanthorpe (1929–)

Ursula Askham Fanthorpe was born in London in 1929. She studied at St Anne's College, Oxford from 1949–53, and then at the University of London Institute of Education from 1953–4 where she obtained a teaching diploma. Fanthorpe became an assistant English teacher, and later head of English at Cheltenham Ladies College in Gloucestershire. She found teaching demanding and left in 1972 to take a post as admissions clerk at a Bristol hospital, where she remained until 1983. Her first volume of poems *Side Effects* was published in 1978 when she was nearly fifty. She has been a Writing Fellow at St Martin's College, Lancashire, and a Literary Fellow at

the universities of Newcastle and Durham. U.A. Fanthorpe has published ten volumes of verse and an audio cassette *Double Act* (Penguin Books, 1997) in which she reads from her work.

Growing Up

prescribed for Ordinary Level exams in 2005 and 2006

I wasn't good
At being a baby. Burrowed my way
Through the long yawn of infancy,
Masking by instinct how much I knew
Of the senior world, sabotaging   5
As far as I could, biding my time,
Biting my rattle, my brother (in private),
Shoplifting daintily into my pram.
Not a good baby,
No.   10

I wasn't good
At being a child. I missed
The innocent age. Children,
Being childish, were beneath me.
Adults I despised or distrusted. They   15

Would label my every disclosure
Precocious, naïve whatever it was.
I disdained definition, preferred to be surly.
Not a nice child,
No.   20
I wasn't good
At adolescence. There was a dance,
A catchy rhythm; I was out of step.
My body capered, nudging me
With hairy, fleshy growths and monthly outbursts,   25
To join the party. I tried to annul
The future, pretended I knew it already,
Was caught bloody-thighed, a criminal
Guilty of puberty.
Not a nice girl,   30
No.

(My hero, intransigent Emily,
Cauterized her own-dog-mauled
Arm with a poker,
Struggled to die on her feet   35
Never told anyone anything.)

I wasn't good
At growing up. Never learned
The natives' art of life. Conversation
Disintegrated as I touched it,   40
So I played mute, wormed along years,
Reciting the hard-learned arcane litany
Of cliché, my company passport.
Not a nice person,
No.   45

The gift remains
Masonic, dark. But age affords
A vocation even for wallflowers.
Called to be connoisseur, I collect,
Admire, the effortless bravura   50
Of other people's lives, proper and comely,
Treading the measure, shopping, chaffing,
Quarrelling, drinking, not knowing
How right they are, or how, like well-oiled bolts,
Swiftly and sweet, they slot into the grooves   55
Their ancestors smoothed out along the grain.

Notes

[17] **Precocious:** exhibiting mature qualities at an unusually early age

[17] **naïve:** showing a lack of experience or good judgement

[24] **capered:** to leap or prance about in a playful manner

[32] **intransigent:** refusing to compromise

[32] **Emily:** reclusive American poet Emily Dickinson

[33] **Cauterized:** to burn in order to stop bleeding and/or prevent infection

[42] **arcane:** obscure, mysterious

[47] **Masonic:** secretive; (Freemasonry is an international organisation of men, united by a common code of morals and beliefs and of certain traditional 'secrets'.)

[49] **connoisseur:** a person with great experience and appreciation of something

[50] **bravura:** showing brilliance

[52] **chaffing:** becoming irritated and impatient

Explorations

Before reading

1. Imagine that you have been asked to write your autobiography, list the chapter headings you would use and write a line summarising each one.

First reading

2. 'I wasn't good
   At being a baby.'
   What does the author mean by these lines?

3. What evidence is there in the poem that the poet was 'Not a nice child,'?

4. Do you think that the narrator found adolescence traumatic? Look carefully at stanza three.

5. What qualities does the author admire in her heroine 'Emily'?

6. Why do you think the poet 'wasn't good | At growing up.'?

7. 'But age affords
   A vocation even for wallflowers'
   Consider the lines above. Do you get the impression that the narrator has found her own niche in adult life.

Second reading

8. Do you think the poet has a sense of humour? Explain your answer.

9. What evidence can you find in the first two stanzas that the poet felt the need to conceal her true nature and character?

10. How do you react to the third stanza? What lines or images did you find particularly striking?

11. How did the author cope with the difficulties she experienced talking to people?

12. In what way is the author a 'connoisseur' of 'the effortless bravura | Of other people's lives'?

Third reading

13. How does the mood of the poem change in the final stanza? Examine the poet's choice of words and images.

14. What have you learned about the author's character from reading this poem?

15. Write a diary entry that the poet might have written at any stage in her 'growing up'.

16. Comment on any three features of Fanthorpe's style. You might consider her imagery, her use of language and her tone of voice.

Fourth reading

17. Write a paragraph giving your personal assessment of the poem. Are you glad you read it?

18. Discuss how Fanthorpe deals with the theme of alienation in 'Growing Up'.

19. Robin Lane Fox wrote: 'I name U.A. Fanthorpe as the poet who can suddenly hit below the heart'. Give your reaction to this view.

Ted Hughes (1930–2000)

Ted Hughes is well known as a poet and as the husband of Sylvia Plath, recognised in her own right as a poet. His work deals not just with nature, where he shows insight into the hidden cruelty of its existence, but he has also reworked a considerable number of writings from Greek and Latin writers. Chief among these are the *Metamorphoses* of Ovid and Seneca's *Oedipus* as well as some Greek plays. His range of poetry is impressive and its uncompromising depiction of the less pleasant aspects of creation remains in stark contrast to the more urbane poetry of many of his contemporaries.

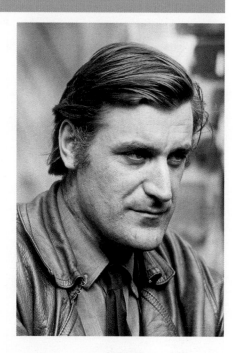

Snowdrop

prescribed for Ordinary Level exams in 2003 and 2004

Now is the globe shrunk tight
Round the mouse's dulled wintering heart.
Weasel and crow, as if moulded in brass,
Move through an outer darkness
Not in their right minds,   5
With the other deaths. She, too pursues her ends,
Brutal as the stars of this month,
Her pale head heavy as metal.

Explorations

First reading

1. 'Now is the globe shrunk tight'
   How does this line suggest the effect that winter has on the earth?

2. The poet refers to three creatures: the mouse, the weasel and the crow. Based on the images the poet creates, how would you describe their lives in winter? Support your descriptions by reference to the poem.

Second reading

3. Choose three words from the first five and a half lines of this poem that you feel clearly suggest the picture of winter the poet wants us to see.

4. Bearing in mind your answers to questions 2 and 3, can you suggest what it is that keeps the mouse, the weasel and the crow going in this harsh environment?

5. 'Brutal as the stars of this month'
   In what way could the 'snowdrop' be considered to be brutal? Does it have anything to do with the environment that she has to grow and flower in?

6. 'She, too pursues her ends,'
   The poet seems to be suggesting that every living thing in the poem has a purpose that helps it to endure the winter. Can you suggest what this purpose is?

7. The poet uses the word 'brass' in connection with the weasel and crow, and 'metal' in reference to the snowdrop. Why does the poet want us to link living things with non-living 'brass' and 'metal'? What qualities could they possibly have in common? Refer back to question 6.

Third reading

8. There are a number of disturbing images in this poem. Choose two images that you find unsettling and discuss why they create this effect.

9. Do you think that 'Snowdrop' is a suitable title for this poem? Why? Can you suggest another more appropriate title?

10. Does it surprise you that the same poet wrote 'There Came a Day'? Are there any similarities between the two poems?

There Came a Day

prescribed for the Ordinary Level exam in 2006

There came a day that caught the summer
Wrung its neck
Plucked it
And ate it.

Now what shall I do with the trees?   5
The day said, the day said.
Strip them bare, strip them bare.
Let's see what is really there.

And what shall I do with the sun?
The day said, the day said.   10
Roll him away till he's cold and small.
He'll come back rested if he comes at all.

And what shall I do with the birds?
The day said, the day said.
The birds I've frightened, let them flit,   15
I'll hang out pork for the brave tomtit.

And what shall I do with the seed?
The day said, the day said.
Bury it deep, see what it's worth.
See if it can stand the earth.   20

What shall I do with the people?
The day said, the day said.
Stuff them with apple and blackberry pie—
They'll love me then till the day I die.

There came this day and he was autumn.   25
The mouth was wide
And red as a sunset.
His tail was an icicle.

Explorations

First reading

1. Take the four seasons of the year and write down five descriptive words for each of them. Discuss the type of words that you associate with each season. Do these words suggest that people tend to regard some seasons as more pleasant than others? Can you explain why this might be?

2. What images does the poet use to suggest the changes that take place in the world of nature with the arrival of autumn?

3. 'Strip', 'roll', 'frightened', 'bury'—these are the verbs that the poet uses to describe the ways that autumn affects the countryside. Are they words that you would expect to be used regarding the actions of autumn? Why? What picture of autumn do you get from them?

4. Consider the way autumn affects the world of people. Is this description in any way different to those dealing with the countryside? What does the word 'stuff' suggest to you?

Second reading

5. What is your reaction to the first stanza of this poem? Is it the type of opening you would expect to a poem about autumn? Why?

6. Consider the image of autumn that the poet suggests in the final stanza. When you connect it to the first stanza does it create a pleasant or unpleasant picture of autumn. Describe, in your own words, what you see when you read these eight lines.

Third reading

7. Examine the rhythm of stanzas 2–7. How would you describe the rhythm? Does it remind you of anything you might have read or heard when you were younger? Do you think that the rhythm matches the sense of these stanzas? Why?

8. What tone of voice should be used to read this poem? Do you find it in any way surprising?

9. The poet suggests that there is a difference in the ways that autumn affects the 'world of nature' and the 'world of man'. Discuss why this should be so. Does this difference hold for all the seasons? Why?

10. Has this poem affected your view of autumn? Go back to the words you wrote down to describe autumn in question 1. Would you change any of them? Why?

Jon Silkin (1930–1997)

The significance and importance of Jon Silkin can be seen from the respect he was held in by his fellows; the awards given to him for his role as a professional poet; and his integrity as an editor and promoter of contemporary literature. He travelled widely in his professional capacity. He founded the magazine *STAND* in 1952 and published his own first poetry collection in 1954—from then until his sudden death, three collections of his poems were published. He was awarded the Faber Memorial Prize, the C. Day Lewis Fellowship and elected to the Royal Society of Literature. He had particular interest

in the literature of the First World War and his own work shows a particular sensitivity.

Death of a Son
(who died in a mental hospital aged one)

prescribed for Ordinary Level exams in 2003 and 2004

Something has ceased to come along with me.
Something like a person: something very like one.
And there was no nobility in it
Or anything like that.

Something was there like a one year   5
Old house, dumb as stone. While the near buildings
Sang like birds and laughed
Understanding the pact

They were to have with silence. But he
Neither sang nor laughed. He did not bless silence   10
Like bread, with words.
He did not forsake silence.

But rather, like a house in mourning
Kept the eye turned in to watch the silence while
The other houses like birds   15
Sang around him.

And the breathing silence neither
Moved nor was still.
I have seen stones: I have seen brick colour
But this house was made up of neither bricks nor stone   20
But a house of flesh and blood
With flesh of stone

And bricks for blood. A house
Of stones and blood in breathing silence with the other
Birds singing crazy on its chimneys.   25
But this was silence,

This was something else, this was
Hearing and speaking though he was a house drawn
Into silence, this was
Something religious in his silence,   30

Something shining in his quiet,
This was different this was altogether something else:
Though he never spoke, this
Was something to do with death.

And then slowly the eye stopped looking   35
Inward. The silence rose and became still.
The look turned to the outer place and stopped,
With the birds still shrilling around him.
And as if he could speak

He turned over on his side with his one year   40
Red as a wound
He turned over as if he could be sorry for this
And out of his eyes two great tears rolled, like stones, and he died.

---

[1] **ceased:** to stop, come to an end

[8] **pact:** agreement

[12] **forsake:** abandon, give up

Explorations

Your answers to questions 3–6
should help you.

First reading

1. There is a sense of unbearable
   sadness in this poem. Can you
   choose one phrase and explain
   why you find it particularly
   moving?
2. The poet uses an image of a
   house to describe his young
   son. What sort of a picture do
   you get of this house?
3. How does the house that
   represents his son compare
   with the other houses the poet
   describes? Can you explain
   what the major difference is
   between them?

Second reading

4. The poet feels that his son had
   'flesh of stone'. What
   impression of the little boy do
   you get from this phrase?
5. 'He did not forsake silence.'
   How does the poet describe his
   son's silence? Do you think
   that such silence is unusual in
   a one-year-old child? Why?
6. In what way has the poet
   suggested that his young son
   was 'Something like a person'?

Third reading

7. 'And then slowly the eye
   stopped looking
   Inward.'
   Why do you think the poet
   found this an important
   change in his son? Was there
   also an alteration in his
   silence? Do you think that
   there is a connection between
   these two changes?
8. In the final four lines of the
   poem the poet repeats the
   phrase 'He turned over'. Can
   you suggest why he does this?
9. The poet's son shed 'two great
   tears' just before he died. Does
   the intense sadness in this
   poem come from the type of
   brief life the little boy had or
   from the changes that
   happened in his condition just
   before his death?
10. Do you think that such an
    intensely personal poem should
    be studied as part of a
    literature course? Why?

Fleur Adcock (1934–)

Fleur Adcock was born in New Zealand and lived there at various times but has spent much of her life in England. Her volumes of poetry include *The Eye of the Hurricane* (1964), *Tigers* (1967), *High Tide in the Garden* (1971), *The Inner Harbour* (1979), *The Incident Book* (1986), and *Time Zones* (1991). She is considered one of the foremost feminist poets of the age, famous for her 'anti-erotic' style of love poems. 'For Heidi with Blue Hair' is taken from *The Incident Book* and is dedicated to her god-daughter, Heidi Jackson.

For Heidi with Blue Hair

prescribed for the Ordinary Level exam in 2003

When you dyed your hair blue
(or, at least, ultramarine
for the clipped sides, with a crest
of jet-black spikes on top)
you were sent home from school   5

because, as the headmistress put it,
although dyed hair was not
specifically forbidden, yours
was, apart from anything else,
not done in the school colours.   10

Tears in the kitchen, telephone-calls
to school from your freedom-loving father:
'She's not a punk in her behaviour;
it's just a style.' (You wiped your eyes,
also not in a school colour.)   15
'She discussed it with me first—

we checked the rules.' 'And anyway, Dad,
it cost twenty-five dollars.
Tell them it won't wash out—
not even if I wanted to try.'   20

It would have been unfair to mention
your mother's death, but that
shimmered behind the arguments.
The school had nothing else against you;
the teachers twittered and gave in.   25

Next day your black friend had hers done
in grey, white and flaxen yellow—
the school colours precisely:
an act of solidarity, a witty
tease. The battle was already won.   30

 # Explorations

the school's attitude and outlook as revealed in the poem. Do you think it was strict, 'stuffy', 'posh', reasonable, or what? Read the entire poem again before committing yourself.

9. Do you think the poem accurately reflects the demand for conformity found in school life? Do you find it true? Explain.

Third reading

10. Would you consider the father's attitude usual or unusual for a parent? Explain.

11. What truths about the life of a teenager do you find in this poem?

12. Do you think the poem is humorous? Mention two ways in which this humour is created. Is this note of humour maintained all the way through?

13. Make notes on the main themes and issues you find dealt with in the poem.

Brendan Kennelly (1936–)

Brendan Kennelly was born in 1936 in Kerry. He was educated at Trinity College and Leeds University. He is currently Professor of Modern Literature at Trinity College, Dublin. He has always published a lot of poetry and is a well-known personality, something which is unusual for a poet and an academic. He was featured in an ad for a high-profile car manufacturer even though he doesn't drive.

Kennelly is fascinated with the past and the way in which the past re-emerges in contemporary society. He is also interested in giving voice to historical characters who were cast as villains. The best examples of this are in his two long sequences 'Cromwell' and the 'Book of Judas'.

He has also worked on translations from the French as well as updating classical works of Greek drama. He has also published a novel and his selected criticism is contained in *Journey into Joy* (1994).

Night Drive

prescribed for the Ordinary Level exam in 2005

I

The rain hammered as we drove
Along the road to Limerick
'Jesus what a night' Alan breathed
And—'I wonder how he is, the last account
Was poor.'   5
I couldn't speak.

The windscreen fumed and blurred, the rain's spit
Lashing the glass. Once or twice
The wind's fist seemed to lift the car
And pitch it hard against the ditch.   10
Alan straightened out in time,
Silent. Glimpses of the Shannon—
A boiling madhouse roaring for its life
Or any life too near its gaping maw,
White shreds flaring in the waste   15
Of insane murderous black;
Trees bending in grotesque humility,
Branches scattered on the road, smashed
Beneath the wheels.
Then, ghastly under headlights,   20
Frogs bellied everywhere, driven
From the swampy fields and meadows,
Bewildered refugees, gorged with terror.
We killed them because we had to,
Their fatness crunched and flattened in the dark.   25
'How is he now?' Alan whispered
To himself. Behind us,
Carnage of broken frogs.

II

His head
Sweated on the pillow of the white hospital bed.   30
He spoke a little, said
Outrageously, 'I think I'll make it.'
Another time, he'd rail against the weather,

(Such a night would make him eloquent)
But now, quiet, he gathered his fierce will   35
To live.

                        III
Coming home
Alan saw the frogs.
'Look at them, they're everywhere,
Dozens of the bastards dead.'   40

Minutes later—
'I think he might pull through now.'
Alan, thoughtful at the wheel, was picking out
The homeroad in the flailing rain
Nighthedges closed on either side.   45
In the suffocating darkness
I heard the heavy breathing
Of my father's pain.

Explorations

First reading

1. What is the relationship between Alan and the narrator?
2. What is the purpose of their journey?
3. How do you think the two men feel as they go on their journey?
4. How do their reactions differ?

Second reading

5. What is the relationship between the two men and nature?
6. How is the night described?
7. Describe your reaction to the frogs. What do you think is their significance in the poem?

Third reading

8. How does the tone change in the second stanza?
9. Do you get any impression of what type of man the father was?
10. How is the journey home different?
11. Does the road seem different to the narrator?

Fourth reading

12. Why do you think the poet seems to put more emphasis on

The Prodigal Son

prescribed for the Ordinary Level exam in 2004

To go away is not to die
And to return is to begin again
But with a difference.

I had a lot to spend; I spent it;
Men's eyes opened in wonder   5
At my extravagance.

You know what it is to spend—
Ecstatic moments of release
That spring from, lead to boredom.

But in the spending was the joy   10
Those who hoarded never knew—
Know-alls, planners, calculators,

Safe adventurers who watched me as I
Flung my portion, to the wind and women.
Some seemed to love me. They did not. They soon forgot.   15

Lose! Lose!—beat in my ears from dawn to dark,
The only lesson one should learn,
The exacting savage art.

Not forgetting anyone, but outstripping all,
I cross your threshold once again   20
With such a history of loss

It stirs what you believe is your forgiveness.
Forgive yourself, forgiving me.
You offer; I accept.

We'll go into a room, draw up two chairs,   25
Share a bottle till the early hours.
I have things to tell you before I begin.

 # Explorations

Before reading

1. What do you know about the parable of the Prodigal Son.

First reading

2. What do you discover about the speaker in this poem? Describe him.
3. Has his life changed? In what way?
4. How did others see him in his previous lifestyle?
5. Who do you think he is talking to in this poem? Discuss this.

Second reading

6. What kind of relationship does he have with the person he's talking to?
7. What does he want from them?
8. Do they have an equal and healthy relationship?

Third reading

9. How does he feel about what he has done?
10. What does he propose to do?
11. Do you think the other person will agree?
12. Write the poem from the other person's point of view?

Fourth reading

13. Write a paragraph or two about the main ideas or themes in this poem.
14. Do you find this a sad and hopeless poem? Write about your feelings on reading this.
15. 'Kennelly's gift is to be able to write in other people's voices in a very believable way.' Do you agree?

Roger McGough (1937–)

Roger McGough was born in Liverpool and studied modern languages at Hull University. Along with Adrian Henri and Brian Patten, he popularised poetry in the 1960s as part of the MerseyBeat poets based in Liverpool. Their poetry put heavy emphasis on live performance and was therefore funny and accessible. It dealt with real concerns for ordinary working-class people. His poetry has been used a lot in schools and he continues to be as popular today as he was in the 60s. He is often used to promote poetry for events such as National Poetry Day. These days his poetry has become more conventional and he uses it for promoting social and human rights issues.

Let Me Die a Young Man's Death

prescribed for Ordinary Level exams in 2004 and 2005

Let me die a youngman's death
not a clean and inbetween
the sheets holywater death
not a famous-last-words
peaceful out of breath death   5

When I'm 73
and in constant good tumour
may I be mown down at dawn
by a bright red sports car
on my way home   10
from an allnight party

Or when I'm 91
with silver hair

and sitting in a barber's chair
may rival gangsters   15
with hamfisted tommyguns burst in
and give me a short back and insides

Or when I'm 104
and banned from the Cavern
may my mistress   20
catching me in bed with her daughter
and fearing for her son
cut me up into little pieces
and throw away every piece but one

Let me die a youngman's death   25
not a free from sin tiptoe in
candlewax and waning death
not a curtains drawn by angels borne
'what a nice way to go' death

Note

[19] **Cavern:** a
club in
Liverpool
where the
Beatles played
their first
concerts

Explorations

Before reading

1. What did you expect this poem to be like after reading the title?

First reading

2. Which of the poet's ways of dying do you think is the most interesting or the funniest?
3. In your opinion, what type of person is the speaker in the poem?

Second reading

4. Where does the poet use puns in the poem? Are they effective?
5. How does the poet use rhyme?

What effect does this have on the way you read the poem?

Third reading

6. Write an obituary for the poet as if he had died in one of the ways that he envisages in verses 2–4.
7. Do you believe him when he says, 'Let me die a young man's death'? He wrote this poem when he was young, do you think that he still has the same sentiments?
8. Listen to the Robbie Williams song 'I hope I'm old before I die'. Compare the sentiments in both.

Eamonn Grennan (1941–)

Eamonn Grennan was born in 1941 in Dublin. He was educated at University College, Dublin and eventually at Harvard where he did his PhD. He has taught at City University, New York and then at Vassar College. He is now professor of English at Vassar. He has written a lot of criticism on contemporary Irish poetry as well as on Shakespeare, Spenser and Chaucer. He is very influenced by Kavanagh. His poetry aims to tell of 'the miracle of the actual'. He is interested in showing things as they are but focussing on the detail like a painter would. His books include *What Light There Is, So It Goes, As*

If It Matters, translations of Leopoldi and most recently his selected poems, *Relations*.

Daughter and Dying Fish

prescribed for Ordinary Level exams in 2005 and 2006

Cast out on this stone pier, the dogfish are dying
in a simmering sunlit heap of torcs
and contortions, bristlemouths propped open

in a silent scream against
the treacherous element of air, a yawn   5
of pure despair, the soft slap of fantails

sliding the slow length of one another
as spines stiffen, scales shimmer, glaucous
sea-eyes pop with shock and resignation

when my cloudy shadow trawls across them.   10
She stands balancing her twenty months
on twisted arm-thick hanks of rope

and is no more than a moment perplexed
when she bends to touch a spine, those
fading scales, and then goes back   15

to the song she was singing, turning
from what I can't take my eyes off:
their cloudy eyes, the slow weave

of their singular limbs, slubbered
smack of oily skin on skin, the faint heaving motion   20
of the whole mass like one body

beating away from the face of the earth.
How they would glide, barely brushing
one another, bodies all curve and urgency

in their glimmering space   25
and humming chambers, their swift unravellings
of desire or death, who now lie

in the raw elusive air and wait
for what comes next, a hapless
heap of undulant muscle, a faint, fierce   30

throbbing. Gently the sea
slaps at these stone foundations
laid to stand the winter storms

without shaking: smooth as skin,
the granite surfaces gleam   35
like live things in sunlight

where my daughter walks,
a cheerful small voice
still singing.

Explorations

First reading

1. How do the fish look to the narrator? Examine some of the detailed pictures/descriptions.
2. Does the narrator attempt to understand the condition of the dying fish? Do you think he does this well? Explain.
3. What effect do they have on his daughter?

Second reading

4. How does the poet contrast the dying fish with what they are like in their natural habitat?
5. Why can't he take his eyes off them?
6. Why is the pier important?

Third reading

7. There are only four sentences in this poem. Does this surprise you? What effect does it have?
8. How does he use mid-line rhyme to help the poem's movement?
9. Examine a selection of the adjectives that the poet uses. Write about the effect created.
10. Which sounds dominate the poem? What effect do they have?

Fourth reading

11. The fragility of life is one of the themes of this poem. Do you agree?
12. What other themes do you find?
13. Does the daughter need to be in the poem? What purpose does she serve?
14. Write about your own personal reaction to this poem.

Eiléan Ní Chuilleanáin (1942–)

Eiléan Ní Chuilleanáin's first volume of poetry, *Acts and Monuments* (1972), from which 'Swineherd' is taken, won the Patrick Kavanagh Award. Many of the poems focus on the relationship between human beings and the natural world. In later volumes she focuses more sharply on questions of female identity. Among her collections are *Site of Ambush* (1975), *The Rose Geranium* (1982), and *The Magdalene Sermon* (1989).

Swineherd

prescribed for the Ordinary Level exam in 2003

'When all this is over', said the swineherd,
'I mean to retire, where
Nobody will have heard about my special skills
And conversation is mainly about the weather.

I intend to learn how to make coffee, at least as well   5
As the Portuguese lay-sister in the kitchen
And polish the brass fenders every day.
I want to lie awake at night
Listening to cream crawling to the top of the jug
And the water lying soft in the cistern.   10

I want to see an orchard where the trees grow in straight lines
And the yellow fox finds shelter between the navy-blue trunks,
Where it gets dark early in summer
And the apple-blossom is allowed to wither on the bough.'

Explorations

First reading: first stanza

1. What do you imagine are the 'special skills' of the swineherd?
2. Do you think the swineherd is proud of these 'special skills' or somewhat ashamed? Where is this suggested?
3. In what situations, usually, do people talk about the weather? Why do you think the swineherd might look forward to this?
4. In what tone of voice do you think the first stanza should be spoken—excited, tired, determined, or what? What phrases would you emphasise in a reading? Why?
5. Where do you think the swineherd works? Look to the second stanza also for clues.

Second reading

6. Lines 5–7: What do you think of the swineherd's ambitions in these lines? Do you find them unusual? Explain. (A lay-sister was a nun who didn't take full religious vows and was given the more menial tasks in the convent, work such as cooking, cleaning, laundry, etc.)
7. Eiléan Ní Chuilleanáin has said that she based the poem on her experience of a convent in Belgium where her aunt was Reverend Mother and where there actually was a Portuguese lay-sister in the kitchen. She has also said that she envisaged the swineherd as female.
   (a) Do you think it a little ironic that the swineherd might envy the lowly lay-sister?
   (b) What aspects of the theme of women and work does the poem focus on? What is the poem saying to you about this?
8. Lines 8–10: What does the speaker think she would enjoy? What does she want out of life?

Third reading

9. Lines 11–14: What do you notice about the speaker's ideal place? In what part of the world do you think she might find this? Is it real or completely imaginary?
10. What does the poem suggest to you about people's dreams?
11. Do you think the imagery is effective at communicating hopes and dreams, both the ordinary and the more exotic? Comment on any two images from this point of view.

Sharon Olds (1942–)

Sharon Olds is the author of seven volumes of poetry. Her latest work, *The Wellspring* (1996), shares with her previous work the use of raw language and startling images to convey truths about domestic and political violence, sexuality, family relationships and the body. A reviewer of this book for the *New York Times* hailed Olds's poetry for its vision: 'Like Whitman, Ms Olds sings the body in celebration of a power stronger than political oppression.'

Olds is currently an Associate Professor at New York University. She also conducts a number of workshops across the country including at The Omega Institute, The Squaw Valley Writers Workshop, and the 'In the Wilderness' programme. Olds helped to found NYU's creative writing programme for the physically disabled at Goldwater Hospital in New York City.

The Present Moment

prescribed for Ordinary Level exams in 2005 and 2006

Now that he cannot sit up,
now that he just lies there
looking at the wall, I forget the one
who sat up and put on his reading glasses
and the lights in the room multiplied in the lenses.   5
Once he entered the hospital
I forgot the man who lay full length
on the couch, with the blanket folded around him,
that huge, crushed bud, and I have
long forgotten the man who ate food—   10
not dense, earthen food, like liver, but
things like pineapple, wedges of light,
the skeiny nature of light made visible.
It's as if I abandoned that ruddy man

with the swollen puckered mouth of a sweet-eater,   15
the torso packed with extra matter
like a planet a handful of which weighs as much as the earth, I have
left behind forever that young man my father,
that smooth-skinned, dark-haired boy,
and my father long before I knew him, when he could   20
only sleep, or drink from a woman's
body, a baby who stared with a steady
gaze the way he lies there, now, with his
eyes open, then the lids start down
and the milky crescent of the other world   25
shines, in there, for a moment, before sleep.
I stay beside him, like someone in a rowboat
staying abreast of a Channel swimmer,
you are not allowed to touch them, their limbs
glow, faintly, in the night water.   30

Explorations

First reading

1. Who are the people in the poem?
2. What is their relationship?
3. What condition is the man in?
4. Was he always this way? What was he like before this?

Second reading

5. Describe each phase of his life as described in the poem.
6. How does the narrator feel about her father now?
7. Did she always feel this way?
8. How does she feel about their relationship?
9. Why does she feel that she is 'not allowed to touch'?

Third reading

10. There are many impressions of him given. Which strikes you most?
11. Of which impression is she fondest?
12. 'S' sounds dominate the poem. Why is this sound used? What effect does it have?
13. Examine the effectiveness of each metaphor: the glasses, the band, the food, the planet, the swimmer etc.

Fourth reading

14. This poem is about regret. Do you agree?
15. Who do you think the poet wrote this poem for?
16. Is there an overall theme in this poem or is the poet just describing a situation?

Carol Rumens (1944–)

Carol Rumens was born in London and educated at London University. Her poetry is focussed on personal journeys as well as social and historical issues. She has always been concerned with feminist issues. It has been said that she was one of the most astute poetic readers of the Thatcher years in Britain. More recently, she has lived and worked in Ireland and her most recent volume of poetry is concerned with exploring that experience, especially her time in the North. *Thinking of Skins*, her selected poems, is the best introduction to her work.

Passing a Statue of Our Lady in Derry

prescribed for the Ordinary Level exam in 2005

She appears tired, though dressed in fresh, white stone,
And bows the bandaged snowdrop of her head—
Pleadingly to the bus—which hurries on
And leaves her stranded in my childhood,

Mother of small contritions, great hopes   5
And the lyric boredom of the rosary
When miracles seemed at our fingertips:
She is much younger now than formerly,

And in her narrow, girlish hands, she weighs
Not holiness, but a frail, human idea   10
That might accomplish anything—dismiss
An army—or, like childhood, disappear.

Explorations

First reading
1. Describe the statue.
2. The poet associates the statue with certain practices and ideals of her childhood. What are these? Examine lines 4–7.
3. 'She is much younger now than formerly'. How do you think this might be?
4. Why do you think the poet names Derry in the title? Discuss this.

Second reading
5. What does the statue represent to the poet?

6. What does the statue represent to the people of Derry that pass her?

Third reading
7. Are there any dominant sounds in the poem? What do they represent?
8. What is the mood of the poem? Do you think the poet is sad, angry, disappointed, hopeful or what?
9. Do you think the poet is very religious? Discuss this.
10. Write two paragraphs on the main themes of this piece.

Ciaran Carson (1948–)

Ciaran Carson was born in Belfast and educated at Queen's University. He has worked for the Arts Council of Northern Ireland as traditional music officer and as literature officer. He has written many books of poetry. His first, *The New Estate*, went almost unnoticed but the next three were released to huge critical acclaim. In each of these books, *The Irish for No* (1987), *Belfast Confetti* (1989) and *First Language* (1993), he uses a very long line to tell stories and anecdotes about Belfast. It has been said that he writes English as if it were Irish, a reference to the way that his stories and poems ramble about. His most recent books of poetry have been translations from the French.

He has written three prose books that don't really fit into any one category. *Last Night's Fun* is supposed to be about traditional music but also concerns itself with recipes for making a fry! *The Star Factory* is about Belfast but is neither memoir nor travel guide; *Fishing for Amber* is about reading, telling and the power of narrative whether it be in Irish folk tales, Greek epic poetry or Dutch painting. Carson is truly one of the most original writers to come from Ireland since Beckett.

Soot

prescribed for Ordinary Level exams in 2004 and 2005

It was autumn. First, she shrouded
The furniture, then rolled back the carpet
As if for dancing; then moved
The ornaments from the mantelpiece,
Afraid his roughness might disturb   5
Their staid fragility.

He came; shyly, she let him in,
Feeling ill-at-ease in the newly-spacious
Room, her footsteps sounding hollow
On the boards. She watched him kneel   10
Before the hearth, and said something
About the weather. He did not answer,

Too busy with his work for speech.
The stem of yellow cane creaked upwards
Tentatively. After a while, he asked   15
Her to go outside and look, and there,
Above the roof, she saw the frayed sunflower
Bloom triumphantly. She came back

And asked how much she owed him, grimacing
As she put the money in his soiled hand.   20
When he had gone, a weightless hush
Lingered in the house for days. Slowly,
It settled; the fire burned cleanly;
Everything was spotless.

Hearing that soot was good for the soil,   25
She threw it on the flowerbeds. She would watch
It crumble, dissolving in the rain,
Finding its way to lightless crevices,
Sleeping, till in spring it would emerge softly
As the ink-bruise in the pansy's heart.   30

Explorations

First reading

1. What type of house do you think the woman lived in? What do her preparations tell us about her?
2. Was she comfortable having him in her house?
3. How does the chimney-sweep feel about entering the house? Is he comfortable? Does he feel at ease?
4. Do you think he was good at his job?

Second reading

5. Why is the fact that 'It was autumn.' important?
6. Do you think that there is a religious element to this poem? Where is this?

Third reading

7. Describe the mood of the poem. What words and phrases suggest this?
8. What is your favourite image in the poem? Why?
9. Examine the adjectives that the narrator uses. How do they help to set the scene?

Fourth reading

10. 'The poet uses a cinematic technique in this poem.' Do you agree?
11. What part in the poem does the 'soot' itself have?
12. What do you think this poem is really about. Discuss this and then write it up.

Paddy Bushe (1948–)

Paddy Bushe was born in Dublin in 1948. He lived in Australia for a number of years before returning to Waterville, Co. Kerry. He has published poetry in English and Irish. He won the 1990 Listowel Writers' Week Award and was a runner-up in the 1988 Patrick Kavanagh Award. His poems are full of a sense of immediacy and he seems to be conscious of finding a musical sound in his poems.

Jasmine

prescribed for the Ordinary Level exam in 2006

What colour is jasmine? you asked
out of the blue from your wheelchair.
And suddenly the ward was filled
with the scent of possibility, hints
of journeys to strange parts.   5

The question floored us. But the gulf
was not the colours that we couldn't name
but that we couldn't recognise the road
your question had travelled, nor sound the extent
of the blue void to which it would return.   10

The ward remade itself in a hum
of conscientious care. Outside, the usual
traffic jams. We took the long way home.
Father, jasmine is a climbing plant
whose flowers are normally white or yellow.   15

And may the fragrance of its blossoms twine
around the broken trellises of your mind.

Explorations

Before reading

1. What impression does the sound of the word 'jasmine' give you?

First reading

2. Where is the poem set? What gives this away?
3. Who are the two main characters in the poem?
4. What is their relationship?
5. Do you think there has been any recent change in their relationship?
6. Why did the question floor them?

Second reading

7. Why did they take the long way home? Suggest a possible reason.

8. Do you think this poem is too sentimental? Discuss this.

Third reading

9. Explain how the 'jasmine' metaphor develops in the last two lines.
10. How are the senses challenged throughout the poem?
11. What is the atmosphere created in the poem? How is this done?
12. Write about the main idea in this poem.

Fourth reading

13. Compare the poem to 'Night Drive' by Brendan Kennelly.
14. Is this a hopeful poem? Share your views.

Paul Muldoon (1951–)

Paul Muldoon was born in Co. Armagh and educated at Queen's University, Belfast. After leaving college he went to work as a producer for BBC radio in Belfast. He also lived in Dingle, Co. Kerry for a while. Since then he has worked mainly as an academic, much of his teaching has been in the creative writing programme at Princeton University in the US. Recently, he was appointed to the prestigious position of Professor of Poetry at Oxford University.

Muldoon is a brilliant technical poet. He is equally at ease writing sonnets and long poems, lyric or narrative poetry. Some of his poetry is written about the North, but often only incidentally. He is very conscious of using puns and word associations in a very deliberate way. His collections include: *Mules*, *New*

Weather, *Why Brownlee Left*, *Quoof*, *Meeting the British*, *Madoc: A Mystery*, *The Annals Of Chile* and most recently *Hay*. His *Selected Poems* (1968–94) is probably the best introduction to his work.

Anseo

prescribed for the Ordinary Level exam in 2006

When the Master was calling the roll
At the primary school in Collegelands,
You were meant to call back Anseo
And raise your hand
As your name occurred.   5
Anseo, meaning here, here and now,
All present and correct,
Was the first word of Irish I spoke.
The last name on the ledger

Belonged to Joseph Mary Plunkett Ward   10
And was followed, as often as not,
By silence, knowing looks,
A nod and a wink, the Master's droll
'And where's our little Ward-of-court?'

I remember the first time he came back   15
The Master had sent him out
Along the hedges
To weigh up for himself and cut
A stick with which he would be beaten.
After a while, nothing was spoken;   20
He would arrive as a matter of course
With an ash-plant, a salley-rod.
Or, finally, the hazel-wand
He had whittled down to a whip-lash,
Its twist of red and yellow lacquers   25
Sanded and polished,
And altogether so delicately wrought
That he had engraved his initials on it.

I last met Joseph Mary Plunkett Ward
In a pub just over the Irish border.   30
He was living in the open,
In a secret camp
On the other side of the mountain.
He was fighting for Ireland,
Making things happen.   35
And he told me, Joe Ward,
Of how he had risen through the ranks
To Quartermaster, Commandant:
How every morning at parade
His volunteers would call back Anseo   40
And raise their hands
As their names occurred.

Explorations

Before reading

1. What are your own memories of primary school, your teachers, friends and characters in your own class—especially the ones that got into a lot of trouble?

First reading

2. What does the word 'Anseo' mean? When was it used in school?
3. Describe the 'master'. What does his title say about him?
4. Why are Ward's forenames important?
5. What is Ward's life like at the end of the poem?
6. What do you imagine his soldiers' lives are like under his command?

Second reading

7. Why do you think Ward takes such care with the stick? Suggest reasons.
8. The narrator of the poem and the master use puns. Isolate each pun and explain what they are referring to.

Third reading

9. The tone in the first verse is very unemotional. What effect does this have on your reading of the poem? Does the tone change later on? If so, how?
10. What contradictions are in the poem?
11. How do the first and last verse mirror each other? What point do you think the poet is making here?

Fourth reading

12. 'What comes around goes around.' Do you think that this saying is relevant to the poem?
13. What is your own reaction to the life and experiences of Joseph Mary Plunkett Ward?
14. What do you think this poem is saying about life?

Carol Ann Duffy (1955–)

Carol Ann Duffy was born in Glasgow of Irish parents but grew up in Staffordshire, England. She attended university in Liverpool, studying philosophy. Her poetry very often gives voice to the powerless or the mad. She is very adept at putting herself in somebody else's head and then writing from their perspective, be they psychopaths, maids or tabloid editors. Her poetry has a wry humour and a lot of people who would not regularly read poetry are comfortable with her style.

She has won many awards for her collections, which include *Standing Female Nude* (1985), *Selling Manhattan* (1987), *The Other Country* (1990), *Mean Time* (1993) and *The World's Wife* (1998). This last collection featured a series of poems written from the

perspective of the forgotten female: Mrs Midas, Queen Kong, Mrs Lazarus and others.

Valentine

prescribed for Ordinary Level exams in 2003 and 2004

Not a red rose or a satin heart.

I give you an onion.
It is a moon wrapped in brown paper.
It promises light
like the careful undressing of love.   5

Here.
It will blind you with tears
like a lover.
It will make your reflection
a wobbling photo of grief.   10

I am trying to be truthful.

Not a cute card or a kissogram.

I give you an onion.
Its fierce kiss will stay on your lips,
possessive and faithful   15
as we are,
for as long as we are.

Take it.
Its platinum loops shrink to a wedding-ring,
if you like.   20

Lethal.
Its scent will cling to your anger,
Cling to your knife.

Explorations

Before reading

1. What do you associate with Valentine's Day?

First reading

2. What is your first reaction on reading this poem? Discuss the various reactions.

3. The onion is given four times. With what is it associated each time?

4. Is there anything at all romantic about this poem?

Second reading

5. How long will the taste of onion stay on the lover's lips. How long will the couple last?

6. What type of relationship do the couple have? Have they been in love for long?

7. How does the onion promise light?

Third reading

8. How would you feel if you were given an onion for Valentine's Day?

9. The poet uses very short lines regularly in the poem. What effect do these short lines have?

10. Describe each metaphor that the speaker uses to describe the onion?

Fourth reading

11. Read 'My mistress's eyes...' by William Shakespeare and compare it with this poem.

12. This poem manages to be 'cold and passionate'. How?

13. Do you think that this is a good love poem? What makes it good or bad?

14. 'Love is particular to individuals and can't be represented by Love Hearts and Teddy Bears.' Does the poet agree? Do you?

Warming Her Pearls

For Judith Radstone

prescribed for the Ordinary Level exam in 2006

Next to my own skin, her pearls. My mistress
bids me wear them, warm then, until evening
when I'll brush her hair. At six, I place them
round her cool, white throat. All day I think of her,

resting in the Yellow Room, contemplating silk   5
or taffeta, which gown tonight? She fans herself
whilst I work willingly, my slow heat entering
each pearl. Slack on my neck, her rope.

She's beautiful. I dream about her
in my attic bed; picture her dancing   10
with tall men, puzzled by my faint, persistent scent
beneath her French perfume, her milky stones.

I dust her shoulders with a rabbit's foot,
watch the soft blush seep through her skin
like an indolent sigh. In her looking-glass   15
my red lips part as though I want to speak.

Full moon. Her carriage brings her home. I see
her every movement in my head...Undressing,
taking off her jewels, her slim hand reaching
for the case, slipping naked into bed, the way   20

she always does...And I lie here awake,
knowing the pearls are cooling even now
in the room where my mistress sleeps. All night
I feel their absence and I burn.

Explorations

Before reading

1. What do pearls remind you of? What associations do you put with them? What type of person wears them?

First reading

2. Who is the narrator?
3. How does she feel about her mistress?
4. What type of person is the narrator?
5. In what period of time do you think the poem is set?

Second reading

6. How is the act of warming compared to work?
7. Why do you think might the narrator 'like to speak'? Why doesn't she? Write the speech she might say.
8. Compare the two characters in the poem in terms of how they live?
9. When do the two characters come together? How do they come together?

Third reading

10. Where is there jealousy in the poem?
11. Explore the relationship between the two characters. Is it a complex one?

Fourth reading

12. Is this a love poem? Discuss this.
13. What do you think this poem is actually about—love, power, class barriers or what? Discuss this and write up your findings.

Paula Meehan (1955–)

Paula Meehan was born in the Gardiner Street area of Dublin. She was thrown out of school yet managed to study and attended Trinity College, Dublin and Eastern Washington University. She made a huge impact with the publication of her third volume of poems *The Woman Who was Marked by Winter* and then with *Pillow Talk*. Meehan's poetry should be read out loud. She is a mesmerising reader of her own work. Her poetry has harrowing lyrical intensity. She uses regular language confidently yet without making it seem ostentatious or over the top. Many of her poems such as 'The Pattern' or 'The Ghost of my Mother Comforts Me' celebrate women in adversity and give them a voice. She has also written a number of successful plays. The most recent of these was *Cell* (1999) which was written after the poet had spent time giving poetry workshops in women's prisons.

Would You Jump Into My Grave As Quick?

prescribed for Ordinary Level exams in 2003, 2004 and 2006

Would you jump into my grave as quick?
my granny would ask when one of us took
her chair by the fire. You woman,
done up to the nines, red lips as a come on,
your breath reeking of drink   5
and your black eye on my man tonight
in a Dublin bar, think
first of the steep drop, the six dark feet.

Explorations

Before reading

1. Have you heard the title before? What does it mean to you?

First reading

2. What do you think the speaker's granny was like?
3. Who is the speaker talking to?
4. Describe the other woman.
5. Describe the speaker.
6. Which of the two do you prefer? Why?

Second reading

7. Do you know any other similar sarcastic phrases that you have learned from your parents or grandparents?
8. What type of reaction would you expect from the other woman?

9. How does the poet use internal rhyme and half-rhymes in the poem? What effect do they have?
10. In one paragraph explain what the poem is about.

Third reading

11. The poet is also a playwright. Can you see any evidence of her dramatic skills here?
12. Have you ever been in the speaker's position yourself? If so, when? What happened? If not, imagine a similar scene from a TV programme— describe what happened.
13. Do you think there is honesty and real feeling in this poem? Explain your views.

Moya Cannon (1956–)

Moya Cannon was born in Co. Donegal in 1956. She was educated at University College, Dublin and at Cambridge. Her work has been set to music by a number of contemporary composers such as Jane O'Leary, Philip Martin and Ellen Crannitch. She is based in Galway where she teaches at a special school for traveller children. Her poetry is often based in Galway or Clare and is concerned with the topography of those places. She uses the landscape and old customs of these places to layer her poetry. Her collection *OAR* won the Brendan Behan Memorial Prize in 1991.

Crow's Nest

prescribed for the Ordinary Level exams in 2005

On Saint Stephen's day,
Near the cliffs on Horn Head,
I came upon a house,
the roof beams long since rotted into grass
and outside, a little higher than the lintels,   5
a crow's nest in a dwarf tree.

A step up from the bog
into the crown of the ash,
the nest is a great tangled heart;
heather sinew, long blades of grass, wool and a   10
    feather,
wound and wrought
with all the energy and art
that's in a crow.

Did crows ever build so low before?   15
Were they deranged, the pair who nested here,
or the other pair who built the house behind the
    tree
or is there no place too poor or wild
to support,   20
if not life,
then love, which is the hope of it,
for who knows whether the young birds lived?

 # Explorations

First reading

1. Describe the nest the poet came upon.
2. What do you find surprising about the description
3. Why is the poet disturbed about the location of the nest?
4. Do you think she admires crows? Refer to words or phrases to justify your view.

Second reading

5. What is your favourite image in this poem? Explain what it suggests to you.
6. Would you agree that the poet has a very exact eye for detail? Refer to two specific examples.

Third reading

7. Why do you think the poet varies thew line-lengths in the poem? What effect does this have?
8. Is this a positive or negative poem?
9. How does the poet feel about what she has found?

Fourth reading

10. Compare this poem to 'Daughter and Dying Fish' by Eamonn Grennan, which is also in this anthology, in terms of their attitude to nature?
11. Could this be read as a love poem? Discuss this view.

Simon Armitage (1963–)

Simon Armitage was born in Huddersfield and studied geography at Portsmouth Polytechnic. He is a very prolific poet having published seven books since 1989: *Zoom* (1989); *Kid* (1992); *Book of Matches* (1993); *The Dead Sea Poems* (1995); *Cloudcuckooland* (1996); a book about Iceland, *Moon Country* (1996); and a prose book about life in Northern England, *All Points North* (1998). Most recently he edited a major anthology of British and Irish poetry.

He is a very popular poet and is often the youngest writer in many anthologies. A lot of his poems have been influenced by his work as a probation officer. He provides good social observations into the thinking of people, especially young people, who are marginalised. Some of his poetry is said to have been influenced by the work of Paul Muldoon.

It Ain't What You Do, It's What It Does To You

prescribed for Ordinary Level exams in 2004 and 2005

I have not bummed across America
with only a dollar to spare, one pair
of busted Levi's and a bowie knife.
I have lived with thieves in Manchester.

I have not padded through the Taj Mahal,   5
barefoot, listening to the space between
each footfall picking up and putting down
its print against the marble floor. But I

skimmed flat stones across Black Moss on a day
so still I could hear each set of ripples   10
as they crossed. I felt each stone's inertia
spend itself against the water; then sink.

I have not toyed with a parachute chord
while perched on the lip of a light-aircraft;
but I held the wobbly head of a boy   15
at the day centre, and stroked his fat hands.
And I guess that the tightness in the throat
and the tiny cascading sensation
somewhere inside us are both part of that
sense of something else. That feeling, I mean.   20

 # Explorations

Before reading

1. What usually comes after the line 'It ain't what you do.' Would it have the same effect?

First reading

2. There are three things that the poet has not done and three things that he has. Compare them. Which is the more attractive to you?
3. What emotion does he get from living with thieves? How would this compare to the feeling that he would get if he was hiking across America?
4. How does he justify comparing a lake in Manchester to one of the 'seven wonders of the world'?

5. What would helping a boy at the day care centre make him feel?
6. How would the boy feel?

Second reading

7. Have you ever had the sensation that the poet has in the final verse? When? Describe it.

Third reading

8. How does the poet use repetition in the poem?

Fourth reading

9. Is the last sentence in the poem completely necessary?
10. What type of guy do you think the poet is?

Unseen Poetry: Approaching The Question

An Approach to a Poem

Like any other work of art, such as a painting, sculpture, film or building, a poem needs many viewings or readings before we come to appreciate it fully. All the usual techniques we employ when viewing any new or unusual object can be of use here: first noticing the particularly striking or unusual features; then focusing in on a small area of it; drawing back and trying to see the whole structure; circling around it; finding words to describe it to ourselves; asking ourselves what we like about it; and so on. And so by circling the object and zooming in and out to examine interesting features, gradually we pick up more and more of the detail until the entire object makes sense for us. *Many readings are the key to understanding.*

Here are some questions you might ask yourself as you read and re-read:

What do I notice on a first reading?

List any and every thing I notice on first reading the poem. This gives me the confidence to say something about it, even though I don't yet understand the full picture.

What do I see?

- Where is it set? What scene or scenes are featured?
- What pictures strike me as interesting? Focus on a setting or an image. What are my thoughts on it?
- Follow the images through the poem. Is there a sequence or a pattern? Have the images anything in common?
- Do the images or settings suggest anything about the themes or issues the poem might be dealing with?
- What atmosphere or mood is suggested by the visual aspects? Which words or images are most powerful in creating this atmosphere?

What is the poem doing, and how is it structured?

(1) **Does it tell a story?**

- Is there a narrative structure to this poem? If so, what is happening? What is the sequence of events? Am I clear about the story line?
- What is my reaction to this story?
- Is there a main idea behind the narrative? What is the poet's central concern?
- What do I notice about the shape of the poem?
- If a narrative poem, is it in the genre of a ballad, epic, allegory, etc.?
- Is it serious, humorous, satirical, or what?

(2) Is it a descriptive piece, re-creating a scene?

- Is its primary purpose to re-create the atmosphere of an event or the mood of a moment?
- Is it mainly decorative? Or has it a point to make, or a moral to transmit?
- How does the poet want me to feel? What mood is created in this poem? What words or phrases help to create this mood?
- If a lyric poem, is it in the form of a sonnet, ode, villanelle, sestina, or what?
- What is the poet's central concern (theme)?
- Leaving technical terms aside, how would I describe what the poem sets out to do?

The speaker

- Who is the speaker in the poem? What kind of person do I imagine him or her to be? What state of mind is the speaker in? What words or phrases reveal most about the attitude and state of mind of the speaker? Consider the tone of the poem and how it is created.
- What point of view is being put across in the poem? Am I in sympathy with it or not?
- Who is the speaker addressing in the poem?

What do I notice about the poet's style?

- Does the poet rely heavily on images? If so, what do I notice about them?
- Does the poet use the musical sounds of words to create effect: alliteration, assonance, onomatopoeia, etc.? Does he or she use rhyme? What is the effect? What do the sounds of words contribute to the atmosphere of the poem?
- What do I notice about the type of words (diction) most frequently used—ordinary, everyday, learned and scholarly, technical, or what?
- Does the poet use regular metre (rhythm or regular beat in the lines) or do the lines sound more like ordinary conversation or a piece of prose writing? What is the overall effect? Explore the rhythm of the language.
- Are any of these features particularly noticeable or effective? What do I like?

What is my reaction to it?

- Can I identify with the experience in this poem? Has there been any similar experience in my life?
- What are my feelings on reading this poem, and what words, phrases, images or ideas spark off these reactions in me?
- How do I react to it? Do I find it amusing, interesting, exciting, frightening, revolting, thought-provoking, or what?
- What seems to me most important about the piece?

- At a critical level, do I think it is a well-made poem? What in particular do I think is effective?

Some basic questions

A final line-by-line or stanza-by-stanza exploration should bring the poem into clearer focus and facilitate answers to the basic questions:

1. What is the poem about (theme)?
2. Is it an interesting treatment of this theme?
3. What is important about the poem?
4. How is the poem structured (form and genre: narrative or lyric, ballad, ode, sonnet, etc.)?
5. What are the poet's feelings and attitudes (tone)?
6. How would one describe the atmosphere or mood of the poem, and how is it created?
7. What features of poetic style are noticeable or effective?
8. What are my reactions to the poem?

Comparing a newly read poem with a prescribed poem

Which ideas are similar? Which are different?
Which poem made the greater impact on you, and why?
What insights did you get from each poem?
What is the attitude of the poet in each case? Are there similarities or differences in tone?
How does each poet differ in use of language, imagery, etc.?
Comment on the form and genre in each case.

Practice

To practise answering similar questions on unseen poems, use any of the poems in this anthology which are **not** on your prescribed course.

Acknowledgments

For permission to reproduce copyright material grateful acknowledgment is made to the following:

Harvard University Press for poems by Emily Dickinson reprinted by permission of the publishers and the trustees of Amherst College from *The Poems of Emily Dickinson*, Thomas H. Johnson, ed., Cambridge, Mass: The Belknap Press of Harvard University Press, copyright © 1951, 1955, 1979, 1983 by The President and fellows of Harvard College;

A.P. Watt on behalf of Michael B. Yeats for poems by William Butler Yeats;

Harcourt Publishers for poems by Robert Frost;

Faber and Faber Ltd for poems by T.S. Eliot, Séamus Heaney and Sylvia Plath and also for 'The Horses' by Edwin Muir, 'Funeral Blues' (Twelve Song ix) by W.H. Auden; 'Snowdrop' (from *Lupercal*) and 'There came a Day' (from *Seven Songs*) by Ted Hughes and for 'Anseo' (from *Why Brownlee Left*) by Paul Muldoon;

The Trustees of the estate of the late Katherine B. Kavanagh, through the Jonathan Williams Literary Agency, for poems by Patrick Kavanagh;

Farrar, Straus and Giroux Inc. for poems by Elizabeth Bishop from *The Complete Poems 1927–1979* by Elizabeth Bishop, copyright © 1979, 1983 by Alice Helen Methfessel;

Michael Longley and Lucas Alexander Whitley Ltd for poems by Michael Longley;

The Gallery Press for poems by Derek Mahon, and for
'Crow's Nest' (from *Oar*) by Moya Cannon;
'Would You Jump Into My Grave As Quick?' (from *Pillow Talk*) by Paula Meehan;
'Swineherd' (from *The Second Voyage*) by Eiléan Ní Chuilleanáin;
'Daughter and Dying Fish' (from *As If It Matters*) by Eamonn Grennan;
'Soot' (from *The New Estate and Other Poems*) by Ciaran Carson;
'The Reading Lesson' (from *Collected Poems*) by Richard Murphy; and
'The Cage' (from *Collected Poems*) by John Montague.

Carcanet Press for poems by Eavan Boland and for
'The Red Wheelbarrow' (from *Collected Poems*) by William Carlos Williams;
'Hedges Freaked with Snow' (from *Collected Poems*) by Robert Graves;

'Request to a Year' (from *Collected Poems*) by Judith Wright;
'Strawberries' (from *Collected Poems*) by Edwin Morgan and
'The Voice' (from *Collected Poems*) by Patricia Beer.

George Sassoon and Barbara Levy Literary Agency for 'Everyone Sang' by Seigfried Sassoon;

Elizabeth Barnett, literary executor, for 'What Lips My Lips Have Kissed' (from *Collected Poems*) by Edna St Vincent Millay, copyright 1923, 1951;

James MacGibbon for 'Deeply Morbid' (from *Collected Poems*) by Stevie Smith;

David Higham Associates for 'Autobiography' (from *Collected Poems*) by Louis MacNeice;
'One Flesh' (from *Collected Poems*) by Elizabeth Jennings;
'Do Not Go Gentle Into That Good Night' (from *Collected Poems*) by Dylan Thomas;

The Blackstaff Press for 'The Green Shoot' by John Hewitt;

Bloodaxe Books for
'Night Drive' (from *Breathing Spaces: Early Poems*) by Brendan Kennelly;
'Heidi with Blue Hair' (from *Poems 1960–2000*) by Fleur Adcock;
'It Ain't What You Do, It's What It Does To You' by Simon Armitage (from *Zoom!*); and
'What Were They Like?' by Denise Levertov;

Thomas Kinsella for his poem 'Mirror in February';

Peterloo Poets for 'Growing Up' (from *Selected Poems*) by U.A. Fanthorpe;

Random House Group for 'Death of a Son' (from *Selected Poems*) by Jon Silkin and 'The Present Moment' (from *The Father*) by Sharon Olds.

Brendan Kennelly for his poem 'The Prodigal Son';

PFD for 'Let Me Die A Young Man's Death' by Roger McGough
and 'Passing a Statue of Our Lady in Derry' by Carol Rumens;

Dedalus Press for 'Jasmine' by Paddy Bushe;

Anvil Press Poetry for 'Valentine' and 'Warming Her Pearls' by Carol Ann Duffy.

COMPACT DISC

CD recordings are by permission of Faber and Faber Ltd (poems of Séamus Heaney), Lucas Alexander Whitley Ltd (poems of Michael Longley), The Gallery Press (poems of Derek Mahon) and Carcanet Press (poems of Eavan Boland). The kind co-operation of Séamus Heaney, Michael Longley, Derek Mahon and Eavan Boland in recording their poems is gratefully acknowledged.

ILLUSTRATIONS

Picture Research: Anne-Marie Ehrlich and Gay Brocklesby

Page 1	National Portrait Gallery, London
Page 20	Bridgeman Art Library/Guildhall Library, Corporation of London
Page 22	National Portrait Gallery, London
Page 23	Art Archive/Royal Holloway College
Page 26	Bridgeman Art Library
Page 34	Art Archive/Tate Gallery
Page 41	(top) Art Archive/Birmingham City Art Gallery
Page 41	(bottom) Bridgeman Art Library / Derby Museum and Art Gallery
Page 49	Amherst College Library
Page 54	'Junction of the Erie and Northern (Champlain) Canals' (c. 1830) (artist: John Hill)–New York Historical Society
Page 59	Trustees of Amherst College
Page 83	National Portrait Gallery, London
Page 89	Bridgeman Art Gallery/Birmingham Museum and Art Gallery
Page 101	Bridgeman Art Library
Page 103	Raymond V. Schoder S.J.
Page 107	Raymond V. Schoder S.J.
Page 117	Natural History Photographic Agency
Pages 125/126	All photos by Raymond V. Schoder S.J. [*note*: the publishers wish to acknowledge the kind assistance of Fr Peter Milward S.J. in locating the photos by Fr R.V. Schoder which appear in this anthology. They appeared originally in their book *Landscape and Inscape: Vision and Inspiration in Hopkins's Poetry* – text by Peter Milward S.J.; photography by Raymond Schoder S.J. (Elek Books 1975)]
Page 136	Hugh Lane Municipal Gallery of Modern Art, Dublin
Page 144	Bord Fáilte
Page 145	Dúchas: The Heritage Service
Page 153	Hugh Lane Municipal Gallery of Modern Art, Dublin / Sarah Purser copyright holders
Page 159	Art Archive / Dagli Orti
Page 165	National Library of Ireland

Page 301	Robert Harding Picture Library
Page 317	Radio Telefís Eireann
Page 326	Photo: Bryan Rutledge
Page 328	Silkeborg Museum, Denmark
Page 337	Ulster Folk and Transport Museum / Museums and Galleries of Northern Ireland
Page 344	Leon McAuley
Page 350	Imperial War Museum, London
Page 355	Michael Viney
Page 371	Derek Mahon
Page 379	Ulster Museum / Museum and Galleries of Northern Ireland
Page 392	Kevin Dwyer
Page 395	(both photos) Royal Georgraphical Society
Page 399	The Irish Times
Page 413	Victoria and Albert Museum, London
Page 415	Sheelagh Flanagan
Page 435	National Portrait Gallery, London
Page 440	National Portrait Gallery, London
Page 442	National Portrait Gallery, London
Page 447	National Portrait Gallery, London
Page 450	National Portrait Gallery, London
Page 452	Camera Press
Page 454	National Portrait Gallery, London
Page 457	Hulton Getty
Page 459	Mark Gerson
Page 462	Bettman / Corbis
Page 464	Hulton Getty
Page 466	Camera Press
Page 470	Mark Gerson
Page 472	Camera Press
Page 475	Victor Patterson
Page 478	Camera Press
Page 481	Coward of Canberra / Carcanet Press
Page 483	Network Photographers
Page 485	Bloodaxe Books / Chris Felver
Page 488	Mark Gerson
Page 491	Carcanet Press
Page 493	John Minihan
Page 495	Kenny's, Galway
Page 498	Peter Fallon / The Gallery Press
Page 501	Peterloo Poets / Rosemarie Bailey
Page 504	Network Photographers

Page 508	David Savage
Page 511	Camera Press
Page 513	Bloodaxe Books / Eimear O'Connor
Page 518	Camera Press
Page 520	Kenny's, Galway
Page 523	Macdara Woods
Page 525	David Bartolomi / New York State Writers Institute
Page 527	Bloodaxe Books / David Hunter
Page 529	Pacemaker, Belfast
Page 532	Paddy Bushe
Page 534	Kenny's, Galway
Page 537	Picador / Sue Adler
Page 542	John Minihan
Page 544	Mike Shaughnessy
Page 546	Bloodaxe Books